# 100 Questions
## Every First-Time
## Home Buyer Should Ask

# 100 Questions
## Every First-Time
## Home Buyer Should Ask

WITH ANSWERS FROM TOP BROKERS
FROM AROUND THE COUNTRY

FOURTH EDITION

## Ilyce R. Glink

 THREE RIVERS PRESS • NEW YORK

Originally published in trade paperback in the United States in 1994, in a revised edition in 1995, and in second and third editions in 1999 and 2005 respectively by Three Rivers Press, an imprint of the Crown Publishing Group, a division of Penguin Random House LLC.

Library of Congress Cataloging-in-Publication Data
Names: Glink, Ilyce R., 1964– author.
Title: 100 questions every first-time home buyer should ask : with answers
from top brokers from around the country / Ilyce R. Glink.
Other titles: One hundred questions every first-time home buyer should ask
Description: Fourth Edition. | New York City : Three Rivers Press, 2018. | Revised edition
of the author's 100 questions every first-time home buyer should ask, ©2005.
Identifiers: LCCN 2017032095 (print) | LCCN 2017044136 (ebook) | ISBN 9781524763442
(e-book) | ISBN 9781524763435 (paperback) | ISBN 9781524763442 (ebook)
Subjects: LCSH: House buying. | Residential real estate—Purchasing. | House buying—
United States. | Residential real estate—Purchasing—United States. | BISAC: REFERENCE /
Consumer Guides. | BUSINESS & ECONOMICS / Personal Finance / General.
Classification: LCC HD1379 (ebook) | LCC HD1379 .G58 2018 (print) | DDC 643/.12—dc23
LC record available at https://lccn.loc.gov/2017032095

ISBN 978-1-5247-6343-5
Ebook ISBN 978-1-5247-6344-2

Printed in the United States of America

Book design by Nicola Ferguson
Cover design by Alane Gianetti
Cover photograph: Image Source/Getty Images

10 9 8 7 6 5 4 3 2 1

Fourth Edition

For Sam, Alex, and Michael,
*Wherever you are, is home.*

And for all home buyers,
*looking for their own corner of the sky.*

And in memory of Gene "Genna" Galperin,
*whose stories of real estate buyers and sellers were legendary,*
*and who we miss everyday.*

# CONTENTS

# Contents

# PREFACE

Twenty-five years ago, I sat down to write the first edition of this book. It was 1993, and for the first time since World War II, mortgage interest rates had dropped below 7 percent for a thirty-year fixed-rate mortgage.

The implications of that were significant. So many more home buyers would be able to afford to buy into the American Dream of homeownership. All of the stakeholders—Realtors, home builders, mortgage lenders, professional home inspectors, contractors—were thrilled. The stock market cooperated. The 1990s, primarily the years when Bill Clinton was president, were a time of great wealth-building, as the stock market bull run lasted 117 months, the longest in history (thanks to the tech boom), increasing 473 percent (though it fell 49 percent before climbing further). Consumer confidence rose with the stock market, and lots of people, including a whole bunch of first-time buyers, were buying homes.

Sam bought his first condo in 1986, seven years earlier, after he graduated from law school. He was 26 years old, and was moving to Chicago to take his first job. His oldest brother was, at the time, a trader at the Chicago Board of Trade, and told him to buy as close to downtown Chicago as possible and as close to Lake Michigan as he could afford. It was good advice, and Sam ended up in a vintage (in Chicago, anything built before the Great

Depression is called "vintage") one-bedroom condo in a brick, three-story, twenty-one-unit walk-up building in Lincoln Park, about a half block from the Lincoln Park Zoo and the Conservatory. It was a lovely spot, about three miles north of the Loop, where Sam worked.

I didn't know him yet. Like many of today's Millennials, I had just graduated from college with a degree in English literature and rhetoric, and a minor in music, and was living at home with my mother, who was already a successful real estate agent working in Lincoln Park and the Gold Coast. I didn't have a job and didn't know what I wanted to do. All of the jobs I was looking at didn't pay much, and I didn't have any savings to speak of. Thankfully, I didn't have student loans from my years at the state university (thanks, Mom!), nor did I have credit card debt (credit cards were just becoming a thing).

I found a job as the building manager for a commercial real estate company, got fired (long story), wrote freelance articles for local newspapers and a woman who ran a small public relations firm, and then found a job as an editorial assistant with a local Chicago book publishing company. I was earning $14,000 (yes, but it's 1987 dollars), worked in an alcove of a building overlooking Michigan Avenue located about four miles from my apartment, and spent my days acquiring, rewriting, and editing books.

Two months later (a little over a year after I graduated from college), I met Sam. My mother decided to get married again, and I decided to look for an apartment to rent. (That's by far the more traditional path to homeownership: You live with your parents, then rent an apartment, and then sometime later—much later, now—you buy a starter home.) I found an ad for a sublet apartment in the local newspaper, a little west of where I grew up, which at the time was a sort of sketchy neighborhood (which is where you live when you find a two-bedroom apartment for $700 per month). I lived there with a college friend for about six months, until our third-floor walk-up was broken into. I was completely freaked out, and we decided to move to a more secure location, in a building with an elevator and doorman. At the last minute, she backed out and I wound up in a large one-bedroom apartment on the sixteenth floor of a building about two blocks from the vintage co-op in which I grew up, with a room that looked west (great sunsets, high electrical bills in the summer!). It was $600 per month, which was much more than I could afford, but I loved living there. I took the 151 bus to the office (an easy commute), walked home when the weather was nice, and had Lincoln Park and Lake Michigan out my back door.

The following January, Sam proposed. We started talking about living together and quickly came to the conclusion that we needed to buy a different place, that living in his second-floor, one-bedroom walk-up wouldn't work for me. So, we started looking for a place to buy together, our first joint home purchase, my first experience in buying anything larger than an item of clothing.

Boy, did I have a lot to learn.

Lots of folks buy homes, but first-time buyers are a breed apart. Brokers say the moment first-time buyers walk into the house of their dreams and realize it's affordable, a glow of complete satisfaction settles on their faces. It is the thrill of finally achieving their American Dream. Whether you're a first-time buyer, or purchasing your first investment property, your first newly constructed house, or your first house in thirty years, you've come to the right place.

This book is for anyone who feels even a little unsure about the process of buying a house: buyers who've bought homes within the past few years but had trouble with their agents, their lender, the negotiation process, the sellers, the inspection, the closing, or any of the pieces that go into the complex game called real estate.

As I have said in past editions, the idea for this book came to me as I was writing an article for the Your Place section of the *Chicago Tribune* at the start of my career as a real estate and money journalist, many years ago. The article was supposed to be about the questions first-time buyers ask, which the brokers I interviewed told me were posed over and over again. I easily culled a dozen questions from my interviews with them. And then another dozen. Over the years, I've added to, and refined, questions on that list. In this fourth edition, I've added a new chapter (called "Fast Pass") with the nine questions you really must answer before you start the process of buying a home. I've combined, eliminated, and changed another dozen questions. But all of the answers contain new information, because we are finally at a place where Millennials are entering their prime home-buying years.

As I'm no doubt sure you've heard, Millennials are a *very* different generation. Equally important, we have just come through the worst housing crisis and recession (referred to as the Great Recession here and elsewhere) since the Great Depression. So many things have changed since the last edition of this book—and I've tried to address them all.

One thing remains loud and clear: Home buying is complicated and becomes more so every time the government tries to "simplify" the process. First-time home buyers often don't know what questions to ask. Even seasoned home buyers don't remember to ask every question they should. And in real estate deals, those unasked, unanswered questions are the ones that cause the most trouble.

This new edition of *100 Questions Every First-Time Home Buyer Should Ask* leads you through the maze of purchasing property by answering questions that pop up at different checkpoints along the way. Want to buy a home online directly from an FSBO (someone selling by owner)? Moving across state lines? Buying new construction? Looking for a deal? Buying an investment property? Trying to negotiate a mortgage? You'll find all of the answers to those questions here, plus helpful listicles in the Appendix. But be aware that laws and rules affecting home buyers change frequently. So, after this book goes to press, I'll continue to update those lists, and add new information as it becomes available, on my website, ThinkGlink.com/book-updates. Or, go to the navigation bar and under the Real Estate tab, you'll find Book Updates.

There are admittedly more than 100 questions in this book, but I've tried to phrase them in the way that you would think about them and ask them, explaining the answers in a way you would understand and recognize. There are three ways to use this book: You can read it cover to cover, starting with the introduction; you can just read the Fast Pass chapter and get going; or you can pick it up when you have a question and find your answer. This book is for you, and you should read it in the way you'd find most helpful.

Good luck, and happy house-hunting!

Ilyce R. Glink
January 2018

PS: Buying a home is an extraordinary experience. If you'd like to share your stories, or if you have questions or comments, please email me at Questions@thinkglink.com. If you'd like to hear from me regularly, please sign up for my free weekly e-newsletter at ThinkGlink.com.

# 100 Questions
## Every First-Time
## Home Buyer Should Ask

# INTRODUCTION

Here come the Millennials. Finally. And, according to the entire real estate industry, not a moment too soon.

For the past decade, since the Great Recession forced so many Americans to put their lives on hold, the world of real estate has been praying for the arrival of Millennials on the home-buying scene to begin buying, selling, fixing up, and financing property. It's been quite the waiting game: when I first started writing about real estate, the average age of a first-time home buyer was 26. Today, it's nearly 34.

There are a lot of explanations for the delay: Millennials who graduated from college in 2008 to 2012 found a weak job market. Many of them moved home instead of moving out with a friend (or by themselves) and renting their own place, typically a precursor to home buying. Roughly a third of them are still living at home. Older Millennials watched as parents lost jobs, tapped their 401(k)s to survive, and took jobs that paid less (and often didn't offer benefits), and their families struggled to make ends meet. Millions of home-owners couldn't sell when they needed to and lost their homes to foreclosure, destroying credit histories and confidence in the process. When you lose confidence in yourself and your ability to pay the bills, it's awfully hard to make the commitment to buying something as large and as permanent as a house.

But Millennials also have cash flow issues, thanks to their student loan problem.[*] About 44 million Americans are paying off student loans these days, to the tune of $1.4 trillion total. The average amount of student loan debt has tripled over the past twenty years, and most 2017 graduates were carrying about $36,000 worth of student loans as they made their way out of college and into their adult lives.

Here are some facts about Millennials and student loan debt that make the real estate industry very nervous:

- Some 58 percent of college graduates[†] reported having student loans;
- 44 percent don't know the difference between private and federal loans;
- 45 percent don't know what percentage of their budget goes toward paying down student loans;
- 37 percent don't know what interest rate their loans carry;
- 15 percent don't even know how much they owe;
- Default rates are running between 7 and just over 11 percent, depending on the type of loan and whether the school was private or public, according to the Department of Education.

For those Millennials who are making their payments, paying off student loans can delay home buying because monthly debt service payments are deducted from the amount someone has available to repay debts.[‡] That, as we'll discuss later in the financing section of the book (or, turn to page 152 to start calculating your available income right now), leaves you less income to qualify under the government's Ability to Repay rules.

Finally, one of the great drivers of homeownership is the next generation. Along with everything else, Millennials have time-shifted marriage and children. They're marrying later than any generation and having kids when they're older. If you're single, or even if

---

[*]  As do their parents and, in some cases, their grandparents.

[†]  According to a Harvard Kennedy School study. http://iop.harvard.edu/student-debt-viewed-major-problem -financial-considerations-important-factor-most-millennials-when.

[‡]  Paying off a student loan is typically a ten-year exercise, unless you refinance or consolidate your payments into a thirty-year term, which makes student loans feel like a mortgage and why you have Gen Xers and Baby Boomers still paying off student loans. Some Baby Boomers have already paid off their own student loans but have signed for their kids' loans and are now paying those off.

you're in a long-term relationship but without kids, you're probably not looking for a house in the suburbs with a good school district. And, because you're changing jobs fairly frequently,* having a longer-term commitment to real estate isn't particularly high on the list.

But times they are a-changing. According to the latest figures from the National Association of Realtors, Millennials accounted for 34 percent of home buyers in 2016, the latest year for which data is available. And almost all of them were buying homes for the first time.

## Who Are Millennial Home Buyers?

According to the Pew Research Center, Millennials (81 million of them) are those individuals born in 1981 and later, up until today. But other researchers cap the era of Millennials at those born between 1981 or 1982 and 1994 or 1995,† which would put the youngest Millennials at around age 22 or 23 (as I write this), up until about age 36 or 37. That makes sense to me, since I see Generation Z (the generation younger than the Millennials) as a next-gen group that some are already calling Digital Natives. (I tend to refer to them as "the generation born with a chip built into their brain.") In short, the oldest Millennials will remember life before Google and what a telephone's busy signal sounded like. Gen Z (including my own kids) won't.

Around the world, Millennials are considered one of the most consistent generations. Much of this has to do with the Internet; this cohort is the most tech-savvy, and technology has flattened much of the world. Information flows freely, is adapted to life seamlessly, and has profoundly (and quickly) changed life for them and their parents. It's certainly changed how people shop for, buy, sell, finance, and invest in real estate.

Unsurprisingly, according to the 2016 Survey of Home Buyers and Sellers, an annual report published by the National Association of Realtors, first-time buyers fall directly into the Millennial sweet spot:

---

* Millennials are known as the "job-hopping generation," and typically have had at least four jobs by the time they're 32 years old or in their first decade out of college, according to a Gallup poll and a LinkedIn study, both conducted in 2016.

† Demographers William Straus and Neil Howe define Millennials as born between 1982 and 2004. Gen Z follows Millennials, and in 2015 made up about 25 percent of the population, which means they'll one day be the largest cohort.

- They're a median 32 years old. (All home buyers lumped together are a median 44 years old.)
- Their median income is $72,000.
- The median price of a first-time buyer's home purchase is $182,500, although that ranges from just about $161,000 for unmarried couples to $208,500 for married first-time buyers.
- 72 percent are married, or an unmarried couple.
- 6 percent is the median down payment.
- 60 percent have no children.
- 95 percent either rent or live with their parents before buying their first home.
- 1 percent purchase the home they had previously rented.
- 87 percent were born in the USA.

Is this you? Then you might be ready to buy your first home (even if you don't realize it yet).

One of the last things I did as I was sending the first edition of this book off to press in 1993 was get an AOL email.[*] I think AOL had fewer than 100,000 people who were signed up for email at that time, but almost as soon as this book was published in 1994, I started receiving messages from readers. We were the "early adopters" of our generation. Then, no one would have thought to look for a house online (the early photos were black-and-white shots of the front of houses, basically reused from listing books that were typically published every two weeks, and jealously protected by real estate companies), much less buy without ever seeing it in person. There was no Google, no Zillow, no Trulia, no agent websites to speak of. (What did happen, in 1993, is that mortgage interest rates dropped below 7 percent for the first time since World War II, and basically haven't gone back above 6 percent for more than a few months since.)

How far we've come. Today's Millennial home buyers have demanded tremendous and continuous technological change from Realtors, lenders, and others in the real estate community. You can do just about everything you need to do to shop for, buy, and close on a

---

[*] I still have it: IlyceGlink@aol.com.

home with your phone, including download and read a digital copy of this book (and link to ThinkGlink.com/book-updates for updates). That's still tough for your Baby Boomer brokers to get their heads around. The tech world has delivered, and made billions of dollars in the process.

So, it's never been easier to find, buy, and finance the right house: as long as you have great credit, sizable savings, little or no debt, and plenty of income. And that's where first-time buyers typically fall short. Since the Great Recession, millions of homes have been swooped up by investors. Prices have risen 41 percent in five years (2011–16), while incomes have only risen 11 percent. Interest rates seem poised to rise above 4 percent for a thirty-year fixed-rate mortgage (and were briefly above that at the beginning of 2017, before falling back). Affordability is worse.

With these changes come new (and important) questions you should be asking as you set out to explore the world of homeownership: Should you buy a home now or rent? Should you buy with someone or on your own? Is your job (and income) stable over the next five to ten years? Should you spend every last dollar the mortgage lender says you can?

To borrow a phrase from Oprah, here are some things about residential real estate I know for sure:

1. Over the past twenty-five years, homes have appreciated in value. Not every home, and not everywhere, but for the vast majority of Americans in much of the United States.

2. Twenty-five years from now, the real estate market as a whole will be worth substantially more than it is today. Buy smart and you'll not only have a better quality of life, but you'll enrich yourself and your family.

3. The above point is true because a home continues to be the centerpiece of a family net worth. Every mortgage payment you make is like enforced savings. (When you rent, you're paying the mortgage of the investor.)

4. And finally, the younger you are when you buy your first home, the wealthier you'll be later in life.

Let's get started.

# CHAPTER 1

# Fast Pass: 9 Questions You Must Answer Before Buying Your First Home

Here's my basic philosophy about home buying: You've got to be honest with yourself. Honest about how much money you spend (and where you spend it), about your priorities in life, about how and where you actually want to live. You may have noticed that the Facebook/Instagram/Pinterest life people portray has only a tangential relationship to reality. But when it comes to making the single biggest investment you're going to make (until you buy your *next* house), being truthful with yourself is crucial to help you find the right house at the right price and on the right terms.

These nine questions are must-asks. What I mean by that is, you must understand the answers to at least these nine questions to have any chance at buying your first home successfully. Take some time and work through them. (Think of them as an extended checklist or listicle, if that helps.)

## Question 1: Should I Rent or Should I Buy?

After reading this question, did you just jump over to Question 2? I wouldn't blame you if you did. After all, you've just forked over some cash in order to buy this book, so you *obviously* want to buy a home. Right?

I get it. But just because you have (or think you have) the down payment cash available and interest rates are still low, that doesn't automatically mean you should buy your first home right now. Homeownership is expensive. It's a big responsibility. It's illiquid (meaning, you can't turn around six months later and decide to rent without potentially losing a fair amount of money). Not only do you buy the property and then become obligated to make 180 or 360 monthly mortgage payments,[*] but you also have to maintain and even improve it. That's a big commitment of time and money, even if you're buying a condominium with a building engineer to handle plumbing issues or basic problems, or a townhouse or single-family house in a maintenance-free community (hint: the phrase "maintenance-free" only applies to the exterior of the house and the land that surrounds it).

Let's walk through the issues you should think about when trying to make the decision about whether to rent or buy your next home:

**WHERE DO YOU WANT TO LIVE?** Most people want to live close to where they work.[†] And while the myth is that Millennials want to live in urban areas, the truth, according to census data,[‡] is that more Millennials are moving from the city to the suburbs than the reverse. That's true even of younger Millennials who are in their early twenties. While there's a desire to be close to the action—living near bars, great restaurants, and recreational opportunities—many Millennials want to be close to family and friends, too. If you're part of the work-from-home cohort, you may be able to live anywhere but your spouse or partner may not. You each have to decide where you want to live, how much of a commute you want to have, what you can afford in a particular neighborhood, and what trade-offs you're willing to make. (For more details, see Question 10, Should I Make a Wish List? What About a Reality Check, on page 38.)

**CAN YOU AFFORD TO BE A HOMEOWNER?** Homeownership is expensive. And, under the new Ability to Repay rules that most mortgage lenders have to live by, it's tough to get qualified unless you have excellent credit and at least a two-year track record of working in a job that gives you sufficient income to pay your mortgage, property taxes, and homeowners' insurance premiums. (Real estate industry observers often joke that the easiest way to get approved for a mortgage is to prove you don't need one.) If you're self-employed, you'll need to provide tax returns for at least the past two years showing you

---

[*] 180 monthly mortgage payments translates into a 15-year loan. 360 monthly payments translates into a 30-year loan.

[†] So do Gen Xers and Baby Boomers, by the way, because who really wants to sit in traffic?

[‡] Released in 2015.

have sufficient income to pay your bills. You'll also need cash in the bank: enough for the down payment, closing costs (unless those are financed), and at least three months of cash reserves. Lenders want to make sure you're not spending every last dollar to buy the property, only to lose your job (and the house) a few months later. If you're weak on the cash side, you should rent for another year and focus on building up your cash reserves.

**WHAT KIND OF LIFESTYLE DO YOU WANT?** When you're in your twenties, you might like being closer to other twentysomethings. That's why WeWork, a company that provides shared workspace, community, and services for entrepreneurs, created WeLive, which provides rental, dorm-style living for adults (albeit with their own kitchens and bigger beds), with shared community amenities and services.* It's why some Silicon Valley tech companies offer its summer interns dorm-style living accommodations that are in close proximity to their headquarters. When you rent an apartment in a rental building or a condo, you're getting congregate living—everyone together in one big property with shared walls, ceilings, floors, elevators, and parking facilities. There's a pretty good chance you'll hear something you don't want to hear (through walls or in the elevator) or see something you'll wish you could unsee. On the other hand, there's the potential for built-in friendships and partnerships to form (the WeLive theory), and you may feel safer than if you live in a single-family home. But if you rent a townhome or single-family house (whether it's in the city or suburbs), you'll have more privacy, and you may well get some sort of outdoor space and the ability to have pets.†

**DO YOU KNOW WHERE YOU'LL BE WORKING FOR THE NEXT FEW YEARS?** As I've already said, buying a home is illiquid. You can't just move at the end of the lease or sublet if you get a job somewhere else. Renting is transitory. If you want to be footloose and fancy free for another few years, or if you don't know where you're going to be working or how much you'll earn, you should seriously consider renting rather than buying. If you buy and have to sell within the first couple of years of homeownership, you'll probably lose money due to the costs of sale (broker's fee, transfer taxes, and other fees that could add up to 10 percent of the sales price of the home). It's generally far less expensive to rent

---

* There are many other companies that have created rental properties in the WeLive mold. They're not cheap to live in, but provide a particular lifestyle experience that would be difficult to create.

† Many rental buildings limit your ability to have pets. And if they allow pets, they may regulate the type or size of pet you're permitted to have. In the rental properties we own, we don't allow pets of any sort. The one time we did, we wound up having to resand the floors due to the renter's dog having repeated "accidents" in the unit.

than buy a home if your timeline is short, because it takes years for a property to appreciate enough to cover those costs of sale. On the other hand, if you (and your spouse or partner) are now happily working in jobs you love, in a location you want stay in for at least the next five to ten years, then you might be better off buying than renting.

**DO YOU WANT YOUR HOME TO REFLECT WHO YOU ARE?** Years ago, a Berkeley professor named Clare Marcus wrote a book called *House as a Mirror of Self*, in which she examined our relationship with our homes and what the aesthetic and stylistic choices we make say about ourselves and our souls. When I first read this book years ago, her observations confirmed my belief that one of the primary reasons people buy homes is that they want their living space to reflect who they are. When you own your own home, you can do whatever you want to it. I've been in condos that were originally four bedrooms and the owner had rebuilt the interior to be a massive one-bedroom apartment. I've also been in tiny saltbox houses that were added on to, renovated, and remade into something completely different. When you own property, you get to decide what to do and whether to make what might turn out to be a good or bad investment. Not so with rentals: Landlords often limit what you can do to the property to make it your own. You might be able to paint the walls pink and install orange bathroom tile, but undoubtedly the landlord will want you to restore the property to its original state when your lease is up. And don't expect the landlord to reimburse you for the costs of those improvements. Those are on you.

> **TIP:** You might read online that it's cheaper to rent rather than own a home if mortgage interest rates are more than 5 percent for a thirty-year fixed-rate loan, but the calculation is difficult because so much goes into it. Your mortgage payment will typically include 1/12 of your homeowners' insurance premium plus 1/12 of your taxes, or a little more since lenders are allowed to keep up to two months' cushion in your tax and insurance escrow account. You may also have monthly assessments (if you live in a condo, co-op, townhouse, or single-family home that is part of a homeowners' association). And then there's the maintenance and upkeep. The thing to remember is that when you rent, you're paying all of those expenses for someone else; it's just that they may have bought the property twenty years ago, so their break-even amount is less. When you rent, you don't build equity in any property, so you have to be a disciplined-enough investor to make sure you set aside that "extra" cash each month that you're not plowing into building the equity of your home. The only time renting is almost always cheaper than owning is if you plan to buy and sell in less than five years. That's how long it takes for typical home appreciation (just over the rate of inflation) to overcome the costs of sale.

# Question 2: Should I Buy with Someone or on My Own?

According to the 2016 Profile of Home Buyers and Sellers, published by the National Association of Realtors, first-time buyers accounted for 35 percent of all home buyers that year (the most recent numbers available as I was writing this book). Their median age is 32, and 72 percent are married couples or unmarried partners. Eighteen percent are single women and just 8 percent are single men.[*] The median income of first-time buyers (which includes the income of all buyers in the transaction) is $72,000 and the median price of a first-time home purchase is $182,500.

What does that mean? That it's tough to qualify for a home. You need to have sufficient income in order to meet the Ability to Repay rules that most mortgage lenders live by. That's why the vast majority of first-time home buyers are made up of couples (married or life partners) or multiple buyers who are not romantically attached (parents or other relatives, often siblings and friends).

In short, the vast majority of first-time buyers purchase homes with other people for all of the reasons we've discussed thus far: Homes are expensive to buy and maintain, and the older you get, the more likely it is you'll be partnered up (married or not).

The question for you is whether you should take the plunge and buy your first home as soon as possible, assuming you're still single, and how your long-term relationship (if you're in one) should factor into that decision. You may also need to have a co-borrower (in addition, perhaps, to your spouse or partner) to overcome any credit or income challenges you have. (More on that in a moment, or turn to Question 41, How Does My Credit Score Affect My Ability to Qualify and Be Approved for a Mortgage?)

> Randy,[†] an attorney who has developed a successful practice, bought his first home when he was 29. He had been practicing law for three years, and had won enough cases to have set aside a substantial amount of cash for a down payment. But, he had been dating Patti for a long time, and thought

---

[*]   For those of you math savants playing along at home, the final 2 percent in the survey is "other," which usually refers to multigenerational buyers, such as parents and children.

[†]   All of the home buyers in this book have had their names changed to protect their privacy, unless otherwise noted.

they might end up together. While he wasn't ready to propose, he was ready to stop paying rent and move into a more "grown-up" place. So he enlisted his girlfriend's help to find a two-bedroom apartment in a neighborhood that would potentially work for both of them if they moved in together. He bought on his own, but with her help, knowing that she'd be happy if they wound up together.

If you're in a relationship that you expect will go the distance, you need to involve that partner in a discussion of what kind of home they envision living in. Here are some questions you should ask each other:

1. When you imagine the word "home," what comes to mind?

2. Where do you imagine living in the next five to seven years? What about longer-term?

3. Do you imagine having or adopting children in the next five to seven years? (This speaks to the size of home you'll need.)

4. Do you want to have pets? What kind? How many? (Pets may limit your ability to rent and may require you to own a property instead.)

5. How much of your income do you spend on rent? If you live together, what portion of your joint income should you spend on rent or owning a home?

If you decide to buy a home, there are many more issues you'll need to go through (separately and together), and you can find them in Chapter 2, The Beginning: How Do I Know What I Want to Buy?

## The Other Way to Qualify

If you can't qualify for a home on your own, first-time buyers sometimes need their parents, siblings, or friends to "lend" them their signature and co-sign mortgage documents. This can be very helpful to the buyer (who otherwise wouldn't qualify for the mortgage) but very risky for the person lending the signature. If the buyer doesn't make regular payments (or make any payments at all), the co-borrower is on the hook legally for *all of the mortgage payments,* not to mention real estate taxes and insurance premiums.

Consider this email I received from a reader a number of years ago: "I co-signed for a mortgage with a friend of mine and then transferred my interest in the property to her. Her name is on the deed while mine is on the mortgage. She has now stopped making payments on the mortgage and this is killing my credit. She says I have no recourse since her name is on the deed and mine is on the mortgage. Is this true?"

One missed payment could destroy the co-borrower's credit (not to mention the first-time buyer's), so I urge you to think carefully before you decide to either borrow or lend a signature.

## Question 3: How Should I Think About My Home-Buying "Time Horizon"? (And Avoid Making a Big Timing Mistake?)

When it comes to buying a house, two guiding principles seem to apply to almost every situation: "Timing is everything" and "Luck is perspiration + opportunity."

Stumble upon the right house? That just means you're putting in the time searching, whether that means driving all over your neighborhood of choice or letting your fingers do the walking online. Manage to close on the day your lease expires? That just means you started looking at the right time. Did you blindly call or email a real estate office on a listing and get an agent who happened to be taking (what used to be known) as "floor calls," who became a lifetime friend?

Here is an example (one of many) from my own life: When Sam and I stumbled upon the house we've now lived in for nearly twenty-four years, we had already seen more than 100 houses, maybe even 150. There was something about this 1880s blue and white farmhouse that just called to us. But the owner wasn't ready to sell. He wanted about $100,000 more than the house was worth—way more than we could afford to pay. We made an offer. It didn't work out. The timing wasn't right.

Several months later, on Memorial Day weekend, we were still driving around looking at houses and impulsively decided to stop and knock on the front door. Over the past couple of months, everything had changed for this couple. He had lost his job. His mother-in-law had fallen and needed them to move in with her. He was ready to say "Yes" to the right offer, which was right at the top of our price range. And we were ready to spend every cent we had at the time, to buy the home where we would raise our family. We made a deal standing on his manicured lawn and shook hands. Paperwork followed, and we closed in October.

So much happens when the timing is right. And yet, timing is one of the top ten mistakes that every home buyer makes. Worse, it's particularly tough for first-time buyers to time the purchase of their first home correctly.

Here's what typically happens: First-time buyers sign a year lease, and then go look for a house. They usually find one quickly (because they've been searching for months online before contacting a real estate agent), make an offer, get it accepted, line up the financing, and close in the span of a few months. And then they realize they have six months of a lease to pay while also taking care of their mortgage, real estate taxes, insurance, and assessments (if they're in a condo or homeowners' association). It's one of the reasons first-time buyers struggle financially during the first few years of homeownership.

Later in the book I talk about something I call the "Cycle of Life" and how this reflects the timing of so many moves you'll make in your life. Quite simply, every five to ten years, you shift into a new life phase, which brings new challenges, pleasures, and requirements. (Remember how much you hated when your parents told you that you were entering a new "phase" of life? I do!) Here's how it usually works:

**PHASE 1: 20s TO 30s.** Graduate from college or graduate school. Within five to ten years, you'll figure out where you want to work. If you haven't moved out from your parents' place, you'll rent an apartment and then a year or two later figure out that you're ready for your own place. If you're not in a relationship of some sort but want to be, you'll probably find one within this decade, and you'll discover that your apartment is suddenly too small.

**PHASE 2: 30s TO 40s.** You decide to buy a bigger place with your significant other. Maybe you decide to marry. Within five to ten years, you decide whether to have kids, and—if you want them—you may decide to sell and move to the suburbs where homes are more affordable and the school districts are better. If you don't have children, but you do have dogs, you might make the same choice to move to the suburbs or buy a bigger place in the city. You might also make a move for work. You could buy one or two homes during this phase.

**PHASE 3: 40S, 50S, AND 60S.** This phase might go a little longer, depending on how old you were when you had your children (and how many you had). If you start having children at 33 and have your last when you're 40, you might stay in your home until you're 60 or 65. If you have children when you're in your mid-40s, you might stay in your home until you're 70 (or you might never leave it). In this phase, you might trade up because of a promotion, because your children need a different sort of school district, a lifestyle choice, or because your parents decide they want (or need) to come live with you.

**PHASE 4: 60S, 70S, AND 80S.** Your kids, if you had them, are grown and you and your spouse or partner are contemplating retirement. This is where you typically decide you don't need such a big house, or at least a house with as many stairs. You sell and decamp to a city, a senior-only community, your retirement home (often purchased initially as a vacation home in Phase 2 or 3), or a rental apartment (because you're tired of maintaining your home and just want the building super to take care of it).

I don't mean to suggest that everyone will automatically fall into one of these buckets, but the truth is, most do. Or, at least, they did. There is a generational change happening now that is pinching housing markets and worrying Realtors: Now that Millennials are showing up to buy, homeowners whose kids are grown, who should be retiring and trading down to a ranch-style home or moving into an apartment, are staying put. They're not selling. That means that not only are there far fewer homes (particularly starter homes) for Millennials to buy; it means that there is far more competition for the homes that are available. Prices are rising even as mortgage interest rates are moving up, too.

Why aren't sellers selling? My best guess is that it comes down to money and time: In the Great Recession, when you could get a thirty-year fixed-rate mortgage for just over 3 percent and a ten-year mortgage for about 2.75 percent, plenty of homeowners refinanced. Sam and I did, and it became supercheap to own our house. But now, ten years later, we've seen prices rise dramatically. Trading down to a smaller home might mean we pay more for less, or leaving a community of neighbors and friends we've come to love, neither of which we're inclined to do. (We also have offices that are two blocks from our home.) Even after nearly a quarter century in this house, I can't imagine us selling anytime soon, and I suspect there are a lot of folks like us. That's one reason why home improvement spending has jumped: Our next move is as likely to be another major renovation of our 1880s farmhouse, to take it through the next twenty years, as it is to sell it and move elsewhere.

That's our future. What about yours? How should you think through the timing issue so you don't make a mistake you can't undo (at least, undo without costing you a whole lot of money)? Let's engineer the process of home buying in the broadest possible terms:

**STEP 1: What can you afford?** Estimated time: One to three months to calculate your budget, play around with numbers, use mortgage affordability calculators (we have one at ThinkGlink.com/calculators), talk to lenders, and start the preapproval process.

**STEP 2: Where you do want to live?** Estimated time: One to two months to figure out your neighborhood(s) of choice. If you're moving across state lines, this could take longer, so plan accordingly.

**STEP 3: What do you want to live in?** Estimated time: One month. Typically, type of housing stock is dictated by the neighborhood. For example, if you want to live in a condo but your neighborhood of choice is a suburb with an excellent school district, there's going to be a mismatch. Conversely, if you want to live in a single-family home, suburbs are filled with them, but finding a single-family house in a good school district in a major metropolitan area will be tougher.

**STEP 4: Find an agent, find a home.** Estimated time: Starts at one month and could last a year, or more. Depending on how much time you have to put against the search, and how much of a buyer's or seller's market mentality rules your neighborhood(s) of choice, this could take a few weeks or several months.

**STEP 5: Closing and moving.** Estimated time: One month to several months. In Georgia, it took Crystal just three weeks to close on her home. Over the same period of time, it took one of Sam's clients nearly four months to close, mostly because the sellers wanted to wait until their daughter finished the school year.

At a minimum, if you compressed all of the steps as much as possible, it would still likely take three to four months to find, qualify for, and buy your first home. On the outside, it would take a year or more. To avoid making a timing mistake, reverse-engineer the process. Start with when you'd ideally want to close and work backward.

For example: Closing in December means your offer is accepted by October. Which means you probably started shopping for a home in June, July, or August. And made the decisions about where you want to live and what you wanted to live in during April or May. And went through the mortgage qualifying process in March or April.

Just remember two things: You should take as much time as you need to find the right home, because it's the single biggest purchase you'll ever make (until you buy the next one); and don't sign a year lease if you intend to start the home-buying process in the next twelve months. If you do, it's quite likely you'll wind up paying rent and mortgage at the same time, for longer than you'd like.

## Question 4: How Much Should I Spend vs. What Banks Say I Can Afford?

Your real estate agent may deny it, but there's a lot of pressure in the home-buying process to spend more than you should.

Why? The way economists (and real estate agents and brokers) think about it, your earning power is going to go up while your mortgage will be locked in for fifteen or thirty years. So, they think, spend until it hurts now and your income will catch up later.

While that seems to make some sense on the face of it, this line of reasoning ignores the three realities of life:

1. There are other costs of homeownership besides your mortgage, including real estate property taxes, homeowners' insurance premiums, and the upkeep and maintenance of the property. (Note: I'm not even including the cost of fixing up your home, which every homeowner wants to do, even with new construction.)

2. These costs always go up over the years.

3. The rest of your life is also going to get more expensive.

Over the past dozen years, I created this chart to help explain how life just gets more expensive, until all of your costs drop dramatically—which will happen eventually. As

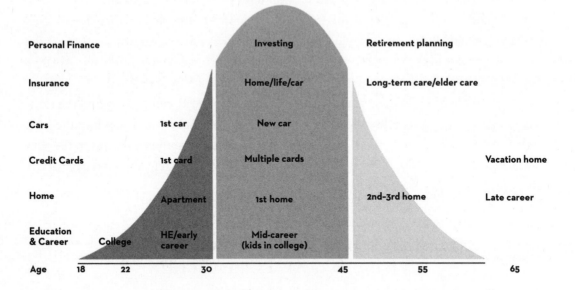

| Personal Finance | | | Investing | | Retirement planning | |
| Insurance | | | Home/life/car | | Long-term care/elder care | |
| Cars | | 1st car | New car | | | |
| Credit Cards | | 1st card | Multiple cards | | | Vacation home |
| Home | | Apartment | 1st home | 2nd-3rd home | | Late career |
| Education & Career | College | HE/early career | Mid-career (kids in college) | | | |
| Age | 18    22 | 30 | | 45 | 55 | 65 |

you can see above, costs rise during your mid-career, then drop dramatically after the kids get out of college. What's changed for Millennials? Student loans that start in your 20s and may continue (if you consolidate them) until your 50s, at which time you might start taking on additional student loans for your future children. (Yikes!)

When most of my older Think Glink Media clients see this, they nod their heads. They get it. They've lived it—or are living it right now. What most Millennials don't understand is the reality of the pile-on to come during their 30s and 40s. What's different now, from when I started describing this concept some fifteen to twenty years ago, is that Millennials have time-shifted the middle section to a much longer, inverted curve. By delaying marriage (or long-term partnership) and children to their mid-late 30s, and 40s, the downward swing might not happen until the late 40s or early 50s, pushing off the years where you begin to catch up financially and prepare for retirement.

In other words, if your last kid doesn't graduate from college until you're 60 and you're thinking of retiring at 65 or even 70, you may not leave yourself enough time to catch up financially. One of my clients is in his late 40s with a 5-year-old (his oldest is 14). He'll be in his mid-60s when his youngest is finally finished with undergrad—and that's assuming she doesn't want to go to grad school.

That's why overbuying (my term for spending more than you should on a house) is problematic. You buy a house that's just a little too expensive, given your existing and expected lifestyle, and you spend the next twenty years treading water as your raises (and perhaps bonuses) don't quite cover your wants and needs. And if, as we learned in the Great Recession, there's an economic downturn, and you lose income or even your job, and then can't find another, there's nothing to fall back on. After all, around two-thirds of Americans don't even have $500 in savings.[*]

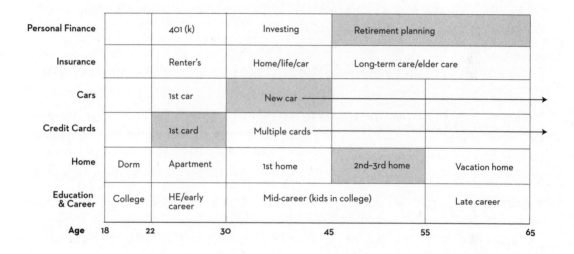

So, how much should you spend? It depends on what your real (as opposed to your dream), expected earning curve looks like. I'm all for risks, but they should be calculated risks. Before you make an official decision about what you want to spend, think hard about these questions:

- What do the next five to ten years look like for work? Are our (if you're part of a marriage or are buying with someone) jobs stable? Will we get regular increases and bonuses? How likely is it that our industry could withstand an economic shock (like 2009 rather than 2001)?
- What do we think we'll earn over the next five to fifteen years?

---

[*] BankRate's 2015 and 2016 survey.

- Will we continue to work (assuming we can) if we have children during this time period? How will we manage the additional childcare expenses if we decide to continue with our jobs?
- What other expenses will we have if we move to our neighborhood of choice? (Will we need a second car? Will we need a gardener?)
- What are our priorities in terms of saving for retirement? Buying a vacation home or investment property? Helping elderly or indigent family members? Building an emergency fund?
- How much house do you really need versus what you really want? (See Question 10 on page 38 for a deep dive into this topic.)

These are the sorts of conversation starters (or stoppers, in some cases) that can make it difficult to move quickly from making that first home-buying decision to closing on an actual house. If you're buying with someone, add time to the process to really think through your various options. If you're buying by yourself, be sure to do the numbers. Sometimes you have less available wiggle room in your budget than you think.

How much will a lender give you? Supposedly, with the Ability-to-Repay rules now in force, you shouldn't be allowed to borrow so much that your mortgage becomes a liability. The problem is that lenders don't look at lifestyle. They look at percentages.

I'll go into detail on this much more, later in the book, but let's start with the basics:

- Conventional mortgage lenders will allow you to borrow up to 28 percent of your gross monthly income to spend on your mortgage, real estate property taxes, and homeowners' insurance. And they'll allow you to spend up to 36 percent on your total debt (including car loan, student loans, credit card debt, and other debts). After taxes and deductions for health insurance or qualified retirement account deposits, that could be more than 50 percent of your take-home pay.
- FHA (Federal Housing Administration loans, part of the Department of Housing and Urban Development) and VA (Department of Veterans Affairs) loans will allow you to borrow more: up to 42 or even 43 percent of your gross monthly income. That could translate into almost 60 percent of your take-home pay. (Ouch!)

That's why it's so important to understand not only how you spend the rest of your paycheck today, but what kind of paycheck you think you'll be bringing in over the next five to ten years.

 **FIRST-TIME HOME-BUYING TIP:** Don't get so caught up in home prices you see online that you forget to think about your own lifestyle. If you can't give up your weekly massage, for example, then make sure you subtract that expense from your available house-hunting budget. A mortgage lender won't know to do that. The calculators you play with online, just like the mortgage lenders you speak to in the office, will assume that every dime you have can be assigned in service of homeownership. But that's not how real life works. It is absolutely how first-time home buyers wind up spending far more than they should, only to get caught in the time-expense vise shown above.

# Question 5: How Will My Credit Affect My Mortgage Options?

The most important thing to know when it comes to mortgage and credit is this: Lenders always want to lend money to those who don't need it. In other words, if you have excellent credit and plenty of money in the bank, you won't have trouble qualifying for a mortgage. Everyone else, well, that's a different story.

## A Brief History of Credit Histories and Scores

Credit reporting companies like Dun & Bradstreet[*] have been keeping financial data about companies for more than a hundred years, and currently collect and disseminate information on more than 250 million companies worldwide. Equifax, which was founded in 1899, is the oldest of the three major credit reporting agencies (CRAs) in the

---

[*]  Dun & Bradstreet was founded in New York, in 1841.

United States and collects and disseminates financial data on more than 800 million consumers worldwide.

Collecting information is one thing. Understanding the value of that information is another. Fair, Isaac and Company was founded in 1956 by Bill Fair and Earl Isaac in San Jose, California. Bill and Earl developed a rating system to score credit reports, which used to be literal collections of paper in a file (which is why you might hear your credit report referred to as a "credit file"). That rating system ultimately developed into a product known as the FICO score, which lenders use to figure out how risky a borrower you'll be. Fair, Isaac shortened its official name to FICO, and now sells its scores around the world, including to 95 percent of the largest financial services firms in the United States.

## What Your Credit History Contains, According to the CFPB

**PERSONAL INFORMATION.** Your name and any name you may have used in the past in connection with a credit account, including nicknames; current and former addresses; birth date; Social Security number; phone numbers.

**CREDIT ACCOUNTS.** Current and historical credit accounts, including the type of account (mortgage, installment, revolving, etc.); the credit limit or amount for each account; account balance; account payment history; the date the account was opened and closed; the name of the creditor.

**COLLECTION ITEMS.** Any account that is currently in collection (meaning, the creditor has charged it off and either sold it or given it to a collection agency).

**PUBLIC RECORDS.** Liens; foreclosures; bankruptcies; civil suits and judgments. Also, a credit report may include information on overdue child support provided by a state or local child support agency or verified by any local, state, or federal government agency. Not all CRAs will report all public records, although some may include library fines.

**INQUIRIES.** Companies that have accessed your credit report either to pitch products (mortgage, credit cards, auto loans, etc.) to you or in response to you applying for credit. You may hear this referred to as "pulls." There are hard and soft inquiries that may be listed, but only the hard inquiries (meaning, a creditor has pulled a copy of your credit history in response to your application for credit) count against you.

## How This Information Translates into Getting Your Mortgage

FICO weights the information in your credit history, based on how much each factor affects your ability to repay a mortgage or some other form of loan. While the actual details of how the FICO score (or its Vantage[*] counterpart) weights your credit history is a trade secret, here's what FICO reveals on its website, MyFico.com:

**35% = PAYMENT HISTORY.** Do you pay on time every month or are you late?

**30% = HOW MUCH DO YOU OWE** relative to how much credit you've been extended?

**15% = LENGTH OF CREDIT HISTORY.** How long have you had your oldest line of credit?

**10% = YOUR CREDIT MIX.** Do you only have one credit card or do you have multiple credit cards, a car loan, and a school loan?

**10% = NEW CREDIT.** If you've opened up several new lines of credit recently, that could indicate a higher risk of default.

The FICO basic scoring model runs from 300 to 850, and while I've spoken with many people whose credit scores were in the 400s, I can't remember ever seeing a score in the 300s. To get a score that low, you'd have to not only stop paying every bill, but file for bankruptcy or have some other extremely negative pieces of information on your credit

---

[*] The Vantage score was created by the three credit reporting agencies (CRAs), Equifax, Experian, and Trans-Union, ostensibly to compete with FICO, even though the three CRAs use and offer the FICO score. A classic case of "frenemies" or collaborators who compete. The Vantage top score was originally 990, while the FICO score tops out at 850, but due to confusion and a low adoption rate, Vantage changed its scoring model to mimic FICO's more closely. How's *that* for confusing?

history. On the upper end of the spectrum, FICO says nearly 20 percent of consumers have credit scores of 800 or above.[*]

What you need to remember is that the higher your score, the better, and the less you'll pay in interest on your loan (mortgage, auto loan, student loans, or credit card debt).

But wait: Here's where credit gets even more confusing. There are many different versions of the FICO score. Creditors (like banks, mortgage lenders, and credit card companies) will use a version of the FICO score to help them decide whether to lend you money and at what interest rate. They'll "pull a copy" of your credit report to see how much credit has already been extended to you and how you've used that credit. Mortgage lenders have one score (that more heavily weights any home loans you've had in the past, for example, and auto dealers have another version that more heavily weights any car or truck loans you've paid over the year).

No matter which version you're looking for, you can't see it unless you get turned down for credit based on your credit history, in which case the creditor who turned you down has to show it to you.[†] The only version of the FICO score consumers can see is to go to MyFico.com (the consumer version of the FICO score) and pay for a copy of your credit history and score. But even that isn't the version a mortgage lender will use to decide whether you're credit-worthy. You might as well get a free version of your credit history from AnnualCreditReport.com, which the three credit reporting agencies (Equifax, Experian, and TransUnion) are required to provide once a year under federal law.

Although you'll have to pay for the credit score that comes with it (about $10, as I write this), this is the better deal (meaning, it's cheaper) by far. The credit score you get is the version that each credit bureau has, based on your credit history. It's sometimes referred to as an "education" score.

There's so much to unpack about credit histories and credit scores, so let's focus on what you most need to know. Whether you get the Equifax, Experian, TransUnion, or even My-Fico credit score, or whether you get it for free from one of your credit card companies, doesn't

---

[*]  In a 2012 press release, FICO said 18.3 percent of consumers had credit scores above 800, which was the highest since 2008's Great Recession. However, the number of consumers with scores between 700 and 799 had not quite rebounded to pre-2008 levels. Overall, half of consumers had credit scores above 700.

[†]  This is part of the Fair Credit Reporting Act (FCRA), which is administered by the Federal Trade Commission. This law governs how Credit Reporting Agencies collect, use, and disseminate your credit information. Together, the FCRA and Fair Debt Collection Practices Act are considered the bedrock of consumer protection law in the United States.

matter. What does matter is where you fall, generally speaking, on the 300 to 850 spectrum. If you're above 780, for example, you're in very good shape. If you're below that, well, it depends on where you fall. Every drop down changes how much you'll pay for your loan; the interest rate you pay rises every time your credit score falls down into a lower bucket.

Each lender's bucket is a little different. For some mortgage lenders, the highest category of credit scores starts at 780. For others, it's 760. On the other end, you're theoretically able to get an FHA loan with a 580 credit score, but in practice you'll have a hard time finding a lender willing to give you a mortgage with a credit score lower than 600 (and for some lenders, that number is 660). In that case, you may have to spend six months to a year working on ways to fix your credit history, including making sure your report is error-free, and raise your credit score to a place where a lender will give you a loan.

## If You Don't Have a Credit File

Some people have what's known as a "thin file" or "no file." It doesn't mean their credit has been dieting! It means that you don't really have enough of a credit history for an electronic file to have been formed for you. If you go to AnnualCreditReport.com and there is no credit history for you, that will be a problem when it comes time to get a mortgage.

Lenders are supposed to use alternative data to judge your credit-worthiness. That means looking at whether you've paid your other bills—the ones that don't show up on your credit history—on time, including your rent, utility, and cell phone service bills. Lenders can't gather that kind of individual data, so there are other companies that have started to pull it for them, like eCredable,* which gathers your utility payments and other alternative data and fashions it into a score that some lenders will use to qualify you for a mortgage, credit cards, and auto loans.

You can also take some steps to build up your credit history (which will, in turn, raise your credit score over time):

1. Pay all of your bills on time every month. Don't ever be late.

2. Pay all of your bills in full each month, if possible.

---

* Full disclosure: I sit on an advisory board for eCredable and am an investor in the company.

3. If you have to run a balance on a credit card, make sure it's less than 30 percent of the total available credit limit. For example, if your credit card has a $10,000 limit, keep your running balance under $3,000. If you need to charge more, separate the balance onto two cards, so that you're using less than 30 percent of the available credit limit on each card.

4. Keep your credit accounts open, even if you're not running a balance. I got one of my credit cards in 1987. I don't use it very often, but having that kind of longevity on my credit history is extremely important to having a high credit score because it shows that you have the ability to manage credit well over a long period of time.

5. Avoid negative information. So, don't go bankrupt, go into foreclosure, go through a short sale, default on an auto loan, have a car repossessed, etc.

6. Make sure your credit history is error-free. If you pull a copy of your credit history and notice an error, you'll need to file an affidavit and go through the process explained on the CRAs website to get it removed.

(I have loads of additional information on credit at ThinkGlink.com, but these basics should get you almost entirely down the road.)

Here's the bottom line: If you have poor credit, you'll have almost no chance of getting a mortgage. If you have mediocre credit, you'll qualify (although maybe just for a government-backed loan like an FHA loan) but the interest rate will be higher than what you see on websites or hear about in the news. If you've got great credit, everyone will clamor for your business. So, pull a copy of your credit history and credit score first and make sure your score is as high as possible *before* you apply for a loan.

## Question 6: Should I Use My Friend Who Is an Agent?

The shortish answer is, of course, "Are you out of your mind?" In my experience, buying a home is stressful enough without laying friendship on the line and complicating everything.

This isn't to say that there aren't *some* friends *somewhere* who might make great agents and are able to separate personal from professional. But that's rare. Most often, you use a friend who is young (like you are) and who hasn't seen your particular movie before. So, mistakes are made, open houses are missed, misunderstandings about what you really want and need occur. You get mad or frustrated, and your agent-friend seethes quietly. Pretty soon, your agent-friend doesn't want to call because it's unpleasant, and the only thing you can talk about are houses you've seen or not seen and what everything is selling for. The friendship begins to crack and when you finally do find a house to buy, all that's left is for your agent-friend to ask you to refer him or her to other friends who might be buying. And while everyone has to start somewhere, you don't have to be the guinea pig or a training ground for your friend, particularly in a hot market, where experience can give you the upper hand in a tough negotiation.

I know you think I'm overselling this. Trust me. I'm not. And it's far worse if you use a relative. (So *don't*.)

When does working with friends pay off? If your friend has been in the business for a while, has a track record you can verify independently, and has the kind of impressive, can-do mindset where he or she is an overachiever in every sense of the word, it *might* be okay.

The best thing you can do is interview your agent-friend as well as a handful of other agents who work regularly in your neighborhood of choice. For a fair point of comparison, consider stacking up your agent-friend against someone who has been in business (successfully, full-time) for at least fifteen to twenty years. Pick agents to interview who are from big, well-known firms and do a full interview where you ask for a resume, talk about what kind of homes they typically help buyers purchase, and what mistakes they've seen their buyers make. And then, choose the agent with whom you have great chemistry. Buying a house is a lot like a short-term marriage—lots of ups and downs, angst and agony. You spend a lot of time with this person for as many months as it takes to find the right home and make an offer that gets accepted. Pick someone who makes you laugh, who is smart and knowledgeable. Who shows you he or she is listening by the types of homes you go to see.

If you do pick your friend, do a "pilot," or a test where you agree to spend a couple of weeks or a month looking for property and then evaluate where you are with the relationship (assuming you haven't already found and bid on a property). If your agent-friend doesn't agree, then I wouldn't bother starting the process. It's already doomed to fail. But if your agent-friend agrees to an initial limited term, then sure, give it a try. Just don't be afraid to say something if it's not working.

# Question 7: What Tools and Websites Will Make It Easier to Shop for or Buy a Home?

Studies show that 95 percent of all home buyers start their search for a home online. That makes sense, given how much time everyone spends staring at their phone. (Apparently, the remaining 5 percent of buyers simply drive by a sign, or hear from their parents, friends, or relatives that a house is for sale in their subdivision.)

But with more than a million websites that show homes for sale, how do you know which ones to use? Residential real estate websites divide into several big categories:

1. **Aggregator or portal sites.** These are sites like Realtor.com, Zillow.com, Trulia .com, and HomeFinder.com. Information comes from Multiple Listing Services (MLS) that upload listing information, and from agents who may provide separate data. Zillow owns Trulia and together they claim to have more than 100 million visitors each month. Realtor.com, which was sold by the National Association of Realtors to a company owned by Rupert Murdoch, claims to have the most listings. On each of these sites, you'll find homes for sale, homes that are not for sale but the owners would entertain an offer, and homes for rent. You'll also find interesting information about neighborhoods and be offered lots of opportunities to get a mortgage, a credit card, your credit history or score, and other items for sale.

2. **Agent or broker sites.** Each agent typically has a website, as do the brokerage firms they work for. Those agents who work for a national company, like Redfin, Century 21, Re/Max, Berkshire Hathaway, Coldwell Banker, Better Homes & Gardens, and Compass, may also have their listings featured on those "parent" sites, as well as any sites that are fed by the local MLS to which they belong. (That's how the data gets to sites like Realtor.com and Zillow.)

3. **Redfin and other discount brokerage companies.** There are also websites like Redfin, which is a discount brokerage company. If you're selling your home (I know, you don't even own your first home yet, but let's imagine), you can list your

property there for 1.5 percent,[*] which is a lot less than you'd pay to a full-service real estate brokerage company. That sort of discounting has helped the company attract listings in many major metropolitan areas. For buyers, it allows you to easily search their database by the usual bedrooms, bathrooms, and list price, but you can also search by other features, including school district. That's cool and helpful. Redfin offers home buyer and seller classes as well, and I'm hearing more buyers talk about getting listings from them.

4. **Auction companies and Auction.com.** In 2014, Google invested $50 million in Auction.com, and in 2016, the company renamed its holding company Ten-X and rebranded itself as the "Future of Real Estate." What's fun about Auction.com is picking a city and seeing how little it would cost to buy property. Not that you'd want to live in some of these neighborhoods, but the day I searched, there were houses in Chicago with minimum bids for as little as $250 to $1,000, a condo in Phoenix with a starting bid of $35,000, two very broken down–looking single family houses in St. Louis with a starting bid of $100, and more than two hundred homes coming up for auction in Las Vegas, where starting bids for single-family houses ranged from nothing (the bidding began at $0) to over $200,000.

5. **Other kinds of apps or mobile home-search websites.** HomeSnap (take a photo of a home and get details back; you can search more than 90 million homes but not in every market), Dwellr (which provides information powered by the US Census Bureau), Doorsteps (powered by Move.com, which owns Realtor.com, Doorsteps has been described as "the Tinder of Real Estate" because you swipe to use it), Xome (a form of discount broker where buyers get 1 percent back), ForSaleByOwner.com (which lists homes that are for sale without an agent), and almost an unlimited number of others.

6. **Other helpful sites or apps.** What if you want to search for a home by school district? You could use Redfin, or you could go to GreatSchools.org. You could also go to NCES.Ed.gov, which allows you to search the National Center for Education

---

[*] That was the pricing advertised as this edition of the book went to print.

Statistics through the Department of Education's database. If you're searching for a HUD home (an FHA foreclosure), you'd want to try HUDHomeStore.com, which is the official website for HUD homes. If you wanted to search best sports in schools, because you think your future children could be NBA stars, you might go to MaxPreps.com. NeighborhoodScout.com and Movoto.com offer information about neighborhoods and crime statistics. NextDoor.com helps you identify neighborhoods you might want to live in and connect with neighbors, while Safewise .com helps you figure out how safe that neighborhood is.

Research shows that today's home buyers (Millennials) are much more adept at using technology than previous generations, and that they expect their Realtors to be as fluent in tech as they are. That's a problem, because many real estate agents and brokers are older and not as fluid in using technology to aid the real estate process. That's why tech companies have stepped in, making billions of dollars in profits.

But here are some things to keep in mind:

1. At the height of the market before the Great Recession (roughly 2004 to 2006), around 6 million existing homes were sold each year. About 1 million new construction homes were sold in each of those years, too.

2. If you spend enough time looking at various websites, you'll figure out that most of them list the same homes for sale. Sure, there are some differences, but the primary bulk of listings is fed by the same multiple listing services.

3. Some websites are faster than others at delivering new listings to you. Some have better pictures. Some allow you to search by more variables, and some try to be everything to everybody.

What's the right website or mobile app? The one you (and your friends) like best.

 **FIRST-TIME HOME BUYER TIP:** There's a tendency to believe something if we see it online. But that's why Snopes, and other websites that verify facts, exist. In 2017, a real estate attorney in Glenview, Illinois, filed a lawsuit against Zillow because she said their Zestimate (essentially, a guess based on publicly available information) was actually an appraisal and that the Zestimate was valuing her townhouse at more than a hundred thousand dollars less than she thought it was worth. She sued Zillow for providing what she called an unlicensed appraisal that is incorrect because it isn't including more accurate comps, causing buyers to misjudge the true value of her property. While the case was dismissed, the question of how accurate Zestimates are is intriguing. Clearly, buyers and homeowners rely on Zestimates, but by Zillow's own admission, they aren't accurate 100 percent of the time. While the company says the vast majority of Zestimates are within 10 percent of the selling price of the home, independent third parties have stated that a significant number could be wildly inaccurate. I've found that in some cities, Zestimates are extremely close to accurate while in others, it's more than 20 percent off. When you're looking for a home, you should certainly look at a Zestimate. But remember that it's only an estimate of value, and doesn't replace an appraisal or what an experienced agent who works regularly in that neighborhood says the true market value is likely to be.

# Question 8: Where Can I Find a Deal?

In the aftermath of the Great Recession, there were incredible real estate deals almost everywhere. Home prices had fallen 25 to 75 percent in different areas and there were so many homes for sale that investors started scooping them up for pennies on the dollar, in some cases tens of thousands of homes at a time.

Today, it's a lot harder to find a steal on a home. Sure, they exist, especially in places that are high in crime or with poor school districts. Or you might get lucky and find a HUD home (an FHA foreclosure) or an REO (bank-owned real estate acquired by a foreclosure or a deed-in-lieu of foreclosure), or even a seller who is desperate to sell (yes, occasionally those exist).

You can also find deals if you're willing to buy a home that doesn't look like an HGTV set. HGTV went on the air on December 1, 1994, which was approximately eight months after the first edition of this book was published. Not many people watched the channel then. Today, it's become synonymous with all things home. You can see new trends unfold in front of your eyes (*Tiny Homes*, for example, or all the Fix and Flip shows), but they're also great examples of how homes are transformed through staging and minor renovations into showstopping examples of ideal real estate before the agent (let alone the buyer) walks through the door. Sellers have learned that if they want to unload their homes for the most money and in the shortest time frame possible, they'll have to follow HGTV (if they don't watch it already, their agents will often recommend it) and make sure their homes look like they're in perfect shape.

But not all sellers have the time, talent, or cash to remake their houses into a home that looks like it could be a developer's model. And therein lies an excellent opportunity to buy an ugly home in a great neighborhood, fix it up, and then live there or sell it. (Yes, some home buyers have made significant money in flipping their first homes, and have gone on to make it a nice side business, since every two years you can keep all of your profits tax-free.) Several houses down from mine is a 1960s single-story house that had great "bones."* The owners retired to Scottsdale, Arizona, and bought a lovely home during the tail end of the Great Recession at a dramatic discount. But they had an unrealistic expectation of what their older, not-fixed-up home would fetch, even though it was in a pricey, great school district suburb. In the end, the buyers (a Millennial couple with a baby) purchased the property for just over the land value and are fixing it up so that it has a new kitchen, new bathrooms, and feels completely remodeled. When they're done, their home will likely be worth a lot more than they put into it. In short: a steal.

You might also look for a deal by purchasing a small apartment building, often called a "multifamily" building. The idea is that you live in one of the units and rent out the others to help defray the cost of owning a larger, more expensive property. Ideally, you'll eventually start to make money from the rentals and will move on to a larger property (multifamily or perhaps a house) while continuing to rent all the units in the first building. Why is this a deal? Because it allows you to leverage (or control) a larger, more expensive asset that will ultimately bring in more revenue and profit over the years.

The bottom line is that there are many ways to think about a great real estate deal and where to find them:

1. **Location.** Buying on the edges of a great neighborhood, since gentrification tends to push outward, block by block, or in a neighborhood that isn't great now but is turning due to an investment in infrastructure (roads or schools), amenity (near a recreational asset like a revamped park, library, High Line, bike path, or mall).

---

* Agents like to talk about a home's "bones," which is shorthand for the basic structure of a house. It's everything you wouldn't change if you were doing a cosmetic remodel, even though some nonstructural walls might be removed.

2. **Condition or size.** Smallest, ugliest, or most outdated house in the neighborhood.

3. **Desperation of the seller.** A seller who is desperate to sell might give you an extra-special deal, especially if the seller can get the bank to agree to a short sale.

4. **Bank-owned real estate.** Foreclosures or properties that were acquired by banks through deeds-in-lieu of foreclosure might come on the market as a deal but may not be offered through typical real estate channels.

5. **Auction.** Sometimes a seller just wants to unload an asset quickly, and there may be a deal to be made.

6. **Multifamily/multi-use properties.** Buy a building with multiple residential units and live in one while renting out the others. Or, buy a building that offers commercial space on the first floor and multiple living units above.

7. **Family and friends.** Finally, sometimes a member of your extended family or a friend will help you find a deal. Someone might pass away and the heirs will decide they want to keep the property in the family and will offer it to you at a below-market price. Or a friend who lives in your neighborhood of choice will tell you about an owner near them who is thinking about putting a property on the market and you get an introduction and buy the property before it is officially listed. And, in case you wonder whether this really happens, read the story below of what happened to Fred's house.

 **FIRST-TIME HOME BUYER TIP:** Fred was selling his house and wanted to maximize his profits, so he asked me what to do. I told him to put a detailed listing sheet under everyone's door in the neighborhood and ask them if they knew anyone who wanted to buy near them. Since people always want people they know (and like) to live near them, Fred soon got a call from his neighbor across the street. He wound up renting the property to the neighbor's son, who eventually bought the property from him. What's the lesson for you? Once you've decided on your neighborhood(s) of choice, find out if you know anyone (or if your friends know someone) who lives in the neighborhood who can let you know if they hear of a property that might be coming on the market. In a hot market, sellers are often looking for a way to minimize the commission they'll pay and are often happier to just sell the property for a fair price (minimizing the hassle as well), which might give you a deal.

# Question 9: How Do I Know I've Found the Right Home for Me?

First-time buyers (and, frankly, even home buyers who are on their fourth or fifth home purchase) often look for that elusive "right" house. They'll search high and low, obsessively check listings online, and run each property through a nearly unending checklist of "must-haves." But sometimes, even after an exhaustive search, they're unable to pull the trigger and put together an offer.

While there's nothing wrong with looking at 100+ homes (after all, I'm the poster child for being thorough!), I'll often tell buyers that there is no "right" choice. Nearly any house that meets your needs and some of your wants, and also falls into your price range, might be a good home for you to buy now. (In the next chapter, Question 10, Should I Make a Wish List? What About a Reality Check?, I'll discuss the difference between what you want in a home and what you can't live without.)

The important word to focus on is "now," as opposed to later. I think the act of buying a home is a confluence of timing, money, wants, needs, trust, and luck. There's certainly an element of "right place, right time"—but I'm also a believer in the adage that "luck is what happens when preparation meets opportunity."* Today's buyers do a lot of the work required to buy a home well before they even contact their first agent. According to the National Association of Realtors' Home Buyer and Seller Generational Trends survey, first-time home buyers spend an average of three weeks searching for a home (which might well fall outside of an unknowing home buyer's true price range) online before contacting an agent. There are hours spent walking through neighborhoods and open houses and reading online blogs (or, one hopes, books like this!) about the process of buying a home.

But nothing replaces the real work (and panic) that starts once you know what you can afford and begin looking at homes that are most assuredly in your price range (or just a bit above). Add to that pressure cooker the knowledge that there aren't that many homes you can afford in your neighborhood of choice; or that there are likely to be bidding wars (with homes selling in a day with multiple offers) where you're up against a very experi-

---

* This quote is attributed to Lucius Annaeus Seneca (c. 4 BC–AD 65), often known simply as Seneca, or Seneca the Younger. According to Wikipedia, he was a Roman philosopher, statesman, dramatist, humorist (hard to imagine given the time frame), and the son of Seneca the Elder.

enced investor with a pile of cash, no financing contingency, and a fast closing date. The fun of simply looking through website listings and scrolling through photos or driving past homes you've seen online evaporates. What's left is a vise through which reason often escapes.

So how do you know it's the right house? For some people, it's about a feeling they get when they see the outside for the first time. For others, it's a feeling they get as they walk through the interior. For some, being comfortable enough to sink into the seller's living room sofa and daydream about where you'd put your own couch and table is telling. And for the rest . . . well, they don't know. They just hope for the best and comfort themselves with the knowledge they can always sell and the worst thing that will happen is they'll lose some money.

Remember when I told you about the time Sam and I were looking for the house we live in now? We had seen maybe seventy-five houses and were driving around a suburb that was a bit north of where we had been looking, a place of just 8,000 residents that felt a lot more like a small town than a proliferation of strip malls. We had been having a discussion about what we liked and what we didn't like in the houses we had seen, and (surprise, surprise) we had some very different views. But all of a sudden, we came up to a street, stopped at the corner, and looked up. There, on a tiny swell, was a small blue and white farmhouse, sitting on a perfectly manicured lot. I pointed and said to Sam, "I like that one." He looked up and said, "Me, too." There was something about the look of the house on the little swell, the grass and tall trees rolling up to it, that felt like home. We called the agent, made an appointment and went to see the property a few times, but we couldn't make a deal with the owner, who was asking $100,000 more than we eventually paid. We saw another 50+ houses, and four months later came back to this house and made a deal on the front lawn.

Later, after we closed, I remember walking around the backyard. "I think there's gold here," I said to Sam, who started laughing at me.[*] But what I meant was, this house and its land felt like the kind of place on which we could build our future, raise our family, settle down for the long run. The house wasn't much to see (five years later we would go down to the studs to renovate and expand it), and it would take virtually every penny we had to buy it. But it felt like home from the moment we saw it.

---

[*] A common occurrence, I can assure you.

How do you know it's the right house? You might not, but use these questions to help you get close enough to decide whether to make an offer:

1. Does this property meet my needs? How does it match up to my reality check? (See Question 10 for details on wish lists and reality checks.)

2. Do I get some of the things I want in a home if I buy it?

3. Can I afford it? Remember that the cost of buying a home doesn't just include the mortgage, real estate property taxes, and insurance premiums, but a host of other maintenance and upkeep expenses, assessments for condos, townhomes, and home-owner association members, and whatever you do to decorate the place. (See Chapter 5—How Do I Know What I Can Afford to Spend?—for details.)

4. How easy will it be to sell it? Today's hot seller's market (where there aren't enough homes for all the buyers who want them) could easily turn into a hot buyer's market. And if you're on the other side of that, you could have trouble selling. So, think about how easy it will be to sell your home before you make an offer, and if there is anyone besides you who would want to live there. (See Question 32—How Do I Become Selective When Choosing a Home?—for more on this topic.)

5. Am I in love with this property? I once wrote a piece for *Chicago* magazine and included a story about a commercial building that a local developer had built. I put in the story that the developer was "in love" with his property, and he got so mad at me for including that detail. I thought it was interesting and revealing, and entirely appropriate—he did love that building and the details he had put into it, but apparently he didn't think it was appropriate for a developer to admit that in public. But the cliché "love is blind" can be true in real estate, too, and as it was for that developer, you have to be able to separate how strongly you feel about a property (or even one facet of the property, like the kitchen or a view) to make sure you're not blinding yourself to the other realities of living there.

If you answer them honestly, these five questions should protect you from making a horrible mistake. Will you wind up with the best house? Maybe not. But will you wind up with the right house for now? You almost certainly will, especially if you dig into the details and "own" the process of buying.

# CHAPTER 2

# The Beginning: How Do I Know What I Want to Buy?

As we learned from the last question, the difference between being a wannabe and a successful home buyer may boil down to nothing more than knowing the difference between what you *want* in a home and what you *can't live without*.

You're thinking, "It can't be that simple." Ah, but the difference between what you want and what you need requires the ability to recognize what's really important to you—and to be able to compromise on the rest. Unfortunately, the ability to compromise is often lost between two spouses, partners, or people who forget that they can't afford to satisfy their every whim.

(And for those of you who think that having a million dollars to spend will buy you everything you've ever wanted in a house: It doesn't. By the time you get there, inflation and your ever-expanding to-do list will make the acquisition of your "wish list" a virtually impossible dream. But before you get depressed, here's what does happen for most: You learn to be content with what you have, which is my definition of happiness.)

 **20/20 HINDSIGHT TIP:** It might make you feel better to know that the inability to compromise isn't limited to first-time buyers. Each time we buy a home, we feel that *this* is the time we're going to get everything we want. We work hard and deserve it, right? But life doesn't work that way, and neither does home buying. The next few questions are designed to give you some insight into what's really important to you and your family.

# Question 10: Should I Make a Wish List?
# What About a Reality Check?

The best real estate agents and brokers will ask their first-time buyers to create a wish list detailing everything they'd love to have in a home, including:

- **Location.** Think about where you like to shop, where your children will attend school, where you work, where you worship, and where your friends and family live.
- **Size.** Think about the number of bedrooms you want, the size of the garden, the extra room you may need for expansion or family flexibility, where you'll do the laundry, and what kind of storage space you need.
- **Amenities.** Think about the garage, kitchen and bathroom appliances, swimming pool, fireplace, air-conditioning, electrical wiring, furnace, and hardwood floors.
- **Condition.** Do you want a home in move-in condition? Or are you willing to put in some "sweat equity," to borrow a *This Old House* phrase, to build in value?

First, you need to figure out exactly what constitutes your wish list. That may involve ranking things like: granite, marble, quartz, slate, or perhaps inlaid, stained concrete kitchen countertops; a wood-burning fireplace; three-car garage; four-person whirlpool; views of some body of water; views of the mountains; the best school district in your state; a five-minute walk to work; four, six, or eight bedrooms; a master suite with his and her custom-built, walk-in closets; and vaulted, tray, or bare-beamed ceilings. You get the picture. (If you don't, check out Pinterest, Zillow, Trulia, HGTV.com, or a million other websites that show incredible images of homes' exteriors and interiors.)

At first glance, many of these items may seem to be in conflict with each other: You want to be close to a transportation network so it's easy to get around, and yet you want a quiet and peaceful neighborhood. You might want to walk or bike to work, but when you come home, you want your neighborhood to be dark, silent, and secure. You want a wide variety of shopping opportunities, and yet you also need to be close enough to your health club to use it on a regular basis. (And who wants to drive a couple of miles for milk and eggs?) You want to take advantage of the city, yet live in the suburbs.

But that's the whole point of a wish list. If you're honest about what you want, the inconsistencies and conflicts will emerge. Most first-time buyers are confused by all of their choices. They take on that "kid in a candy store" mentality; many have difficulty choosing between different styles of homes. One broker says she always has a few first-time buyers each year who need to see at least one of everything in the area: a California ranch, an old Victorian, an in-town condo, and several new subdivisions. It takes a tremendous amount of time, but it's never wasted. Even if the buyer decides ultimately to go with a loft, you're learning what you don't want, and that's extremely useful.

Some agents and brokers also use reality checks to help their clients define their needs as well as their wants. Brokers often say that "buyers are liars." Of course, that isn't really what they mean. They mean that home buyers, particularly first-timers, don't understand the difference between what they want and what they need. So they share their wish list, or ask for whatever their friends on Facebook are buying, or they look backward in their life and request a loft when really they need a four-bedroom house in the suburbs over the next five to ten years. A reality check helps buyers understand how to think about what they can't live without.

Joanne, a real estate sales associate in New Jersey, says that she asks her first-time buyers very specific questions about what they need to survive in their first home. "I just know their pocketbook will not allow them to have everything they want. I tell them they'll begin to get what they want with their second home. Not the first."

Here are some of the questions a savvy real estate agent might ask (or, that you can ask yourself):

- How many bedrooms do you need?
- Do you and/or your spouse or partner work from home, or do you like to have a formal space in which to work while you're home?
- How many children do you have or are you planning to have while you live in this home?
- Is a garage absolutely necessary? How many spaces do you need?
- Why do you need a home with a basement or attic?
- Do you use public transportation on a daily basis? Do you bike to work?
- How close to work do you need to be?
- Does driving on a major expressway or in traffic make you crazy?
- Do you want to care for a garden or would you prefer a maintenance-free home?
- Where do your friends and close family members live?

- Is being close to your house of worship important to you?
- Do you need to have great cell phone service?

By asking specific questions about your daily lifestyle, good real estate agents can center in on the best location, home size, and amenities for your budget. They can read between the lines on your wish list. And they can reality-check.

But wish lists and reality checks have another use. By prioritizing the items on these lists, a good real estate agent can tell which items you might be willing to trade off. For example, if the first wish on your list is to have a four-bedroom, two-bath house, and the thirty-eighth item is a wood-burning fireplace, then the broker knows you'd probably prefer a four-bedroom two-bath house without a fireplace to a three-bedroom, two-bath home with a fireplace.

The bottom line is this: Unless you win the lottery or are independently wealthy, you're probably going to have to make some of those trade-offs when buying your first home.

And sometimes you're going to make a mistake.

**NEW CONSTRUCTION TIP:** The general rule about new construction these days is that you'll get a brand-new place with new appliances, new windows, and the rest, but you'll likely have to make some trade-offs to swing it. If the average existing home costs $250,000 in a major market, the average price of new construction typically tops $300,000. So if you can only spend $250,000 and you want a new construction property, the trade-offs will generally include the overall size of the home and where it's located. Also, don't be fooled by the list price of a new construction home. The typical new construction buyer spends 10 to 15 percent above the "list" price in upgrades, all of which usually have to be paid in cash, up front, so be sure to factor that into your budgeting.

### ILYCE AND SAM'S STORY

When Sam and I bought our first place together (a vintage Chicago co-op built in the 1920s), we didn't own one. Since we lived in the city, overlooking Lake Michigan, and had easy access to public transportation, we couldn't even envision that one day we might change our minds and purchase a car. So our wish list included a parking place, but it was low on the list, maybe around the twentieth item.

On the other hand, a wood-burning fireplace was pretty high up there, about number five. You can guess what happened. When we were given that Volvo a few years later, and began hunting and pecking for parking spaces on the street, we were sorry (particularly on cold, snowy, below-zero Chicago nights) that we didn't have a space in which to park the car. But not as sorry as when we went to sell our unit and discovered that most home buyers in that area wouldn't even consider a building that doesn't have parking. Fewer people cared about the fireplace—although we did.

You can bet that a two-car garage was right near the top of our list for the next home we purchased.

Brokers say the best wish list should include everything you want in a home, such as location, schools, shopping, and distance to work. If your initial list says "nice house, four bedrooms," try asking yourself these questions to stimulate your true desires.

How often do I go to the city? Suburbs? Country? Where would I rather be?

How long do I want to spend driving to work each day?

Do I have frequent guests? Do I need a separate guest room?

Do I work from home? How often? Does my spouse or partner? Do we need separate office spaces?

Do I want a special play area for my children?

Will my children take a bus to school, walk, or will I have to drive them?

How far away is my house of worship?

Do I want a big garden?

Must I have a garage? For two cars? Three cars? Do I need a dedicated parking space?

How far away is the airport? Grocery store? Dry cleaners? Gym? Train station?

What is my favorite form of recreation and how far away from it am I?

Where does my family live? Where do my friends live? How far away from them do I want to be?

Do I want a home that is in mint condition (also called "blue ribbon" condition by some people in various parts of the country)? Or, do I want to buy a small house on a large lot and fix it up or even add on to it over time?

Questions of lifestyle are crucial components of a wish list. Do you and your spouse/partner like to stay in on Saturday nights? Or do you prefer to be "close to the action"? And will that change over the years? Are you a single woman or married with children? Are you a single parent? Gay or lesbian couple? Do you have dogs/cats/other animals? Do you travel frequently? Do you own a car? Do you own, or are you contemplating purchasing, a boat in the near future? Will you want to be within fifteen minutes of the marina?

### PERRY'S STORY

When Perry was looking for a house a few years ago, a dock was near the very top of her wish list. It ranked about even with choosing the right school district for her daughter. Her husband is a sailor who sails competitively, they own several boats, and he basically lives on the water. After looking at more than a hundred homes up and down the coast, the house she and her husband wound up buying near Washington, D.C., has four docks and an incredible view of the sunrise—and is in a great school district. (To be fair, Perry wasn't buying her first home. Depending on where you're looking, you may have to make additional trade-offs to get waterfront property.)

You can see how personal preferences feed into the list. Each spouse or partner has to create his or her own wish list and reality check and prioritize them. Some parents even ask their older children to think about what they want and need in a home. Then, together, you and your spouse or partner should discuss each of your lists and how to prioritize them into one wish list and one reality check. Use the worksheets that follow to guide your discussion (and feel free to open something really delicious to drink in order to "lubricate" the discussion).

# WORKSHEET
## *Your Wish List*

You and your spouse or partner should each create your own wish lists and reality checks (see next worksheet for how to create a reality check). After you're done, sit together and work through each item. Since you'll only be able to afford one home, you should create one wish list and one reality check from which to start your search.

| WISH LIST ITEM | YOUR RANK | SPOUSE OR PARTNER'S RANK | CHILD/OTHER BUYER'S RANK |
|---|---|---|---|
| 1 | | | |
| 2 | | | |
| 3 | | | |
| 4 | | | |
| 5 | | | |
| 6 | | | |
| 7 | | | |
| 8 | | | |
| 9 | | | |
| 10 | | | |
| 11 | | | |
| 12 | | | |
| 13 | | | |
| 14 | | | |
| 15 | | | |
| 16 | | | |
| 17 | | | |
| 18 | | | |
| 19 | | | |
| 20 | | | |

NOTE: if your list exceeds twenty items, continue on a blank sheet of paper (or pull out your laptop or tablet) until you've put everything you've ever wished for in a home in writing. Be as specific and detailed as possible. Being specific will make it easier for your agent to assist you in finding the right home.

Once you get the information down on paper, try to organize it into a concrete sentence: "I want a four-bedroom, three-bath home with a large garden, a fairly new kitchen, loads of closet space, a wood-burning fireplace, and a two-car garage, within a fifteen-minute commute to the office and church, down the street from the high school, and in such-and-such location."

That's a start. Now, prioritize the items in your wish list and think about which items you'd trade off for others. For example, would you give up a wood-burning fireplace if it meant having a two-car garage? Could you get by with a smaller house if it meant you'd be in a better school district? Would you prefer to be closer to work even though it means giving up a large garden? What if you had to live in a condo but could walk to work? Keep comparing each item with the other until you've got a coherent wish list of items that makes sense to you.

(It's okay if the top five or even seven items are of equal importance. But figuring out the handful of things you most want to have in your new home will help *enormously* down the line when you're actually seeing real properties and your emotions come into play.)

## WORKSHEET
### *Your Reality Check*

Again, if a wish list is everything you want in a home, a reality check is everything you can't live without. For example, you may want a four-bedroom home, but you absolutely need three bedrooms. You may want a large garden, but you really need a place to hang out outside, have your children or dogs play safely, and grill hotdogs and burgers for your friends. Your reality check may include many of the same items as your wish list, but perhaps in a pared-down version. This is the place where you want to be completely honest about the minimum you need to live comfortably in your new home.

Ideally, each spouse or partner does his or her own reality check. Afterward, you should sit together and work through each item. You'll be able to afford only one home, so you should end up with one list of basic needs and one list of wants.

| | REALITY CHECK ITEM | YOUR RANK | SPOUSE OR PARTNER'S RANK | CHILD/OTHER BUYER'S RANK |
|---|---|---|---|---|
| 1 | _____ | _____ | _____ | _____ |
| 2 | _____ | _____ | _____ | _____ |
| 3 | _____ | _____ | _____ | _____ |
| 4 | _____ | _____ | _____ | _____ |
| 5 | _____ | _____ | _____ | _____ |

6    _____   _____   _____   _____

7    _____   _____   _____   _____

8    _____   _____   _____   _____

9    _____   _____   _____   _____

10    _____   _____   _____   _____

11    _____   _____   _____   _____

12    _____   _____   _____   _____

13    _____   _____   _____   _____

14    _____   _____   _____   _____

15    _____   _____   _____   _____

16    _____   _____   _____   _____

17    _____   _____   _____   _____

18    _____   _____   _____   _____

19    _____   _____   _____   _____

20    _____   _____   _____   _____

 **20/20 HINDSIGHT TIP:** No two people are alike. No matter how compatible you and your spouse or partner are, you are two individuals and you're going to end up with two different (sometimes *really* different) lists. Rather than denigrate each other's wish list or reality check items, try to view the lists as a statement of each person's priorities (again, this is where libations can be extremely helpful, or do something that relieves stress, like taking a walk while you talk). Some of each person's priorities should make their way into your final wish list and reality check. If either list is too one-sided, you're headed for home-buying trouble.

From your reality check list above, create a single sentence that represents your basic needs for a home. If you're a single woman, your reality check might include: "I need two bedrooms (mostly for resale purposes), two bathrooms, a dedicated parking space or attached garage, some sort of outdoor living space, security in the building, and a twenty-minute drive to work or less."

These details give you and your broker something to work with. You can go online and use a portal to search for a home that has some of your parameters. (While today's home shopping portals are good, the search parameters will become even more specific and helpful over the next few years.) Meanwhile, your real estate broker or agent can take your wish list and begin to match it to homes listed in your local multiple listing service.

Are creating a wish list and reality check worth the time and effort? Brokers say they are. Even though a good broker should spend an hour or two divining the same information, writing up a wish list and reality check will help focus your mind on what you really want and what you can't live without.

Trust me. An honest wish list is the road map to finding the house of your dreams.

 **FIRST-TIME BUYER TIP:** How long you plan to stay in your home is critical to making all kinds of successful decisions when it comes to buying a home. It affects everything from where and what you buy to how you wind up financing your home. Although you may have one timeline in mind when you create your wish list and reality check ("We won't move until our youngest finishes high school" or ". . . our home-based business requires larger office space"), later years may bring surprises. I'll talk about time-based planning throughout this book. For now, think carefully about your timeline when creating your wish list and reality check.

## Question 11: How Do I Figure Out Where I Want to Live?

Finding the right location is a problem for many buyers, not just first-timers. In part, the answer will be decided in the spot where your bank account meets your wish list. Neighborhoods being what they are, you can almost certainly find something in your price range in or near an area in which you'd want to live.

In a story I once did for WGN-TV before the Great Recession, I took at look at what was available for $220,000 in several different parts of the Chicago metropolitan area. What I found is that you could buy something in almost every location, from the fanciest suburbs to a more modest city neighborhood. What you'd have to do, however, is trade size or amenities for price. For example, when I did that story, $220,000 bought you a tiny one-bedroom apartment with an okay view just off Michigan Avenue. Or, you could spend the same amount of money and buy a three-bedroom ranch-style home in Haines-ville, about two hours out of Chicago, with a lovely garden, fireplace, sunken tub in the master bath, and a fully finished basement. (Today, $220,000 *might* get you a studio in the 60611 zip code, which encompasses North Michigan Avenue.)

The same thing is true in almost every other urban area. For example, I'm sure that you could find a relatively affordable studio or one-bedroom condo in an area that also in-cludes million-dollar homes. Buildings in Manhattan that contain apartments costing $10 million or more are right next to buildings in which the apartments go for a fraction of that amount. But if you must have three bedrooms, that expensive suburb or building will most likely be out of your price range.

The point is, you can find something affordable in nearly every neighborhood. Whether it meets your reality check is another story.

The first thing to do is to find a suburb or neighborhood that offers homes (condos, townhomes, or single-family houses) that meet your needs at prices you can afford. Some-times the easiest way to find what you're looking for is to cross out options that don't work, for one reason or another. Start by asking your broker to cross-match your price range with your reality list, or go online to one or more of the big real estate portals and enter your price range and the part of your metropolitan area in which you think you'd want to live. The price range, combined with the number of bedrooms and bathrooms that you must have (from your reality check), should instantly narrow your choices to several sub-urbs or neighborhoods. Now, take a close look at these areas, and apply some of the fea-tures of your wish list: Is one in a better school district? Is another closer to work? Does one have more character or better shopping? Is one located on a golf course? Is one nearer (or farther away from) your parents or in-laws?

Once you've narrowed down your choice of areas to two or three suburbs, neighbor-hoods, or even streets, take an extensive driving tour of these areas. Get out and walk around the streets. Sit on a bench and watch the people go by. After all, these might be your future neighbors. Get a coffee at the local coffee shop and watch who comes in. Next, start looking at some of the houses in the neighborhood, perhaps during a Sunday open house tour. If you begin to see homes you like in an acceptable, affordable neighborhood, you're on the right track.

**RESOURCES:** The Internet has made shopping for a community a much easier task, particularly for out-of-state home buyers. There are sites for most major metropolitan areas, and many brokerage sites (both national and local) contain a fair amount of community information. You can shop for a home by going to a site and simply keying in some of the items on your reality checklist. For example, you can request all listing information for homes that match a particular description (say, four bedrooms, two baths, under $300,000) within a certain location. If nothing comes up that meets your needs at the price you can afford, it may mean (1) the neighborhood is too expensive for your price range, (2) the type of housing in which you're interested doesn't exist, or (3) you need to try another website.

## Question 12: What Does Location, Location, Location Really Mean?

Among real estate industry professionals, "location, location, location" is called the broker's maxim. It's certainly a cliché, but you might even call it the Realtor's Mantra. It's the credo that all real estate agents live by, and during the days, weeks, and months when your broker helps you search for a home, you're likely to hear this phrase more than once. But what does it really mean?

Here's how I've always taken it: The first location is the right city or suburb. The second location is the right neighborhood. And the final location is where on the block the property is located (or if you're buying in a high-rise, where in the high-rise your condo is located and what view you have). Brokers say that successful buying and selling is linked to the location of the home. You can usually change everything about a home except its location. Think about it: You can paint, decorate, gut the interior of the house, replace the asphalt shingles with slate, put on new siding, add a deck, repave the driveway, and plant flowers. But you can't uproot the entire thing with a bulldozer and drive it two towns over.

(Of course, some houses literally can be picked up and moved. People do buy houses that are slated to be torn down and move them to new locations. And there are mobile homes or manufactured homes that come prebuilt from a factory and are built onto a lot in a day or two. That's not what we're talking about here. You're not going to move an apartment from midtown Manhattan to New Jersey. And no one takes a 150-year-old brick townhouse from Boston's North End and moves it to Newburyport, Massachusetts.)

If the house of your dreams is located next to a railroad yard, you should probably just go back to sleep and try to dream up something else. A poor location will severely limit any property's ability to appreciate in value and will hamper your ability to sell the property quickly in the future. If a home is priced very low or has been for sale for a long time, a poor location may be the reason.

**ED'S STORY**

Ed, a real estate attorney, bought and sold several homes before he purchased the one that backed up to Chicago's famous elevated train tracks, known as the "El." It was an 1880s brick two-story house with a nice yard that desperately needed some TLC.

But—it backed up to the El. Trains run by there every ten to fifteen minutes, faster in rush hour. The whole house shook. Ed stood for a while inside the house. He didn't seem to think it would be a problem. "You get used to it; I hardly even hear it." He made an offer.

He proceeded to completely renovate it, even putting in a sauna. When he decided to move to Texas a few years later, he put the house on the market. Two years later, it was still for sale, waiting for someone who wanted to spend several hundred thousand dollars buying an overimproved house in a good neighborhood, but in a very poor location. (It finally sold, and has since sold again.)

What is a poor location? Defining "poor" is often a matter of taste, and it's very localized. To local brokers, a poor location means a home may be difficult to sell because it is located:

- Next to a railroad yard;
- Near a toxic waste or municipal garbage dump;
- On top of, or next to, a freeway, expressway, or interstate highway;
- In the center of nightlife activity;
- Near a busy intersection, or on the busiest street in town, even if that street is a comparatively quiet rural lane;
- Next to a school;
- In the midst of gang territory, or an otherwise high-crime area;
- On a run-down block or in a deteriorating neighborhood;

- In a city, town, or suburb having significant budget problems, poor public schools, or a lousy local economy;
- Backing up or next to a type of housing that is different from the rest of the neighborhood. (For example, if you're looking at a single-family house and all of the other single-family homes back up onto other single-family homes, but the one you like backs up to an apartment complex, that could be a geographical problem.)

Of course, plenty of people can spin what might normally be called a poor location into a positive selling point. If you buy a home in a run-down neighborhood that is surrounded by yuppie housing, you might be able to turn a nice profit as the neighborhood improves over the years. Being located next to a noisy high school may mean you can keep an eye on your children throughout the day. Twenty-five years ago, you could have picked up a large, old house in or near downtown Denver for a song. In 2017, Denver was one of the hottest housing markets in the country, with hardly a For Sale sign to be seen in any of the lovely neighborhoods that now surround downtown.

A good location, on the other hand, is one that allows the owner to thoroughly enjoy every aspect of his or her home. It will be located close, but not too close, to shopping, restaurants, work, transportation, good schools, etc. A good location is one that you can easily sell to someone else, giving you additional flexibility (not to mention peace of mind). If when you're looking for homes, you're faced with the choice between a beautiful home in a lousy location, or a slightly smaller, less beautiful home in an excellent location, which one will you choose?

You have to be careful. You might not think that being on the busiest street is a problem, if you're moving to a smaller town from Fifth Avenue in New York City. But if you're trying to sell that home and you've overpaid for it, the financial consequences could be severe. The same principle applies to condos. When Sam and I bought an investment condo off the blueprints more than ten years ago, we were careful to buy above the floor that had partially obstructed views. For a condo building that had some amazing views, you'd never want to own a condo where the views were obstructed. That will always be considered one of the worst units in the building.

 **20/20 TIP:** "Location" doesn't just refer to the particular suburb or neighborhood in which you live. It also refers to the block on which your home is located, and even to your home's placement on that block. If corner lots are more valuable in your neighborhood, and you live in the middle of the block, that's a geographic factor you're not going to be able to change. Since you can't, always think about how easy or difficult a home may be to sell *before* you make an offer to purchase.

 **NEW CONSTRUCTION TIP:** When you buy in a new development, you are often looking at a large, vacant cornfield with perhaps a spec house (one that the developer builds and furnishes to show you what the other homes in the development will be like). From that, you're supposed to extrapolate what the neighborhood will look like. When it comes to new construction, location is even more important than usual. Certain lots will be deemed "premier," and the developer will charge a higher fee for them. For example, on a golf course development, lots that face the golf course might be two to three times as costly as lots that face the outside street. But they might also appreciate in value at twice the rate of a nonview lot. Should you buy the most expensive option? Brokers say it depends on what you want and what you can afford. If you want to live on a golf course, and a golf course view is important to you, and you can afford it, then go ahead. If your choice is to buy a nonview lot or live outside the community, you might want to give up the view just to get inside the gates. When you look at the developer's master plan for the area, think through which lots are most and least expensive and try to understand the developer's reasoning behind his or her pricing strategy. That could be important information when it comes time to sell.

## Question 13: How Long Do I Plan to Live in My Future Home?

This may be the single most important question for you to answer in this book. Why? Because the answer directly affects the size and type of home you buy, where it's located, as well as the type of mortgage you use to finance your purchase.

Times have changed since our parents bought their homes. Chances are, unless they've retired or are in professions where they are required to relocate to different parts of the country from time to time, your parents are still living in the home in which you grew up. (Maybe, if you're at the upper end of the Millennial spectrum, and your parents were older when they had you, it's possible that they're either just planning to move or have just completed a move to a retirement property.)

My mother, Susanne, lived in the same Chicago co-op apartment building for nearly forty years. It was the first (and only) home she and my father purchased together. After more than twenty years as a top-selling real estate agent, she began to look around for a new place to buy. She finally found a brand-new building going up just a block and a half west of Michigan Avenue, on Chicago's near north side, in a neighborhood known as River North. At the end of 2003, the building was finally completed and she moved into her new condo, which she refers to as her "retirement home." A few months later, she finally sold the co-op in which I was raised.

Aside from being one of the top real estate agents of her day, my mother's experience in homeownership is pretty typical of her generation. But it will likely be quite different from yours. Statistics from the National Association of Realtors (NAR), a national trade association based in Washington, D.C., reveal that before the Great Recession people lived in their homes only about five to seven years on average. A lot of that was due to the buying and selling (fixing and flipping) that took place from around 1999 through 2006, when the real estate industry was last on a tear.

Today, a slightly smaller percentage of Americans own their own homes: The national rate has fallen from a high of 67.4 percent in 2009 (which is similar to other industrialized nations) to about 63.5 percent in 2017. There are a number of reasons for this, but mostly it's because homeownership is becoming less affordable to more Americans, despite historic low interest rates, since home prices have risen faster than wages from 2010 to 2015. In 2017, home prices rose twice as fast as wages. Millennials, who would naturally be the first-time-buyer generation, are facing a mountain of student loans, not to mention credit card debt. And they're marrying later and starting families later (if they're having children), which are two triggers for home buying. So if you also factor in the number of homeowners who lost their homes during the Great Recession, whose credit was subsequently destroyed, the lower number of homeowners begins to make sense.

Another thing that's different: People are once again living in their homes longer. Whether that's due to rising prices or low interest rates or inventory being so short that they can't figure out where they'd rather live, Americans who are buying homes are keeping them and, in some cases, renting out a room or two (thanks to websites like Airbnb and VRBO) to make ends meet.

**ANDY AND KATIE'S STORY**

Andy and Katie met when he returned from years of working in Europe, and she was recently divorced with two young boys. They decided to get married and move from the Chicago suburb in which she lived to one five miles away, which would be closer to where Andy worked.

But it didn't work out. The schools weren't right for Katie's boys, and they started to fail out of their classes, so she signed them up for private school. She and Andy had their first baby together, and she got pregnant with a second right away. Suddenly, Katie thought about how much money she would be spending to send four children to private schools.

Instead, they sold their new home and moved back to the suburb where she and her children had been so happy for so many years. The compromise will be Andy's commute, which he is willing to make for the sake of their children.

How are you supposed to know how long you're going to live in your home? I suppose there's no way to know for sure—unless you're hiding a crystal ball from me. For some general guidelines, refer back to the Cycle of Life on page 14.

## Moving as a National Pastime

The average family moves five to seven times. In addition to accommodating fluctuating family sizes (grown-up children, grandchildren, aging parents, etc.), buying and selling homes is one of the best ways to accumulate wealth.* By purchasing a home, fixing it up, and selling it every five to seven years (or even seven to ten years), you should be able to increase the size of your equity (the cash you have in your home) significantly over the course of your lifetime.

---

\* People also move because of divorce, death, or because their children's needs aren't met by their local school district, or because of a new job.

**TED AND SUSAN'S STORY**

Ted and Susan decided they were going to make money by buying fixer-upper properties, putting the time, effort, and cash into making them beautiful, and then selling them for a profit.

It's a good plan, and one that countless home buyers have made use of. But Ted and Susan were so successful, they ended up making hundreds of thousands of dollars in profit from the sale of each home. In one case, they bought a 6,000-square-foot apartment that had been foreclosed on, gutted it, and sold it for more than $2 million. They traded that for a house in a nearby suburb that cost $2.8 million. Over the next fifteen months, they gutted that and put it on the market for $9.5 million.

Ted and Susan made millions on that property. The Tax Reform Act of 1997, which allows an individual to keep up to $250,000 ($500,000 for married couples) in profits tax-free, provided you've lived in your home at least two of the last five years, helps home-owners cash in on fixer-upper deals, although you pay long-term capital gains on the rest. You might not make millions from the sale of a home you've fixed up, but you'll get to keep a far larger portion today than was possible under earlier tax regulations.

## But Wait! Here's Another Reason to Think About How Long You Plan to Stay

Knowing how long you plan to live in your house is also crucial to choosing the correct mortgage. If you think you're only going to live in your home for five years, why would you choose a thirty-year fixed rate mortgage? Think it through this way:

1. **Will I actually stay for five years?** It's amazing how fast time flies.[*] Seven or ten years might go by before you look up, in which case, you might be happy to have had a longer-term loan.

---

[*] As I update this fourth edition, I continue to be amazed by this. It's been twenty-five years since the first edition was written, in 1993!

2. **Could I rent this property once I'm done living here?** If you get a thirty-year loan, that mortgage amount (though not the property taxes) will be fixed for thirty years. Renting the property may become extremely profitable down the line. If you can swing a fifteen-year loan, you may see that property become a cash cow even sooner.

Although the Great Recession and subsequent housing crisis killed innovative but dangerous mortgage options like the pay-option adjustable-rate mortgage (ARM), there are excellent, though slightly less flexible, loan options that provide you with the stability of a fixed-rate loan (for as long as you'll need it) at a less expensive interest rate.

If you're going to stay in your home for ten to fifteen years, or you can afford the slightly higher payments, you might want to lock in a fifteen-year fixed-rate mortgage. When you sell the house, you'll own it free and clear and have a sizable amount of cash for your next purchase. Or, you might get a thirty-year fixed-rate loan and simply add a little extra to your monthly mortgage payment. (It's called prepaying, and can be an excellent way for you to cut down the term of your mortgage and save yourself thousands of dollars in interest. I'll talk more about this later, in the financing chapter.)

## Look Before You Leap

Before you start to look for a home, think about where you are in the Cycle of Life, and where you'll be (or hope to be) in five or seven years before you start to look for a home:

- Is marriage, a life partnership, or living with someone else a possibility?
- How many children do you plan to have?
- Are your children near or at school age? Have you chosen the school district you want for them?
- Is it likely you'll be transferred for your job?
- Do you have an aging parent in another part of the country who may require your close supervision or attention?
- Do you have an aging parent or post-college-age children who might be moving back home with you? Will you need flexible living space that your current home can't provide?

# Question 14: What Are the Different Types of Homes?

Your home is supposed to be your castle. But unless your name is Windsor, it's unlikely you'll end up living in one.

There are several basic types of homes that are commonly available in all parts of the country. They may, however, be called different names. For example, a "two-flat" in Chicago might be called a "two-family" in Boston, or a "duplex" on the West Coast.

**FIRST-TIME BUYER TIP:** If you don't know exactly what you're looking for, or what it's called, don't be shy about asking your agent. Most good real estate agents or brokers would rather work with a buyer who isn't afraid to ask questions, even if they have to fill in the buyer's intelligence gaps along the way. You can also learn a lot about your local market by searching for homes online before you start working with an agent.

If you decide to buy a home, you'll end up choosing from some form of condominium, townhouse, cooperative apartment, and a single-family home. There are numerous differences between each of these home types, from the rights of ownership to the way the property is maintained. As the saying goes, the devil's in the details—so, here is a detailed look at each type of property and some things you might want to keep in mind as you shop for the right one.

## Condominiums

Usually found in urban centers or densely populated suburbs, condos became popular in the 1970s when state legislatures passed laws allowing their existence—before, condo buildings didn't allow homeowners to own the land beneath the building, so a new type of homeownership had to be invented. An apartment building is converted to a condominium by means of a condominium declaration (often called a "condo dec"). New construction condominiums must also have a condo dec.

This declaration divvies up the percentage of ownership, defines which areas are commonly held by all owners, determines who is responsible for the maintenance of the property, and states the condo rules.

One of the most important things to remember about a condo is that you don't actually own the unit in which you live. Instead, you own the air space inside the walls, ceiling, and floor of the unit, possibly the plumbing within your unit, and perhaps a parking space. (In new construction condos, you sometimes have to buy your parking space separately.) With your neighbors, you also jointly own what's known as the common elements of the property, which may include the roof, plumbing, common walls, lobby, laundry room, garden area, garden, or garage.

Condos don't always look like tall buildings. Condo developments can take the form of townhouses, duplexes (condos stacked two-by-two), or four-plexes (condos stacked four-by-four, also known as quads). You might get a two-family (or two-flat) house that's been turned into a condo. Or, you can have a single-family, maintenance-free community in which the houses are actually condominiums. Suburban condos tend to stretch out longer than higher. City condos tend to be in mid- or high-rise buildings because the land is so valuable, and cities tend to permit taller buildings than in suburban or rural areas.

**NEW CONSTRUCTION.** Developers building new construction condos, or renovating an old apartment building to turn it into condos, may keep control of the newly formed condo board or homeowners' association, until a certain percentage of the condos have been sold. This can present some difficulty, especially if there is a physical problem with the units (such as a leak) and the homeowners decide to sue the developer. Another issue to think about is that financing new construction can be tricky. Usually, the developer hooks up with a lender to fund the loans. But the national secondary mortgage market leaders (Fannie Mae and Freddie Mac) require that a large percentage of the units be occupied by homeowners before they will fund a loan.[*] So if you decide to refinance before that number of the units are occupied, you may run into some trouble. You should also know that

---

[*] This number has shifted over the years. When I was writing the third edition of this book, Fannie Mae and Freddie Mac required that 70 percent of a condo building's units be "owner occupied," that is, the owners had to physically live in the building, in the units. After the Great Recession, that number fell to 50 percent, when it became clear that many condo owners were underwater and couldn't sell. Currently, the number is 50 percent, but if you decide to buy a condo with the idea of renting it out, you need to watch this number over the years so you don't get caught in a tight spot. It's unclear how Fannie Mae and Freddie Mac will treat the "renting by the day," which is how Airbnb and VRBO are viewed at the moment or if they will be able to tell that this has happened. Technology is having a huge impact in the real estate industry on so many levels and I expect this will continue.

to finance a condo unit, Fannie Mae and Freddie Mac will require that no more than a specific percentage of the building is rented. If you're thinking about buying and renting out that condo, and there are too many renters in the building already, you may have to get in line to rent or be forced to sell at an inopportune time.

**MAINTENANCE FEES.** A condo association raises money for maintenance of the common elements through monthly assessments. The building's expenses (including the portion of your monthly payment that goes into the building's emergency reserve account) are tallied, then divided by the percentage of ownership, and then divided by twelve. So if your annual share of the building maintenance cost is $2,400, you will pay $200 per month in assessments in addition to the costs of your mortgage and real estate taxes.

**FIRST-TIME BUYER TIP:** If you choose to buy a condo or a co-op (see below), you must understand that the lender will take into account the extra monthly payment you'll have to make and will readjust the amount it is willing to lend you. For example, the lender might tell you that you can purchase a $160,000 house or a $130,000 condo.

**FIRST-TIME BUYER TIP:** The condo declaration will divide up the ownership of the property. You, as a condo owner, will own a certain percentage. Typically, the tax assessor will levy a property tax on your entire condo building. Your share of the tax is typically equal to your percentage share of the building. That's why condo owners are often unable to protest their individual property tax bill unless the building hires an attorney to fight the tax levied on the entire property.

## Cooperative Apartment

Before there were condos, homeowners owned their units by purchasing shares in a corporation that owned the building in which that unit was located. As my friend David puts it, if you own a condo, you own real estate that you can use to secure a mortgage. If you own a co-op, you own shares in a corporation that owns the real estate in which your apartment is located. The shares give you the right to lease your unit from the corporation. You pay a monthly assessment (often called a lease payment or rent) based on the number of shares you own in the corporation.*

One sticky issue with co-ops is control. For many years, co-op boards used their power to reject potential buyers at will to keep a firm grip on who moved into the building. Unfortunately, a little of that unpleasantness continues to this day, particularly in swanky neighborhoods and in buildings whose owners have, shall we say, certain "attitudes" about people of color, certain religions, genders, sexual preferences, and single parents. In addition, co-op rules often require a higher cash down payment (30–50 percent is not uncommon), and sometimes refuse to allow purchases financed with a mortgage or that are made by trusts. You also get very high-end co-ops that may even reject celebrities or wealthy people with a high profile. Fortunately, many co-ops have relaxed their restrictions in recent years.

If you're looking for an abundance of co-op units, try New York City, Chicago, and, to a lesser extent, San Francisco, although there are a fair number spread out over the rest of the United States.

**JANICE'S STORY**

After looking for a home for nearly a year, Janice came upon a co-op conversion, located in the town in which she was living. The co-op was asking for a 50 percent down payment, and wanted to see her finances.

"Literally, they asked me to sign a piece of paper that allowed them to do a full credit and financial background check on me," Janice said. "They wanted past addresses, names of references they could call, my current and past jobs, bank account statements, and my Social Security number."

Although Janice had a good amount of cash saved up for her down payment, 50 percent was pushing it just a bit. She decided that the financial obligations with this particular co-op were too onerous, and ultimately declined to make a purchase offer.

---

* Unless you're living in New York City, where many buildings are formed as co-ops and brokers deal with them all the time, I find that younger or newer real estate agents and brokers have a tough time understanding (and thereby showing and marketing) co-ops. I'm not sure why they don't get it, but many of them don't, and they might shy away from showing them to you.

In the best light, all of this screening should hopefully make for a better neighbor, right? But co-op boards sometimes make mistakes, too. In one New York co-op, the board voted in a family that had impeccable credentials. On paper, they had it all: the best schools, best awards, terrific family history, and glowing letters from the board of the building in which the owners previously lived. Later, after several incidents with these particular owners in which the police had to be called, board members discovered that the former building was only too glad to rid itself of these individuals and wrote the letters hoping to get rid of a problem that had caused tremendous upheaval and unrest.

 **20/20 HINDSIGHT:** If you don't "pass the board," as it is commonly called, don't feel bad. Even famous celebrities and politicians are often voted down for various reasons. While it's illegal for a co-op board to reject you because of your race, religion, or sex, more often than not, you'll be told you simply don't have enough money or it's a "personality" issue. It's hard not to take the rejection personally, but you have to ask yourself if it was really the kind of place that's right for you.

**NEW CONSTRUCTION.** It's rare that a co-op is built from the ground up these days, although it does happen in New York from time to time. More commonly, you'll see an existing rental building converted into a co-op.

**MAINTENANCE FEES.** Like a condo, your monthly assessments cover the general maintenance of the property. But because the corporation pays the real estate taxes as a whole, your share of the taxes is normally included in your monthly assessment.[*] That means your assessment is going to look pretty steep when compared side-by-side with a condo building assessment notice. For a fair comparison, you'll have to break out the costs. When looking at a co-op listing sheet, remember that the assessment generally includes property taxes (which is often where newbie real estate agents and brokers get confused).

---

[*] Which also makes it impossible for you to contest your co-op property taxes individually.

## Townhouse

A townhouse development can take several different forms, but it often looks like a group of slender houses attached in a long row (which is why in some areas townhomes are called "row houses." Generally, you share a wall in common with each of your neighbors. Townhouse developments will have groups of these attached buildings.

This difference is in the way the property is held. Most row houses built in the first half of the twentieth century are held "fee simple," meaning you hold legal title to your home and the land on which it sits. You are also responsible for the property's real estate taxes, even though you share a common wall with your neighbors. Today, many newly built town homes are constructed as condominiums, complete with a homeowners' association.

**NEW CONSTRUCTION.** A popular trend in the construction of townhouses is a maintenance-free community. Essentially, this means that while you own your own property, the homeowners' association manages the exterior of the property, as well as the common elements, and takes care of it for you. So if the townhouses need painting, there's no need for you to do anything. On the other hand, they'll typically choose the color without consulting you.

**MAINTENANCE FEES.** Even if you hold your property fee simple (the way you'd normally own a single-family house), you may have to join a homeowners' association. Your monthly maintenance costs would cover the common areas not immediately on your property, such as a garage, playground, laundry room, party facilities, workout area, or swimming pool.

## Mobile Homes

Once the poor stepchildren of the real estate industry, mobile homes and manufactured housing (see page 63) have become a way for first-time buyers and others with few resources to purchase a home and stop paying rent (although you may have to rent the land on which the mobile home sits). While you might not choose to purchase a mobile home if you could afford a regular home, you might do so if your only other option was renting, or if you needed to live somewhere remote where there aren't enough homes to rent or buy.

First, let's talk about what a mobile home is. It's designed to be transported (hence the term "mobile") in one piece to a plot of land, often within a mobile home park. These parks might contain hundreds, if not thousands, of mobile homes. The home comes with bedrooms, bathrooms, living room, and a kitchen, and might be of standard width (approximately 12 to 15 feet wide), or even a double-wide width (approximately 30 feet wide). Typically, you purchase the mobile home and rent the land (receiving water and power hookups).

Mobile homes weren't built too well in the past, which is why they have such a shaggy reputation today. They didn't last long, and they didn't hold up too well, particularly in tornadoes. Today, they're being built to better standards (and yes, there are some mobile homes that are all tricked out and might even be considered "high-end"). Some mobile home parks have very strict rules in order to help increase the value of the homes located there. If the mobile home park in which you're interested has these sorts of rules, it's good thing.

### MAITA'S STORY

A Guatemala native who became an American citizen more than twenty-five years ago, Maita rented her home when she first came to this country. With three small children, she finally decided to stop renting and buy a home. She bought a used mobile home for $12,000 and rented a spot for it in the only mobile home park near a tony suburb outside of Chicago. But the rent for her space kept going up and up. After living there for nearly a decade, she decided to sell her mobile home and buy a house.

Like many Hispanics, Maita saved prodigiously throughout the years, and parked her cash in a bank account. When she found the house she wanted to buy, a two-bedroom, one-bath home near the Wisconsin border, it cost around $120,000. She took out a $40,000 mortgage and paid the rest in cash (and still had cash leftover in her bank account). In the first two years of homeownership, she was able to pay down her loan by $10,000. Her house has also increased in value by about $15,000. Today, it's paid off.

To Maita, the best part of the transaction was how much money she was able to get for her mobile home: When she sold it, she received $14,000, a "profit" of $2,000.*

---

* Technically, there was no profit on the home because Maita had to rent her space in the community and had fixed up the mobile home through the years she owned it. Still, getting a little more than she paid for it felt like a win, and so she celebrated.

## Manufactured or Modular Homes and Tiny Homes

Manufactured housing is a different, but fast-growing, part of the new construction industry. While these homes may be left on wheels, they aren't generally intended to be "mobile." They're typically built on an assembly line, transported to a location, and then installed permanently on a foundation, where you may not be able to tell that they were constructed elsewhere.

The process of building a manufactured home is fascinating. Homes are built in sections, called "modules," and are put together on airplane wheels. The sections are wheeled through various parts of an enormous factory, as the walls, floors, wiring, plumbing, drywall, cabinets, doors, hardware, windows, trim, and exterior siding are installed and finished. Most manufactured houses consist of four to eight modules, and are completely built in about a week. (I was lucky enough to visit a manufactured-housing plant in central Wisconsin, for a story I was working on for WGN-TV. It was a fascinating, if dusty, day. Later, we had cameras rolling on a frozen, windy Chicago spring day as the home was installed on a prefab foundation.)

The completed sections are then loaded onto flatbed trucks and driven to their permanent location. The modules are lifted up by crane, and delicately put into place. The entire house will generally be installed in a day (or two, if it's a very big house) on a permanent concrete foundation. Once the house has its mechanicals connected, and the exterior work and landscaping are finished, you'd be hard-pressed to tell the difference between a manufactured house and a stick-built home.

Manufacturers say that because the homes are built under controlled conditions (inside a factory where the building conditions are not at all affected by weather), are built to withstand the delivery (which could be up to several hundred miles), and are watched so closely, they tend to have fewer problems than regular stick-built new construction.

Another reason to consider a manufactured home is the price. Most new homes cost a minimum of $125 per square foot to build but can cost much more than that. In major metropolitan areas, the average might run from $150 to more than $800 (or a lot more) per square foot for a top-of-the-line home, depending on the finishes (and excluding the cost of the site). Manufactured homes cost between $80 to $200 per square foot, depending on the finishes and the costs of installation (including fees to the local municipality, foundation costs, and transportation and installation costs), or about half of what it costs to build a comparable stick-built home. If you're watching your pennies, and want to build a home from the ground up, this may be an option you'll want to explore.

## Tiny Homes

Since the last edition of this book was written, the tiny home phenomenon has developed, thanks in part to the Great Recession of 2008–09, where so many people suddenly found themselves in foreclosure or out of a job (or just shedding the last vestiges of consumerism), and to a fairly addictive show on HGTV, where couples who (supposedly) can't afford to buy a normal house or condo where they want to live figure out a way to build a truly tiny home (perhaps as small as 175 square feet) that they can transport wherever they want (as long as they can find power and water hookups), or plant in a friend's backyard (with a fabulous view, natch!).

How big a "thing" are tiny homes? In part, it depends on how you define it. Wikipedia says that homes under 500 square feet fall into the "micro-home" or tiny house category, which it describes as an "architectural and social movement," in the United States. Sarah Susanka—an award-winning architect who wrote her first book, *Not So Big House,* in 1998, and has gone on to write many subsequent books on the topic—has made her career leading the charge in support of building smaller, higher-quality houses in favor of larger homes. As I write this, HGTV's *Tiny House* series is wildly popular. There are tiny house blogs, tiny house conferences, and even, apparently, tiny house life coaches who can help you downsize from a full-size life into something that will fit into a trailer-sized residence (and presumably will help you learn to avoid hitting your head on the ceiling of your new tiny home).

But how many of those homeowners love living in extremely cramped quarters for a larger period of time? My guess is not too many. In 2017, the *New York Times* published a story about a couple living, somewhat unhappily, in a "micro-home," which was a 492-square-foot rental studio in Manhattan. The writer described how their life felt "shabby," and how they were using up their furnishings more quickly because they used them so frequently. But the trade-off was, apparently, living in the right neighborhood in Manhattan. Location, location, location.

A former editor of mine worried (rightly, as it turned out) about losing her job as the head of content for a division of a tech company. She wanted to find a place to live with her husband and twin sons that was affordable even if she lost her job and a new one wouldn't pay nearly as much. So they moved to a one-bedroom sort-of tiny house, with just 800 square feet. She and her husband slept on a pullout couch in the living room and gave the boys the bedroom to share. They live in Southern California, so you could argue that the house's outdoor space helps in ways that the garden in a colder-weather climate wouldn't, but still. Four people in 800 square feet. Before you make that move as a homeowner, you'd certainly want to try it out for size.

**NEW CONSTRUCTION.** A newly built manufactured home will last a lot longer than an old one, thanks to certain regulations builders must follow. Still, even brand-new mobile homes can be upended by tornadoes. Because manufactured homes are connected to permanently installed foundations, they should be able to withstand nature's fury just as well as a stick-built home.

**MAINTENANCE COSTS AND FEES.** Even if you're renting the land underneath your manufactured home, you're typically responsible for the hookups to cable, water, and sewer and for garbage pickup. If you own the land but are living in a manufactured-home community, you may have monthly or annual maintenance fees, so be sure to factor that into your budget when you're shopping around. You'll also have to maintain your house, mow the grass, and, depending on where you live, shovel snow. And if you're buying a manufactured home and then moving it to a piece of land you own, you'll still need to account for a variety of expenses, including transportation expenses, local municipality building or permitting fees, foundation expenses, electrical and water hookups, etc. Be sure to engage a builder who has done many of these installations so that you know you're going to wind up with a house you can live in.

## Single-Family House

Far and away the most common form of home is the detached, single-family house, which is available in all sorts of shapes, sizes, and prices. The most defining feature of single-family homes is that the house sits by itself, on its own piece of property. Legally, this type of ownership is referred to as "fee simple."

**NEW CONSTRUCTION.** In some developments, you may have homes clustered together, while a large portion of the development sits as open land—a golf course, nature preserve, or man-made lake. Again, you'd own your own plot of land and the house that sits on it, but may have to join a homeowners' association and pay monthly dues for the maintenance and insurance of the common areas, which could include everything from a clubhouse, pool, and workout facility to parking facilities for cars and bicycles.

**MAINTENANCE COSTS AND FEES.** Single-family homes can be wonderful! But, boy, they can also be a lot of work. And you, the homeowners, are responsible for all of the expenses associated with ownership and maintenance, including real estate taxes, garbage removal, water, and sewage. Unless your house is in a subdivision, however, you probably won't have monthly or annual maintenance fees to pay.

**FIRST-TIME BUYER TIP:** I'm often asked which appreciates fastest: a single-family home, a condominium, or a co-op? The answer is, actually, any of them.

It depends on how much you pay for the home, and what happens to the other homes in your surrounding neighborhood. Generally speaking, single-family homes appreciate faster than condos or co-ops. That said, if you buy a condo that has been foreclosed on and then fix it up, you may realize a gain of 100 percent or more in a short period of time. Or, if you buy a home as a pioneer, in an area that hasn't developed yet, you may realize an enormous gain if your neighborhood suddenly becomes "hot." But while it's seductive to think about buying a home and making a fortune on it, you have to think about whether or not you'll be comfortable living there, day in and day out. We'll talk more about this later in the book.

## Question 15: Should I Buy a New Home or an Existing Home?

Before the Great Recession, approximately one out of every six home buyers purchased a newly constructed property in any given year. In the years since, that ratio has been severely out of whack, contributing to a significant shortage of homes for sale.*

---

* Approximately one million new homes per year were built in the fifteen years prior to the 2008–09 recession. In the first few years after, roughly 360,000 to 400,000 homes were built, or about a 75 percent reduction in new construction. By 2017, the number of new construction homes sold reached about 600,000, which is still 40 percent less than prior to the Great Recession. What has increased dramatically is the number of multifamily properties built, primarily for rentals.

Buying new homes is tempting because, well, everything is new. No one has ever used the toilet, refrigerator, closet, stove, or sink before. When you move in, everything is as pristine and polished as it gets.

Many home buyers love the idea of buying a new home because they get to be the first people who will live in it. Just remember, the day after you move into a new home it becomes an "existing" or "newer" home. But here's the good news: Unlike buying a new car that loses a third or even half of its value the moment you drive it off the lot, new homes can be an excellent, long-term investment. In some areas, newly constructed homes (often referred to as "new construction") appreciate faster than existing homes.

Should you buy a new home or an existing home? I'm asked this question frequently. It's difficult to answer because where you want to live and what your housing options are factor into the decision. But I'll try to outline a few things for you to think about before you make your decision:

1. **New construction generally costs more than existing housing.** Typically, you'll pay more for a four-bedroom newly built house than for a similarly sized home that was built five, ten, twenty, or even fifty years ago. That premium can be partly explained because new houses tend to be larger than homes built twenty to forty years ago. You'll typically have two and a half to three baths in a four-bedroom home, compared to four bedrooms and two baths (in a home built twenty years ago) or even three bedrooms and only one or one and a half baths (for one built fifty years ago). Today's newly built homes typically contain central air, loads of appliances, fireplaces, and lofted spaces. You may have a two- or three-car garage, upgraded wiring (perhaps with smart-home capabilities), double-paned windows, granite or marble countertops, and a basement with a high ceiling. You might even have solar power or a superpowered charger in your garage for an electric vehicle. One of the reasons your new house is so expensive is that you're typically paying a portion of the impact fees, charged to developers by the community to cover the costs of development (including sewer lines, more roads, and more students in the local schools). If money is an issue, you'll probably want to find an existing house that you can later fix up with all the amenities of a newly built house.

2. **New construction typically takes place in cornfields, far away from urban areas.** That's because it's difficult to find a vacant, large infill plot of land in a city, and it

isn't as profitable for large, production developers to build homes piecemeal. So developers looking to put up 100 to 500 homes at a time typically purchase acreage farther and farther out from the city center. While whole new communities spring up, the retail and service development for them usually lags behind; when you first move into a new community, you might have to drive five miles for a gallon of milk. (And if you have young kids at home, all those milk runs can really run up the mileage on your car.) Also, developers sometimes pick less favorable school districts or communities in order to find affordable land, so your brand-new home may not be in the best school district, or even in your suburb of choice. Does that mean you shouldn't buy a home in a new development? Of course not. It simply means you need to think about where you're going to go shopping, work out, drop off the cleaning, fill up the car, and school your children before you sign the purchase offer.

3. **Make sure your developer is well funded**. One of the dangers in buying new construction early on in the life of the project is that the developer may run out of cash before the project is done. (Back in 2003 and 2004, that happened to several high-profile brand-new condo buildings in Chicago. The developer went broke and the finance company had to take over the buildings.) If that's the case, your home could plummet in value, as the investors look to recapture their investment by selling the homes below the price you paid. While few developers are going to give you their financial statements to look at, be sure to thoroughly check out the background of the developer by searching the Internet for news about the developer, checking with the Better Business Bureau, and even contacting your state to check out any possible complaints filed against the company. You shouldn't have trouble with a large, well-known company that has completed various successful projects over many years, but do your homework. Visit residents who live at other developments the builder has completed, and see how well the homes have held up. Also, ask if the owners have any complaints about the developer or the development. A series of disgruntled homeowners should be a red flag.

4. **Quality new construction may appreciate at the same speed or even more rapidly than an existing home.** If you purchase a home from a reputable, quality developer, and the development itself is a quality project, your home should not only retain its value but appreciate, even though other, newer projects have opened up. But beware: In a low-quality development, homes can come apart faster than the time it

took to build them originally.* While your home may still go up in value, you may spend more than the appreciation you gain if you have to repair big problems.

Do you want to live in a new home or do you want to fix up an older one? New construction means everything is about as perfect as it's going to get and you'll be the first to use it. These days, no matter what the price range, you should be able to customize your new home to some degree, take advantage of options and upgrades, and choose your own colors and carpet. You also get a home specifically designed to your needs. If you require a home office, for example, most new construction house plans feature a first-floor space that could function as a separate home office. Hopefully, your newly constructed home will require almost no maintenance. (Why? Everything is new.) So if you're looking for a house that's about as maintenance-free as can be (without going into a maintenance-free community we talked about earlier), new construction might be perfect for you. But when you buy new construction, your home will appreciate only as fast as the general area. If you are looking to build in value, you'll probably want to choose a fixer-upper home. (See Question 16 for more information on finding and buying fixer-upper homes.)

**MATT AND ANNIE'S STORY**

Matt and Annie bought a brand-new house for $400,000. They spent another $70,000 to build out the attic, add some beautiful landscaping, and spruce up the family room.

Five years later, they sold their house for $800,000! Why did they do so well? They were among the first to buy in what ended up becoming a very hot, trendy, expensive development. Their lot, although not directly on the water, had a nice view from the second floor. And it was easily accessible to the nearby downtown metro area.

Matt and Annie pocketed a lot of cash, but what they did next was make an even smarter move. They bought another house for $500,000 in cash, in the same general area but a less expensive neighborhood. As a result, instead of making monthly mortgage payments,

---

* In our neighborhood, a one-year-old multimillion-dollar house is being taken apart brick by brick in order to fix massive leaking caused by a design flaw. The owners have had to move to another house while extensive repairs take place.

they are using the cash they would have spent on a mortgage to build up their children's college funds, create a solid emergency fund, and take a vacation. Location, location, location indeed.[*]

 **FIRST-TIME BUYER TIP:** This old adage is really true: If it seems too good to be true, it probably is. And that goes for everything, from new construction to stock tips. So if the developer is promising you the moon, and you can't get any independent confirmation that this person is an honest, reputable businessperson, watch out. Also, if you can't overcome some misgivings about the value you're getting for an investment in a property, don't sign the papers. At a minimum, finish reading this book before you make a final decision on purchasing a new or existing home.

## Question 16: What Are the Advantages and Disadvantages of Buying a Home That Needs Renovation? How Much Should I Spend to Improve the House? What Do Brokers Mean by "Overimproved"?

Brokers like to say there are three kinds of homes you can buy:

1. **Move-in Condition.** This is a house that's about as close to perfection as possible. There's no decorating or renovation required. All you have to do is move in your furniture (or purchase the sellers' furniture, if that's an option) and start living.

2. **Good Condition.** When you hear brokers refer to a home like this, it generally means the home's "bones," or structure, are in fine shape, and the amenities and appliances are in good working order. On the other hand, you might not like the décor. Gold velvet–flocked wallpaper and olive green shag carpeting might be your

---

[*] One of my best friends lives in Los Angeles. She and her husband bought their house fifteen years ago, and it has more than doubled in price. She's now looking to find a smaller home in a different neighborhood for about half of what she can sell her current home for, and use the proceeds to buy an investment property.

taste, or it might not. In this type of house, which accounts for most of the homes on the market, you might need to repaint the walls, strip the floors, or replace the carpeting.

3. **Handyman's Special, or the Fixer-Upper.** With a handyman's special (no offense intended to all of the handywomen out there), you can expect to see anything from a home needing minor repairs to one that requires a gut job.

When it comes to the advantages and disadvantages of buying a home that needs renovation, the answer depends on how much money you have to spend. Most first-time buyers have limited cash reserves. The down payment is usually a stretch, let alone finding money to decorate or renovate. Also, fewer people today have the time, know-how, or interest to actually do much of the renovation themselves, and hiring someone to renovate or decorate for you can be expensive. If the option of buying a new home is available to you, purchasing new construction can be cheaper and easier in the long run.

If, however, you have the time and cash to put into renovating a home, there are significant advantages to be gained: You might be able to purchase a bigger home in a better neighborhood, with better school districts, that is closer to work. You may be able to purchase a two-flat or two-family home and fix it up, then rent out one unit and live at a far reduced cost. One of the best reasons to buy a fixer-upper is to maximize the investment.

### ANGELA AND TOM'S STORY

When Angela and Tom went looking for houses, they realized they couldn't afford to buy anything worthwhile in their top choices for location. So instead of looking at single-family homes, they looked for a two-family house.

They found one that needed a lot of work. But they also could see that it would make a terrific single-family home once they could afford to do the renovation and live without the additional rental income. So they bought the property, rented out one of the units, and lived in the other.

After six years and several substantial increases in their joint annual income due to job changes, Angela and Tom finally had the cash to do the renovation and combine the two units together and live without the renter's monthly contribution to the mortgage. Best of all, the neighborhood had appreciated tremendously in value. By renovating their home to just above the neighborhood standard, they were able to significantly increase its value. Today the house is a showpiece they love living in, and Angela and Tom are busy squirreling money away for their young daughter's college education.

## But It Doesn't Always Work Out This Well

There are also disadvantages to fixing up a home. Renovation and decorating create mess and chaos; understand ahead of time that during the period of the renovation (and for some time thereafter), your house will never be clean. Construction and renovation almost always take more time and money than you think they will, and more than one relationship has been known to end over the turmoil and tumult.

When you look at a home that needs renovation or a gut job (taking a house down to its structural bones or guts), you need to understand exactly how much work would be required and acquire a realistic ballpark estimate of how much that work will cost.

**20/20 HINDSIGHT:** Unless your broker is also a contractor, his or her estimate of how much renovation work will cost will likely be dead wrong. Do *not* rely on his or her estimate. Instead, consult with or even hire a contractor or architect to tour the home with you before you make an offer. A contractor's or architect's ballpark estimate will be close enough for you to decide how much you want to pay for the home. Just remember, when renovating, expect the unexpected—and add 10 to 15 percent to your expert's ballpark, especially if you're buying a much older house.* Renovation almost always costs more, and takes more time, than you think it will. One contractor's best guess: Double the time and add 25 percent to the final bill and you won't be sorry.

For example, if you're in a neighborhood of renovated homes that sell for $375,000, and you see a house that requires a new kitchen, new electrical wiring, repainting, refinishing

---

* A top professional home inspector once told me that older houses tend to have more expensive problems, which Sam and I have found to be true over the years.

of floors, and three new windows to make it livable, you must take into consideration the cost of construction and subtract that from the list price. If the house is listed for $275,000 and you figure the renovation will cost $50,000, then the effective list price of that house for you should be $225,000. And, depending on whether the market is fast or slow (that is, a buyer's or seller's market), you might offer something in the high $210,000 range. If, however, every house in the neighborhood needs similar renovations, then $275,000 might be an appropriate price for the property.

Another problem with renovation is that buyers sometimes think they can buy a cheap house and create the house of their dreams. Sometimes that strategy works, but when it doesn't, watch out. When the time comes to sell the house (in five to seven years), they find they have a white elephant: a house whose value far outstrips the other homes in the neighborhood.

This is called overimproving your home, and you can overimprove to the point where you'll never be able to get your money out of it. It's best to try to avoid the situation of selling a $400,000 house in a $250,000 neighborhood.

## DANIEL'S STORY

About twenty years ago, Daniel bought a house that needed a new kitchen. He loves to cook, so he put an $18,000 kitchen into a $160,000 house and planned to do other repair and renovation work. One day, his broker stopped by to say hello and look at his construction work. After admiring his beautiful new kitchen, the broker cautioned Daniel not to spend so much money that he would want to ask more than $250,000 for the house.

"The neighborhood won't support a house that's worth more than that. I'll have trouble selling it," the broker told Daniel. At that point, he hadn't overimproved the house, but he had to be careful about where he spent his renovation dollars.

A few years later, Daniel sold his house for $230,000 and made about $30,000 in profit, after expenses. It was nice to pocket some profit, but his timing was a little off. His neighborhood was about to pop. When I was writing the third edition of this book, some fourteen years ago, I heard that the house he used to own recently sold for more than $500,000. Today it's probably worth a million or more, because the neighborhood has become so popular. If Daniel had stayed in his house a few extra years, until the neighborhood values caught up with his improvements, he would have pocketed hundreds of thousands of dollars in profits.

While not all neighborhoods explode in value the way Daniel's did, many houses do have the potential to increase in value—if you make the right home improvement choices.

> ### SALLY AND ANDY'S STORY
>
> Sally and Andy make a great living. Together, they earn nearly $550,000 per year. When they decided to buy a home (it was their third), it was a 4,000-square-foot condominium in a nice building. They paid $600,000 for the condo and spent another $700,000 completely gutting the place. They created a fancy one-bedroom apartment, with a den that also functioned as a guest bedroom, and a gourmet cook's kitchen.
>
> And then one day, at age forty-eight, Sally got pregnant. Realizing their home wouldn't work for a baby and a nanny, they decided to sell. They put the condo on the market for nearly $1 million, even though nothing in the building had ever sold for nearly that much. Had they sold for that price, they would have lost about $300,000 in renovation costs, not to mention another $60,000 in broker's commission.
>
> But the condo didn't sell. They lowered the price another $100,000. Finally, after a year, it sold. By that time, the couple had bought a house elsewhere, and had been carrying two loans for nearly nine months. They lost a substantial amount of cash on the transaction.

 **FIRST-TIME BUYER TIP:** If you're thinking about buying a home that needs renovation, be careful to consider what other renovated homes in your neighborhood are selling for in the marketplace.

# Question 17: Should My First Home Be an Investment?

There seems to be both a different attitude and a higher level of sophistication among Millennials about finances. They are more aware of their debts (what with tens of thousands of dollars in student loans waiting to be repaid) and more aware of the need of investing for retirement (although most don't believe they'll ever be able to retire). Some also seem to look at real estate differently, and are more open to making their first purchase a vacation or investment home.

**RENEE'S STORY**

Renee bought her first house a couple of decades ago, in what was then a somewhat dicey neighborhood in San Francisco, where it was affordable, even on her salary as a freelance editor. When she moved to New York, she rented out the San Francisco house, which in the twenty-plus years she has owned it has increased in value to the point where she would never be able to afford to buy it today. While living in New York City, she bought a vacation property several hours away. After a few years of using it, she starting renting it out and then finally sold it, doing a little better than break even. She then bought a condo in Brooklyn that she and her husband have slowly renovated over the years. When she makes her next move (which she is planning to do in the next few years), she is already thinking about whether to rent out the Brooklyn condo or sell it (it has more than doubled in value) and keep the profits tax-free.

Real estate has long stood the test of time as a good investment. It generally appreciates slowly, at just above the rate of inflation. In fact, portfolio managers have long used real estate to hedge their other investments, since it typically moves out of sync with stocks and bonds. But for most of us, our single biggest investment will be our own homes.

What if you're not quite ready to live in a house but it makes financial sense to own one? That's where buying a first home as an investment property can make a lot of sense. In some ways, real estate is a rather flexible (though not liquid) investment: You can buy a single-family house, a townhouse, a condo, or a multifamily building that may have as few as two units in it or as many as six or eight units; multifamily units are nice investments over the long run because you can live in one of the units and rent out the others. You can rent out the property some of the time or all of the time (as long as multifamily rules permit it). As rents rise, you can, and should, have the long-term goal of raising your own enough to cover the amount you pay to live—and more. Low interest rates are a boon to home buyers, and in the ten years since the end of the Great Recession, mortgage interest rates have been rock bottom, boosting your home-buying power.[*]

---

[*] Thirty-year mortgage interest rates have been around 6 percent or below almost consistently since 1993, according to Freddie Mac data. They have been below 5 percent since 2010, and in mid-2017, you could get a thirty-year fixed-rate mortgage for 3.70 percent. Interest rates are expected to rise to about 5 percent in 2018, although mortgage experts and housing industry economists have been projecting this for the past few years.

Michael's story is typical of the letters I often receive from ThinkGlink.com website visitors:

---

**MICHAEL'S STORY**

Michael had been renting a one-bedroom condo in a building on Chicago's lakefront. He had been thinking about buying a place, so when the owner of another unit in the building decided to sell, Michael bought it, thinking he'd move into it.

But the owner of the condo Michael was renting offered him a fabulous deal to stay. He looked at the numbers and decided he could make at least 10 percent on his money by simply renting out the other unit, which was more than he could make by keeping the money in the bank or investing it in the stock market. So he continued to rent the one-bedroom in which he had been living and rented out the other unit.

Yet another condo in the building came on the market, and Michael bought that one as well, and rented it out for a substantial profit. Finally, a third unit came on the market, and Michael bought it and finally moved into his own home. He later moved to Kansas City and rented out all three condos, which had tripled in value since Michael originally bought them.

---

There are thousands of stories like his. When I was in Atlanta speaking at a personal finance conference for WSB radio,[*] I met a woman who started out like Michael and ended up owning forty properties.

"You should tell people that it really works," she said. When I asked her why she was attending the conference (instead of giving one of her own), she replied, "Because I always learn something from someone here. And if I don't learn anything at least I feel like I already know more than most people here."

I thought that was an amazing lesson: A heaping dose of self-confidence is key to making a successful investment, whether in real estate or the stock market. Do your home-

---

[*] I was a radio talk show host on Sunday mornings and filled in for the *Clark Howard Show*, among other shows, on WSB Radio, in Atlanta, from 1998 to 2015. I also had a short-lived Sunday morning talk show on WGN Radio, in Chicago, where I currently sit in weekly with Steve Cochran's morning show and am a guest and fill-in host for the *Wintrust Business Lunch*, hosted by Steve Bertrand.

work, make sure the numbers add up, and then step forward. The younger you are when you buy your first home, the wealthier you'll be later in life.

### JERRY'S STORY

Jerry put 10 percent down on a building that was being converted from industrial space to condominiums. He intended to move into the property, but when the building finally opened (several years after he had put down his cash), he realized the unit had appreciated so much that there was a huge profit to be had by selling. Then he realized he could more than cover his expenses by renting it out at the current market rate. So that's what he did. He kept the rental unit and ended up buying a second property (a single-family house) not too far from where he worked. Today those condo properties have generated six-figure profits.

But before you think that buying investment property is a one-way road to riches, keep in mind that the road can be quite bumpy along the way.

### ED'S STORY

Ed also put down cash on a building that was being converted from rental units to condominiums. Like Jerry, he originally thought he would move into the unit. When the time came, he realized the market rents would more than cover his investment, so he rented out the condominium.

And that's where the trouble started. After two months of rental payments, Ed's renter skipped out, causing some minor damage to the unit and leaving Ed with a mortgage payment, real estate taxes, and a homeowners' insurance bill but without any investment income. To cover all that, plus his own rent each month, Ed ran up a few thousand dollars on his credit card.

So Ed decided to sell. Except that he couldn't sell the unit right way. Real estate is what is known as an illiquid asset, and it took nearly eight months to sell. Lesson learned: Real estate is a far less liquid (meaning, easily salable) investment than a share of stock because on any given day there will be someone who wants to buy your share of stock, but there may not be anyone who wants to buy your condo, townhome, or house.

The good news is that overall, Ed wound up making about 30 percent on the cash he originally invested in his property. The property had appreciated significantly, and when all was said and done, he pocketed more than $35,000 for his efforts.[*]

# Investment Property Gotchas

Before you buy a home as an investment, here are a few things to keep in mind:

- **It's still all about location.** Whether you're buying your first home to live in or rent out, location counts. Read Question 12 (What Does Location, Location, Location Really Mean?) to understand why agents say it doesn't just matter what suburb or neighborhood you choose but where your property is placed on a block. If you're buying a condo or townhouse, location refers to where your unit is placed inside the building as well. (One of Ed's problems was that his rental condo was on the first level, rather than higher up in the building.)
- **Make sure the numbers work before you sign the contract to purchase.** Whether you live in your new home or rent it out, real estate costs money to buy and maintain. Make sure you feel comfortable with carrying the costs of the rental unit (assuming you can't get it rented) over a period of months. Talk to local rental agents about how much rent they think the unit could fetch. If there are monthly condo or homeowners' association fees, make sure you add those in, too. Have a backup plan in case the property suddenly can't be rented.
- **Give yourself a financial cushion.** You want to have some extra cash on hand, just in case something breaks or you're without a renter for an extended period of time. One of my own rental properties was vacant for nine months after the terrorist attacks on September 11, 2001.

---

[*] Sam and I have had mixed success with our investment properties. The one we bought because we had a real need has done well over the years and will bring in a substantial amount of cash when the mortgage is paid off in the next few years (we've been prepaying this mortgage). But the condo I bought at an auction, spur of the moment, gave us trouble and while we came out just about even, it was a pretty rocky ride. The condo we bought off the blueprints could have been a disaster, but a strong rental property market has saved us from losing big bucks when many of the units went into foreclosure following the Great Recession. I don't think we'll make money when we sell this one, but at least we won't lose our proverbial "shirts." And, of course, we've done very well with our primary residence.

- **Create an exit strategy for yourself and the property.** You probably won't keep this rental property for the rest of your life. At some point, you'll want to sell. Figure out what has to happen to trigger the sale. You might want to use the cash for a different property. Or you might move to another state. If you can't rent it for several months or a year, then perhaps you'll list.
- **Think about how difficult it will be to sell this investment property before you buy it.** If you buy a home that's been on the market for a while, there's probably a reason it hasn't sold. Figure out the reason and see if it can be corrected—before you make an offer to purchase. If you can't fix "the problem" with the property, but know it will make a great investment, then you should buy. But remember that if you purchase a property priced well below similar homes in the area, and whatever problem or drawback the property has can't be fixed, you may find that it appreciates much more slowly than neighboring properties and could take a lot longer to sell.

# CHAPTER 3

# How Do I Look for a Home?

## Question 18: How Do I Start the Search for the Home of My Dreams? Should I Look on the Internet? Do I Have to Get off My Couch?

There are two good ways to find the right home: You can work with a real estate broker or you can do it yourself. Most of this book is geared toward buyers who work with third-party agents, but let's spend a few minutes examining how you can find a home on your own—and why you might choose to do it that way.

### FSBOs

If a seller chooses to sell his or her home without the assistance of a real estate agent or broker, it's called "for sale by owner." (You might also see the acronym FSBO, which is pronounced "fizz-bo.") Homeowners choose to sell their homes themselves for two reasons: (1) they think they can handle all the details, and (2) they won't have to pay a commission to real estate agents once a deal is made.

As I have already noted, the Internet has completely changed the real estate game over the past twenty-five years, and I'm quite sure there will be more change and compression as the

Internet of Things really gets going. In 1993, as I was writing the first edition, the Internet barely existed. AOL was just becoming a "thing." There was no Zillow, Trulia, or Realtor .com, or even Auction.com. Realtors controlled all the information, were at the center of the real estate buying and selling universe, and doled out information in careful dribs and drabs. If you wanted to find information about homes for sale, the only place to go to was your local Realtor's office. If you wanted to sell your own home, you could put a sign in your yard and then (because there were no cell phones) sit by the landline waiting for someone to call.

How many homes are sold as FSBOs? No one really knows. The best studies seem to suggest that anywhere from 8 to 15 percent of homeowners (it varies by regions) choose to sell without a broker. The National Association of Realtors (NAR) will tell you the number is closer to the 8 percent range. Other industry observers suggest the true number of FSBOs ranges quite a bit higher than that. Some experts suggest that as the Internet matures, the number of FSBOs will naturally increase, but so far, the only thing I see increasing are the number of websites where sellers can list their homes FSBO.

You'll find FSBOs listed in your local newspaper's real estate classifieds, under "Houses for Sale." You might also find them in alternative newspapers, weekly or monthly neighborhood newspapers, and local magazines. Of course, since 1996, the Internet has exploded with literally thousands of real estate–related websites. One bunch dedicated solely to FSBOs includes sites like ForSaleByOwner.com, which is still a widely recognized FSBO site; there are also thousands of local FSBO sites. And homeowners and investors are using sites like Zillow and Trulia to put up their own listings, hoping to attract some of the 100 million eyeballs that sites like those get each month.

With the Internet, however, things change frequently. When I wrote the second edition of this book, a website called Owners.com was the leading FSBO site. It basically invented the genre. Several years later, it went out of business and the guy who started it sold the website name. Today Owners.com helps home buyers connect with FSBOs and other homes that are for sale. Instead of working with a traditional real estate agent, you work with someone called an "Advisor," who helps manage the transaction and functions like a discount agent, so when you close you get some cash back.

While ForSaleByOwner.com may be a leading FSBO website[*] as we go to press at the beginning of 2018, that could change in the future. Don't count out Auction.com

---

[*] ForSaleByOwner.com bills itself as the "World's Largest By Owner Site," which it might well be in 2018.

(which has benefitted from substantial investment from a division of Alphabet, the parent company of Google). There's a growing website and Facebook page called FSBO-Local. Redfin, a real estate company, also lists FSBOs. And it's pretty easy to put up a website these days with a URL that is the actual address of the property. If you decide to look for a home that is for sale by owner in your neighborhood, the best idea is to go to Google or another search engine and type "FSBO" into the search browser. Most consumers have geolocation enabled, so Google knows that you're searching in your immediate area. If you want to search for a home elsewhere, you'll need to type in "FSBO [location]."

While FSBO sellers will sometimes buy an ad in the classified section of your local paper, one of the best ways to find a FSBO property to purchase is to walk around the neighborhoods you've targeted as being acceptable. FSBO homes usually have a sign posted outside letting prospective buyers know they are for sale.

If you decide you want to tour the inside of a FSBO, simply call the telephone number in the advertisement or on the sign and make an appointment. The homeowner will then give you a tour of his or her home. This can be awkward, as you should be looking for every fault and every reason not to buy the home. And yet you don't want to insult the homeowner, just in case you do want to buy the home. Internet listings are helpful here, because many websites allow you to see photos of the home's exterior and interior, videos and floorplans, and even (thanks to drone technology) the property from above.

For more on how the Internet is changing the real estate game, skip ahead to "Using the Internet to Find Your New Home," on page 87.

## Going It Alone

One new—and rather disturbing (to me)—trend is that more home buyers, especially first-time buyers, are looking for property on their own, without the benefit of an agent representing them. Why does this happen? When first-time buyers go to a new construction development, they often go by themselves. The moment you sign in without an agent, you are considered "unrepresented" and it may be difficult to later introduce an agent into the process. From that point on, you are dealing with the developer on your own, usually through a salesperson who represents the developer exclusively. Other times, home buyers simply (and mistakenly) believe they'll get a better deal if they approach a seller about his or her home (whether it is listed or not). They figure the seller will only have to pay a half commission and that leaves 2.5 to 3 percent of the purchase price negotiable.

But that's not how the real estate game works today. Here's what really happens: Whether you come with an agent or not, the seller has already signed a commission agreement with his or her agent promising to pay the total commission regardless of whether the buyer comes with an agent or not. That's a legal agreement that you can't change. If the buyer has an agent, then the seller's agent agrees to split the commission paid with the buyer's agent. Otherwise, the seller's agent gets it all.

And here's why it's disturbing: When it comes to FSBOs, buyers (again) believe they'll be better off without an agent. Today's Millennials want to do everything fast, preferring to ask their friends for advice on buying a home (even if their friends rent or live with their parents) rather than hire an agent. But buying a home isn't like buying a dress, bicycle, or even a car. First-time buyers often don't understand how a local marketplace works and don't have a clear idea of what a property is worth. You could easily wind up overpaying for your home or missing the signs of future trouble.

Now that you know that, why would you want to look for a home without an agent? Frankly, I don't think you should. There's no benefit to you as the buyer. You're in the enviable position of having buyer brokerage (where the agent owes his or her fiduciary duty to you, not the seller—see Question 22 for more details) available to you, without having to pay for it out of pocket (the seller still pays the commission). Why wouldn't you want to have a smart person, who supposedly knows the area and housing stock, take you around and share a career's worth of knowledge?

It seems obvious, and yet I hear more and more stories every day about buyers going it alone. All sellers, but particularly FSBOs, tend to be greedy. They're hoping to save the 6 or 7 percent commission, but they don't want to share it with you. So when you start the negotiations, they may come down 6 or 7 percent because they've started out with a higher price than the competition. But you could still wind up paying more than you should, and not reaping the benefit of the commission savings.

Many home buyers like searching for FSBOs in addition to homes listed for sale because it makes them feel as if they are seeing everything that's out there on the market. They aren't, of course, because the vast majority of homes for sale are also listed with brokers in a computerized system called a Multiple Listing Service, or MLS. Access to the MLS used to be restricted to member brokers and their clients. In the days before the Internet, access to the MLS data was so tightly guarded that brokers weren't even allowed to give listing books (yes, there were black-and-white, telephone-book-size listing books printed *every other week* with the new listings) to their clients to peruse. But today you can find almost all listing information online at any number of websites, all available at the click of a mouse.

So, no, you don't really have to get off your couch to find a home. (At least, you don't until the showing.)

> **FIRST-TIME BUYER TIP:** If you're buying a FSBO, be sure to use a real estate attorney, even if you're in a state that doesn't typically use real estate attorneys to close residential deals. You'll need an attorney to help you draft the contract, advise you on local laws that will be helpful (such as disclosure laws), make sure the proper paperwork is filed, and protect you in case something goes wrong.

## Buying New Construction on Your Own

Here's what happens when you shop for a newly built home: Developers, who have already set aside an amount of money to pay commission to a broker, love it when consumers come without representation. That's because they save the 3 percent they would have paid to the buyer's broker, they typically get a higher commission or a bonus, and are better able to sell you all sorts of options and upgrades, which, as I pointed out earlier, is all paid for up front and in cash.

As a buyer, however, you'll find it easier and less time-consuming if you go with a buyer's broker or agent to see a bunch of new construction developments. Developers will tell you that you don't need a broker—but they'll pay the commission should you choose to use one. I'm going to reiterate an important point: If you don't bring a broker with you when you go to a development or if you don't protect your broker by signing in under his or her name when you first tour a development, you may not be allowed to bring in that broker later. You will have, effectively, no representation in your deal.

Every once in a while, the developer will lower the cost of the new construction by the amount that he would have paid in brokerage commission fees. Usually, though, he (developers are still mostly men) won't. More likely, he'll give you extra upgrades for free or at a reduced cost. And the truth is, a good broker may be able to extract the same concessions or more—that's what the negotiation is all about!

**FIRST-TIME BUYER TIP:** If you're buying a new construction home without an agent, I think you also need to hire a good real estate attorney who can eyeball your new construction contract (the standard "forms" typically favor the builder and give the buyer few, if any, rights or recourse).

**NEW CONSTRUCTION TIP:** Although it isn't common to hire an inspector for new construction, it's an excellent idea to have someone look in during the four crucial stages of building: (1) after the foundation is poured; (2) after the framing is up; (3) after the house is wired and plumbed; and (4) just before the walls are closed in. By having your professional home inspector stay on top of the builder during the construction, you'll have someone who can point out mistakes or shoddy workmanship while these errors can be remedied less expensively—and on the builder's dime, not yours. You'll also want to do a final walk-through before closing and make sure you have your punch list (your list of items that still need to be finished before the house is completed) together.

## Using a Real Estate Agent or Broker

If you decide you don't want to look for a place to buy by yourself, your other option is to use a broker. Brokers come in all different shapes, sizes, and personalities, but there's one constant: The benefits of using one are significant.

- **They're your eyes and ears.** A good agent is supposed to be your eyes and ears, prescreening homes on the market, finding out why the home is for sale, and selecting the ones he or she thinks might be right for you.

- **You'll get off the couch less.** Your broker is supposed to do at least some (if not most) of your legwork, and walk through these homes to further eliminate those that won't meet your needs and wants.
- **Pave the way.** A good broker will make your appointments for you, chauffeur you around from showing to showing, help you understand the good and bad of a house and neighborhood, find potential opportunities, provide you with enough information to create a winning offer (though that may not always work, particularly in a hot market), and then present that offer to the seller and selling broker and shepherd the deal through to the closing.

By tapping into the local Multiple Listing Service (MLS), brokers can pull up all kinds of information, including:

- A list of all homes available in your price range, or in your desired location;
- The homes' amenities, square footage, most recent tax bill, number and size of bedrooms and bathrooms;
- How long a particular home has been listed for sale;
- The original price plus any price reduction;
- The home's address and the listing broker's telephone number;
- Photo of the exterior of the home, possibly the interior, perhaps even a video tour or floorplan, and maybe even an aerial shot of the property;
- A list of similar homes that have sold recently and the relevant data;
- Other pertinent and interesting facts and figures, such as the lot size, the way the house faces, and the listing broker's description.

 **FIRST-TIME BUYER TIP:** Real estate brokers and agents are only as good as you let them be. If you choose to use a broker or agent, you'll have to learn the difference between conventional, buyer, and discount brokers. You'll also learn how much to tell your broker, and when complete honesty may not be entirely appropriate.

 **FIRST-TIME BUYER TIP:** Everyone comes with baggage. That is, we all carry around our own personal collection of aches, pains, and life problems. And the older we are, the more baggage we seem to tote around. It works the same way with a home: The older the home is, the more likely it's going to have problems, quirks, oddities, and other things that make it seem less than perfect. If you expect the home you buy to be flawless, you're in for a rude awakening. There are no perfect homes. Really. I'll talk about this more as we move through the home-buying process, but remember this: While buying a home is the American Dream, the reality of the property is what you have to live with.

## Using the Internet to Find Your New Home

Up until, say, 1996, the way people bought homes had been fairly static for decades. All of the information about which homes were listed for sale and how much they cost resided with a few licensed real estate agents and brokers, who zealously (some might say jealously) guarded it. Access to the information was severely limited. How limited? As I've mentioned, as late as the late 1980s, books of house listings were printed every other week. Agents who were members of the local Multiple Listing Service (there were typically a dozen or more in a major metropolitan area) would have a copy and you could make an appointment with the agent to see the current listing book. If the agent really liked you, you might be given an old copy of a listing book under cover.

You wanted to buy a house? You either worked with a licensed agent or (actually, and) you spent the weekend looking through pages of classified newspaper listings over the weekend looking for FSBOs.

But in the mid-1990s, computers and the Internet began to open up new opportunities to companies wanting to move in and disseminate real estate information on a larger scale. Tiny Multiple Listing Services began to merge into one or two metropolitan MLSs, which cooperated fully with each other and gave all licensed agents who were members (no matter where they were located) access to the data.

Internet companies put everything up on the Web, free to anyone who had a computer and modem. After a few expensive false starts, the data about which homes were for sale started getting posted on the Internet for anyone to see. Suddenly, by going to Yahoo! or Realtor.com, you could tap into as many as 2 million listings and find out the list price of property for sale, the number of bedrooms and bathrooms a house or condo had, how much the seller paid in taxes, and all sorts of previously private information.

Both the industry consolidation and the Internet advances were met with a great deal of skepticism and cynicism by both agents and brokers, as well as the real estate reporters who covered the industry.

The key to making real estate brokers happy about the dissemination of the listing data was to put in their email address as the contact name for more information about the property. (And not putting FSBO properties on the same sites that carry Realtor listings.)

 **FIRST-TIME BUYER TIP:** Which is fine, except it sets up one of the biggest problems for consumers shopping for a home on the Internet: If you contact the listing broker for more information about a particular listing and you are either not represented or you do not inform the listing broker at the time of contact that you are represented, there is a very real chance that you will end up in a dual agency situation, with the listing broker owing her loyalty to neither you nor the seller. That would mean you'd be spending the largest amount you've ever spent on anything without anyone guiding you along the way.

Which brings us to today, and the (literally) millions of real estate–related sites that exist on the Internet.

## The Best and the Worst of Today's Internet

The Internet is a good place to:

- **Identify potential cities or neighborhoods.** Google Maps and other similar sites allow you to look at the geographical shape of an area and make selections based on distance to work, school, or your house of worship. It will tell you how long it takes to get to work, and where hotels, schools, restaurants, and the closest Starbucks are. You can even see what the neighborhood looks like and "drive" along streets to get a sense of the area.
- **Learn more about that city or neighborhood.** Many cities have their own websites, which discuss everything from sports and recreational opportunities to schools, cultural offerings, shopping, and restaurants. Other companies, such as a

local real estate company, may also put up neighborhood information, while local brokers will blog about great shopping and restaurants.

- **Choose a school district.** GreatSchools.org, SchoolDistrictFinder.com, and Moving.com (owned by the same company that owns Realtor.com) will all help you find the right school district for your children (if you have them). And many school districts host their own websites, which include dates, contact information, teacher resumes, calendars, photos of students, and other information that can help you evaluate a school. (This is useful even if you don't have or want children, since living in a good school district will be an important asset when it comes time to sell.)

- **Get a taste of what's on the market.** You'll be able to see some, even most, of the homes that are for sale in a given marketplace. Many websites offer a plethora of color and 360-degree photos, floorplans, and videos of the interior and exterior of the houses.

- **Check out the demographics and statistics that define a neighborhood.** Search "crime statistics" and your neighborhood or city and you'll quickly track down the information you're looking for.

- **Shop for a home loan.** You can easily apply for a mortgage online with all types of lenders, including a portal lender that aggregates many mortgage lenders into one site, individual mortgage brokers, national lenders, or with Internet companies that offer a slew of the top lenders from which to choose. DocuSign and Adobe (among others) allow you to sign loan documents with an electronic signature. This means that you'll be able to close on your home electronically someday, without paying a visit to a local title or escrow company.

## The Bad News

Unfortunately, today's Internet:

- **Doesn't necessarily offer complete information on every home that's for sale in every neighborhood.** So if you rely solely on the Internet to shop for a home, you're probably missing some, if not a lot, of homes, and you'll likely miss crucial data points on homes that are listed.

- **Might be out of date.** Although some sites claim to update their information daily, if not several times during the day, the truth is that they can't update anything unless the information has been sent to them from the individual brokerage firms. In some cases, that might happen weekly or even monthly. In a hot seller's market, like the one we're experiencing in 2017 and 2018,[*] keeping listings up to date is tough, if not impossible.

- **Expect to get steered toward the seller's broker for more information.** While the seller's broker knows what's going on with the property (you hope!), you don't want to end up in a dual agency situation—which is what might happen if you email a seller's broker for more information about a particular listing and you don't mention that you're already represented by a buyer's agent. Or the seller's agent could continue to work only for the seller—in which case you would wind up with no representation at all!

- **It isn't a substitute for walking around a neighborhood.** While getting to know a city or neighborhood through an Internet site is a good idea, it isn't even close to going there in person and experiencing the area as a would-be resident. You may like a house on the Internet but be horrified by the actual neighborhood once you get there. Until you visit and see for yourself, you'll never really know.

- **Can overwhelm you with information.** What the Internet does best is to provide you with information so you can make an informed decision on your own. And you can access that information at any time of the day or night. Want to apply for a loan or sign your closing docs at 3 a.m.? No problem. On the other hand, with hundreds of thousands of real estate–related websites to peruse, you can get easily overwhelmed if you don't know where to go and what to look for.

- **Can be a huge waste of time.** Either the information is duplicated on larger websites, or you're getting information that is supposedly objective but is provided by someone who wants your business.

And yet, according to the latest figures, more than 93 percent of Americans start their search for a home on the Internet. Another new trend is that home buyers are purchas-

---

[*] And like the one we experienced during the latter half of the 1990s and into the early 2000s, when homes sold in a matter of days (or minutes).

ing houses—sight unseen—through the Internet. In my mind, you're taking a huge risk (what if the home isn't what it seems to be?), but sometimes it works out.

> **FRED'S STORY**
>
> Fred lived in the San Francisco area and was told at work he was being transferred to Boston in the next two weeks. The problem was, Fred was going to be traveling nonstop for work and didn't have time to fly out to look for a place to live.
>
> Late one night, he went to his home office, fired up his computer, and started searching Boston real estate in his price range. He looked up neighborhoods and the different types of homes that were available and found a few things he liked. Next, he went to a couple of mortgage sites and ended up applying for a loan online.
>
> By the next night, he was approved for his mortgage and had called several agents to talk to them about various properties they represented. By the third day, when he left for a two-week business trip to Asia, he had made a successful offer on a property without ever seeing it. At the end of his trip he came back to San Francisco, packed up, put his stuff in storage, and flew to Boston. He closed on the property a few weeks later, and had his things moved into his new place.
>
> Fred likes the home he bought and, because of a hot seller's market in the Boston neighborhood he chose, felt he had to move quickly. Time constraints and travel prevented him from visiting Boston ahead of time, but fortunately, it worked out okay.

If you're going to buy a home sight unseen, keep these issues in mind:

1. **Protect yourself as best you can.** Hire a real estate agent to help. Put in the usual inspection and financing contingencies as well as an attorney approval rider (see Question 71 for details). If, for some reason, the seller won't accept a mortgage contingency, try to include a contingency that allows you to withdraw from the sale if the house doesn't appraise out in value (that is, if the bank's appraiser comes back and says the house isn't worth what you're paying for it).

2. **Find out as much as possible about the neighborhood and block.** Look up crime statistics, try to find photos of the neighborhood and area online, look for a neighborhood or block association that can provide more information, and try to talk to

someone who lives nearby. Talk to the local village hall or building department to make sure no new highways, train depots, commercial developments, or dumps will be located nearby. Study local maps to figure out whether your property will be surrounded by other similar properties or something entirely different.

3. **Ask the agent to send you any rules or regulations for the property.** That way, if you're buying a condo, co-op, or townhouse (or in a subdivision), you'll know what, if any, rules you'll need to live by (such as the number of pets permitted and what they can be).

**20/20 HINDSIGHT:** No matter how much you think you love a house you found online, don't make an offer until you've actually stepped through its portals in person. If you must make an offer sight unseen, be sure you include the regular home inspection, financing, and attorney approval (if applicable in your state) contingencies in order to protect yourself.

## Question 19: What Is the Difference Between a Real Estate Agent and a Real Estate Broker? What Is a Realtor?

Real estate professionals go by a few different names, although the distinction shouldn't matter much to you. The only caveat here is to make certain the broker or agent you choose to work with is a licensed real estate professional; all real estate brokers and sales agents are licensed and regulated by each state. Most states have laws that require brokers and agents to post their licenses in a visible place. If you're not certain your agent is licensed, simply ask to see the license. Or you can call the state agency that regulates real estate agents and brokers in your state and verify the license.

What's the difference between a real estate agent and a real estate broker? To the average home buyer or seller, there isn't much difference. Either an agent or a broker can help you successfully complete your home purchase. To become a real estate agent, an individual must complete the required number of hours of classes and pass the agent's exam. To become a broker, the agent must then take additional classes, have a specified amount of experience in the field (usually a year), and pass another exam. Both agents and brokers are typically required to take a certain number of hours of continuing education courses, and they may also take additional courses to garner a few extra letters after their name.

Having a real estate broker's license confers certain privileges, including the right to open, run, and own a real estate office, and to work independently without an office. A real estate agent must work for a broker, who is responsible for that agent's actions.

Is it better to work with a broker than a sales agent? Not necessarily. Although it would seem that a broker may have more experience or be more knowledgeable than an agent, that isn't always the case. Plenty of excellent sales agents have chosen not to become brokers because they have no intention of ever running their own office. (For example, my mother, Susanne, a top-selling agent in Chicago for more than twenty years, has never taken the broker classes or exams.) The experience and knowledge of an agent who has been working in an area for fifteen years will far surpass that of a brand-new broker. You should find the most experienced professional to work with you, regardless of their official title.

## Realtors vs. Non-Realtors

What is the difference between a broker who is a Realtor and a broker who is not? A Realtor is a broker or agent who belongs to the National Association of Realtors (NAR) and subscribes to that organization's code of ethics and conduct. There are around 2 million real estate agents and brokers in the United States, working for 86,000 (plus or minus a few) brokerage offices, of which approximately 1.2 million are, according to NAR, dues-paying Realtors.

**FIRST-TIME BUYER TIP:** If you're searching for a home online, you may run across other people who offer to help you buy a home. Some of these may call themselves "facilitators," or have some other sort of name. They typically work for newer-model tech-based real estate platforms that are attempting to disrupt the real estate industry. The questions you should always ask are: "Who do you represent?" and "How (and how much) do you get paid?" That should tell you all you need to know about their loyalties.

# Question 20: How Do I Choose the Right Agent or Broker?

Finding a broker or agent who meets your needs and personality can be tougher than it sounds. Those buyers who have the worst experiences are often those who just walk into or call their neighborhood shop and ask for anyone at random. That's not the best way to find a good partner, and odds are against you having a great experience.

Connie is the director of career development and advertising for a real estate firm located in Overland Park, Kansas. She has her broker's license and has sold real estate for more than fourteen years. Connie believes that every buyer, but especially a first-timer, should carefully interview several agents and brokers. "Have them describe to you how they go about assisting a buyer. Try to get a feel for the agents' philosophy on working with buyers. Try to get a feel for their background and experience level. And be sure to ask them for a resume. If you're thinking about letting someone represent you in the transaction, I think it's reasonable to expect to see a copy of their resume."

Connie says she'd be leery of any agent who lets you walk into his or her office and then immediately bundles you into his or her car and shows you homes. The agents need to interview you, she says. "And first-time buyers generally need an education on the purchase process and understanding what their options are in the transaction."

Although Connie recommends working with a heavily experienced agent ("Why should you be the guinea pig?" she asks), she says sometimes brand-new agents offer excellent service. "That depends on their training and support. It can be a good situation. But more often than not, the more experienced the agent, the more transactions he or she handles in a year, the more situations they're confronted with, the more insight into the closing process they will have."

## Making a Good Match

In addition to looking for an experienced agent, try to find one who suits your personality. If you're an early bird, don't choose someone habitually late. If you're allergic to smoking, don't choose a smoker. If you're extremely organized, don't choose a broker who is constantly losing his or her keys. Over time, or on long days of multiple showings, these little personality quirks will make you crazy.

It's also important to find someone who won't push you into making a decision before you're ready. You want a broker who will tell you the facts and help you compare the differences between properties, but you don't want someone who will scare you or pressure you into purchasing a home. Unfortunately, some brokers and agents do pressure buyers to buy—especially in a hot seller's market where there are very few homes and a lot of competition. If that happens, you need to be tough enough to back away from that pressure and find yourself a new agent. You can also call a meeting with the agent's managing broker to talk about the situation. This can be a very effective strategy: One of the managing broker's jobs is to smooth out the bumps between agents and their buyers and sellers.

 **FIRST-TIME BUYER TIP:** I've often said that working with a real estate agent is a little like a short-term marriage in that you see over time the best and worst characteristics of the other person. Even in the best of circumstances, the pressure will mount and you may not always like what's happening, or how a situation is being handled. But since you'll be in such close proximity for an undetermined amount of time—often at least three to six months from start to closing—it's a good idea to find someone with whom you're compatible.

How do you find a good broker or agent? Try this:

- As in choosing a doctor or an attorney, most people are referred to an agent or broker by their friends or a family member who has recently bought or sold a home and had a good experience.
- If you're moving across state lines and don't know anyone in your new town, you may want to contact a relocation company, who can assist you with the sale of your existing home (if needed) and the purchase of your new home.
- There are also plenty of portal sites, like Zillow, HomeFinder, and Realtor.com (formerly owned by the Realtors and now owned by a company controlled by Rupert Murdoch), and national real estate companies like Coldwell Banker, Redfin, Century 21, Re/Max, Berkshire Hathaway, and Better Homes and Gardens Real

Estate, which provide listings online and can link you to the listing agents, allowing you to take the interview process from there.

- If your company is moving you, the company may have an ongoing relationship with a broker or brokerage firm in your new location.

Although it's certainly wise to interview a broker who is referred by someone you know, also interview several other agents who frequently work in your area. Aunt Jeanne's suburban agent may not be the most effective agent to help you find a downtown loft.

**FIRST-TIME BUYER TIP:** Don't let your mother, father, or sibling foist someone on you or try to guilt you into using a family member or friend. This almost never works out. If one of your relatives is a real estate agent, by all means sit down and interview them. But make sure that's only one of a small handful of agents that you interview before you make a final decision. I typically recommend talking to three agents to start, and adding a fourth or fifth if you still don't feel as though you've found the right person.

Here are a few other suggestions for finding a great agent:

- Open your local neighborhood newspaper to the real estate section and see who runs the biggest ads, week in and week out.
- If you ask friends, neighbors, or relatives for referrals, make sure they had a great experience with the agent they used. You don't want to use someone who doesn't give good real estate.
- Visit open houses and spend some time talking to the real estate agents about homes in the neighborhoods. Ask these listing brokers to define what makes a great buyer's agent. Ask them who, in addition to themselves, they'd want their own children to use.
- Call your local board of Realtors and ask for the names of agents who sold the most property last year, then try to match those names up with the agents who work in your neighborhood of choice. If the local board can't (or won't) help, you can call the real estate companies in your area whose signs you see the most often and ask which agents do the most business in your neighborhood.

## 17 Questions You Should Ask Agents Before Hiring Them

Despite any horror stories you may have heard, the vast majority of first-time buyers have good, if not great, experiences with their agents. But to ensure you're working with the right person, you'll have to take on the responsibility of interviewing several agents before you make your final selection. Here are some questions you should ask each time you interview a real estate agent:

1. How many years have you been in the real estate business?

2. How many years have you been with this company?

3. How many real estate transactions did you complete in each of the last two years?

4. What was the dollar volume of your transactions in each of the last two years?

5. What percentage of your business is with home buyers vs. sellers? What percentage of your home buyer business is with first-time buyers?

6. How old are your clients, on average? Do they have children? (You're trying to find someone who represents buyers who look like you.)

7. What was the price range (lowest to highest) of the homes you helped your clients buy and sell last year?

8. What would you say is the average price of the homes you helped your clients buy and sell?

9. Are you an exclusive buyer's broker? Do you ask home buyers to sign an exclusivity contract? Do you charge an up-front fee that is later applied to the commission?

10. What are the primary neighborhoods or communities in which you work?

11. How familiar are you with the schools, crime statistics, and demographics of the various neighborhoods? (Hint: Brokers are forbidden from "steering" you to one neighborhood or another for any reason. For this reason, they may choose to tell you where to go to get information on crime or schools but opt not to tell you themselves.)

12. What style of home do you most frequently work with? (If you're looking for a four-family apartment building and they're more familiar with single-family houses, it might not be a good fit.)

13. Are you a smoker or a nonsmoker? (If this is important to you.)

14. How many home buyers or sellers do you work with at a given time? (You're trying to find out how much time you'll get from the agent.)

15. How frequently will I hear from you? How do I reach you? Can I email you? Or phone you at home? Are you planning any extended vacations in the next six months?

16. Do you work with an assistant? Will I be working with the assistant or with you?

17. How long has it been taking your clients to find a property they like well enough to construct an offer? (You're trying to gauge how fast the local market is moving and if the buyers are successful in their quest to find a property.)

 **FIRST-TIME BUYER TIP:** You can find out a lot about an agent just by the way he or she answers these questions. If he or she bristles and seems reluctant to share information with you, that may be a sign of things to come. If he or she is open and friendly, and you develop a connection on the phone, you may have found someone with whom you'll enjoy working.

## Going It Alone

I know I'm repeating myself here, but Millennials (and I know I'm generalizing here) believe they can learn almost everything they need to know online. And, that's true and not true because the Internet contains a lot of false or misleading information designed to point you in one direction or another. There are many technology companies (and more starting up each year) that are banking on Millennials wanting to do everything themselves, including buying a home. While technology helps, and may one day lower the commission that is paid, there really isn't a benefit to buying a home without a buyer's broker's help. While more and more buyers tell me they are shopping on their own, if they purchase something that's listed on the local MLS, they are not necessarily buying on their own. They are buying with the assistance of a dual agent, also known as a transactional agent, a facilitator, or non-agent, depending on which state you live in. (For more information on dual agents, transactional agents, facilitators, and non-agents, see Question 23.)

And what that means is you're essentially making the largest single purchase of your life without any representation at all. And that's just foolhardy.

## Question 21: What Is a Seller's or Conventional Broker? What Are the Seller's Broker's Responsibilities to Me?

First things first: There is a wide gulf between a seller's broker, also known as a conventional broker, and a buyer's broker. Buyer's brokers (and exclusive buyer's brokers) represent the interests of the buyer (see Question 22). Seller's brokers represent the interests of the seller.

It seems obvious, but there's a lot of crossover that makes it confusing.

The theory goes that the broker works for the person who pays his or her commission. A seller's broker means the seller pays the commission. A buyer's broker means the buyer is responsible for paying the commission.

But wait! Didn't I just say that even if you use a buyer's agent, the seller will pay the commission? Yep. And, in practice, that's generally how it works. In many states, any broker who works with a buyer, who is not a dual agent, automatically becomes a buyer's broker—even if the seller pays the commission. But if, for some reason, the seller doesn't pay the commission, the buyer would then be responsible for paying it. It doesn't happen very often, and you can usually negotiate around it—if you know what your financial responsibility might be.

Since I wrote the first edition of this book in 1993, buyer brokerage has gone mainstream. In the early 1990s, there were more conventional brokers, but today buyer brokerage has been accepted by the National Association of Realtors (NAR) and written into almost all state statutes. We'll talk more about this in Question 22.

When a seller or a conventional broker brings the buyer to the deal, he or she is also called the subagent. Even though a subagent will take you, the buyer, around to see various houses, and appear to work in your best interests, your broker is still a seller's broker.

Being a seller's broker means that he or she has a fiduciary responsibility to the seller, rather than to you, the buyer. The seller's broker is required by law to represent the seller's best interest—not yours. These distinctions have caused a tremendous amount of confusion for buyers, who quite naturally assume that the person taking them around, showing them houses, telling them the inside scoop, and buying them coffee and dinner, works for them.

Let's be clear on one point: If you haven't hired a buyer's broker and signed an exclusivity contract with him or her, and if you're not living in a state that mandates buyer brokerage, you're most likely working with a seller's or conventional broker.

> **FIRST-TIME BUYER TIP:** Subagency has been all but eliminated in all states, except in a particular circumstance: when you (the buyer) are unagented (meaning, you're acting alone) and go to visit a home that is listed by a seller's agent. The seller's agent owes his or her fiduciary duty to the seller, but you become the customer in a subagency arrangement. To be clear, this means you have no one acting on your behalf in the transaction (a potentially dangerous circumstance), and the seller's agent gets both sides of the commission. In this case, the subagent (who is bringing the seller and buyer to the table simultaneously) is known as a dual agent.

## Agency Disclosure

It's all so confusing—far more than it needs to be. To counteract some of the confusion, many states have adopted "agency disclosure" laws that require brokers to disclose to the buyer whom they actually represent in a given deal. In some states, brokers and agents must make that disclosure in writing and will ask you to sign it. When you sign the form, you're saying that you understand who is working for you, and whether the agent is working for you or for the seller. If you don't understand what the form says or what it means, don't sign it.[*]

---

[*] When it comes to legalese, this is actually a good rule of thumb: Don't sign anything you don't genuinely understand. It's entirely possible that it will come back to bite you!

## Things a Seller's Agent Cannot Do for You

If you're a buyer working with a subagent, there are certain things seller's brokers cannot legally do, which varies slightly from state to state. In general, he or she:

- **Cannot tell you what to offer for the property.** Because they work for the seller, subagents are supposed to help the seller get his or her list price. If you're in an extremely hot market, like during the latter half of the 1990s, you may pay list price or even more. In a soft market, one that favors the buyer, you'll probably pay less than the list price, maybe even a lot less. Either way, how much you pay will put you in conflict with the obligation the seller's broker has to the seller.

- **Cannot tell you which home to buy if you are deciding between two.** A seller's broker works for each seller and may work for multiple sellers. If a seller's broker, for example, shows you five houses in a given day, he or she has technically worked for five sellers. That's confusing, but it boils down to this: If you like two homes, the seller's broker actually works for the two sellers simultaneously and so should not help you choose one home over the other. (Can you see now why buyer brokerage is so much more appealing?)

- **Cannot point out the defects of a home, unless they are material, hidden defects.** The seller's broker cannot say anything or do anything that will influence you not to buy a property. Material hidden defects must be disclosed, however, because they are not visible to the naked eye. For more information on seller disclosure, see Question 80.

- **May only provide you with comparable data upon request.** Seller's brokers must provide you with all the information you need to come up with a reasonable offer, so ask your broker to provide you with: a list of "comps" detailing how much other homes in the neighborhood, similar in size and amenities to the one you like, sold for in the past six months; a list of current similar listings and their list prices (it's important to know the difference between the asking and sales price of homes in the area); and the average number of list days. This will help you figure out whether you're in a fast market (seller's market) or slow market (buyer's market).

Of course, some seller's brokers will give you all these things without you asking for them. It's understandable why they do it: A broker relies on referrals in order for his or her business to grow. If everyone refers two buyers or sellers, the agent's or broker's client list pyramids, and after a few years he or she could have a client list numbering in the hundreds.

Just remember this: All agents, including seller's agents and brokers, want you to have a good experience when you buy a home.

They want it to be easy.

They want you to like them.

They want you to refer your friends to them.

 **20/20 HINDSIGHT:** Before you start believing that conventional brokers won't be able to help you buy a home as effectively as a buyer's broker, let me reassure you that is not always the case. For dozens of years, conventional brokers were the only game in town, and they've helped millions of buyers successfully purchase homes. But if you have a choice, or can declare your preference, go with a buyer's agent.

Many seller's brokers pride themselves on being full-service firms, and since they have every incentive to close the deal—after all, they get paid only at the closing—the broker should be delighted to provide you with the names of various mortgage brokers, inspectors, and attorneys (they probably keep a list of "recommended" service providers). You'll want to get several recommendations for each service. That way you can properly interview the prospective attorney or inspector and choose the best person for the job. In addition, many real estate companies now own mortgage firms. Undoubtedly, they'll give you the name of their in-house or affiliated lender, who may or may not give you a great deal. But you won't know that until you shop around and compare prices.

The various changes in state laws governing brokers who are subagents of the seller require that you be more aware of the shifting nature of the relationship. However, a good broker (whether buyer's or seller's) will be responsive to your needs. That puts the onus on you to be well-informed about what you want and how you intend to get it.

# Question 22: What Is a Buyer's Broker? What Is an Exclusive Buyer's Agent? Should I Use One?

We've established that traditional (also known as seller's) agents and brokers work for the one who pays the commission: traditionally, the seller. But in the late 1990s, an increasing number of sophisticated buyers recognized that the conventional broker's role posed a conflict of interest. They asked: "How can a broker have my best interest at heart when he or she is being paid by the seller? How can a broker help me find the best property at the best price when he or she is bound legally and financially to serve the seller's best interest?"

That's how buyer brokerage really started to take off. In the latter half of the 1990s, many states around the country changed their laws to allow *buyer agency*. Here's what that means today: If you're a buyer and are working with a broker, that broker automatically becomes a buyer's agent. If you're a seller, the broker functions as a seller's broker.

But we're getting a little bit ahead of ourselves. A buyer's agent is one who is ethically and legally bound to put the buyer's interests ahead of all else in a real estate transaction. The buyer's agent owes the buyer his or her fiduciary duty, not the seller—even if the seller will ultimately pay the agent or broker's commission.

The buyer's agent's duties are not at all dissimilar to the way a nice seller's broker might have treated you. The buyer's broker will hunt for homes that are appropriate for your needs and budget. He or she will help you negotiate every facet of the contract, striving to get you the best price and terms. Some buyer's brokers will even help you find the best mortgage and homeowners' insurance with the most favorable terms. Then the broker will help you with any of the other niggling closing details and show up at the closing to collect his or her check.

A buyer's broker may want you to sign an exclusivity agreement. This agreement states that you will not work with any other buyer's agents within a defined period of time. As with all real estate contracts, it is negotiable. The agent may want you to put down a fee of some sort (refundable at closing). Whether or not you pay it is up to you; however, I don't think a fee is necessary to prove that you're committed to working with a particular buyer's agent. Likewise, I would make sure that the exclusivity agreement includes a definite time limit and allows you to cancel the agreement if you decide not to purchase a home or simply because you've found someone else you'd rather work with.

## There Are Buyer's Agents and There Are Exclusive Buyer's Agents

The most common form of buyer's agency is designated agency, which means that the agent is a buyer's agent when working with a home buyer and a seller's agent when working with a seller.

But that means your buyer's agent might also be a listing agent and may, in fact, have several homes currently listed for sale that may be right for you. The possible conflict of interest is, of course, that you'll be shown one of these listings and find yourself in a dual agency situation—where the same agent is representing both sides in the same transaction. While you can ask your buyer's agent to give you to another agent in his or her office to go through the offer/counteroffer process, you may feel bad because you've developed a strong attachment to your buyer's agent and, more important, you've probably told him or her some personal information about how much you can really spend on a house. The problem there is that if your buyer's agent becomes a dual agent, you have to trust him or her not to reveal your financial secrets to the seller. That kind of disclosure could really destroy your negotiating power.

**FIRST-TIME BUYER TIP:** We all talk too much about ourselves to our buyer's agents. It just happens because you spend so much time together. Don't lose any sleep if you've let slip some vital piece of financial information. But try not to talk exactly about how much you're prepared to spend on a house, just in case the quoted amount comes back to haunt you.

Another way around the potential dual agency conflict of interest is to hire an *exclusive buyer's agent*. An exclusive buyer's agent never takes listings. They represent only buyers. In the mid-1990s, exclusive buyer's agents were viewed with skepticism and scorn by the regular brokerage community. In Massachusetts, for example, there were even stories (which I was unable to verify directly) that exclusive buyer's brokers were discriminated against when it came to setting up showings. One exclusive buyer's agent claimed he had been assaulted by another real estate agent who was unhappy with his client's bid for a property. He claimed this agent physically attacked him!

Fortunately, those stories are few and far between, and in the years since I published the second edition of this book they have pretty much faded away completely. But what is clear is that exclusive buyer's agency has become much more accepted over the years, although it remains far more popular on the east and west coasts than in the center or southern sections of the country. Best of all, where before you might have found only one or two exclusive buyer's agents in an entire metropolitan area, more have joined the ranks so that home buyers have a larger choice of people with whom they can work.

**RESOURCES:** If you're looking for an exclusive buyer's agent, you might want to check out the National Association of Exclusive Buyer Agents (naeba.org), a nonprofit organization dedicated to improving the image and numbers of EBAs around the country. They can recommend you to their members who must abide by their tough code of ethics. Most EBAs will also be members of the National Association of Realtors (NAR), which didn't even recognize buyer's agency as a legitimate form of real estate agency until the early 1990s.

## A Difference in Perception

If you're wondering how a buyer's broker might treat you differently from a seller's broker, you're not alone. If the seller's broker breaks the law by providing you with insights and information about various sellers and their homes and advises you on which house to bid and on how much to offer, then there may not be a great difference in service. (Then again, the seller's broker could be liable to the seller for breaching his or her fiduciary duty to the seller. But that's not your concern.)

On the other hand, a buyer's broker is completely on your side, bound by contract and the law to provide you with all of the information you need to buy your dream house at the lowest price possible and on the most favorable terms.

Sharon, a sales agent in west suburban Chicago, says: "When I'm working for the seller, my job is to bring in the best offer. When I'm working as a buyer's broker, I feel free to give that kind of advice as well as to suggest different pricing (strategies) my clients may offer."

Experts say buyers generally have trouble with two facets of buyer brokerage: the exclusivity agreement and the payment for services rendered. When a buyer opts for buyer brokerage, he or she is often asked to sign an exclusivity agreement. According to most of these contracts, the buyer agrees to work only with the buyer's broker for a certain length of time. If the buyer purchases a home within the exclusivity period, he or she will owe the broker a fee.

Sounds simple enough, but buyers, who are used to changing agents at will, sometimes find the idea of exclusivity disquieting. If you feel that a ninety-day exclusivity period is too long, offer a thirty-day term that is renewable. A good buyer's broker will understand your nervousness (you're not the first to feel this way) and should be happy to make you feel comfortable. Thirty days will be enough time for you to decide if you like the buyer's broker's service.

Payment of the buyer brokerage fee is another issue buyers struggle with—particularly first-time buyers who are often short on cash. You should know that it is the fee that guarantees the buyer's broker's loyalty. Buyer brokerage fees can be paid either as a flat payment, hourly, or as a percentage of the purchase price of the home.

## The Real World

In the real world, however, the buyer's broker's compensation often ends up being paid by the seller. What happens is the seller's agent agrees to split the commission with the buyer's broker, just as the seller's agent would agree to split the commission with a conventional broker. Where the fee issue might come into play is if you end up buying a FSBO with the help of your buyer's agent. But there, too, it usually gets worked out. Either the seller pays a half commission (2½ or 3 percent) to the buyer's agent or the purchase price of the home is raised to cover the commission.

## Other Issues and Concerns

Do buyer's brokers ever pressure their clients to buy something if their exclusivity contract is about to expire? Most brokers say no, but first-time buyers Dawn and Bill don't agree. They said they've had a nasty experience with a buyer's broker who applied enormous pressure and even took the couple to court. (The judge threw the broker's case out of court and forced him to pay both sides' legal fees.) Some real estate attorneys confide that they've seen some agents present their clients with a choice of four houses and pressure them to purchase one quickly. Again, reputable agents do not act in this way. Your job is to find a reputable agent.

There are many reasons to choose to work with a buyer's broker, but the most obvious one is hardly ever mentioned: Because the buyer's broker is paid by the buyer, he or she is free to bring the buyer to any property that is available, including FSBOs.

---

**MARK'S STORY**

Mark is an architect who purchases homes and small apartment buildings for rehabilitation and resale. He is always on the lookout for a deal, and has a couple of agents who specialize in these types of properties looking for him in different parts of town. While he has had some luck calling sellers directly, he has directed the agents he works with to pursue FSBO properties. He guarantees them their share of the commission, should the deal go through, and he frequently purchases FSBO properties with a buyer's broker. In fact, he recently closed on just such a house. "The property wasn't listed in the multiple listing service. A conventional broker wouldn't have even found it," he said.

---

Is buyer brokerage the right choice for you? That depends on how comfortable you are with the concepts of exclusivity and being responsible for the broker's commission. When Mark buys a FSBO property, he makes sure the seller will pay his broker the half commission she's entitled to. If the seller won't, Mark adjusts his offer and pays the commission out of his own pocket.

More buyers, especially first-timers, are choosing buyer's brokers because they like having someone represent them. Some companies who transfer employees from one location to another and pay their moving costs ask the relocation company to give their employees a buyer's broker option. Even some websites, which originally put only the listing broker as a contact, now suggest you might want to contact your own buyer's broker first.

As when making any selection, interview a buyer's broker and (if it's an option, because it isn't in many states) a conventional broker and decide who will be able to help you the most.

# Question 23: What Is a Dual Agent? What Is a Transactional Broker? What Is a Non-Agent?

Dual agency occurs when the same real estate broker or agent represents both sides in the same transaction. A dual agent is the agent representing both the buyer and seller in the purchase and sale of a single property.

The problem with dual agency is the inherent conflict of interest in having the same person represent two sides of a single deal. How can the buyer's broker have a fiduciary relationship with the buyer, and do everything in his or her power to help the buyer purchase the home for the best possible price and on the best possible terms, if he or she is also acting as a seller's broker, trying to get the seller the most money possible? It's impossible for a single broker or agent to represent the best interests of opposing sides in a single transaction—no matter what anyone tries to tell you!

Another form of dual agency occurs when the selling broker and buyer's agent work for the same firm. Although not all states recognize this as dual agency, some do because it's possible that the listing agent and buyer's agent will share confidential information in some informal exchange that could be harmful to their client. The firewall separating buyer's agents and seller's agents can seem dangerously thin (or nonexistent) in some offices.

Because of the inherent conflicts of interest, the National Association of Realtors has tried over the years to give new names to dual agency that appear to lessen this inherent conflict of interest.

Two terms of choice have emerged: transactional brokerage or non-agency. If your buyer's broker happens to bring you to one of her listings and you fall in love with it and want to make an offer, the buyer's broker may cease to become your broker and may assume the role of a transactional broker. This means that the broker will help the transaction through to the close, without having a fiduciary duty to either the buyer or seller.

The problem with transactional brokerage is that the buyers and sellers lose and the broker wins. Neither the buyer nor the seller has a broker in their pocket to guide and advise them, but the seller pays the full commission, as if he and the buyer were receiving everything they bargained for from their full-service brokers.

Non-agency is another name for transactional brokerage, except it's more honest. Again, the agent does not work for either the buyer or seller but shuffles papers back and forth and helps the deal go through.

Is dual agency a bad thing? Sometimes, because the broker knows both sides very well, he or she can help smooth over a difficult situation and find the common ground that permits the deal to happen. In that case, dual agency is definitely a good thing. But when the buyer and seller have developed a trusting, personal relationship with their agent, and then suddenly find themselves nonrepresented by their agent who is stuck in the middle, the lack of representation can cause real problems.

What should you do if you're presented with a dual agency situation? Here's your best option: Ask your agent to choose whether they want to represent the seller or you. If the agent chooses the seller, ask the agent or the managing broker of the firm to assign another agent to you. That way, you'll have full representation in the construction and negotiation of your contract.

## Question 24: What Is the Typical Real Estate Commission? How Is It Split?

Sellers are always focused on the commission. And why not? It's a huge chunk (usually 4 to 7 percent) that comes straight out of the sales proceeds.

But it's also important for buyers to be aware of how much commission is actually being paid. By law, there is no standard real estate commission. It's entirely negotiable—and real estate agents must tell you that. They might, however, give you a general range of commissions, say 4 to 7 percent, or tell you it's 6 percent (hoping you won't negotiate). Whatever the commission rate, the seller's agent typically winds up splitting it with the buyer's commission, sometimes equally, sometimes not.

Even though it is the seller who typically pays the commission, buyers should be aware of the commission rates and whether it is a buyer's or seller's market in their area. If it's a seller's market—where there are more qualified buyers than homes for sale—the commission might be somewhat below what is typically acceptable for that area. If the commission is normally 6 percent, it might be 5.5 percent or less, since the demand is high for the seller's property and the seller's broker doesn't have to work too hard to make the sale. Since the Great Recession, sellers have pushed for lower commissions, especially if their properties didn't have any equity (or very little, meaning they were functionally a short sale and had to bring cash to the closing in order to walk away even).

You might also see far more FSBOs in a seller's market. If there is a huge demand for property, sellers may put up a website featuring information about their home, use portals (with free and/or paid listings), advertise in the local neighborhood newspaper (if it still exists), and put up a large For Sale sign on their front lawn. Savvy sellers will hope that they can get away with paying only a half commission (2.5 to 3 percent) to the buyer's agent and pocket the other half of the commission they'd normally pay to the listing agent.

If there's a buyer's market—where there are more sellers than qualified buyers—you might find the seller offering more than the typical commission (or even extras like free trips and cars) to entice agents and brokers to bring their buyers. If the typical commission is 6 percent, you might see the seller offering 7 percent, with 4 percent going to the agent who brings the buyer to the table. Although most agents won't try to sell you a piece of property just because it has an extra-high commission (or other bonuses) attached, they might bring you to see it.

 **20/20 HINDSIGHT:** A disturbing new trend creeping up is the unequal distribution of the commission between the seller's and buyer's brokers. While typically the commission is split 50/50, sometimes the seller's agent will take a larger portion of the commission. I've seen deals where the seller's agent gets a 3 percent commission and the buyer's agent gets just 2 or 2.5 percent. While this new trend wouldn't seem to affect you, a home buyer, it actually might. While I'm not suggesting your agent would ever pressure you to buy a home strictly because of the commission split (although this, in fact, does happen once in a while), you will likely be shown homes where the commission split is equal or favors the buyer's broker before you are shown homes where the reverse is true. Sellers who permit this kind of unequal commission split to go on are doing themselves no favors. You, the buyer, should insist on seeing everything that's available in your price range.

## Question 25: What Is a Discount Broker? When Should I Use One?

The idea that you can buy something for less than its market price is extremely appealing in America. We have discount clothing stores, food stores, drugstores, and whole towns built up around outlet malls. And then, of course, there's Amazon, which in the past ten years has emerged as the first (and often last) stop for pricing products and finding deals. So is it surprising that the demand for discount real estate brokerage has continued to grow? Not really. To me, the surprise is how long it's taking for the Internet to definitively impact traditional real estate sales models.

In a discount brokerage situation, the discount buyer's agent gives you the names and addresses of properties for sale from the local Multiple Listing Service (MLS), but you do all the legwork, look at every home that might possibly be right for you, work out your own mortgage, present your own contract, submit your own counteroffer, arrange for your own inspectors, and do your own walk-through. For your "sweat equity," the discount broker will give you a portion of the commission he or she receives.

Why should the discount broker receive anything if you're doing all the work? Good question. To begin with, the discount broker has access to the MLS, which lists all the properties for sale in the area and which lists a lot of information, including a home's size, price, and number of bedrooms and bathrooms. It's a very useful list to have, and access to all of these details is strictly limited to member agents and brokers and their clients. By sharing the commission with the discount broker, you're essentially buying access to the local MLS.

But wait! you say. What about the Internet? Can't I get all the listings from a website?

Possibly. And sometimes you'll get enough information (address, specific information about the size of the lot and house, or the amount of last year's tax bill) all in one place. This is why so many people are going to Zillow as a first stop on their digital home shopping tour: You can put in a zip code and instantly see all of the homes that are listed for sale or rent.

But if you click through and contact those agents, you won't have any representation. You'll automatically enter into a non-agency arrangement, where the seller's agent is also representing you, the buyer. It isn't much, but with a discount buyer's agent, you still get a bare minimum of representation.

## The Dollars and Cents of Discount Brokerage

Here's a look at how the dollars and cents of discount brokerage works:

Discount brokerage firms give buyers up to 50 percent of their share (which might be

2 to 3 percent of the sales price) of the commission at closing.* On a $100,000 property, your share might be as much as $1,500. That $1,500 might well pay the points for your mortgage (unless you get the seller to cover closing costs), or cover the cost of repainting the interior of the house after you move in. And while $1,500 may not seem like it's worth the effort, discount brokers say that there are those home buyers, particularly first-time buyers, who need every nickel to buy a home and are willing to put in the time and effort.

A discount broker may split its share of commission with you, minus any "extras." And this is where you need to take care. The discount brokerage firm often puts a price tag on every service it provides for you, including every telephone call or each showing. A minimum number of showings are usually included in the deal, but if the broker shows you additional properties, the fees for these pay-as-you-go services are deducted from your portion of the commission.

For example, there is a discount brokerage firm in Chicago that charges somewhere between one and four percentage points off the commission refund for each service it performs for you. So if you need the broker to place a follow-up call to your lender, the company would reduce your refund by 1 percent for each call. If the total possible refund is $1,500, each phone call would cost you $15.

### SANDRA'S STORY

A first-time buyer, Sandra needed every penny to put into the purchase of her home. She saw an ad for a discount broker and called. She thought it sounded like a great deal.

Later, she told me she had been thinking that she'd just do some of the work and receive about $2,000 back from the agent.

But as it happened, things didn't turn out quite as she had planned. First, it was a really tight seller's market, and by the time the discount broker got around to setting up showings, the homes had sold. Sandra spent hundreds of hours scouring neighborhoods, real estate classified advertis-

---

* Revenue splits with agents have become much more complicated. In some real estate companies, the split between the company and the agent is quite uneven. A top-producing agent may receive as much as 90 or even 95 percent of the commission received by her real estate firm. Re/Max agents get 100 percent of the commission, but then have to pay for services the company provides. Even the splits between buyer's and seller's agents may be unequal, with seller's agents keeping a higher proportion of the commission for themselves even if it would be in the seller's best interest for the buyer's agent to get a bigger share.

ing, the Internet—anywhere she thought there might be an appropriate home for sale. But all of that time turned out to be wasted.

Additionally, after a few short weeks, the discount broker informed her that she had used up her allotment of "free time" and would now be charged for everything the broker had to do, from phone calls to setting up appointments. She would even be charged for the ultimate negotiation of the contract.

"I'd given myself a thorough education of the marketplace, and for that I'm grateful," Sandra said later. "But I also realized the value of a full-service agent in a market that's so tight that you need to be in the inner circle of agents to have any chance at all of a successful bid."

Sandra fired the discount broker and hired a full-service broker who worked with the biggest company in town. Within a few weeks, she'd found a house and made a successful offer to purchase.

**FIRST-TIME BUYER TIP:** The general caveat for real estate services holds true here also: If you've decided that a discount agent is the way to go, don't necessarily use the first one you find. Try to locate more than one discount broker in your area and then interview each at length. Ask for a resume and references. Then call those references and ask them both how much time they put into their home purchase and how much money they received back from the broker. Discount brokerage is best used by home buyers who have a clear idea of what they want or who have been through the process before. But first-time buyers who are willing to put in a little "sweat equity" might be able to save a little money.

## New and Improved? Or Just New Packaging?

If you type "discount real estate broker" into an Internet search engine, you'll get nearly one million results. Some of these are for discount fee real estate companies, and others are articles about the phenomenon. New discount fee brokerage companies are springing up daily. As I was writing the fourth edition of this book, I got a press release pitching a "new company ready to truly use tech to put sellers in charge (and put more money in their pockets) in much the same way that Uber and Airbnb disrupted their respective industries."

The company, called Reality,* launched in New York in mid-2017 and promises to make skyrocketing commissions a thing of the past by "putting the power" back in the hands of sellers, saving them "tens of thousands of dollars" by paying a low flat fee instead of a commission. Sellers pay a flat fee of up to $14,950 and do all of the work themselves. When I pointed out to the public relations person that this sounded just like ForSaleByOwner.com, he agreed that there were "similarities" but stressed there are "differences, too." Meanwhile, yet another FSBO company, Homie, also started up in Utah in 2017, promising to do exactly the same thing with even better technology, but only cost sellers $1,000. On Homie's website, the company claims to have saved Utah residents $10+ million in commissions. On the other hand, it is also looking to attract buyers and do mortgages, which are extraordinarily profitable.

And this: Zillow's Instant Offers, OfferPad, and OpenDoor are all just out of the gate, and could potentially be game-changers because of how they offer ways for buyers and sellers to connect directly. Here is a bit more about each of them:

**OFFERPAD.** The company was started in 2015 by two real estate investors who have bought thousands of homes in the Southwest and Florida in the wake of the Great Recession and housing crisis. OfferPad uses online data and technology to make an almost instant cash offer to sellers whose houses meet their criteria: single-family homes, including condos and townhouses, properties in age-restricted communities (maximum purchase price up to $325,000), gated communities, site-built after 1960, valued up to $500,000, are owner-occupied, located in certain communities, and don't have foundation issues. You put in your address, the valuation comes back, there's an inspection, and then the closing is scheduled.

**OPENDOOR.** This company makes an offer for homes within twenty-four hours and then schedules an inspection. Any work that the inspector (which the company pays for) deems necessary will be deducted from the offer price. Buyers can work with OpenDoor as well, going to see homes that are listed at any time, from 6 a.m. to 9 p.m. If you work with an agent, the agent will receive a commission of 0.75 per-

---

* This is how I know I'm getting old: It feels as though every new tech company continues to re-spell the English language, mangling it further.

cent (which is 25 percent of a normal commission, or what a traditional full-service agent would receive).*

**ZILLOW INSTANT OFFERS.** Not to be outdone, Zillow has created a new platform to enable sellers to get not-quite-instant-but-still-fairly-quick offers from investors looking to buy homes. At press time, there didn't seem to be a way for buyers to take advantage of the process and make an offer on these homes, although I'm sure the company is working on it. Meanwhile, traditional Realtors are up in arms: They collectively pay millions of dollars in revenue to the company and see this as taking business out of their pocket.

Will these newer models survive? I think that the Internet and technology will eventually change the way we buy and sell real estate, crushing the commissions paid to real estate agents and brokers. Today's buyers (and in particular Millennials) believe they know what they want and that the Internet can school them in what they don't know. They want to move quickly, and the Internet facilitates that. The problem is understanding exactly how everyone gets compensated and who, exactly, represents your best interests. I think that's still worth paying for, but not everyone in the real estate industry agrees.

The point is that there are only so many ways to buy and sell real estate: doing it yourself, using a discount broker of some type (and I include Internet-based companies in this category), or using a full-service real estate agency.

Don't let anyone hoodwink you into thinking it's more complicated than that.

## Question 26: How Much Should My Broker Know About the Amount I Can Afford to Spend on a Home?

Let's recap what you now know about real estate agents and brokers:

1. All conventional or seller's brokers have a fiduciary responsibility to work on the seller's behalf. That means they must do everything they can (legally, morally, and ethically) to get the seller the highest price from the buyer.

---

* Likewise, if you're a seller, you'll have to pay a 1–3 percent commission, which the company will deduct from the proceeds of the sale.

2. Buyer's brokers have a written fiduciary responsibility to the buyer. They must do everything in their power to help the buyer purchase the home for the best price possible and on the best possible terms.

The reason for this separation of duties is clear: The seller pays the commission of both brokers, the one who lists and shows the property, and the subagent (or buyer's agent), who brings the ready, willing, and able buyer to the table.

But since most seller's agents act as buyer's agents when working with buyers, the whole notion of agency representation is a bit sticky. The smartest thing you can do is play it safe with your financial information: *When it comes to buying a home, NEVER disclose to your agent the maximum amount you can afford to pay for a home.*

Why? Although the buyer's broker is supposed to hold your intimate thoughts, feelings, and finances in confidence, that buyer's broker may show you one of his or her listings and then become a dual agent. Or your buyer's broker might decide to represent the seller, and you'll be assigned another buyer's broker to handle your negotiation. Either way, your former buyer's broker now knows how much you can afford to spend—and you may end up spending that, even if you didn't intend to.

### MARK AND AMY'S STORY

Mark and Amy were searching for the perfect home on Long Island. Like most first-time buyers, they had a general idea of the process but only a vague concept of the fine lines the real estate world has drawn between broker-seller and broker-buyer relationships.

They found a beautiful house in a tiny, wooded community on Long Island, about an hour and a half from Manhattan. The house was listed at $350,999. They put in a lowball offer for $260,000, but told "their" agent (who in fact was a seller's broker and not a buyer's broker) that they would go as high as $300,000. That turned out to be a strategic mistake. By telling the broker that they were willing to spend as much as $300,000 for the property, they were precluded from getting the property for less.

Why? "Their" broker was obligated to bring the seller the $260,000 offer but should have also informed the seller that the buyers would go as high as $300,000. If the seller had responded favorably to the lower bid, he or she might have been persuaded to sell the property for less than $300,000. But once informed that the buyers would go as high as $300,000, the seller had no incentive to make the deal for less than that amount.

If, as required by law, Mark and Amy's broker actually told the seller that the couple was willing to bid as much as $300,000, then their effective bid would have been $300,000, rather than the $260,000 they actually offered.

As it happens, Mark and Amy didn't buy that particular house. After this episode, they changed to a buyer's agent and simply didn't disclose any information about their finances.

## Exclusive Buyer's Brokers and Agents

As you can see, there is a danger in disclosing any information about your finances to either a conventional or buyer's agent. But what about an exclusive buyer's agent? An EBA will never represent a seller, so there's no potential conflict of interest, right? That's the general idea.

But it's possible that your EBA will represent other home buyers interested in the same neighborhood, home type, and price point that you are. If you make an offer for a house and your EBA has another set of clients who are also interested in that property, and you've disclosed how much you can pay for the house, the EBA might (I'm not saying "would," I'm saying "might" because things happen and people talk) let it slip how much you can pay. And then the other couple may have a slight advantage when it comes to putting together an offer.

## Protecting Yourself

The best way to protect yourself turns out to be the easiest:* Don't disclose your financial situation or intent. Never tell your broker what the top price you'd be willing to pay for a piece of property is. In fact, you might simply want to reassure the agent that you've been preapproved for a loan and you're interesting in looking at homes priced from, say, $200,000 to $250,000. Always assume that whatever financial information you convey to

---

* And, the hardest for some people who have a difficult time keeping some information private.

the broker might be transmitted (perhaps inadvertently) to the other side. If your agent or broker offers to assist you in getting a mortgage (or asks directly to see your financial statements), politely accept the name of a few lenders he or she does business with regularly and then decline to go into specifics.

Although I hope nothing bad happens to you in your search for, and purchase of, a home, the best protection is to prepare for the worst.

 **20/20 HINDSIGHT:** Brokers will often tell me that they can't represent a home buyer effectively if they don't know how much the buyer(s) can spend on a home. I'm not sure that's true. Some of the best agents I know simply like to be in complete control of the situation, and that includes knowing about their client's finances. But *wanting to know* and *needing to know* are separate issues. Just because you're asked how much you can afford to spend doesn't mean you have to give out a top number. You can provide a general range. Also, just because you've been told you can spend a certain amount doesn't mean you'll want to go that high. As long as you can truly afford to spend whatever range you give your agent (and getting preapproved for a loan is a good way to go), then the agent needn't know anything else. Which may make for awkward and uncomfortable moments if he or she asks you specifically how much you're willing to spend on a home.

# Question 27: How Do I Know If My Broker Is Doing a Good Job?

Whether you wind up using a buyer's broker or subagent, a discount agent, or a full-service agent, the agent's number one job is to assist you in finding a property that's suitable and affordable.

Your broker or agent is doing a good job if he or she listens closely to your wants and needs and asks you thoughtful follow-up questions that may prompt further introspection and explanation. Whether or not the agent is doing a good job becomes more apparent once you start seeing some homes: Do the homes you're being shown match up with what you've told the broker you want and need? Do they match up with the priorities on your wish list and reality check? Do you like him or her?

If your broker is totally off the mark, you might then assume she hasn't been paying attention. Or perhaps you didn't communicate effectively and honestly with him. If you aren't honest with yourself about what you want and need, it'll be hard to discuss it openly with someone else, so your broker may end up showing you the wrong kind of property.

## Get a Clue

Here's how to know if your broker is doing a good job:

1. **Do you feel the broker is paying attention to you?** Or does his or her attention wane when you're speaking?

2. **Does the agent ask you a lot of questions?** Has the agent ever asked you why you're looking for a four-bedroom home or one that has an exercise studio? By asking, the agent may be able to better understand your motivations and can present a suitable substitute.

3. **Is there a mismatch in what you're seeing?** If you've worked with the agent several times and all the properties you've been shown weren't even close to what you'd hoped you would see, you might have a problem.

4. **Nothing seems to be secret.** If you're working with a buyer's broker and the seller suddenly seems to know your every move during the negotiation, your agent might be spilling the beans (perhaps unwittingly), and breaking his or her fiduciary duty to you, the buyer.

5. **Can you hear me?** If your broker never returns your phone calls, or takes several days to do so, that's a clear signal that he or she is not being conscientious.

## Don't Wait to Take Action

If you decide that your agent isn't doing a good job, don't hesitate to speak with the agent's managing broker. Again, one of the most important functions of the managing broker's job is to make sure the customers of the firm are happy. If you're not satisfied with the response you receive from the managing broker, feel free to file a complaint with the agency that regulates real estate agents in your state.

In any case, unless you've signed a buyer brokerage exclusivity agreement, you have the option to find another agent or broker at any time. Most agents will allow you to break an exclusivity agreement if you're really unhappy, since they don't want you to cut into their referral business by discussing how displeased you are. But if you can't break your exclusivity agreement, or the agent wants you to pay him or her additional money to break the agreement, simply wait out the expiration date of the contract. No one can make you work with someone you don't like.

## Question 28: How Can I Help in the Search for a Home If I Use a Broker?

Brokers across the country say the most important thing you can do as a buyer is to be honest about the difference between what you really want in a home and what you actually need. (It always comes back to creating your wish list and reality check.)

After honesty, they ask that buyers be flexible with their time and responsive to their calls. If a broker agrees to spend an entire Saturday with you and sets up a day of showings, it's extremely frustrating if you decide to cancel at the last minute.

(Of course, it's perfectly acceptable to cancel if there is a true emergency. And if that's the case, communicate that to the broker and reschedule. But remember, weekends are prime time for real estate agents and if they set aside the time for you and you cancel, it's not just lost time to them—it's lost money.)

Here's a short course on home buyer etiquette:

1. **Honesty is the best policy.** Whether it's telling the broker what you really want or need in a home or telling the agent specifically why you did or did not like a particular home, if you're not honest and open with the broker, you make the job tougher than it has to be.

2. **Be available.** If you're going to be out of town on business, or tied up in meetings, let the broker know you're not going to be available to look at property or talk about prospective homes. On the other hand, you should return your agent's calls

promptly, and have a backup number in case the agent calls with an urgent message about a property. You might have either received an answer to your offer, or a new, hot property has come on the market in the neighborhood you want.

3. **Except when it comes to your finances.** As discussed, play this hand close to the vest for your own protection.

4. **Don't have unrealistic expectations.** Your agent may be the best in town, but she's not a miracle worker. She can't gin up a collection of houses in a hot seller's market. If you call her up on Saturday morning and ask her to book in a day of showings, it's probably not going to happen. The weekends are the busiest times for an agent and they fill up quickly. Also, booking open houses (even if both sides use Internet-based house-showing software) takes time and some back-and-forth. If you want to spend a Saturday or Sunday looking at open houses, make sure you reserve your agent's time at least a few days, if not a week, in advance.

5. **Be loyal.** Agents like loyal buyers. Don't work with two full-time agents at the same time. The real estate community is small and word gets around fast. Also, if you've taken up six months of an agent's time, and things are going well, it's not nice to suddenly switch to your relative or to a discount broker to close the sale. Legally, of course, you may have the right to switch at any time (barring an exclusivity agreement), but the seller may be obligated to pay your original agent the commission, and not Aunt Edna, who steps in at the last moment promising to give you a portion of her commission back.

## Helping Out

If you're like every other first-time buyer, the moment you decide to get serious about buying, you'll be energized—if not consumed—by the process. You'll want to do everything in your power to find the right home fast!

Once you know what you want, what you need, and what you can afford, you can help your agent by looking through the Internet at properties that might be for sale and then bringing them up for discussion. Ask the agent if she thinks the house might be a good fit for you, and if not, why. Long-term agents have generally seen most of the houses in their area come up for sale at least once in their career, and may know something about the history of the house that could be helpful.

**FIRST-TIME BUYER TIP:** You'll probably be tempted to go visit some open houses as you walk around the neighborhood. That's fine, but be sure to sign in as represented by your agent. That's called "protecting the broker." By signing in as someone's client, you're putting the seller and seller's agent on notice that you are represented. If you don't sign in your broker at an open house, and you later try to go back with your agent and make an offer, the selling broker might put up a fight and say that you were his or her client for that particular house—making the listing broker a dual agent—and entitled to the entire commission. So make sure you sign in your broker at each and every open house.

## Question 29: What Do Descriptions in Listing Sheets *Really* Mean?

The key to understanding real estate ads is to assume that the broker is putting the best face on a bad situation.

That's not to say that there aren't some fabulous homes out there. There are, and they may be worth every penny of their list price. And I'm also not saying that brokers are being dishonest—most of them aren't. But if Mr. Smith's apartment has a four-inch-wide view of the ocean sandwiched between two towers, I'll bet you money that Mr. Smith's broker will put "ocean view" somewhere in the newspaper ad.

Brokers know that most people want to have a good view from their windows—even if they're going to be away at work during the day and will only see it at night. (Actually, I've always been amazed at people who want to have a view of Lake Michigan or any other body of water . . . it's completely black at night and you can't see anything anyway!) The most expensive property is usually congregated around whatever view is the star attraction: In Chicago, it's Lake Michigan; in Boston, it's the Charles River; in San Francisco, it's the bay; in New York . . . well, in New York, everything is expensive. But the Manhattan buildings that overlook Central Park are *really* expensive.

When you read an advertisement, how do you distinguish between an apartment that really has a great view from one that has a six-inch-wide strip of blue? How can you tell a home that's really in move-in condition from one that needs to be completely redecorated?

That's the tough part. But remember: The broker will usually be very specific about a true feature. If the kitchen is new with top appliances, the ad may say, "Gourmet kitchen with top appliances." If the view really does include Lake Michigan (or Central Park, the river, the bay, or whatever), it will say so.

## Be Sure to Read Between the Lines

If you don't know a specific building or neighborhood well, you might want to try to read between the lines of an advertisement. Here's a list of key phrases to watch out for and what they may mean (in a tough, cynical world):

| PHRASE | WHAT IT MIGHT MEAN |
|---|---|
| Fantastic view | Could be the best view of your life; or there might be little, if any, view, and you might have to crane your neck out the window to see it. |
| Treetop view | The apartment is about four floors up. During the summer your view may be blocked by leaves. |
| Just renovated | Probably needs a minimal amount of redecorating—unless the seller's red walls and chintz everywhere don't agree with your ideas about good taste. |
| Move-in condition | May be in pristine condition, or you may just need to paint. |
| Needs work | Could mean anything from a home that needs new paint and carpet to major structural renovation. |
| Handyman's (or woman's) special, aka "fixer-upper" | Probably a gut job; it's likely the home needs serious renovations and may even be unlivable. |
| "As is" condition | The home may have some serious problems that will emerge with a home inspection report; the house may be filthy, and the seller doesn't want to clean it up; or, the seller simply wants to be done with the deal, without having a prospective buyer try to negotiate the price down because of the condition. Or a combination of all three. |
| Bright and sunny | Maybe the home has a southern exposure, or maybe every room is painted bright yellow, or maybe there's 10,000 watts' worth of lightbulbs, all of which will be turned on during your showing. |
| Dollhouse | A word brokers often use to describe a home that is too small to accommodate a growing family; it may also be too small to accommodate a regularly sized individual. |

| PHRASE | WHAT IT MIGHT MEAN |
|---|---|
| Tiny home | Could be used to describe new category of homes, the under-200-square-foot special, as made popular through the HGTV series. |
| Oversized rooms | Don't expect Queen Elizabeth's great hall; could mean truly large rooms or anything over 9 by 9 feet. |
| Street parking | The broker is telling you the home doesn't come with a parking space and that you can park easily on the street. However, if the home is located in a congested metro neighborhood, or an area that doesn't permit street parking from 2 a.m. to 6 a.m., or an area that doesn't allow parking on the street in case of a "snow emergency" (or anything over two inches), don't believe it unless you see for yourself. It isn't always easy or desirable to park on the street. |
| Deeded parking space | You get a parking space. It could be indoors, outdoors but covered, or simply outdoors, but it's yours—even if it is too small for your Chevy Suburban. |
| Round-the-clock security | Could mean a twenty-four-hour doorman (though brokers usually say this), a nighttime security person patrolling the premises, a television security system, or a buzzer system. |
| Newer mechanicals | Might've been replaced last year or five years ago. You may have to replace expensive mechanical systems within five years. |
| Newer roof | You may have to replace the roof within five years, or it may be just fine. |
| Needs new roof | Don't be surprised to find signs of water damage from recent roof leaks. Check for brown water marks on the ceiling and buckling hardwood floors during your showing. Ask how many layers of roof are on the house and if the next replacement is a "tear-off," where several layers of old roofing must be pried off and replaced. Or, could you, for a lot less money, add another layer of asphalt shingles? |
| Oversize lot | In Chicago, which has one of the smallest "regular" lot sizes in the country, an oversize lot could mean something as small as 30 by 125 feet. (A standard lot in Chicago is 25 by 125 feet, so you'd be getting a few extra blades of grass.) |

## What About Square Feet?

The concept of square footage requires a bit more explanation. As you tour different homes, brokers will give you a listing sheet for the property. On it, you'll see that the size of the unit is given in square feet. You'll remember from your high school geometry class that a square foot is a two-dimensional square measuring one foot by one foot. You'll often see it expressed as 1x1 or 10x10 (a room measuring 10 feet by 10 feet, or 100 square feet).

Real estate is measured the same way.[*] But the truth is, the actual square footage of a home as presented on paper can be a bit deceptive. Over the years, I've received dozens of letters from readers who felt that the square footage was misrepresented on the home—particularly in a condo, where a proportionate share of the hallway may be included in "your" square footage—and they paid a larger amount because they thought the house was actually bigger than it is.

Pricing a home based on its square footage isn't exactly the best way to go, and should be considered only along with other methods of determining value. Here's why: If your listing sheet says a particular home has 2,000 square feet, you may assume it's a big house. But when you get there, it may not feel that large. Why? Because a home's square footage is supposed to be calculated by measuring the exterior perimeter of the home. So in addition to losing the interior wall space, you also lose the exterior wall space. Although it doesn't sound like much, it all adds up. You'll also lose space to closets, appliances, and chimney vents.

Brokers want you to think you're getting the most for your money, so they'll put down the largest number for the home's square footage that they can get away with. In my former residence, a vintage co-op built in the 1920s, our unit was listed as having as few as 1,700 square feet to as many as 2,300 square feet. Six hundred square feet is an entire condo in New York City![†]

---

**BOBBI'S STORY**

When Bobbi bought her Manhattan condo, the property was listed as having 1,800 square feet, but felt smaller. When Bobbi bought the apartment next door and planned to add it to her unit, that unit was advertised as having at least 500 square feet. Together, Bobbi thought she had 2,300 square feet.

---

[*]  Commercial space is measured in square feet as well. But in a world where many employees work from home, or are placed into "cubes" (a derivative of square footage if there ever was one), lawyers and other executives still measure the relative value of their power by counting ceiling tiles, which are generally one by one square feet, so they can be assured of their place in the pecking order of the firm. (It's an old joke that actually isn't funny to most lawyers!)

[†]  In fact, when my older son, Alex, lived in New York the summer between his junior and senior years of college, he and a friend rented a 550-square-foot "two bedroom" (I had to put that in quotes) apartment on the ground floor of a brownstone in Chelsea.

When the architect she hired did the drawings to combine the units, the new unit turned out to have only 2,000 square feet. Why? The original unit actually had 300 square feet of living space less than was originally advertised. The larger number could be justified if you measured around the exterior of the unit rather than the actual space inside (and perhaps included a share of hallway space and the storage closet in the building basement).

**FIRST-TIME HOME BUYER TIP:** Don't rely on the listing sheet for an accurate assessment of a home's true square footage. If you want to know how many square feet are in the home, either measure the house's exterior, or ask if the sellers have an architectural plan of the unit. After a while, you'll have a sense of how big 2,000 square feet really is, and will be able to "guesstimate" how large other homes are based on how big they feel. Still, if you have to rely on square footage to know whether a property is going to be right for you, you're probably not looking at the right metrics.

**NEW CONSTRUCTION TIP:** Developers have their own set of tricks for increasing a home's square footage on paper. For example, some developers will include an attached garage when calculating square footage. Others will include the attic or a crawl space. Others will include the basement, whether it is or isn't finished. So what is the true measure of square footage? If you want to be technically accurate, you should measure around the perimeter of the house or condo and use that as a base. Also, garages (whether attached or not), basements (even if they look like aboveground space), unfinished attic spaces, and other spaces that are not legal by local code are typically not included in the square footage assessment. Use the architectural drawings that accompany the information kit the developer has prepared and make your own determination of size.

**20/20 HINDSIGHT:** If you make an offer based on a certain price per square footage and later find out the unit doesn't have quite that much space, don't beat yourself up about it. Remember, if the house was big enough for you when you thought it had 2,000 square feet, it's still probably big enough even if it only has 1,850 square feet.

## Question 30: Now That I Can Shop for a Home on the Internet or Buy from a Developer, Do I Need an Agent? Can I Get a Better Deal If I Buy a House Without an Agent or Through an Auction?

We've been living in a DIY world for a while now: Stroll up and down the aisles of Home Depot or Lowe's, ask a few questions, watch a few videos and maybe an episode or two of *This Old House* or any of the HGTV fix-and-flip shows, and you suddenly feel capable of tackling any home-related project. Regrout the tile in the bathroom? No problem. Install cabinets or a hardwood floor? Sure! Rewire the house? Why not? Home improvement stores have plenty of experienced staff on hand to help you plan out your renovation or home improvement project down to the tiniest detail. As you walk through the exit, with hundreds or even thousands of dollars in materials and equipment, your confidence level is high. You know you can complete the project, and that it's going to look great.

Then, as you start carrying the bags in from the car, reality sets in. A little later, when the caulk pops out in a big goop and you can't seem to smooth the seam in a way that would make your plumber proud, you know you're in trouble. It isn't quite as easy as it looks. It'll still get done, but it may take you a whole lot longer, cost more, and cause more angst than if you hired someone with experience to help.

When it comes to buying a house, many home buyers feel they have the knowledge, tools, and savvy to buy a house on their own. For sure, the Internet has made a huge amount of information like house listings, interest rates, mortgages, and credit scores easily accessible. And knowledge is power.

The only thing the Internet doesn't do is provide years of experience to filter the vast amount of information that's available. It doesn't tell you who to trust.* In my mind, that's the biggest benefit you'll receive by hiring a great agent to help with this purchase. Because even though you're reading this book, and I'm walking you through the process of buying a home, I'm not there, in person:

---

* What it does is leave you with the *impression* of trustworthiness based on how much money a company spends on Internet advertising, which isn't at all the same thing. And fake news abounds in online real estate, with similarly disastrous consequences, just as it does everywhere else.

- To point out the stain on the ceiling that could indicate the presence of a leak, or the mold on the basement walls, or the absence of gutters.
- To remind you that even though you're "in love" with this house the other one you saw four days ago better suits your needs and wants.
- To be your eyes and ears when new properties come on the market so that you don't waste your time seeing homes that aren't right for you and your family.
- To tell you the ugly wallpaper, cat-scratched floor, and diaper stench can be removed and the house buffed and polished back to pristine condition, building in extra value for your hard-earned dollar.
- To make sure the seller gives you all of the state-mandated disclosures.
- To be the buffer between you and the seller when the negotiations get tough, or the seller pulls a fast one, or the inspection doesn't go well.
- To tell you there will always be another house, and even though it seems like this was the "perfect house," the next one that comes along will be even better.

It's true that with an agent, you may not be able to move as quickly as you'd like. But that's probably a good thing when you're buying the single biggest, most expensive purchase of your life to date. Now that I'm finishing my third decade watching the world of real estate evolve, I'm here to tell you there are great benefits in slowing it down a little and taking the time to accommodate someone else's schedule (who isn't going to be working at 3 a.m. when you're up, scrolling through listings online because you're so excited you can't sleep).

You may feel dragged down by the weight of having someone else on board. But when you're considering the single biggest, most expensive purchase of your life, there is a benefit to *not leaping before you look*. An experienced agent will offer you the perspective of someone who has seen the house you think you want to buy go on and off the market a half dozen times over a couple of decades.

Can you buy a house without an agent? Absolutely. There is no law requiring you to use an agent to buy or sell real estate. But for home buyers, particularly first-time buyers, it seems foolhardy. After all, you get the benefit of all this experience for nothing because the seller typically pays the commission.

As for getting a better deal, you won't get one with a property that's listed. As we've discussed earlier, on day one, the seller signed a contract agreeing to pay his or her agent a set commission (typically a percentage of the sales price) when the home is sold. It doesn't matter whether you're represented by an agent or you come solo. It's unlikely that you'll get a better deal out of a seller when you are negotiating on your own behalf.

What about a FSBO? There's a good chance you'll overpay for the property, simply because you haven't seen all the properties on the market, because online portals like Zillow provide guesstimates of value, not a true appraisal, because the technology is ginned to make the home that's for sale look highly desirable, even when it's not. Because even if you live in your neighborhood of choice already, you might not know what is the true value of a home that is for sale.

### JACKI'S STORY

Jacki owns a house on a double lot. She also owns a building with three apartment units. One day, she called my husband, Sam, who is a real estate attorney, to ask how complicated it would be to swap her three-unit building for the property next door to the house she owns. "It would be an even trade," she said.

Sam asked her about the property next door. It turned out to be a little run-down. On the other hand, her three-unit property is in pristine condition, the apartments are bigger, and it's fully rented. Sam said it seemed to him that her rental property might be worth more than her neighbor's property. He advised her to have a real estate agent come out and take a look, especially because the neighbor's property was already listed with a real estate agent.

Even though she had lived in the neighborhood for thirty years, next door to this property, Jacki wasn't sure how much everything was worth. If she traded her property evenly, she might have lost a quarter of a million dollars of value.

Almost all home buyers, but particularly those buying for the first time or purchasing new construction, will do better by having a smart, experienced buyer's agent on their home-buying team. And, as I write this in 2018, I don't think real estate agents are going away anytime soon. There's too much money at stake. Real estate is a multitrillion-dollar industry. The National Association of Realtors (NAR), the National Association of Home Builders (NAHB), and the Mortgage Bankers Association (MBA), among other for-profit, quasi-governmental, and publicly traded entities, are extremely strong nonprofit trade associations who lobby hard on behalf of the industry. They're formidable opponents, and while they don't win every battle, they've won enough so far to keep industry control out of the hands of tech giants.

But it may not be that way forever. The question you'll need to ask is whether you'll get good enough help using a technology-enabled platform like OpenDoor (or whatever comes after) to buy a home that's in your best interest.

Only time will tell.

## Question 31: What Do I Need to Know About Buying a House That's for Sale by Owner (FSBO)?

Whether you buy a property that's listed by an agent or is a FSBO, most of what you have to do stays the same. The questions in this book should be asked about all sorts of properties. Here are ten truths about FSBOs that you need to know:

1. **It's easy to overpay for a FSBO.** The biggest mistake home buyers make when buying FSBOs is overpaying for the property. It's not just that you can't compare one house to another in terms of size and amenities. With a FSBO, you need to think about the possible financial impact of issues and neighborhood changes that aren't readily apparent. For example, if the developers of a six-story apartment building have received approval to build on the lot behind the FSBO property, the seller may not be legally obligated to share that tidbit of information with you—but it could dramatically (and most likely negatively) affect the value of the property. If you don't know what's going on in the immediate vicinity of the property, it could hurt you.

2. **The seller won't automatically reduce the sales price.** Another mistake home buyers make is thinking the seller will reduce the sales price by the amount of the commission he or she isn't paying. If you believe the home is worth what you're offering, as opposed to what the seller is asking, you may need to back that up with some relevant sales data.

3. **Some properties come with problems attached.** There are two reasons homeowners sell without a broker, and both have to do with money: (1) the seller doesn't want to pay a commission and (2) prospective agents have told the seller that the prop-

erty won't sell for as much money as the seller wants, so the seller decides to sell by owner in order to set a higher price (and hopefully catch a fool for a buyer). When the seller and prospective agents differ on the value of a property, it often has to do with the seller not realizing that any problems that may be attached to the property might lower the intrinsic value. In other words, if the property backs up to a corn-field, that fact might have a positive effect on the price. But if the cornfield is slated to be turned into a subdivision of townhouses, it could have a negative effect on the price. Do your investigation ahead of time and then, before you make an offer, think about how hard it might be to resell this property in the future.

4. **Don't undernegotiate.** Often, first-time buyers don't know whether it's a buyer's market or a seller's market, and regardless, markets flip in a matter of weeks. Not knowing can undercut your negotiation power when it comes to dealing with a FSBO. Make sure you know what you want out of the deal and how much you're willing to pay, and then hold firm. Don't allow a seller to talk you into paying more than you want (or can).

5. **Make sure the seller gives you the required disclosures.** State laws require sell-ers to make various disclosures. If you're buying directly from the seller, without an agent, make sure you get all of the disclosure forms you're entitled to receive. If you work with an attorney (which I think is an excellent idea anyway, but particularly if you're not working with an agent), he or she should help guide you in this area. If not, talk to your escrow or title company about forms and contracts.

6. **Don't give the seller your earnest money.** When you make an offer to purchase, you'll typically include a good-faith deposit check along with the signed contract. If there are no brokers involved, you have to figure out who will hold the earnest money. Never pay it directly to the seller. Instead, see if the escrow company, title company, or another third party will act as an intermediary and keep the funds safe. Another op-tion is to have one of the attorneys (either yours or the seller's) hold it for you.

7. **Make sure you buy an owner's title policy in addition to the lender's title.** In some states, the buyer pays for the title insurance policy. In other states, it's up to the seller. If the seller traditionally buys the title policy, make sure yours does. If the buyer pays for the title in your state, you can work with your escrow agent or title officer to order it.

8. **Get your documents in order.** In many parts of the country, real estate agents help buyers and sellers get their documents organized so that the property can close. These days, they even charge a "doc prep" fee for handling the paperwork.* If you're doing this on your own, you'll want to check with your attorney or escrow agent or title officer to be sure you haven't forgotten anything. You don't want to show up at the closing and find out there's a problem.

9. **Be careful which contract forms you use.** If you're using an attorney, he or she should be able to provide you with a contract and contingencies that protect your rights. If you aren't using an attorney, you can ask the escrow agent or title officer to help you gather the contracts and forms you need. While some, or maybe all (depending on the state), of these contracts and forms are on the Web, you have to be careful about which form you use. Whether you are in an escrow state (where escrow agents or title companies have forms), or in other states (where forms are on the Web), take care in selecting the contract, because these are the words, sentences, and paragraphs that are supposed to protect you in this huge purchase.

10. **Don't take the seller's word—check it out yourself.** A common mistake home buyers make is taking the seller or the seller's broker at his or her word. When you're spending a few hundred thousand dollars, it's important to check everything out yourself. Insist on a professional home inspection and a final walk-through. If something doesn't look right or doesn't pass inspection, spend what you need to in order to be sure the house is okay. Once you close, it's expensive and heartbreaking to have to sue the seller. The time to do it is now.

---

* Which, by the way, I think is outrageous. Because if you don't have documentation, you can't actually buy the property. But now that many of the companies that own real estate companies are publicly traded (Coldwell Banker, Century 21, Better Homes and Gardens Real Estate, Berkshire Hathaway, etc.), they're looking for every last dollar to make shareholders happy. That means they've ultimately pushed more costs onto their real estate agents, who have turned around and pushed them onto buyers and sellers.

# CHAPTER 4

# How Do I Identify What I Like and Need in a Home?

Knowing which of two or three different properties is right for you is the key to being selective. Over the next few questions we'll talk about ways to hone your natural sense of selectivity and apply it toward your home purchase.

## Question 32: How Do I Become Selective When Choosing a Home? How Do My Wish List and Reality Check Help Me?

The issue of selectivity is very tough if you're a first-time buyer. Nearly every home is going to look at lot better than the cramped one-bedroom apartment you've been renting for the past five years (or better than your old room at home where you've been living rent-free since college).

But it's important not to jump at the first house that appears to meet your needs. Why? Because you might also be able to get a few things you want in addition to the basics. And if the house later turns out not to have met as many needs as you first thought, you'll be glad you gave yourself a few days to get over that first rush of house adrenaline.

**JOANNE'S STORY**

Joanne set up ten showings for a couple who were first-time buyers. The couple went to the first home and fell in love with it. They wanted to make an offer on the spot. But Joanne, an agent in Pompton Plains, New Jersey, has a policy: Never let a first-time buyer purchase a home at the first showing.

"First showings are all about emotion," she says. "You have to get some distance and some perspective before choosing the right home."

Joanne showed the rest of the homes to the couple. They liked three of the ten, including the first. And then they had to choose. They ended up choosing the first, but for reasons that hadn't even occurred to them when they first decided it was "the home."

Millennials know that relatives and friends can lend perspective, and soliciting community commentary is second nature. But older folks see the value in community commentary as well, because it helps the decision-making process become less scary, particularly if you're buying on your own and not as part of a couple or a partnership. These days, Millennials will often solicit their parents' and friends' advice when they're looking at listings online. If a friend or relative lives near a home that's on the market, the first-time buyer might dispatch the friend or relative to take a look in real-time. Or the friend or relative might take the initiative and go see the property themselves, or dig online to find other helpful information, such as tax records or prior owners.

Mike, a sales associate in York, Pennsylvania, says family members can help first-time buyers become more selective about a home, especially if they come to the first showings. If they come to the first showing, they feel like they're part of the process. "If they come only for the second showing, they feel compelled to find something wrong with the house," he explains.

But learning how to be selective doesn't just mean relying on your friends or relatives to tell you which way to turn. While listening to their advice and opinion (especially if it conflicts) will help develop your selectivity (particularly if you become selective about whose advice you're going to take), selectivity is also about defining and refining your own tastes and trusting your own judgment. It's about putting aside emotion in favor of reason and logic, and becoming objective when looking at property.

## Starting the Process of Selectivity

How do you become selective?

1. **Start by casting a wide net.** Look at everything online in your neighborhood of choice. Have your agent show you a wide variety of homes, including ranches, condos, townhomes, and a subdivision under construction.

2. **Compare the styles and feel of each environment.** Once you've identified which housing style you like best—maybe it's even the subdivision under construction— have your broker set up a showing of a handful of houses that fall into your price range, size, location, and amenity requirements.

3. **Next, compare what you like and dislike about each of the homes you've seen.** Take a few photos of each home (including one of the house number so you can keep track) and mark up the listing sheet with what you liked or disliked after each showing.

4. **Keep a running list of your top five favorite homes.** After showing her buyers five or six homes, "I ask them to prioritize the top two or three they're most interested in," Joanne says.

5. **Ruthlessly eliminate those homes that don't meet your needs and have fewer wish list items than other homes.** Try to keep the list of homes you love to no more than two or three. If another "fabulous" home comes up, compare it to the others you "love" and try to sort out which are the new top two.

 **FIRST-TIME BUYER TIP:** When you're in a hot seller's market, the process of learning how to be selective might mean that homes in which you're interested wind up selling to other parties. That's because hot housing markets move faster than you do—*or should*! While it's painful to lose a house that might be right, it's more painful to purchase a home quickly, just for the sake of doing it, and then realize that it *isn't* right.

**20/20 HINDSIGHT:** Being selective isn't easy. It forces you to make decisions about what you like and don't like. Also, some of the issues aren't clear-cut. Each home will have pluses and minuses: One may be in a good school district; another might have four oversized bedrooms and a nice backyard. Your wish list and reality check really do help. If you've been honest about your priorities and understand that reality will temper the amenities you'll get with your first home, the lists should help you step back and take most of the emotion out of the decision. (For more information on how to make a wish list or reality check, see Question 10 on page 38.)

---

**BILLY'S STORY**

As a young lawyer fresh out of law school, Billy found himself with a huge salary and no deductions. He'd lived in rental apartments all his life (his parents never bought) and decided to purchase a home before his work assignments got too busy.

Of course, work kicked in immediately at the firm, and Billy ended up taking quick looks (if that) at apartments and making blind offers. He relied on his agent to do the looking and then made an offer based on her assessment of how good or bad the condo was.

Needless to say, it wasn't a great way to go. And Billy ended up buying a condo that was just so-so and was never that happy living there. After his career settled down, he found the time to do a much more thorough search and bought a new home a few years later.

---

Let's compare that to Michael's search for a home. When Michael decided to buy his first home, he looked at neighborhoods all over Chicago. He spent weekends and nights over many months going to showings with his real estate agents and open houses on his own, or with his mom, sister, or girlfriend. Once he decided on a particular neighborhood, he looked at what his dollars would buy. He knew he needed at least a two-bedroom condo, and he was in a serious enough relationship that he wanted his girlfriend's input on the property. After a couple of failed offers, he finally found a two-bedroom, two-bath condo. It was at the higher end of his range, but it met all of his needs and a lot of his wish-list items. He couldn't be happier.

**NEW CONSTRUCTION TIP:** If you're thinking about buying new construction, you've got to focus even more on selectivity. You need to be selective about the contractor or builder or developer you choose. You need to be selective about the location within the development, as well as where the development itself is located in the neighborhood or suburb. You must then be selective about which options you add on to the purchase price—or you'll quickly go broke trying to upgrade everything in the home. New construction involves so many decisions that it's easy to get confused. Again, go back to your wish list and reality checklist and figure out what selective means to you in the context of a newly built home.

## Question 33: When I Go to a Showing, What Should I Look For?

The most important thing you can do at a showing is to step back and view the home objectively. For your purposes, that house, condo, or townhouse isn't a home but a physical dwelling: four walls, floors, and a roof. Brokers say first-time buyers often get caught up in the moment. There's a rush of attention thrust upon you, with brokers willing to do almost anything to get you to like them and their properties.

Mary, a sales agent in San Antonio, Texas, says that she tries to have people look dispassionately at the homes that are for sale. She tells her first-time buyers to inspect everything: every nook and cranny, every corner of the house. Pick up the rugs to inspect the condition of the floor, she recommends. Open every door. Poke through the closets. "I actually prefer to show a vacant house rather than one with furniture in it because by the time the buyers get halfway through, they're looking at the antique sewing machine, not the bones of the house. Inevitably, conversation turns to the great bedspread or grandfather clock," she says.

For some people, seeing through the decoration is the hardest part of buying the right home. If you have an aversion to bright colors, prints, checks, or plaids and you see a house with blue, yellow, and orange walls, you may have trouble focusing on how beautiful the structure of the home is because you're repulsed by the decoration. Your emotional reaction might be to turn and walk right out the door and miss a potentially terrific house simply because someone has different taste.

**SARA AND JEFF'S STORY**

Sara and Jeff are minimalists. It's an understatement to call their taste spare, because it almost looks like no one lives in their home. They prefer white walls, hardwood floors or white carpeting, and a few pieces of starkly designed furniture and artwork arranged artfully in a room. Living in their home is quiet and peaceful, Jeff says. It's almost a Zen-like experience.

So imagine their frustration when they went house-hunting: brightly colored rooms, loud-print wallpaper, and more mess and clutter than they'd ever seen. They looked at beautiful homes but were unable to visualize how a can of white paint would've helped calm down a red room, transforming it into something they'd enjoy living in.

Eventually, they ended up purchasing a loft in a commercial building that was being renovated and converted into residential units. They found it easier to deal with blueprints than transforming reality.

## Your First Showing

By the time you get to the first showing, you may already feel as though you know the property inside and out. With today's online listings, you may have already seen color photos of each room, 3-D images, Google Street View, floorplans, a video, and other information about the property. But when you walk through the front door, remember that you're looking for a home that meets your basic needs:

- Is it within the right distance to work, church, family, and friends?
- Does it have enough bedrooms and bathrooms?
- Is there enough storage space?
- Is there parking?
- Is it safe?
- Is it in the right school district?

If the home meets the basic requirements, then start to look for how many wish list items it includes. (Note: These are my suggestions and are to be used as an example. Go back to your own wish list and reality check to remind yourself about what's important to you.)

- Is there an extra bedroom and/or bathroom?
- Is there a double vanity in the second bathroom?
- Is there a garden or deck?
- Is there a separate laundry room?
- Is there a basement or crawl space? Is it convertible into usable space?
- Is the garage attached?
- Can the kids walk to school and after-school activities?
- Is there a wood-burning fireplace or a gas fireplace?
- What is the condition of the house, its appliances, roof, foundation, walls, wiring, etc.?

Remember, start with the general items and then get more specific.

## Question 34: How Can I Remember Each Home When I've Seen So Many?

It's difficult to keep all the homes straight in your head, particularly if you've seen more than ten houses in a single day. Brokers know that after buyers see just five or six homes, their ability to separate the properties diminishes. My mother, Susanne, who for years was a real estate agent in Chicago, once showed a couple twenty different properties over a day and a half. They were visiting from out of town and had requested to see everything that was available on the market in their neighborhood of choice that they could afford. By the end of the second day, my mother said they were completely frazzled—and more than just a bit confused about which property had which amenity.

New subdivision developers know that prospective buyers might visit as many as five different subdivisions, each with five to eight model homes, in a weekend. That's twenty-five to forty model homes to keep straight—a virtually impossible task!

Is your head swimming yet? If you don't create a method to organize this sort of real estate madness, it will be soon. Here are a few suggestions for keeping the houses organized in your mind:

- **Document it digitally.** Use your phone (a more powerful computer than the ones that sent the first astronauts to the moon) to take photos, notes (you can talk to your phone as you walk through the property), and video of the property to help you remember it. Include the date you saw the house, the time of the showing, and who was there (your broker, the seller's broker, the owner, your mother, your father-in-law, etc.).

- **Map the neighborhood.** Create an enlarged map of your neighborhood of choice and highlight it to mark the streets you've looked at. Use a different color to mark the various homes you've actually seen (in person) in the area. You'll also want to mark the local schools, shopping, transportation routes, and houses of worship. When my husband, Sam, and I were looking for the house in which we now live, Sam marked the train lines and train stations in red and drew half-mile circles around them. Since we only had one car at that time, he knew he'd be walking to the train station, and about a half mile was the maximum amount of distance he was willing to go.

- **Create a house-hunting file in the cloud.** Whether it's Google Drive, Dropbox, or some other online storage area, collect your listing sheets, photos and videos, and links to other relevant information you've gathered and organize it by the address of each property. Share the file with everyone who has seen the house and ask for feedback.[*]

 **FIRST-TIME BUYER TIP:** If you're having trouble remembering which home had more of the features you want, or are finding it difficult to rank the homes based on their amenities, try this simple rating system: assign five points to each item in the top five spots on your wish list and reality check. Assign one point to the remaining items on each list. As you go through each house, check off all the features it has on the wish list and reality list. Add up the points and put that number at the top of the listing sheet. This method should help you nonemotionally rank the homes you've seen. If you want to be more specific, make a few cop-

---

[*] As I'm writing the fourth edition of this book, I continue to be amazed at how different the world has become since the third edition. Over the past twenty years, Google, Facebook, Apple, and Amazon have completely changed the world. The cloud has become a supertool that's available and affordable, and technology continues to disrupt one industry after another. My own career journey from freelance writer to software company CEO wouldn't have been possible even twenty years ago. But that's another story. . . .

ies of your wish list and reality checks and attach the checked-off copies to the individual listing sheets.

## Question 35: How Do I Know When It's Time for a Second (or Third) Showing?

Whether or not you go for a second showing depends on your initial reaction to a home. If the house appears to meet your needs and wants, and you like it, your agent may set up a second showing.

Brokers say you'll know when you're ready. It usually happens after you've seen four to five houses. You may have followed all the suggestions for remembering which house is which, but you can't seem to place that one house you remember really liking. Or you'll find that you still like a particular house better than all the others you've seen and will want to go back for an extended look.

Brokers may schedule first showings twenty minutes apart so that you can see five to six homes in a morning or afternoon, including travel time. Fifteen minutes should be enough time for you to decide whether the home is a possibility. You'll say either "maybe" or "forget it." (As you get further along the path, you may be able to make up your mind in five minutes or less, but that's a lot of pressure to put on a first showing, especially when you're new to the game.)

Second showings take longer. Expect to spend at least thirty minutes. During a second showing you'll want to reconfirm that the things you liked about the house the first time are still appealing. Or you may decide that the house really isn't right and cross it off your list. If you do like the house, the second showing is where you should begin to examine the home's structure and mechanicals. Although you'll hire a home inspector to do a professional home inspection on the house, each inspection will set you back between $300 (for a smaller condo in a smaller metropolitan area) and $800+ (for a larger property in a larger metro area). If you know what to look for, you can spot problems early on in the game and save yourself some money.

Here are some physical things to check out while you're on your second showing:

- **Overall impression of the exterior.** Does the house seem in good shape? Is it sound? Now, step back: Are the lines of the house straight? Does the roof sag?

If the house is brick, is the mortar between the bricks cracked or chinked? Is the paint peeling? Is the aluminum siding dented, dirty, or in really good shape? Is the sidewalk cracked around the house? Does it appear to pitch in toward the house (which might cause leaking into the basement) or slope away from the house?

- **Roof.** Are the shingles curling or lifting? Ask the agent (or owners, if they're there) to find out how old the roof is and if there have been any problems. A new roof, if properly installed, should last between fifteen and twenty-five years. If the house has a tile or slate roof, it could last for fifty to a hundred years or more, but might be expensive to fix or replace.

- **Windows and door frames.** Are they in good shape? Are there storm windows? Has the caulk dried out and pulled away? Are they cracked? Can you feel air blowing in? Are the frames square? Are there cracks in the plaster above the door frames?

- **Overall impression of the interior.** Does the home appear to be sound? Do the wood floors creak when you walk on them? Are they pitched in any one direction? Are the stairs shaky? Is the kitchen or bath linoleum tile peeling or bubbled? Are there discolored patches on the walls or ceiling? Are there other signs of leaks? Is the plaster cracked? Is the paint or wallpaper peeling? Are the walls and ceiling straight? Do doors, cupboards, and drawers open easily? Is the house clean?

- **Attic or crawl space.** Is there insulation? Has it been laid out properly? Is there a fan? Are there air leaks? Is there poor ventilation?

- **Plumbing and electricity.** Turn on all the faucets, showers, and bathtubs. Is everything working? Do they drain well? How's the water pressure? Does the water have a funny smell? Does the home use city water or have its own well? Do the lights seem to work? Check the fuse box or circuit breaker. Are there enough electrical outlets? Or is everything connected with extension cords? Are there enough telephone jacks?

- **Basement.** Are there cracks in the walls or foundation? Does it smell musty, stale, or damp? Does the basement leak? Is the house in a floodplain?*

---

* Don't count on your listing agent knowing the answer to this question. With global warming changing weather patterns, you should verify by looking at the latest floodplain maps online at FEMA's website (FEMA.gov). Your state, county, and even your local municipality may post online floodplain maps. The seller telling you that the house is or is not in a floodplain should not be trusted, simply because this information may change from year to year.

- **Mechanicals.** How old are the hot water heater and furnace systems? Is there an air-conditioning system or are there window units? How old are the window units and do they come with the house? Does the listing agent have any information on the heating, electricity, or water bills?
- **Pests.** Is there evidence of termites? Cockroaches? Mice? Check any wooden beams for tiny holes or piles of sawdust.

## Seat Yourself

Second showings take the selectivity issue we've been talking about a step further. In a second showing, you should sit down on the furniture and try to imagine living in the home. You should look around and think about where you would put your furniture. Ask yourself these questions:

- How would you feel about coming home after a hard day's work?
- Where would you relax?
- Can you see yourself cooking in the kitchen?
- Will your armoire fit into the living room?
- Is the bedroom quiet enough for sleeping?
- If you're looking at a house, go outside to the garden and sit for a while. Will you feel comfortable grilling in the backyard? Do you like the garden as is or will you want to redo the landscaping?
- Open up the windows and listen to the sounds of the neighborhood. Are there noisy wind chimes? Children? Dogs? Dump trucks? Airplanes? Is the house on a flight path? Are you listening to a nearby or distant highway? Local traffic? Frequently used train tracks? Are there other noises?
- Do you feel relaxed in the house?

At this point, you might be able to make up your mind about the house. For some first-time buyers, the second showing clinches it and they make an offer. However, other first-time buyers need a third, or even fourth, showing.

## Third Showings

After living in our co-op for a few years, Sam and I decided to sell and buy a house. We put the apartment on the market and a couple came and looked at it on five separate occasions. By then, we were really annoyed. The unspoken rule of thumb is, if you don't have a contract in hand when you come for the fifth showing, don't come at all. If you ask for a third showing, the brokers and seller are naturally going to think you're extremely interested. They're going to expect you to make a serious offer.

If the third showing comes and goes and there's no offer, the seller is going to begin to get impatient. If you then call and ask for a fourth showing, the brokers will have to persuade the seller to go along with it. It's a lot of work preparing a house for a showing. The seller will have to clean up the house, pack everyone off, and clear the decks. It's a major maneuver because most of our homes don't look like those featured in *Architectural Digest*, *House Beautiful*, or HGTV (and my apologies to those of you who do maintain homes to these standards).

By the time you ask for a fifth showing, the seller has given up on you and is more interested in the next buyers who are scheduled to come through the door. If you do put in an offer after a fifth showing, the sellers may not treat it very seriously, especially if it's a lowball offer, just because you've wasted their time (and everyone else's).

I can hear you howling, "But I wanted to be sure! It's a big investment—the single biggest investment of my life!" All that's true, but five showings is a great inconvenience to a seller, particularly if there's no offer. I don't want you to rush and make a bad decision. And the seller will deal with it. But over time, as you become more familiar with the process of buying a home, your ability to make a decision will naturally speed up.

By the way, our fifth-showing buyer never made an offer. We eventually took the home off the market and lived there for three more years before selling to a doctor who was moving to Chicago from New York.

## Making an Offer After the First Showing

Some brokers say first-time buyers don't really need a second, third, or fourth showing. They say, if you've been honest with the broker and honest with yourself in filling out your wish list and reality check, the broker will lead you to several homes, each of which could work for you.

Mike says he tries to eliminate the need for second showings by picking homes that most closely match the buyer's needs and wants. He does, however, encourage second showings if the buyer initially sees the house at night. "If I've done a good job," he notes, "they'll be ready to make an offer after only two outings. My first-time buyers rarely need to see more than ten properties [to find the one they love]."

Some immigrant first-time buyers, who speak little or no English and work with agents who speak their own language (Coldwell Banker once boasted it had agents who, between them, spoke at least seventy-five different languages), get fewer choices than that. Over the years, my husband, Sam, has worked with many Hispanic buyers who were shown two or three houses and told to choose between them. They were so grateful to be able to buy a house—any house—that it didn't even occur to them to ask if there were others on the market that they could look at.

If you've never bought real estate before, you'll want to see more than two or three properties before making an offer. That's rarely enough. Ten homes might be the right number for some buyers, but 50 or even 110 homes might be the right number for you.

When Sam and I were looking to buy the house we now own, we looked at perhaps 125 or even 150 houses over a four-year period. Many were open houses on the weekends. Some were showings. None were right, especially as our way of thinking began to evolve. We changed neighborhoods and locations and finally made our way to a suburb of Chicago, some eighteen miles north of where we lived when we were first married. On the other hand, when we were deciding to purchase a loft for Sam's office, in downtown Chicago, his need to be close to the train, in a certain part of town, and for a certain price, eliminated everything but one building. And that building only had one condo for sale that met our price and size criteria. We made that decision almost instantaneously.

 **20/20 HINDSIGHT:** When you're going through the process of buying a home, it's easy to get sucked into the buyer/broker relationship and start letting the broker make your decisions for you. Try not to think about whether the broker thinks it's a good choice.

What you really have to do is step back and analyze whether or not this home is right for you.

# Question 36: When Do I Know I've Found the Right House?

What is the most important thing you can learn about buying a home? *There is more than one right home for you.*

Reread and remember those two lines. Some buyers get so overcome with emotion that they become fixated on one particular property. They focus all of their energy and attention on one property that: (1) they may not get, or (2) they might pay too much for.

There is more than one right home for you.

When you go out looking, stay calm. Don't get emotionally involved with the seductive process of buying a home. Don't get intellectually tangled up in the thousands, even hundreds of thousands, of dollars you're going to spend. Don't worry about whether you've secured or damaged your prospects for a golden retirement.

Real estate attorneys routinely advise their clients not to fall in love with a piece of property. "It's not wise because if you fall in love with a house and then have the inspection and something's terribly wrong, you're going to want to buy the house anyway, and that may not be in your best interests," says one attorney.

Sometimes, real estate agents or brokers will seem to encourage you to fall in love with a house. They'll say things like "Isn't it beautiful?" or "I could spend my whole life here" or "You'll be so happy here" or "Don't you just love this place?"

Of course, they want you to fall in love with this house. Then you'll buy it. They'll receive their commission and go on to the next buyer. You, on the other hand, will end up spending the next five to seven years (or longer) in that home. But despite the admonitions not to fall in love with a home, not to become fixated on one particular piece of property, people do it all the time. Including me.

I fell in love with our vintage co-op with a wood-burning fireplace. We could have bought a newly built house we saw on a huge lot (30'x165'; it was big for Chicago) in a nice neighborhood that in the first five years would have nearly doubled in value. But no, I was completely enamored with this twenty-four-hour doorman, no-parking building. I saw all of the pluses and none of the minuses. A typical case of what I now refer to as "first-timeritis."

Twenty-eight years, two homes, three investment condos, thousands of newspaper columns and magazine articles, and more than a dozen books on real estate and personal finance topics later, I can tell you that falling in love with a house is exactly the wrong thing to do. If you don't keep some objectivity during the buying process, you'll be suckered in before you know it.

## About That Objectivity . . .

There is, however, a difference between falling in love with something you've seen and recognizing that you could buy a piece of property and be happy living there for five or ten years.

Agents say that when buyers find a right house (as opposed to *the* right house) you can see a look of joy on their faces. "If they sit down on the couch, it's a good sign. If they're trying to decide where to put their furniture, it's a very good sign. If they've got a special glow on their faces, it's the right house," they say.

You may not be the type to blush easily, but you get the idea. You'll have a chemical reaction to a house that's a good choice. And there may be more than one house to which you respond in this way.

Over time—say, in a few years—the home that's right today may seem small and cramped for your growing family. You'll change, and as your fortunes increase, today's dream home may seem a little like a starter home. You'll reset your sights on that golf course development or a better neighborhood or school district. Your cozy kitchen will suddenly seem too small for your growing family.

"Where did all that space go?" you'll wonder. And then it will be time to find your next "right" house.

# CHAPTER 5

# How Do I Know What
# I Can Afford to Spend?

## Question 37: How Much Can I Afford
## Based on My Lifestyle?

How much house can you afford? There's certainly an answer to that question, but you might want to answer another one first: How much can you afford to spend on a house based on your lifestyle?

The answer most real estate experts give is this: If you can afford to rent and have enough cash for a down payment, you can probably afford to buy. But, as with all things, that's not a hard and fast rule. If you lead an expensive lifestyle and aren't prepared to trade that for a house, then you'll either have to buy a less expensive home or change the way you live.

Let's start with how much you can afford based on just your income and cash on hand for a down payment. The easiest way to know this for sure is to get prequalified or preapproved for your loan.

When you get *prequalified* for your loan, you essentially tell the lender (either on the phone, in person, or through an online calculator) how much you earn and what debts you have. The lender crunches those numbers through a formula and comes up with an actual mortgage amount you can afford to support. When you get *preapproved*, you'll need to provide the lender with documentation like checking or bank account statements, a pay stub from work, or perhaps the last two years of income tax forms. (If you go online for your preapproval, online lenders will either do a "lite" version, requiring only that you answer the questions truthfully, or ask for your approval to pull verifications from the IRS and Workforce Solutions, a company owned by Equifax that keeps employment records on 70+ million employees and provides verifications for creditors, lenders, and employers.)

I wrote this as I was preparing the third edition: "As technology continues to advance, it will likely be possible for you to get preapproved for your loan within seconds on an Internet mortgage lending site." I went on to say that "my guess is that all of this will not only happen, but become routine, before I write the next edition of this book." And so it has. QuickenLoan's Rocket Mortgage allows you to get approved for a mortgage or a refinance in less than eight minutes, and almost all loan companies prefer that you complete their online application.

Just make sure that you know whether you're getting prequalified or preapproved: When you get preapproved for your loan, the lender *commits in writing to funding your loan* providing the house appraises out in value (and, of course, that your paperwork checks out). With a prequalification, *there is no commitment from the lender,* but you have an idea of what you can afford (and you might as well use an online calculator like the one on Think Glink.com).

## Prequalification

The nice thing about prequalification is that you typically don't pay an application fee or apply for the mortgage. That means the lender doesn't pull a copy of your credit history and score. You can save that until after you've found the home you want to buy and then you can comparison shop to find the best mortgage deal. Lenders will be delighted to prequalify you in a preliminary way, with no obligation, because it means they get an opportunity to pitch their wares to you.

Whether you do it online or in person, prequalifying is a relatively painless process. The lender will ask you a few simple questions about your debts and assets and apply your numbers to the debt-to-income ratios that are required by lenders on the secondary market. Then, the lender will tell you how much mortgage your income will support.

(You may hear about secondary market lenders during the course of your purchase. These are companies like Fannie Mae and Freddie Mac, which purchase loans from mortgage companies that make loans to consumers like you. By guaranteeing retail lenders a steady source of cash, secondary market lenders help keep the mortgage market "liquid," which keeps mortgages affordable for home buyers. Even though you may see an advertisement for Fannie Mae or Freddie Mac, and perhaps will visit their websites to get more information about the home buying process, you won't do business directly with them (at least not as of the writing of this edition, though lenders are always worried about this). For more information about the secondary market, mortgages, and buying a home, visit these websites at HomePath.com (which is Fannie Mae's consumer website) and FreddieMac.com.

## Figure It Out Yourself

With the proliferation of online calculators, I'm just going to give you an idea of how to roughly calculate this for yourself.* I've made two assumptions:

1. You aren't spending more than 10 percent of your gross monthly income to service your debts (student loans, credit card payments, auto loans, etc.) each month.

2. You have 20 percent in cash to put down on the property.

Assuming this, if interest rates are above 8 percent, you can spend between 2 and 2.5 times your gross annual income on a home. So, if your interest rate is 8.5 percent (which it hasn't been in more than twenty years), and you earn $100,000 a year, you could spend $200,000 to $250,000 on a property with a conventional mortgage.

If interest rates are at 5 to 6 percent, you can spend roughly three times your gross annual income on a home, or $300,000.

If interest rates are 3 to 4 percent, you can spend roughly four times your income on a property, or $400,000 (assuming the same gross income).

Since 1993, when mortgage interest rates fell below 6 percent for the first time since World War II, homeownership has become incredibly affordable. During the Great Re-

---

* Does anyone do math by hand anymore? Of course not. And why would you when it's so much easier and faster to use a calculator?

cession (2008–09, but with a hangover effect that lasted for nearly ten years after), interest rates fell below 5 percent and then 4 percent. Combined with the drop in home prices, homeownership became even more affordable. And it still is a good, long-term bet.

## Debt-to-Income Ratios

How do mortgage lenders determine how much you can afford to pay? Lenders on the primary (the retail companies that lend to consumers like you) and secondary markets have developed debt-to-income lending ratios through years of trial and error.

All conventional lenders follow the same basic ratios. They've determined that you can afford to pay between 28 and 36 percent of your gross income in debt service. That means, altogether, your mortgage principal and interest payments, real estate taxes, insurance, car loan, and credit card payments may not exceed 36 percent of your gross monthly income. They'd like to see you keep your mortgage, real estate property taxes, and homeowners' insurance premium payments to 28 percent of gross monthly income.

If you're getting an FHA, VA, or USDA loan, you will be able to go above these ratios, to as much as 42 percent of gross monthly income. Forty-two percent, of course, may end up feeling like 60 percent of your take-home pay, or more. In Questions 57 and 61, I'll cover these loan options in more detail.

## Calculating How Much Loan Payment You Can Carry

Let's leave aside the issue of the down payment for a moment and talk about how much of a monthly loan payment your income will carry. Some experts suggest you should aim to spend 25 percent of your gross monthly income (GMI) on your housing expenses, while others say you can spend up to 33 percent. Compared to the 36–41 percent of gross monthly income that your lender* may allow you to put toward your total debt payment, 25 and even 33 percent seems sort of conservative. Ultimately, you have to decide how

---

* Government-backed lenders and some mortgage brokers may allow you to get to this level of indebtedness. Whether that's a good idea is up for discussion.

much of your income you want to spend each month on housing. You have to decide how aggressive or conservative you can be without incurring more debt because of your other living expenses (that is, your lifestyle choices).

Get out a pencil and fill in your personal finance facts on the Maximum Monthly Payment Worksheet.

## WORKSHEET
### *Maximum Monthly Payment*

| | | |
|---|---|---|
| Step 1 | Add gross monthly income from all sources | + _____ |
| Step 2 | Multiply by 0.25 for 25 percent of your income | x _____ |
| | 0.33 for 33 percent of your income | x _____ |
| | 0.36 for 36 percent of your income | x _____ |
| Step 3 | Subtract present monthly debt service (add amount you pay monthly in principal and interest on all debts and put on Total Debt line below) | - _____ |
| | credit cards | _____ |
| | car loans | _____ |
| | school loans | _____ |
| | charge accounts | _____ |
| | other personal debt | _____ |
| | Total debt | - _____ |
| Step 4 | Your Maximum Monthly Mortgage, Taxes, and Insurance Payment Amount Equals | = _____ |

Let's say your gross monthly income is $5,000 ($60,000 per year). Divide by four ($5,000 x 0.25 = $1,250) or three ($5,000 x 0.33 = $1,667). Let's say you have a car loan ($150 per month) and you're paying off a credit card balance ($100 per month): $1,250 − $250 = $1,000 or $1,667 − $250 = $1,417.

In this example, you'd be able to spend between $1,000 and $1,417 per month on your principal and interest payments, real estate taxes, and insurance. If real estate taxes are $100 per month ($1,200 per year) and insurance is another $50 per month that will leave you between $850 and $1,267 to spend on a mortgage.

Here's how to calculate the amount of mortgage you can afford to carry: Multiply the net amount you can spend ($850 to $1,267) by twelve (for an annual mortgage amount), then divide that number by the current prevailing interest rate (say, 4 percent for a thirty-year fixed-rate loan).

**25 PERCENT OF GROSS INCOME: $850 x 12 = $10,200 ÷ .04 = $255,000**

**33 PERCENT OF GROSS INCOME: $1,267 x 12 = $15,204 ÷ .04 = $380,100**

So how much house can you afford? Assume you add a 20 percent down payment to each of these mortgage amounts (multiply $255,000 or $380,100 by 1.20):

**$255,000 x 1.20 = $306,000**

**$380,100 x 1.20 = $456,120**

According to these calculations, on a $60,000-per-year income, assuming you have 20 percent to put down in cash, you'd be able to afford a home that costs between $306,000 and $456,120.

Thus, a 4 percent interest rate (plus a 20 percent down payment) allows you to buy a home that is anywhere from five to nearly eight times your gross annual income. If interest rates were 8 percent, as they were for much of the period from the end of World War II to the early 1990s, you'd only be able to buy a home that cost between 2.5 and 4 percent of your income.

The lower interest rates go, the further your hard-earned dollars will stretch.

Use this worksheet to work it out the other way:

## WORKSHEET
### *ESTIMATED Purchase Price*

| | 25 PERCENT GROSS MONTHLY INCOME | 33 PERCENT GROSS MONTHLY INCOME |
|---|---|---|
| Gross monthly income (GMI) | x 0.25 | x 0.33 |
| x 12 months | _____ | _____ |
| / Current interest rate | _____ | _____ |
| = Amount of mortgage you can afford | _____ | _____ |
| + Down payment | _____ | _____ |
| = Total cost of property | _____ | _____ |

## Finding Your Lifestyle Comfort Level

But just because you can afford to spend up to seven or even four times your income doesn't mean you have to. It's extremely important to find a level of payment that's comfortable for you and your family based on how you like to spend your money. Although you may be technically able to afford a $250,000 home, making those payments each month might mean your family will have to give up other luxuries like summer camp or new clothes for school.

 **20/20 HINDSIGHT:** Remember, you might hear that it's in your best interest to spend every penny you can when you buy your first home, but the choice is yours. It's all about what lets you sleep at night.

## Figuring Out Your Budget

Finding your comfort zone is most easily accomplished if you're on top of your expenses. If you know what you spend, you know which expenses can be redirected toward paying the costs associated with homeownership.

The first thing to do is figure out where the money goes each month. Use the Monthly Expenditures Checklist on pages 156 and 157 to help you determine what you're spending your salary on each month.

But be honest about what you're really spending. As I was writing this, a wealthy Millennial became the target of online ridicule by insisting that the reason his cohort couldn't afford to buy a home was that they routinely ate $20 avocado toast! That's insane, but money does find a way to get spent. If you routinely spend $20 a week on coffee and another $100 per weekend on Uber or Lyft, or if you eat lunch out with your friends four days a week, put it in. Later on, when you're trying to figure out how to save enough money for a down payment, you'll know exactly where to make the cut.

---

**BEST MONEY MOVES OFFER:** If you're buying this book in 2018 or 2019 and need help with your finances, I have a special offer for you: Just for buying this book, you'll get a free year of my Best Money Moves plan, which will help you figure out how to identify financial stress and dial it down with information, checklists, cool tools, and calculators. Go to BestMoneyMoves .com/100QFTB4 for information on getting free access to the best tools and information for getting your expenses under control.

---

## Monthly Expenditures Checklist

Use this checklist to figure out exactly where your money goes each month. If you have other expenses that aren't listed, add them in at the bottom.

| EXPENSES | $ SPENT PER MONTH |
|---|---|
| Rent | |
| Electricity | |
| Gas | |
| Telephone/Online | |
| Auto Loan/Lease Payment | |
| Auto Insurance | |
| Health Insurance | |
| Renter's Insurance | |
| Life Insurance | |
| Other Insurance | |
| Monthly Savings | |
| Retirement Contribution | |
| Children's Education Fund | |
| Credit Card Debt | |
| School Loans | |
| Other Monthly Debt Payments | |
| Grocery/Pharmacy/Sundry Bills | |
| Weekly Transportation | |
| Care for an Aging Parent or Relative | |
| Charitable Contributions | |
| Medical/Dental Bills | |
| Restaurants/Ordering In | |
| Entertainment | |
| Health Club/Working Out | |
| Recreation | |
| Child Care/Babysitters | |

Children's Expenses _____

School Tuition _____

Housecleaning Expenses _____

Vacations (divide your annual expense by
twelve to find out the monthly expenditures) _____

Books/Music _____

Online/Offline Subscriptions _____

Laundry/Dry Cleaning _____

Yard Work/Landscaping (for rental) _____

Gifts _____

Major Purchases (technology, etc.) _____

Furniture/Decorating _____

Clothing _____

Miscellaneous Expenses (coffee, snacks,
lottery tickets) _____

Other _____

Note: If you're going to enter in your clothing purchase under "clothing," but are carrying it as a debt on your credit card, only enter it once. If you put it in under "clothing," make sure you enter only the amount of interest you pay on your credit card, not the minimum amount due (which includes a tiny bit of principal in addition to all that hefty interest).

## Adding It All Up

Are your monthly expenditures more than your monthly after-tax take-home pay? Are the two numbers closer together than they ought to be? If they are, you're out of balance financially, which could be a problem when you try to get a loan.

An important part of being a homeowner is taking responsibility for your finances. Most first-time buyers (and even those who are repeat buyers) have to make some trade-offs because homeownership is expensive. By cutting back on your budget now, you'll be steps ahead after you move in and want to spend some more money to dress the place up. Look over the list and begin to determine which expenses can be eliminated or cut down. (For more hints on budgets, credit, and finance, check out ThinkGlink.com.)

# Question 38: How Much Will It Cost to Own and Maintain a Home?

In the movie *The Money Pit,* Tom Hanks ends up throwing his life savings into renovating his home. Maintaining a home often feels the same way.

Calculating the costs of homeownership appears to be easy: If you can afford your mortgage, insurance, and real estate taxes, you can afford to own a home, right? Unfortunately, that's not always the case. There are costs of homeownership hidden from renters that can both lighten the wallet and break the bank.

Calculating these costs is tougher than predicting your mortgage payments because they're variable by nature and given to change. If PITI—principal, interest, real estate taxes, and insurance—are the fixed costs involved with owning a home, utility payments are semi-fixed, and everything else is a variable.

Here are the basic expenses you will be responsible for when you actually buy your home:

- Mortgage payments of principal and interest, paid monthly or bimonthly, if you have a loan that requires you to make payments every other week.
- Real estate taxes, paid annually or in two installments, or paid monthly with the mortgage if you escrow your insurance and taxes.
- Homeowners' insurance policy premium, paid monthly with the mortgage if you escrow your insurance and taxes, but sometimes paid separately from the mortgage annually or semiannually.
- Homeowner's assessments or monthly condo and co-op assessments.
- Utilities, including electricity, gas, cable, cable modem, satellite, online service, etc.
- Trash and garbage collection, including recycling as required by your local municipality.
- Water and sewage (may be separate or billed together).
- Repairs and maintenance of the interior and exterior of the home (which includes everything from washing windows to replacing the roof, to painting the interior and exterior).
- Landscaping and grounds maintenance (including driveway resurfacing, as needed, plus all the regular stuff).
- Snow removal (for those living in colder climates).

How much do these items cost? For some, like landscaping, water, and the utilities, the answer depends greatly on season and usage. Your mortgage and insurance payments will likely be fixed and remain the same. Utilities will go up and down with the seasons and will likely drift higher. Repairs and maintenance of the house depend on the condition the home was in when you bought it. If the boiler is on its last legs when you buy the home, you may have to pay for a new one shortly after the closing.

**20/20 HINDSIGHT:** It is less expensive to keep up with the maintenance rather than to defer it. Plan to put at least $1,000 to $5,000 in a home improvement fund so that you have the cash you need to make emergency repairs or regular maintenance. A new roof could cost $3,000 to $15,000+, while a new hot water heater might cost $600 to $1,500+, plus installation. Consider purchasing a home warranty (for existing homes only, not for new construction). While it doesn't cover structural problems, it will pay to fix or replace any appliance, electrical, or mechanical system that was working on the day of closing through the first year you own your home. Best of all, many sellers will pick up the cost of a home warranty as a marketing tool. See Question 75 for more information.

**NEW CONSTRUCTION TIP:** The whole point of buying new construction is that you won't have to touch the house for the next ten years, right? That may be true with some things, like the roof, mechanical systems, and appliances (hopefully!), but new construction carries with it a whole other set of problems, including the possibility that the builder didn't install some things properly. While you'll find most of these soon after you've moved in, you'll need to make sure that the caulking around the bathtubs, showers, and sinks stays in place, and that you don't let exterior painting go for too long. The last thing you want is a nearly brand-new house looking disheveled and run-down.

## Real Estate Taxes

Real estate taxes are another matter. From every corner of the United States, homeowners cry out that their property taxes are too high. Formulas for calculating property taxes differ from state to state, but the general feeling is that you can expect to pay anywhere between 1 and 3 percent of the market value of the home.

For example, if your home has a market value of $100,000, it's likely that you might pay anywhere between $1,000 to $3,000 or more per year in property taxes, depending on where you live. In Chicago, if you own a $250,000 condo in the Gold Coast (the fanciest part of town), you might pay up to 70 percent more in real estate taxes than the person who owns a $250,000 bungalow on the city's southwest side. Is it fair? Not really. Currently in California, you pay 1 percent of the sales price of the home, no matter when you bought it. So if you paid $100,000 for a California bungalow twenty-five years ago, you're still paying around $1,000 in property taxes (plus a few other fees and taxes).

**FIRST-TIME BUYER TIP:** You can't escape property taxes, but you can fight them. See the Appendix for useful information on how to lighten your property tax burden.

## General Maintenance

What kinds of specific expenses might you encounter in your first few years of homeownership? General maintenance and upkeep of your home can be expensive. Brokers say would-be homeowners often forget to consider the basics for the exterior and interior of the home.

Cold-weather and warm-weather climates exact their own peculiar punishments on a home. Severe winter weather can wreak havoc on driveways, gutters, the roof, and exterior paint, not to mention the time spent shoveling. Depending on the amount of snow, you may want to invest in a snowblower. (Or consider joining your new neighbors to pay for snow removal during the season.) In addition, your driveway may need a coat of sealant from time to time to prevent cracking.

Landscaping and a garden are year-round issues. If you live in the far South, your garden will require constant care and attention to avoid becoming a jungle. In the North, you'll have at least three seasons of gardening.

Another maintenance concern is the exterior upkeep of the home. Brick homes may need expensive tuck-pointing to keep the walls from leaking. Clapboard or shingle houses need painting every few years to stay weathertight, and may require new shingles or boards from time to time. Even homes with aluminum or plastic siding have portions that require some painting or, at the very least, washing. (Aluminum or plastic siding tends to be the cheapest alternative in the long run, as they require little maintenance beyond the occasional cleaning, experts say.)

Repairing or patching the roof can be an ongoing expense, as a particularly severe winter or windstorm can rip shingles right off. If you live in the house long enough, you will eventually have to replace the roof, though the new one should last twenty years and usually comes with a warranty.

**FIRST-TIME BUYER TIP:** It's a good idea to use a professional home inspector or structural engineer to give your home the once-over before you buy. But if you're purchasing an older home, an inspection is almost a "must," even if you're buying in "as-is" condition. A good inspector (and real estate agent) should point out the age of the home and remind you that you might have to replace that roof or other appliances and mechanical systems within the next few years.

Maintaining the interior can also be expensive. Older windows may need recaulking or a new sash. You may want to purchase storm windows to improve energy efficiency. Bathroom tiles may need regrouting. If your wood floors have a polyurethane finish, you'll need to buff them down and reapply that finish every two to three years, or risk damaging the floor. Hardwood floors with a wax finish should be cleaned and buffed every two to three years as well.

Older homes may need rewiring, a new hot water heater, or a new furnace right away, but depending on how long you plan to live in the house, odds are you'll replace most of the major mechanical systems. Even newer mechanicals require yearly upkeep, however, as filters need to be changed and systems need to be cleaned. Although basements and attics might seem like ideal storage facilities, they require maintenance as well. Basement walls may require treatment for mold and cracks. Attics may need extra insulation. Other issues may arise as the house—especially a brand-new home—settles.

**20/20 HINDSIGHT:** Being a good neighbor means being there in case of an emergency, and helping out if you can. But it also means keeping your home looking good so that the neighborhood continues to improve and appreciate in value. Maintenance and landscaping are the essence of that unspoken agreement you make when you buy into a neighborhood. If it's part of the bargain you aren't willing to keep, perhaps you should rethink your homeownership plans, or purchase a different type of home that doesn't require as much work.

## Question 39: What Are Assessments or Homeowners' Association Fees? Do All Subdivisions, Townhouses, Condos, and Co-ops Have Them?

Assessments are fees that you, the owner, pay for the upkeep of property held jointly with other owners. You'll have to pay some sort of monthly or annual assessment if you choose to buy a condo, co-op, or townhouse. If the single-family home you buy is located in a particular type of subdivision that has common property (like a private playground, security gate, pool, parking deck or garage, garden, clubhouse, etc.), there may be a homeowners' association that will assess you for a share of the maintenance, upkeep, and taxes of that common property, or any other shared expenses such as doormen or other staff.

Regardless of the type of property, your proportionate share of the upkeep should be assessed based on your percentage of ownership. If you own 1 percent of the property, then you should pay 1 percent of the upkeep.

Many different areas and amenities may be part of the common area, including a parking garage or parking spaces, recreational amenities (health club or workout facilities, tennis courts, private lake or lagoon), land, the roof and exterior walls of condos, townhouses, and co-ops, lobby, security, etc. Part of the upkeep of these common areas includes liability insurance coverage as well.

### Paying Your Assessment

How do you pay an assessment? Assessments are usually billed monthly by the homeowners' association. Some single-family homeowners' associations bill on a yearly basis;

some bill twice a year. Whenever it comes, the bill is expected to be paid promptly. If it is not, the association is entitled to bill you for late fees and even to take you to court to force you to sell your home to pay for late assessments.

## Assessments Lower What You Can Afford to Spend

If you're thinking about buying a townhouse, condo, co-op, or single-family house that would require payment of an assessment, you should be aware that the lender will consider the assessment to be another fixed expense (like paying down a car loan or credit card balance) and will include the assessment in the debt-to-income ratio. That means you'll be approved for a total amount of mortgage. For example, if you have $1,000 per month to spend on housing expenses and the monthly assessment of the condo you've had your eye on is $200, you really only have $800 to spend on your housing expenses.

Another thing: Assessments almost always go up over the years. Every condo, co-op, or townhouse association has a board of directors that oversees the costs, repairs, and maintenance done to the property. They have the power to impose "special assessments" to pay for large-scale capital improvements, including a new roof, new deck, new elevators, new windows, tuck-pointing, and a hundred other things.

## Protect Yourself: Read

How can you protect yourself? Before you make an offer (and certainly before you close) on a condo, co-op, or townhouse, it's a good idea to request copies of the last two to three years of budgets and board minutes to familiarize yourself with ongoing issues of maintenance, problems, and long-range planning. You should also request a copy of the current year's budget and next year's project budget (if available). Reading board minutes can bore you to tears, or it can be like a juicy gossip rag. You won't know the people, but once you move in they'll be your neighbors.

Reading the board minutes will quickly get you up to speed on any major capital improvements the board may be planning. In that case, you may have an advantage when negotiating the price of the home. If you read the minutes and find out that the board is planning to levy a three-year special assessment to cover the cost of windows that were replaced five years earlier, you should try to get your seller to lower his or her price to at least recoup some of that cost. (After all, the seller enjoyed the use of those windows for five years.)

 20/20 HINDSIGHT: When you ask for a copy of the board minutes, you should also request a copy of the rules and regulations of the building. Many properties have pet restrictions, which you'll want to know before making your offer.

# CHAPTER 6

# The Nuts and Bolts of Financing Your Home

## Question 40: What Is a Mortgage? How Do I Get Information on Mortgages?

If a person agrees to lend you money, it's likely he or she will ask you to put up something to collateralize the loan. The collateral must be something of equal or greater worth than the amount of the loan so that the lender feels secure in giving you the money.

Here's a formal definition: A mortgage is a loan for which you pledge the title to your home as the collateral. The lender agrees to hold the title (or agrees, in some states, to place a lien on your title) until you have paid back the loan plus interest. The lender gives you the money; in exchange, you agree to make monthly installments of principal and interest, home insurance, and real estate taxes. Most people (somewhat mistakenly) call this collective amount their "mortgage payment."

### A Brief History of Home Loans

Before the Great Depression in the 1930s, we didn't have mortgages the way we know them today. Back then, people paid cash for their homes, or they would take out very short "balloon" mortgages, on which they would pay interest for maybe five years and then owe the entire balance in one huge "balloon" payment.

When the stock market crashed in 1929, most people lost their life savings and were unable to pay back their mortgages, so they lost their homes. In fact, many people were unable to pay their real estate taxes and they, too, lost their homes. In 1930, so many people in Cook County (the county in Illinois that includes Chicago) couldn't afford to pay their real estate taxes (less than 50 percent paid), that the city canceled the year's real estate tax collection. That's why Cook County collects its real estate taxes a year in arrears. (In other words, Cook County homeowners pay last year's taxes in the current year. So taxes paid in 2019 will be for taxes owed from 2018.)

## The War Ends

At the end of World War II, many returning veterans had money to spend and were ready to settle down. The US government decided US soldiers were good risks and helped come up with a plan to lend them money to buy homes. The plan allowed them to borrow money for thirty years and pay it back slowly, with interest. The program was such a huge success that commercial lenders soon followed suit.

That was the beginning of the modern mortgage industry. Today, trillions of dollars in mortgages are made every year and are sold on the secondary market. They are such a stable source of income (less than 2 percent of all mortgages fail or go into default, a ratio that held until the start of the Great Recession, when it doubled) that investors—huge pension funds, for example—buy mortgages from banks, savings and loans, and mortgage brokers. This puts money back into the system, where it can be lent again.

Some lenders do keep a small percentage of loans in-house. Called portfolio loans, they typically have more relaxed qualifications for approval. To find out if your mortgage will be kept or sold, ask the person taking your application what percentage of loans are kept or sold. Remember to ask if your loan in particular will be sold. Don't be surprised if the answer is "yes." The vast majority of home loans are resold on something called the secondary market. If your loan is sold, another company may be hired to "service" the loan for the new investor. If your loan is not sold, you will continue to pay and deal with the local folks who gave you your loan.

**FIRST-TIME BUYER TIP:** Even if your loan is sold, it doesn't mean you have to pay back the loan all at once. What the new lender is buying is either the right to service your loan (meaning, to collect the funds) or to hold your mortgage note—or both. If your loan is sold, there will be a period of 60 to 90 days where records get transferred or merged and there may be some confusion. Be vigilant and keep calling for more information if you're not sure about your mortgage balance or account. It's up to you to make sure you're paying the right lender.

## A Big, Scary Scam

One of the more common scams is the mortgage sale scam. Here's what happens: You receive a notice that your loan is being sold and a new company, XYZ Capital, will now collect your monthly mortgage check. You're instructed on official-looking letterhead to send your mortgage payments to the new company.

What you don't realize is that there is no new company. It's a scam. So you send in one, two, or even three months' worth of payments. And go on with your life.

Out of the blue, you get a call from your old mortgage company wondering why you're 60 or 90 days late in paying your loan. Your credit has been damaged, and even though you've already paid out to XYZ Capital, you still owe your regular monthly payment to your real mortgage company.

Of course, you'll contact the Federal Trade Commission (FTC.gov) and file a complaint. But what could you have done to protect yourself ahead of time?

If you receive a letter like this announcing that your mortgage has been sold, be sure to call up your original lender to confirm that information. Get the name and the toll-free telephone number of the new lender from your original. (The new lender is required by law to provide a toll-free number that you can call to check on the status of your account.)

That's all it takes. If you do find out the letter you've received is a fake, call the FTC immediately. With any luck, they'll be able to put the scam artist out of business permanently.

## How Do I Get Information on Mortgages?

Getting the information is easy. Sorting it all out and choosing the best home loan for you is a little tougher.

Here are some good sources of information:

- **Real estate agents and brokers**. Real estate agents usually know which local mortgage companies offer good rates. Heck, your agent's firm probably owns its own mortgage company (not to mention title or escrow company, alarm system company, and perhaps even appraisal company). Your agent should be prepared to give you a list of at least three different mortgage companies he or she knows are good and responsive, including the one her firm owns.
- **Visit a local lender.** Walk into your local bank, savings and loan, or credit union (credit unions typically have really inexpensive mortgages for their members) and ask for their free information (they should have gobs of it).
- **Call your local housing authority.** Your local housing authority is an excellent place for free information. They may also have special programs for first-time buyers. These programs could include down payment assistance or extra-low interest rate loans for families who meet certain income or location requirements. If you qualify, you may be able to get a loan that carries an interest rate that's well below the market rate.
- **Online.** Everything you can get in person is now available on the Web, and then some. It's also available 24/7/365. Just be careful of where you search.

# Question 41: How Does My Credit Score Affect My Ability to Qualify and Be Approved for a Mortgage?

As we discussed in Question 5, if you are gearing up to buy a home, your credit score could mean the difference between a manageable mortgage payment and one that breaks the bank.

That's because your credit score is one of the biggest factors lenders use to determine your mortgage interest rate and how much money you'll have to put into a down payment and pay toward closing costs.

"A credit score really means a lot," a former president of the National Association of Mortgage Professionals told me when I was writing the third edition of this book. "It gives the lender an opinion—based upon that credit score—about the potential risk they are taking."

If you have a higher credit score, lenders may view you as less of a credit risk and assume that you'll make on-time mortgage payments every month. As a result, a lender may offer you a mortgage at a lower, more competitive interest rate—a difference that can add up to hundreds of thousands of dollars saved over the life of the loan (generally fifteen or thirty years).

## A Solid Credit Score Could Save You Thousands

### Scenario 1: FICO credit score, 700 to 759

Let's say that you're applying for a $250,000 mortgage with a thirty-year fixed interest rate, and you have a FICO credit score within the 700 to 759 range. (FICO credit scores start at 300 and go up to 850.)

In April 2017, according to FICO's Loan Savings Calculator, which estimates how FICO scores impact the interest rate you pay on a loan, you would qualify for an interest rate of 3.883 percent. A $250,000 loan at that interest rate would ring in a payment of $1,177, for principal and interest. That is a total of $173,625 in interest over the life of the loan.

At the end of the loan term, you would have paid $423,625—the $250,000 loan amount plus the $173,625 in interest—for your home.

### Scenario 2: FICO credit score, 660 to 679

Now, consider what happens if your FICO credit score is instead in the 660 to 679 range and you apply for the exact same mortgage mentioned above.

According to the FICO calculator, your interest rate would rise to 4.274 percent. At that rate, your monthly mortgage payment for principal and interest would jump to $1,233, and you would pay $194,011 in interest over the life of the loan.

## Question 42: What Is the Difference Between a Mortgage Banker and a Mortgage Broker? How Do I Find a Good Lender? Who Are the People Involved with Making the Loan?

The essential ingredient to a successful purchase is finding a lender you can trust to walk you through the process. Where do you find such a person? To begin with, it's important to understand that lenders come in all shapes and sizes, and they're called by different names.

- **Mortgage brokers** are involved with the origination side of the business. They take loan applications, process the papers, and then submit the files to an institutional investor, typically an S&L or a bank or a mortgage banker, who underwrites and closes the loan. Mortgage brokers usually work with a wide variety of investors—who will buy your loan on the secondary market, providing mortgage bankers and brokers with an almost inexhaustible supply of money with which to make new mortgages—giving them the ability to offer a wide variety of loan packages. Some mortgage brokers seem to have more lending flexibility and can work with those folks who might otherwise have a tough time getting a mortgage.
- **Mortgage bankers** go a step further. They, too, work within the origination side of the business, but they also get involved with servicing the loan and closing the loan in their own name with their own funds. If you went to a bank for a loan, the mortgage banker would take the loan application and lend you the money from the bank's own coffers. Once you closed on the loan, the same company might service your account, collect payments, and make sure your real

estate taxes were being paid. Or the company might sell your loan on the secondary market (to institutional investors) and then relend the money. Mortgage bankers make their money on underwriting the loan. You pay fees and points, which the banker pockets. Mortgage bankers might make additional money on the spread between the rate on your loan and the going rate of loans in the secondary market, which is called the service fee premium.

**20/20 HINDSIGHT:** Be sure to ask your loan officer if your loan carries a service fee premium that is being paid to him or her. The service fee premium should be disclosed. The higher the fee, the greater the chance that your loan's interest rate is actually above the going market rate.

## Qualities to Look for in a Mortgage Company

So how should you select a mortgage company? You should pick a company based on experience, customer service, and recommendations.

The one thing you shouldn't do is to make the decision based solely on which lender is offering the lowest rates. While rates are extremely important, there is a tremendous amount of competition in today's mortgage market. That means that all mortgage brokers and bankers should be offering mortgages at competitive prices.

But if a company is offering a mortgage package that's well below market rates, you should beware. Remember the old cliché: If it sounds too good to be true, it probably is. Almost all conventional mortgage companies generally choose from the same pool of institutional investors. A company offering abnormally low rates might make up the difference by increasing closing costs or tacking on additional settlement fees.

Richard, the president of a mortgage brokerage in Evanston, Illinois, reminds borrowers that the lowest rates do not necessarily mean you automatically get good service (in a perfect world, they might); and fast, efficient service is essential for a smooth closing.

The most important consideration: You want to make sure the lender you choose will be able to deliver the funds to close on your new home. So be sure you do an online search of the mortgage lender's name and add the word "complaint."

## Choosing the Right Lender for You

As with any other part of this process, choosing the right lender will take some time, effort, and lots of telephone calls. Lenders today offer a plethora of mortgage options that are individually tailored to each borrower's financing needs. In major metropolitan areas, there are dozens, if not hundreds, of mortgage brokers and bankers; in smaller communities, the numbers fall proportionately. Still, there should be ample choices and fairly stiff competition among lenders for your business.

 **FIRST-TIME BUYER TIP:** Remember, when going to apply for a loan, you're in the driver's seat. You're giving them your business, not the other way around. If a lender seems condescending or doesn't treat you fairly or with civility, take your business elsewhere.

## Starting Your Search

The first thing to do when starting to look for a mortgage is to find out the current mortgage interest rate. You want to know the following information:

1. The current interest rate lenders are charging for their most common mortgages.

2. How many points (a point is 1 percent of the loan amount) they are charging to make the loan.

3. The annual percentage rate (APR) of the loan (which adds up all the extra costs and fees and amortizes the cost over the life of the loan).

4. What lengths of loans the mortgage company offers (7/23 or 5/25—which are fixed for either seven or five years and then convert into one-year adjustable rate mortgages—or thirty-year fixed, fifteen-year fixed, five-year balloon, etc.; for more information on various mortgage types, see Question 56).

The easiest way to find out what lenders are charging is to go online. And because online advertisers track every move you make, you're probably already seeing current mortgage rates being advertised wherever you look online.

If not, visit the biggest lenders in the country (Bank of America, Wells Fargo, Quicken Loans, Citibank, and Chase) or online real estate and mortgage information aggregators like Zillow, Bankrate, Realtor.com, LendingTree.com, and HSH.com. If you belong to Costco, you can search CostcoHomeFinance.com for special, member-only loan rates.

If your loan is above the conventional amount (whatever it happens to be at the time you apply), you'll have to find a lender that does jumbo or superjumbo loans. Don't worry, they're happy to work with you as long as your credit is good, you have enough for a down payment, and they establish that you have the ability to repay your mortgage each month.

## The Good, the Bad, and the Ugly

How do you find a good mortgage banker or broker? As with finding a good real estate broker, seek out recommendations from friends and family. Your real estate broker may have excellent suggestions, so be sure to ask for a list of lenders. If you have a real estate attorney, ask him or her for a few names. Once you receive several names, go online and check them out (make sure that their licenses are up to date and there are no regulatory actions against them) or go to their office and talk to the manager in charge. Look around— some new mortgage brokers actually work out of their home—and investigate with whom you'll be doing business. Find out how long the company has been in business. Ask them how many mortgages they have closed and for around how much money. It's important to work with a company that has a track record.

 **FIRST-TIME BUYER TIP:** You should feel entirely comfortable with your lender and your loan officer. If you get a funny feeling at the office, leave and find another mortgage company. If you're concerned about its track record, or the way it deals with its customers, don't be afraid to search for details or complaints through the local Chamber of Commerce, or your state's attorney general's office. You can also call the Mortgage Bankers Association (MBA) of America (MBA.org) to see if any complaints have been filed. Finally, feel free to ask for references.

**20/20 HINDSIGHT:** If you feel you are being unfairly treated by a lender, or if the lender has made promises that are not kept when you show up at the closing, you may be in the grips of a predatory lender. For more information on predatory lenders, see Question 66.

# Question 43: How Do I Apply for a Loan? Should I Apply Online for a Mortgage?

Applying for a loan is different from getting prequalified. Getting prequalified before you buy property is like dating. You either go online and play around with calculators, or you go to a lender and talk about what assets and liabilities, income, and credit you have and then, taking your word (usually), the lender comes up with a dollar amount you can borrow.

If you want to get preapproved, you'll have to actually apply for your loan. "Applying" means providing the documentation and proof the lender needs to determine your ability to repay your loan and what kind of a risk you'll be. It means putting in your Social Security number and providing your electronic signature. And you'll probably need to pay an application fee (that may run several hundred dollars and be credited toward the closing costs).

## Handy Information

Having the following information can speed up the process significantly:

- Copies of all bank statements for the last three months.
- Copies of all account statements, including stock brokerage accounts.
- Most recent pay stub for you and your spouse or partner.
- W2 form for the past two years.
- If you're self-employed, the past two years of tax returns plus a profit-and-loss statement for the year to date.
- A gift letter, if part of the money you're using to buy the house has come as a gift

from your parents, friends, or other relatives. This typically is a letter, which does not necessarily have to be notarized, written by the gift givers that states that the cash is a gift and does not need to be repaid.

## Decision Time

There are some important decisions you'll have to make at the time of application.

**What type of mortgage should you choose?** At the time of application, you'll have to decide which mortgage type is right for you. (See Question 56 for a discussion of different mortgage types.) The type of mortgage you choose should depend on two factors: (1) how long you plan to stay in the house and (2) how much risk you are willing to take. That's it.

Here's how to think about risk: Do you prefer knowing how much your loan payment will be for the next thirty years or until you sell the house? Then a fixed-rate loan would probably work well for you. If you don't mind some risk, a two-step loan like a 7/23 or 5/25 might be the ticket. If you've never met a black-diamond run you didn't go for or you dream of climbing Mount Everest, then an adjustable-rate mortgage (ARM) might be a very good choice (and they even have built-in caps on how high the interest rate can jump each year and over the entire life of the loan).

**Should you float the rate or lock in?** When the lender asks you this question, he or she is really asking you if you want to lock in at the current rate, or take a gamble that the rates will drop a bit before you close on the loan.

Here's how the float option works: Let's say you go in on Monday and fill out an application. The rate for a thirty-year fixed loan is 4 percent. You're scheduled to close in two months. You think interest rates are going to drop in the next sixty days, so you opt to float your loan, meaning that at any point in the next sixty days you can call to lock in the rate. If rates drop, you'll get the lower rate. But if rates go up, you'll have to pay the higher rate. If, however, you think that mortgage rates can't possibly go lower than they are before you're scheduled to close, then it's in your best interest to lock in the rate of your mortgage. Locking in means that the interest rate you pay on your mortgage will be whatever the mortgage rate is on the day you make the application.

Lenders today may give you one free adjustment in the rate with a float option, and you'll pay for others. Be sure to ask how the policy works.

**FIRST-TIME BUYER TIP:** Locking in or floating the interest rate has nothing to do with what type of mortgage you choose. You can choose to float the rate or lock in on all types of mortgages, including a fixed or adjustable-rate mortgage (ARM).

**How long should the lock be?** This sounds like the same question as above, but it's not. When you apply for a loan, the mortgage rate offered by the lender is only good for a specific amount of time. You have to choose how long you want the rate to last, while remembering that the longer the rate lock, the higher the interest rate.

Lenders usually offer to hold the rate for thirty, forty-five, or sixty days. You should base the length of the lock on when you're supposed to close on the loan. For example, if you apply for a loan twenty-eight days before you want to close, you might choose to hold the rate for thirty days. If you're going to close in thirty-eight days, you might choose to lock in for forty-five days.

Lenders will rarely offer to hold a lock for longer than sixty days, but if you need to close quickly, they might manage to approve your mortgage and lock a rate for seven days. The shorter the lock, the more important it is to furnish your lender with everything he or she needs to get your loan going.

The reason lenders don't like to lock in rates for extended periods of time is that interest rates fluctuate daily and often change several times each day. With that much activity, it's difficult for lenders and investors to predict how much interest rates will change over the course of two months. To protect themselves, they limit the length of lock-ins. Just remember, the longer you want the lender to hold the lock, the more you'll pay for that privilege.

**NEW CONSTRUCTION TIP:** If you're buying new construction, it's likely that you're buying off of a blueprint, unless you're buying a developer's spec house. It could take anywhere from four months to two years (in the case of some loft or condo conversions) for the property to be ready. If you've got to wait nine months or longer until closing, don't try to lock in on a rate now. You'll pay way too much to lock in a rate today. You're far better off waiting until you're only sixty days out from closing, and then watching interest rise and fall until you decide it's a good time to lock in the rate.

**How many points, if any, do you want to pay?** Another decision you'll have to make is how many points you want to pay at the closing. Most first-time borrowers don't realize that there is an inverse relationship between the points (remember, a point is one percentage point of the loan amount) you pay and the interest rate you receive. You may have to pay some points or fees, but the more points you pay, the lower your interest rate will be. If you pay no points up front, you'll have a slightly higher interest rate, and pay more over the life of the loan.

Points are paid in cash (usually tough for first-time buyers to come by) at the closing, but the federal government allows you to deduct them from your income taxes during the year of the closing. Or you can amortize your points (pay them over the life of the loan), which will ultimately increase your rate. And sometimes the seller will pay the buyer's closing costs.*

 **FIRST-TIME BUYER TIP:** I'm often asked whether points paid for a refinance can be deducted for tax purposes. The answer is, unfortunately, no. You must amortize the points over the life of the loan and deduct a portion of points each year. However, if you refinance your loan, say, in five years, you may deduct any remaining points in the year you refinance.

Why might you want to pay additional points? Let's say you decide to close on your home in November. That means you might only have one month's worth of mortgage interest to deduct in that year. However, if you decide to pay three or four points in cash at closing, you would have more to deduct for the year, and can maximize your deductions. If you decide to pay five points, the lender might lower your rate by a point and a half. That's called "buying down" the loan, and you'll have to ask the lender about that specifically if you're interested.

---

* This generally doesn't happen in a hot seller's market, so don't expect it. You should ask, however. Because even if it is a hot seller's market, there are areas of the country where this happens fairly often.

**NEW CONSTRUCTION TIP:** Some developers use a different sort of buy-down loan to entice first-time buyers to purchase new construction: they'll "buy down" the interest rate for the first two or three years with cash. This doesn't have anything to do with you paying more points up front in exchange for a lower interest rate, though they're both called the same name. You receive two significant benefits from buying down your interest rate: (1) a larger deduction and (2) a lower interest rate for the life of the loan.

Here's how points work: If you need a $100,000 mortgage, each point is $1,000. If you decide to buy down your loan with five points, you'll need $5,000 in cash at closing just to cover the points paid to the lender.

## Good-Faith Estimate of Closing Costs

Every time you put in an application for a loan, the lender is required by federal law (the law is called RESPA, for Real Estate Settlement Procedures Act) to give you a good-faith estimate of your closing costs. That sheet of paper should detail every fee you'll likely pay, and add it all up for you. You may even be asked to sign the document, to prove that you've seen it.[*]

## Something New: TILA-RESPA and TRID

Many first-time home buyers used to feel somewhat deceived by the good-faith estimate because the actual costs at closing were often somewhat or very different from the costs originally listed. That became such a problem that the Consumer Financial Protection Bureau (CFPB) issued a new rule in 2015 that combines the requirements of the Truth in Lending Act (TILA) with the requirements of the Real Estate Settlement Procedures Act (RESPA). It's now referred to as TILA-RESPA. You may also hear it called TRID,

---

[*] That's just one of about one hundred signatures or initials you'll have to provide at your closing, unless you sign your docs electronically.

which stands for (T)ILA-(R)ESPA Integrated Disclosure rule. Someone made this joke at a mortgage convention I attended: Only the government would make an acronym out of an acronym.*

The rule requires lenders to send you your closing documents a minimum of three days before closing so that you have a chance to read them and ask questions in advance. If the documents are not provided at least seventy-two hours in advance (you have to sign to prove you received them or opened your email), then the clock starts all over again and the closing is postponed.

The document you receive is called a Closing Disclosure form, and it is a five-page form that provides final details about the mortgage loan you have selected. It includes the loan terms, your projected monthly payments, and how much you will pay in fees and other costs to get your mortgage (closing costs).

 **20/20 HINDSIGHT:** Once you've finished the application (which you'll probably do online), don't walk away without getting a copy of every document you've signed. It is extremely important to be able to document in writing every step in the application process. If your lender ever gives you trouble, you'll have to prove what was said and what was signed. Also, signing a document signifies that you've actually read it. Take the time to read all documents at the application, and don't be afraid to ask questions. If you're doing the application online, there should be a toll-free number you can call to speak with a live person. Some lenders also do online chat.

## Are Online Applications Okay?

Older Millennials might remember a time before Google, but younger Millennials don't. Regardless, the expectation for all Millennials has been, and will be, this: *We want it now. We want it fast. We want it on our phones.*

And tech companies have complied. They have taken over real estate companies,

---

* Ha-ha. I'd say the joke's on you, except that after a somewhat rocky start, the technology started working well and now everyone in the real estate world is used to the idea that the buyer will know what the closing docs and costs are seventy-two hours before closing—or the deal isn't closing.

started new ones and completely changed how people buy and sell real estate. They're not done yet, but the die has been cast.

So should you apply for your loan online? It's almost certainly going to happen that way. No one wants to retype a million pieces of information into yet another computer screen. Once is enough, and it might as well be you who does the work. Then, the information can be encrypted, visible only to the loan officer, and run through a program that will tell the lender almost instantly whether you qualify for your mortgage.

As I was in the final stages of editing this book, I took a business trip to San Francisco and had breakfast with Dick, a loan officer and friend of more than twenty years who lives and works in the Bay Area. Like so many other mortgage lenders, his company has moved to exclusively doing online loans. "I hardly ever go to see anyone in person," he said. In fact, Dick sold his San Francisco home of forty-plus years (yes, for a huge profit) and moved to the East Bay, where he now works from home. "All of the work I do is by phone or by email," he says. "Sometimes I'll see a client at a closing but typically not even there."

## Question 44: What Kind of Documentation Will I Need for My Application?

If you've spent months searching for the perfect home, the last thing you want are delays in the mortgage approval process. Unfortunately, a delay in getting approved for your mortgage can push back the closing or be a viable reason for the seller to cancel the purchase contract.

One problem that can cause a delay is faulty or missing documentation. Even after going through the pounds of paperwork during the mortgage application process, lenders often request more documentation.

According to one loan officer, most borrowers don't understand exactly how much detailed information the lender will need to approve their loans. Here is a list of documents your loan officer may ask for. You should be prepared to provide these documents, or copies of them, at a moment's notice.

- All W2 forms for each person who will be a co-borrower on the loan.
- Copies of completed tax papers for the last three years; include any schedules or attachments.

- Copies of one month's worth of pay stubs.
- Copies of the last three bank statements for every bank account, IRA, 401(k), or stock account that you have. Bring a copy of your most recent statement for any assets you have.
- A copy of the back and front of your canceled earnest money check. Contact the bank if this has not yet come through.
- Copy of the sales contract and all riders. You'll also need both brokers' names, addresses, and phone numbers, and the same information for both your attorney and the seller's attorney.
- If you are selling a current residence, you will need to provide a copy of the listing agreement and, if the home is under contract, a copy of the sales contract.
- As we discussed earlier, if gift funds are involved, the giver must provide proof that he or she had that money to give, such as a copy of the giver's recent bank statement. You must then show the paper trail for the money, including a deposit slip. The giver will have to either write a gift letter, which is an actual letter, or fill out a gift letter affidavit, available from the loan officer, indicating that the funds were a gift and the gift giver does not expect repayment.
- Complete copies of all divorce decrees.
- Copies of an old survey or title policy for the home you are buying, if available when you apply for the mortgage, or when it becomes available during the purchase process.
- If you are self-employed, you will also need to provide complete copies of the last two years' business tax returns and a year-to-date profit-and-loss statement and balance sheet with original signatures.
- A list of your addresses in the last seven years.
- If you have made any large deposits (that is, larger than your monthly income) into your bank accounts in the last three months, you will need to provide an explanation as to where the funds came from with proof.
- If you have opened a new bank account in the last six months, you will need to provide a letter explaining where the money came from to open this new account.
- Addresses and account numbers for every form of credit you have.
- Documentation to verify additional income, such as Social Security, child support, and alimony.
- If you have had a previous bankruptcy, bring a complete copy of the bankruptcy

proceedings, including all schedules and a letter explaining the circumstances for the bankruptcy.

- For a Federal Housing Administration (FHA) or Department of Veterans Affairs (VA) loan, bring a photocopy of a picture ID and a copy of your Social Security card. Also, bring proof of enlistment for a VA loan.
- If you have any judgments against you, you will need to provide a copy of recorded satisfaction of judgment, and copies of documents describing any lawsuits with which you are currently involved.

## No-Doc Loans, Stated Income Loans, the Housing Crisis, and the Great Recession

A loan that requires almost no documentation is commonly referred to as a no-doc or stated income loan. They were loans designed for people who had cash businesses or who couldn't or wouldn't provide the documentation lenders need to process a conventional loan. Basically, you just put in some numbers (or the lender would put in what was needed to get the loan approved) and the numbers had no basis in reality. In exchange, the buyer typically paid a higher interest rate and fees on the mortgage. These are the loans that helped kick off the housing crisis and Great Recession, which is why they weren't offered for a few years. But now that we're a decade past the start of the trouble, some lenders are again dreaming up creative ways for people who can't afford to buy a home to get a mortgage anyway.

I'm including Carie and John's story because it's a real example of how no-doc loans used to work and why they can be successful.

---

**CARIE AND JOHN'S STORY**

Carie and John decided to leave their jobs in the New York publishing world and move to Denver to be near Carie's family. Like so many New Yorkers, they paid cheap rent for more than a dozen years and had decided long ago not to buy into the Manhattan housing market.

After they resigned from their jobs, they got in touch with a Denver-based mortgage company and a friend who sells real estate. Even though neither Carie nor John had any idea then what they'd do once they got to Denver, they were approved for a reasonably priced no-doc loan.

"I know I wouldn't be comfortable lending to me," Carie said with a laugh. "But I'm glad they said yes."

Carie and John quickly found jobs in Denver, fixed up their house, and moved on with their lives. But for many people who bought in 2006 and a dozen years later were still underwater with their homes, no-doc, stated income, and even pay-option ARM loans were financially devastating.

# Question 45: What Types of Circumstances Might Foul Up My Loan Application? And How Can I Fix Them?

What screws up a loan application? These days, technology has crushed the amount of time it takes to process and verify a loan application. That's a good thing. But if you fall outside of the box that technology can manage, because you're self-employed or have been at your job for less than two years, it may take longer to process and verify your application because a loan officer will have to personally shepherd your application through the process. That could be (and probably will be) extremely painful, slow, and frustrating.

As the buyer, it's up to you to stay on top of things from the day you apply for your loan through the closing. There are often things you can do to help speed the mortgage loan process and meet that pressing deadline.

Any number of things can go wrong during the mortgage approval process: You or the lender can lose documents, the lender may demand more documentation, appraisals may be running late, or verification from banks or your employer may not be processed quickly enough. Mortgage experts agree that problems can surface with interest rates, points, or the up-front fees a lender charges to make a mortgage loan. In fact, they estimate that as many as 30 percent of all mortgage applications will face some problem with the interest rate or points.

## The Rate Lock and Yet Another Scam

To eliminate the uncertainty of changeable interest rates, borrowers may pay their prospective lender for the privilege of locking in a specific interest rate and number of points. The lock is good for a predefined time, usually thirty to sixty days. When you lock in your rate, you must close on your mortgage before the lock expires, or you lose the preset interest rate.

But the mortgage loan process can easily go awry, particularly if interest rates start to fluctuate. Lenders, nervous about their investments and eager to charge the highest interest rate possible, are not as eager to close on their loans as when interest rates are dropping. According to a former director of consumer affairs for the Office of the Commissioner of Savings and Residential Finance (which regulates and monitors mortgage brokers, mortgage bankers, and financial institutions in Illinois), there are many ways for the lender to give you trouble.

"The lender may give you a lock on the interest rate that is intentionally too short given the current market conditions," she says.

A reasonable lock period is forty-five to sixty days. Lenders rarely agree to extend a lock to ninety days (unless they are affiliated with a new construction developer) because of market volatility. But the director says mortgage brokers might "play the float" with your mortgage. Although you think you've locked in at a certain interest rate with a certain number of points, lenders will, in essence, gamble with the rate rather than actually lock it in, hoping that interest rates will slip further. If they do go down, the loan officer and the mortgage company will then split the excess between the current interest rate and the rate you locked into.

## If Rates Go Up

The fun starts when interest rates begin to rise. If the loan officer has been playing the float with your loan, and the rate goes up, he or she will have to pay the difference between your locked-in interest rate and the current market rate out of his or her pocket to close on the loan. And because loan officers are loath to pay out, they will often find something "wrong" with your application at the last minute, forcing you to accept a higher interest rate or more points, says one loan officer.

There are a few things you can do to guard against such situations and to ensure you get the mortgage loan you applied for within the time frame allotted in your application contract.

- **Two can be better than one.** Some experts recommend that buyers apply for two different mortgages at two different companies. Float the rate with one application and lock in the other. "If you have trouble with one of the lenders, you can always play each against the other," says one loan officer. Of course, this method of safeguarding will cost you an additional application fee of $200 to $500, unless you can get the lender to waive the fee until the closing. Even then, you might owe a "breakup" fee.

- **Get the lock commitment in writing.** Never accept a verbal lock. "That way you'll have proof that the lender went against the bargain," suggests the Illinois attorney general's office.
- **Get copies of all docs.** Make sure you receive copies of anything you sign during the mortgage application process before you walk out the door. Don't let the lender mail the papers to you.
- **Secure a good-faith estimate.** Make sure the lender hands you a good-faith estimate of closing costs before you sign anything or pay anything.
- **Keep your lifestyle intact.** Don't make major lifestyle changes after the application has been made and before you close on the property. Don't buy a car. Don't increase your indebtedness in any way. Don't change jobs. It's likely that the lender will pull a second credit report and possibly another employment verification just before closing, and those lifestyle changes could sink your loan application.
- **Keep in touch.** Keep in direct and close contact with your loan officer throughout the process, but at least weekly. Experts say that if you aren't going to be approved for a loan, the lender should know within days, maybe even minutes, but certainly in no more than two to four weeks (four is an extreme case, with a lot of extra vetting required). Typically, lenders can tell you almost instantaneously if you're approved. Credit reports, tax records, and employment verifications can be pulled up while you're sitting in the office (if you do this in person) or electronically (virtually instantly) if you're applying online. If you aren't approved while you're sitting in the lender's office, you'll want to call every couple of days to see if the loan officer needs any additional information.
- **Create a paper trail.** Once your loan officer tells you he or she has all of the documentation required for your loan, you should send an email confirming that and asking for a commitment letter. You'll also want to keep a copy of every bit of paperwork and correspondence between you and the lender.

If, after all this, the loan officer tries to back out of your locked-in rate agreement and force you to take higher rates and points than you originally agreed to, experts suggest you start yelling. Literally. The squeaky wheel gets the grease. If the loan officer tries to make you take a higher rate, you should contact the manager of his office. Have your attorney yell for a while. A few (not so veiled) threats about contacting the state's attorney general's office, the Better Business Bureau, and other consumer-action organizations should get the loan officer to back down.

Of course, sometimes the problem isn't the lender.

## BENNETT'S STORY

Bennett wasn't really interested in selling his house until he was contacted by an eager real estate agent one day. The phone call came in 1999, in the midst of another superhot seller's market, and the agent wanted to know how much Bennett wanted for his house.

Bennett named a sky-high price, and much to his surprise, the buyer accepted. But then the appraisal came back, indicating that the house was actually worth about $50,000 more than Bennett had asked. So, much to the buyer's chagrin, he changed his mind.

A week or so later, the agent showed him the appraisal sheet, and Bennett could see that the appraiser had actually located his house in the midst of a much hotter neighborhood, and used comps (comps are the sales prices of comparable property in the same neighborhood) from a different neighborhood.

So the deal was on again. But then the buyer didn't have enough money for the down payment. Bennett agreed to lend them $10,000, but structure it as a loan to one of the buyers' mothers. The mother, in turn, would gift the money back to the buyers. After the closing, the money would be repaid to the seller.

But then Bennett's attorney got wind of the deal, and it smelled bad. Sellers are not supposed to give the down payment (or any extra cash) to the buyers under the table, so to speak. And if a wacky transaction is structured like this one, the buyer's mortgage lender has to be notified in advance and approve the deal. By not informing the lender, Bennett and the buyers were on the verge of committing mortgage fraud—which the federal government takes quite seriously.

Bennett's attorney ended up saving the deal, but it took quite a while to sort everything out, and it delayed the closing for several weeks.

# Question 46: How Much of a Down Payment Will I Need to Buy My Home? Should I Put Down the Largest or Smallest Down Payment Possible?

These days, the answer starts at zero—actually, less than zero. You can get loans with nothing down; loans where the down payment is a gift from friends, relatives, or a grant; or loans where you actually put down some cash. But you can also get loans for more than the purchase price of the home, either because your loan allows you to fold in the closing costs on the loan or because you got a special FHA loan to help you improve the property.

Zero-down and very low-down-payment loans (where the amount you put down is 3 percent or less) have been around for a while, but since the Great Recession are only available as government-backed loans. But for cash-strapped Millennials, they might be a good choice.

## What You Should Put Down

The standard down payment is 20 percent of the sales price of the home, so if the home costs $100,000, a conventional lender would require that you have $20,000 in cash for a down payment plus closing costs. The reason lenders ask for 20 percent down is that homeowners with a larger equity stake in the home are less likely to default on their mortgage than those homeowners with a smaller equity stake. If you put down at least 20 percent on your home, you will not need to pay for private mortgage insurance (PMI), which can cost between $45 to 60 per month per $100,000 of loan value.

But lenders today recognize that 20 percent of the sales price is a huge amount of cash for most first-time buyers. In San Francisco, where the median price of a home sold in 2017 was well over a million dollars, a first-time buyer condo might cost as much as $500,000. If you're putting down 20 percent on that house, you'll need to come up with $100,000 in cash for the down payment plus another $25,000 or more in closing costs, fees, and reserves. That's unaffordable for nearly all Americans.[*]

---

[*] San Francisco and Santa Clara County have become so unaffordable that tech companies in Silicon Valley are moving chunks of their operations to other cities, as even their highly paid employees are unable to afford to live there.

As a result, several widely available mortgage options will allow you to put down significantly less, although then you'll need the income to qualify. For example, first-time buyers commonly put down 10 or 15 percent of the sales price. Conventional lenders will allow a smaller down payment (anything less than 20 percent) as long as the borrower purchases private mortgage insurance (PMI). PMI is paid monthly, along with your mortgage, until you have about 20 percent equity in the home. The law requires lenders to automatically cancel PMI once your loan-to-value ratio reaches 22 percent. (For more information on PMI, see Question 58.)

If you choose an FHA loan, you can generally put down as little as 3 percent, of which 2 percent may be a gift from a friend, relative, or a grant from a nonprofit housing organization. (You'll need mortgage insurance, however.) While FHA never developed the zero-down loan President George W. Bush promised, it does offer programs for HUD homes (which are FHA foreclosures) that require only $100 down.*

VA loans, which are backed and administered by the Department of Veterans Affairs and are available only to qualified veterans of the US armed services, have a zero-down option. These loans tend to be more expensive than conventional zero-down options. Very low-down-payment loan options (3 or 5 percent) from the VA are more reasonably priced.

Nontraditional lenders are also jumping into the mortgage game. Some investment companies, for example, will allow you to borrow against pledged stock assets to fund a 100 percent mortgage. (Most first-time buyers aren't flush enough to use this solution.)

**20/20 HINDSIGHT:** Borrowing on margin means that you're essentially using your brokerage account (and the stocks, bonds, and mutual funds it contains) as collateral for whatever it is that you're buying. Sophisticated investors have used margin accounts for years, to fully leverage their holdings and invest money they don't necessarily have readily available. The danger with borrowing on margin is that if your assets in the margin account suddenly drop dramatically in value (think 2008–09), there is a risk that you'll be called upon to sell them at a disadvantageous time, in order to maintain a certain loan-to-value ratio in the mar-

---

* You can find out more about HUD homes at HUDHomeStore.com, which is the government-sanctioned website for all FHA foreclosures.

gin account. Be sure you fully investigate how these accounts—their mortgage margin account options—work before you sign on the dotted line.

## Small Down Payment vs. Large Down Payment

Whether you put down a small or large down payment depends on the following:

1. How much cash you have lying around.
2. How nervous you are about leveraging your finances.
3. What you plan to do with your cash instead of putting it down on a house.

**FIRST-TIME BUYER TIP:** There is no right answer when it comes to the question of down payments. Some people can borrow 100 percent of their home's purchase price and invest the rest in obscure technology stocks and still get eight hours of sleep a night. Other people get the jitters just thinking about their 80 percent loan-to-value ratio. And for some folks, the question isn't how much to put down (they have trouble scraping together the down payment) but whether to put extra cash they receive after the closing toward paying down their mortgage or invest it monthly in the stock market.

Generally, first-time buyers are squeezed to the hilt. If they can scrape up a 10 percent cash down payment, they consider themselves lucky. But if you have more cash available, there are two schools of thought on the size of the down payment. Some experts feel that you should purchase your home with the smallest down payment possible. This will leave you with some cash for emergencies, decorating, and any renovation work you may want to schedule. Or you can take out the biggest loan possible and invest the money elsewhere.

On the other hand, you may want to put down a larger down payment in order to cut down the size of your monthly mortgage payments—and save yourself the monthly cost of private mortgage insurance (PMI), which can run $35 to $60 for each $100,000 in purchase price.

The more dollars you put down, the lower the cost of owning the home. Why? You pay less interest over the life of the loan. If you put down 20 percent versus 15 percent, and the difference is $5,000, you should strongly consider putting down the 20 percent—because you'll also be saving the PMI cost, which can really add up.

## Putting Down More, Not Less

When might you be required to put down more cash?

In special circumstances, a higher down payment may be required. Some co-ops may require a 30 or 40 percent cash down payment to prove that the resident has the financial means to cover any capital expenses that may be required in the future. Co-ops may even require a higher down payment than that, if they permit financing at all. (You likely won't run into those kinds of issues, as they're for extremely expensive buildings.) Requiring a high cash down payment is another way for the co-op to filter out those individuals they choose not to have in their building. Fortunately, most co-ops have done away with the higher down payment requirement in order to make the units more affordable.

And there are some cash-rich folks (yes, there are a few first-time buyers with trust accounts) who just don't like the idea that they owe anyone and can't get used to it. These folks should put down as much as they can.

## Making the Decision

The real question you need to ask yourself is this: What am I going to do with the money if I don't put it down on the house?

Stocks hit their Great Recession low of 6,547.05 on March 9, 2009, the lowest point since April 15, 1997. As I write this, the Dow Jones is hitting new highs regularly. It passed 21,000 for the first time in March 2017. At the same time, median home prices in most communities hit new highs as well. Would you have been better off investing in the stock market or in a house?

It's a false comparison. Sure, you might have made more money investing in the stock market during that time, but where would you have lived? If you subtract out the cost of renting an apartment, the returns look much less attractive. For most Americans, their home is the single biggest real estate investment, but once the mortgage is paid off, it's also one of their largest financial assets.

The truth is this: Past performance of any investment is no prediction of future returns. That's true in the stock market, in real estate, in collectibles, and in fine art. What happened in the stock market from 2009 to 2017 may never happen again. Or it might. No one knows.

I'm going to put on my Best Money Moves hat and tell you that the best thing you can do is fully fund your 401(k) (which is invested in the stock market), buy a house, stay there for a decade (or more), and, as you make more money, continue to invest in both your home (or other pieces of real estate) and the stock market. Acquire assets, not stuff, and live as frugally as you can. Having liquid assets (real estate is an illiquid asset because it takes time to sell) gives you options. Your house becomes your home.

## Should You Prepay Your Loan?

The question of prepaying your loan versus investing that extra cash each month in the market is a bit easier to answer.

Every dollar you use to prepay your loan actually earns you your net rate of interest you're paying on your mortgage. For example, if your loan rate is 4 percent, and you don't itemize (you take the standard deduction on your federal income tax form), every dollar you prepay earns 4 percent, a decent interest rate when banks are offering 1 percent on cash. If you were to invest that same dollar in the stock market (either in mutual funds or individual stocks or bonds), you'd need to earn at least enough to meet that return plus pay taxes. So if you're in the 15 percent bracket, you'd need to earn about 6.5 percent on your money. If you're in the 28 percent bracket, you'd need to earn about 8.5 to 9 percent on your cash.

I believe in diversification, and a real estate investment (even if it is your own home) is a pretty good counterpoint to the stock market. So prepay your home loan a bit each month or, if you can afford it, go with a fifteen-year mortgage so you'll benefit from the lower interest rate.

The rest of your extra cash should be used for regular investments in the stock market, either through your company retirement account, a Roth IRA, a 529 College Savings Plan, or another brokerage account.

**FIRST-TIME BUYER TIP:** I firmly believe that buying a house isn't just a decision about where to live. It's a decision about your financial future. Studies show that the younger you are when you buy your first house, the wealthier you'll likely be in your lifetime. When you're buying your first home, or your second, or your third, you should keep your personal finances in mind. If you buy the right house in the right neighborhood, and it goes up in value over time, you've not only made money, you've enhanced your net worth. And that, in turn, enhances your ability to leverage your wealth. Finally, when the average American retires, more than 70 percent of his or her wealth is tied up in his home. Investing in your own home makes a lot of good financial sense.

## Question 47: Should I Borrow from My 401(k) or Other Retirement Accounts to Fund My Down Payment?

Here's the ideal scenario for a first-time buyer: You've been working hard and saving every penny you can in the years before you buy a home. You've accumulated a small pot of cash that you can use as your down payment. You've either paid off your credit cards, or avoided going into debt at all. Your school loans are small and manageable or paid off.

Unfortunately, the people who fall into that scenario are few and far between.

Generally, first-time buyers don't have perfect credit scores or large bank accounts because they haven't been in the workforce for a long time, but they've usually been there long enough to start to accumulate a little bit of cash in their retirement account. (Millennials are different in that typical Millennial first-time home buyers often have a mountain of student debt in addition to some leftover credit card debt from graduation.)

When it comes time to figure out where your down payment cash is coming from, many home buyers turn to their 401(k) and Roth IRA accounts. Borrowing from a 401(k), an IRA, or a different retirement account seems like the perfect solution. The cash is just sitting there, accumulating, and you're years away from retirement.

Of course, there are a few questions you'll have to answer: First up: Can you borrow from your 401(k)? That depends on the individual plan your company has set up. Some companies permit you to borrow from a 401(k), but you may be limited as to how long you can keep that cash out of your retirement account. For some companies, you may be limited to two to five years before the loan must be paid back, with interest. If you don't reimburse your account within the prescribed time, the IRS could look at the loan as a distribution, which would require you to pay a 10 percent penalty plus income taxes.

Other retirement plans allow you to borrow the money for a down payment without a set period of time to pay back the loan. However, if you leave the company for any reason (including getting fired), you'll have just sixty days to pay back the loan no matter where you are in the cycle—or the loan will be seen as a distribution. Check with your plan administrator to see if your company does permit you to borrow, and under what circumstances.

You could withdraw up to $10,000 to use as a down payment on a first home from either a conventional IRA or a Roth IRA. You would have to pay regular income tax on the cash, but would not be subject to the 10 percent penalty.

The real question is: *Should* you borrow from your retirement accounts in order to fund your down payment? I have mixed feelings on the issue. While I understand the desperation many first-time buyers have when they're scraping together the funds for a down payment, the practical side of the equation can't be ignored. You can borrow every dollar you need to buy a house, but no one will lend you a dime for retirement. (I often use this line with regard to paying for a child's college tuition. You can borrow cash to pay tuition bills, but not retirement bills.)

On the other hand, there is that pot of cash just sitting there. If you need to borrow only a small percentage of what you have, and can pay it back within a few years (with interest) and will still be able to put away 401(k) money, then borrowing from your future retirement to pay for your down payment probably won't damage your long-term retirement prospects.

But if the house loan will empty the retirement coffers, you might want to think again. And don't forget, if you leave your job before the loan comes due, you'll have to pay it all back within sixty days, or risk paying a penalty to the IRS on top of taxes owed.

## Question 48: What Fees Are Associated with a Mortgage Application? What Lender's Fees Will I Be Charged for My Mortgage?

There are usually three fees you may be required to pay at the time of your mortgage application:

1. The application fee, which can range from nothing to $500.

2. The appraisal fee, which can range from $200 to $300, depending on where you live.

3. The credit report fee, which ranges in price from $25 to $100 per person.

These fees might be grouped together under the application fee. Many times the lender will apply part of the application fee toward the appraisal and credit report fees. If you're planning to apply for two mortgages (one fixed, one floating), it's best to try to negotiate the lowest up-front fee possible, or find a lender that has no application or up-front fees.

## Online Lending

In 2016, consumers paid roughly $2.5 billion in online loan application fees. Ten years ago, the total was a fraction of that number. In another ten years, I wouldn't be surprised if that number had doubled again (partly from lenders raising the cost to apply online and partly from an increase in the number of applications). Online loan applications are big business, and the trend is to move almost all of the loan application cash online. If you apply online, you may pay just one, smaller fee—say, $500—which will cover your initial application and credit report. Or the fee might be applied toward all of your lender fees. You'll usually be asked to give your credit card on a secured site.

But beyond the online application fee, there's a whole range of lender's fees you'll have to pay in order to close on your loan. (Steady yourself: This list might just make you think about being a renter again.)

## What Are the Lender's Fees I'll Be Charged for My Mortgage?

A long time ago, when buying a home seemed like a simpler process, lenders often charged home buyers a flat fee to close on a loan. But as interest rates (and profits) fell and the call of the Wall Street investor grew stronger, lenders began charging for many different services that were formerly covered by the flat fee. Some mortgage experts say lenders have sought to juice their lost profits with the highbrow business of nickel-and-diming buyers nearly to death.

There has been a push, both from the federal government and from Fannie Mae and Freddie Mac, the two secondary market lenders, to lower the costs associated with home-ownership. By adopting technology and lowering the cost of making a loan, Fannie Mae and Freddie Mac hope to make homeownership even more widely available to more Americans. And yet, it costs more than ever before to close on a home. Go figure!

## The Name Game

Not every bank calls every charge by the same name, which can make comparing lenders as tough as comparing apples and station wagons.

Lenders are supposed to make it easy for you to know and understand their costs of doing business. At the time of the application, the lender is required by the federal Truth in Lending Law to provide a written, good-faith estimate of all closing costs—and it's supposed to accurately reflect your closing costs. Mortgage brokers recommend that you shop around for the best deals before actually applying for a mortgage. You also shouldn't be afraid to negotiate lower fees, and to ask for detailed explanations for each one.

 **20/20 HINDSIGHT:** The time to negotiate fees with the lender is before you sign your application. Once you've signed the application, it's too late: You've made your deal and will have to live with it.

## Lender's Fees

Here are some of the fees that lenders may try to charge you for the privilege of lending you money. The fees cited reflect ranges given by real estate experts across the country, though actual charges may be higher or lower depending on your individual situation and location:

- **Lender's points, loan origination, or loan service fees.** The lender's points—a point equals 1 percent of the loan amount—may also be referred to as the service charge. The points are the largest fees paid to the lender and usually run between 1 and 3 percent of the loan amount. Occasionally, the points will run more than 3 percent, particularly if the borrower chooses to buy down the loan rate. **COST: Usually zero to 3 percent of the loan or more.**
- **Loan application fee.** The money charged by the lender to apply for the loan. The application fee is almost never refundable, which means you'd better be pretty darn sure you want a loan from a particular lender and will actually be approved for it. **COST: Usually between nothing and $500.**
- **Lender's credit report.** The lender may actually pull up two credit reports on you. The first will come just after you've filled out the application and paid the fee; if there is a second report ordered, it will be pulled just before closing, to make sure you haven't made any enormous purchases or gotten into credit trouble during the elapsed time. Most first-time borrowers don't realize there may be two credit checks. However, you only pay once. **COST: Usually between $25 and $75 per person. If there are two people purchasing the property, the cost will be, say, $50 each, or $100. Sometimes the charge for the credit report has been known to run as high as $75 each, which is ridiculous, given that it costs the lender a fraction of that for each report.**
- **Lender's processing fee.** With this fee, the lender is trying to pass on to you some of the cost of doing business. The processing fee is the fee for processing the loan application. **COST: Usually between $75 and $200.**
- **Lender's document preparation fee.** The cost of preparing the loan documents for the closing. **COST: Nothing to $250.**
- **Lender's appraisal fee.** This is the fee lenders charge you to have the home you want to purchase appraised. Lenders supposedly charge you exactly what they're being charged for the service, which is provided by an outside contractor. Electronic appraisals present a new wrinkle to this equation: Lenders search a huge database for comps (the sales price of homes similar to yours that have sold re-

cently) to come up with an approximate appraisal. While electronic appraisals haven't yet been perfected, this is the future of the industry, except for unusual or extremely expensive homes. **COST: Usually from $225 to $400 if the lender does an electronic appraisal; you might only be charged $100, though the lender might pay just a fraction of that.**

- **Lender's tax escrow service fee.** This is a onetime charge to set up and service your real estate property tax escrow (see Question 91). The unfortunate part is that you'll still pay even if you decide to pay your own taxes out of your own account. **COST: From $40 to $85.**

- **Title insurance cost for the lender's policy.** Most times, the title insurer will have a flat fee for the loan policy that will be given to the lender. If you want a title insurance policy that will pay you if there's a problem, that will be an additional, though very worthwhile, fee. **COST: Between $150 and $350.**

- **Special endorsements to title.** If the lender requires extra title endorsements, the buyer must pick up the cost. Some of these might include a condo endorsement (if you're buying a condo), a PUD (planned unit development) endorsement if you're purchasing a home in a development having specific zoning characteristics, an environmental lien endorsement (a statement to the lender that the lender's mortgage on the property won't be affected if the government finds an environmental hazard on the property and files a lien against it so that the owners clean it up), a location endorsement (proves the home is located where the documents say it is), and an adjustable-rate mortgage endorsement. **COST: $25 to $100 each.**

- **Prepaid interest on the loan.** The per-day interest charge on the loan from the day of closing until the last day of the month in which you close. This is paid at closing because the lender has to calculate it by hand. After you pay, you then skip a month and begin to pay your regular monthly balance. This is because the loan is paid in arrears. **COST: Requires separate calculation for each borrower, but your lender should calculate it for you and put it on your good-faith estimate.**

Note: The above charges are only the lender's charges for doing business with you. For a list of all the closing costs you can expect, see Question 91.

# Question 49: What Are Junk Fees? How Do I Avoid Them?

Mortgage brokers say that some of the lender's costs are legitimate. For example, it costs at least $350 to $450 to send someone out to do an appraisal almost anywhere in the country.

But some lenders create "junk fees" purely to increase profits. True junk fees are often difficult to identify because the lender has given them legitimate-sounding names, which can confuse borrowers. As one mortgage banker puts it, "When I see names like 'underwriting fee' and 'commitment fee,' I can tell that these types of fees are being beefed up. When you have an appraisal fee or a credit report fee, you know the lender is being charged by different agencies or companies to do actual things. Those agencies or companies charge the bank, and the customer pays it at the closing. But what is an underwriting fee? If you don't underwrite the loan, you have nothing. Buyers should have the lender explain charges they don't understand, and negotiate to exclude certain extra charges. For example, it's ridiculous to pay for an underwriting fee."

It's even sillier when you realize that, with technology, the lender's time and costs have dropped. (Yes, the lender has invested in new technology, but this goes above and beyond that commitment.) The idea is to pass that savings on to the customer, something that the federal government and secondary mortgage market leaders Fannie Mae and Freddie Mac are actively pushing for. Unfortunately, passing along the savings to the consumer means someone else's profits are being shaved.

The time to negotiate lender's fees is before you pay the application fee. Once you've completed the application, it's too late to renegotiate; you've structured the deal and both you and the lender must live up to the application contract.

 **FIRST-TIME BUYER TIP:** Shopping around is the only real way to know what you should be paying for your loans. It's a competitive world out there, so pitting five lenders against one another and having them compete for your business is the only way to get your fees down to the most reasonable level possible. Using this method, you should end up with the best possible mortgage with the fewest possible points and fees. Online aggregators, like LendingTree.com, claim to do this work for you. But through the nearly thirty years I've been reporting on real estate, I've found there's no substitute for good, old-fashioned shopping around.

How much will it cost you to close? Every year, Bankrate (a website that publishes lenders' interest rate information and makes money every time you click on a link or apply through their site) publishes a survey of closing costs. In the 2017 study, Bankrate found that for a $200,000 mortgage with a 20 percent down payment, closing costs would range from $1,946 in Colorado to $2,648 in New York. And while that $500 doesn't seem like that big a difference, that's the average based on ten lenders in each state. If you don't shop around, you could wind up paying much more—and never know you're being ripped off.

**20/20 HINDSIGHT:** Top lenders say paying about 1 percent of the loan amount in closing costs and fees is fair. On a $300,000 loan, you'd expect to pay around $3,000. On a million-dollar house, you'd expect to pay $10,000, and so on. However, that amount doesn't include things like prepaid interest on the loan (which you can somewhat control by setting the closing date). If the fees are more than 1 percent and your loan is higher than the market rate (considering your credit score), you might want to spend more time shopping for a mortgage.

## Question 50: What Is Truth in Lending?

Under the 1974 Real Estate Settlement Procedures Act (also known as RESPA), the lender is required in most circumstances, within three days of receiving your application, to give you or place in the mail to you a Truth in Lending statement that will disclose the annual percentage rate (APR) of your loan. (See Question 51.)

In many cases, the APR will be higher than the interest rate stated in your mortgage or deed of trust note because the APR includes all fees and costs associated with making the loan. In addition to interest, points, and fees, other credit costs are calculated into the total cost of the loan. The Truth in Lending statement also discloses other pieces of useful information, such as the finance charge, schedule of payments, late payment charges, and whether or not additional charges will be assessed if you pay off the balance of your loan before it is due. This is known as the prepayment penalty.

## A Quick Word About Prepayment Penalties

Many states do not permit lenders to charge a prepayment penalty. But national lenders and federally chartered banks may be able to attach one even if prepayment penalties are illegal in your state.

Prepayment penalties prohibit you from paying off your loan for the first two to four years. Just so we're clear, this also means you cannot sell your home or refinance your loan within the first two to four years without getting penalized, though you can still make extra payments toward the balance of the loan. If you do refinance or sell your home, you'll be subject to a penalty of anywhere from 2 to 4 percent of the entire loan amount. And no, the lender will not let you out of the penalty even if you're just one month shy of the expiration of the penalty period.

On the other hand, the lender will give you a somewhat reduced interest rate if you accept a prepayment penalty. That's the trade-off you're making.

Another reason to avoid prepayment penalties is that they are sometimes associated with predatory lenders, who want to lock you into an ultrahigh interest rate loan for as long as possible. (For more information on predatory loans and how to spot a predatory lender, see Question 66.)

Frankly, I'd rather see you do almost anything than get a loan with a prepayment penalty. If you or your spouse or partner lose your job, or get sick, or get transferred, you'll be limited in what you can do with your property without triggering the penalty. If interest rates drop—too bad! You can't take advantage of that situation either.

## And Now, Back to Our Regularly Scheduled Truth in Lending Statement

Some of the information that the lender is required to disclose may not have been finalized by the time the Truth in Lending statement is sent. In that case, the lender's statement will say it is an estimate. The lender will always provide you with a new Truth in Lending statement at the closing. If you want to know about the charges you'll be paying before the closing, you can call the lender and ask if all the estimates on the statement were correct.

# Question 51: What Is the Annual Percentage Rate (APR)?

Under the Truth in Lending law, the lender must tally up all of the costs involved in making the loan and amortize them over the life of the loan. The APR is what the loan is actually going to cost you. It includes the interest rate, points, fees, and any other costs the lender charges for doing business. If you go to a bank and look at its percentage rate of interest, it will also have the APR for that loan listed. The difference might be considerable: If the interest rate a bank will charge you for your mortgage is 8 percent, the APR might be 8.75 percent or even higher.

The APR is one tool for helping you compare various loans. For example, if Lender A and Lender B each offers you an 8 percent, thirty-year fixed-rate loan with one point, you'll be able to use the APR for each loan to see which loan will cost more.

But keep in mind that a loan that has the higher APR may be better for you than the loan with the lower APR, depending on how long you're going to hold the loan. Also, APR has absolutely no meaning, once you close on your loan.

When you're comparing loans, you're actually better off stripping down the loan to its essential components (basic loan with interest rate, and then costs and fees) rather than using the APR.

# Question 52: What Is a Good-Faith Estimate?

Under the terms of the Real Estate Settlement Procedures Act (RESPA) of 1974, when you file your application for a loan, the lender must provide you with a good-faith estimate of closing costs.

Usually the lender will give you the estimate before you leave the office after completing your application, but your loan officer may also legally send it to you within three business days. If you're applying online, you should get it immediately (or it will arrive in your inbox shortly after completing the application).

The good-faith estimate is based on the lender's experience of the local costs involved with making a mortgage in your area. Any cost the lender anticipates must be stated—except for a paid-in-advance hazard insurance premium (if any), or other reserves deposited with the lender (hazard and mortgage insurance, city property taxes, county property taxes, and annual assessments). The estimate may be stated as a flat dollar amount or a range. The good-faith estimate form must be clear and concise and the estimates must actually reflect the costs you will incur. It is your right to question any estimate of any cost that is provided in a dollar range rather than a flat fee.

If the lender does keep some funds in reserve, they may or may not be included in the estimate. Be sure to add them into your calculations of closing costs. And remember, closing costs can change. Under the new TRID rules, your lender is supposed to send you the final estimate of closing costs three days before you close. It should be sent to you via US mail, overnight courier (like UPS or FedEx), or email (the lender has technology to know whether you've opened the email or not).

## Question 53: What Is a Real Estate Tax Escrow? What Is an Insurance Escrow? How Can I Avoid Setting Them Up?

A real estate tax escrow is an account set up by a lender. Into it goes the amount of money your lender tacks onto your monthly principal and interest payment in order to cover your annual real estate taxes. When the tax bill comes up, the lender takes the money out of the escrow account and sends it to the tax collector. A lender will also collect cash for your homeowners' insurance policy (for noncondo and non-co-op properties), which are included in the fees you pay to the lender to hold in escrow for payment of your real estate taxes and insurance premiums.

### Why Don't Most Owners Pay Their Own Property Taxes and Insurance Premiums?

Historically, government institutions that developed the concept of the thirty-year fixed mortgage collected additional money for real estate taxes and homeowners' insurance. The default rate due to unpaid real estate taxes was low. As private lenders moved into the market, they followed suit.

Today, every state has passed legislation that says that lenders may require real estate tax and insurance premium escrows. Real estate taxes are a priority item for lenders, as the lien for real estate taxes comes before the lender's mortgage lien. That means that if you default on your loan, and the home is sold to pay your bills, your real estate tax bill is paid before anything else, including the lender's mortgage (commonly called the first mortgage). Therefore, it's in the lender's best interest to make sure that property taxes are always paid.

Skeptics will tell you that lenders require escrows because they're a large source of free money. Currently, only fifteen states* require lenders to pay interest on escrow accounts.

But lenders will tell you that tax and insurance escrows help them protect their investment in your home. They also make the argument that most borrowers like being budgeted so they aren't surprised with a huge tax bill once or twice a year. There's some merit to both arguments.

Federal legislation regarding escrows is worded to allow the lender the authority to withhold or impound money to cover taxes and insurance. There are limitations, however, that went into effect in the early 1990s: Lenders are limited to withholding no more than two months' worth of cushion, and they must provide an itemized statement of moneys coming into your account and bills that are paid, similar to a checking account statement.

In other words, if you pay $100 per month to cover your real estate taxes and insurance, your lender may only hold an extra $200—or two months' worth—in escrow.

Fine. So why doesn't your lender pay you interest on that money? Because many states and the federal government don't require lenders to do so. Lenders argue that escrows are complicated and an extra burden to them. They say it's an expense to them to keep in touch with each homeowner's bills, all of which are due at different times. However, these services have long since been digitized, and lenders do charge a one-time escrow service fee that should offset some of these costs.

Many lenders insist on a tax escrow, no matter how much equity you have in a house. They may tell you, if you're using an FHA or VA loan, that an escrow is required under the terms of that mortgage agreement. That isn't quite true. Although both FHA and VA loans contain provisions for real estate property and insurance escrows, the lender has the option to waive it.

According to industry professionals, some lenders will not demand an escrow account

---

* According to Investopedia, the states that do require interest payments on escrow accounts are: Alaska, California, Connecticut, Iowa, Maine, Maryland, Massachusetts, Minnesota, New Hampshire, New York, Oregon, Rhode Island, Utah, Vermont, and Wisconsin. There were two attempts to pass a law (in 1992 and 1993) requiring lenders to pay interest on these accounts, but these failed.

if you have a low loan-to-value ratio. For example, if you put more than 40 percent down (with some lenders, the threshold is 30 percent) in cash, most lenders will cancel the mandatory real estate tax escrow clause. In many states, lenders must waive the escrow requirement if you pledge a savings account with an amount that would be sufficient to pay your real estate taxes. By pledging the account, you can maintain control over payment of your taxes and receive interest (however little there is) on your money.

If you suggest this option and the lender balks, don't hesitate to say you'll be happy to call the state's attorney to check on the legality of the issue. Faced with that threat, the lender should back down. The exceptions are federally chartered savings banks, which claim they are not required to comply with state laws regulating this part of the lending process.

If you are successful in getting your lender to agree not to require an escrow account, you might find yourself hit with a onetime fee, which can run as high as 1 to 2 percent of the loan amount. In some states, charging this onetime fee may violate state law. Ask your real estate attorney for clarification.

**FIRST-TIME BUYER TIP:** Not all lenders charge that much for the privilege of paying your own real estate taxes and homeowners' insurance premium. And you may want to find one who doesn't.

## When Something Goes Wrong

It's important to realize that escrow accounts can easily go awry. There are lenders who have collected enormous sums of money from individual homeowners. One attorney said a lender tried to collect two years' worth of real estate taxes from his client up front. This is, of course, against the law.

### SARA'S STORY

When I was first writing this book, I interviewed Sara, who at that time was a first-time buyer who recently moved to the East Coast. She told me about the lender to whom her bank sold her mortgage, who increased her tax escrow by 46 percent because they needed several months' cushion. At first she refused to pay the overage, instead sending 8 percent over her normal payment.

"I heard from everybody, from the computer people all the way to the president of the company. Finally they started returning my checks. After a few months they make it hard for you. I finally paid it," Sara said, adding that she had almost 30 percent in equity in her property.

Today, that lender couldn't get away with what it did to Sara. The law clearly states that lenders may hold no more than the equivalent of one year's worth of property taxes plus two months extra.

**20/20 HINDSIGHT:** One thing a lender has is the ability to ruin your credit quickly. Even if you're having trouble getting your message through to the lender, don't stop paying your mortgage. Pay everything the lender asks of you while you fight the battle. If you prevail, you'll not only receive your money back, but you'll have kept your credit intact. And in today's digital world, our ability to get a mortgage is almost solely based on our credit history.

## Insurance Escrows

Federal law allows mortgage lenders to require you to buy enough homeowners' insurance to cover the mortgage amount in case of a fire, earthquake, tornado, or other catastrophe. Of course, you'll want to get additional coverage that will also protect your equity in the home plus the cost of replacing your personal possessions and rebuilding your home to today's standards.

To ensure that the homeowners' policy insurance premium is paid, lenders will often require homeowners to pay the insurance premiums in the form of monthly payments that are tacked on to the regular mortgage payments of interest and principal. That money goes into an insurance escrow. Once a year, the lender will dip into that fund and pay the insurance premium. Insurance is one of the four parts of PITI—principal, interest, taxes, and insurance—and is one of the basic costs of homeownership. Overall, the insurance escrow works like the real estate tax escrow, except that you never get rid of it.

## Mistakes Home Buyers and Homeowners Make

One of the biggest mistakes home buyers and homeowners make is not getting enough homeowners' or hazard insurance, or not buying it from a reputable, well-capitalized company. While getting the right kind and amount of coverage may be expensive, it could be the best investment you ever make.

### BILL AND TOM'S STORY

Bill and Tom lived in a beautiful brick home across the street from a golf course in a tiny suburb north of Chicago. One night, when they were in Texas, lightning struck their home and burned it nearly to the ground.

The next day, as Sam and I helped Bill and some neighbors pick through the rubble, he came across the box of "important" papers with the insurance policy they had bought for their home. It turned out to be guaranteed replacement coverage, and not only did it pay for the complete rebuilding of the home, but it also paid for Bill and Tom to live in a rental apartment for two years as the home was being redesigned and rebuilt.

You can't always buy guaranteed replacement coverage, but you should try.

 **20/20 HINDSIGHT:** As your home appreciates in value, it'll become more expensive to rebuild should something happen to it. Make sure your homeowner's policy keeps up with not only in your home's increase in value, but also the increase in the number and value of your personal possessions, including furniture, clothing, artwork, and jewelry.

## Avoiding Real Estate Tax and Insurance Escrows

Lenders will generally forgo the real estate tax escrow requirement if you meet the following criteria:

- **Put down 30 percent or more in cash.** Most lenders use a 30 percent cash down payment as the benchmark for deciding whether or not to forgo the requirement for a real estate tax or insurance escrow.
- **Pledge an interest-bearing account.** If you promise to keep a certain amount of money (enough to cover a year's worth of taxes) in an account at the lending institution, your lender should allow that instead of an escrow account. But you will likely have to use additional funds outside of the pledged account to pay your real estate tax bill.

If you don't meet either of these criteria, you'll probably have to have an escrow account for real estate taxes. However, once you've built up the required 30 to 40 percent equity in your home, you can try to end your real estate tax escrow the next time you refinance (if your lender doesn't offer a procedure for terminating the escrow).

Insurance escrows work almost the same way. Lenders almost always require an escrow account for insurance, and are allowed to by law. Still, you can make this a point of negotiation. Ask your lender what you would have to do to have this escrow waived.

### Fees, Fees, and More Fees

Even if you meet the criterion for avoiding a real estate and insurance escrow, don't imagine you won't still have to pay something. Lenders typically charge a fee for allowing you to pay your own insurance premiums and real estate taxes. According to many lenders, the fee is a onetime computer setup charge to automatically check that you're paying your insurance premium and tax bill.

## Question 54: What Should I Do to Make Sure the Mortgage Application Process Goes Smoothly?

Sometimes, the mortgage process seems to have been set up just to bring out the beast in all of us. It can be a brutal, ego-shattering experience—no one enjoys it. Your number one job is to make the entire process go as smoothly (and as quickly) as possible. You don't want to raise the hackles of your loan officer, but at the same time, you want to remind him or her that you're in control of the situation.

Here are some specific things you can do to make the process go more smoothly:

1. **Straighten out your finances.** If you don't have a grip on what's coming in and what's going out (and where, and why), you may be in for a rough time when you apply for a home loan.

2. **Fix your credit issues.** First, pull a free copy of your credit report from each of the three major credit reporting bureaus from AnnualCreditReport.com. Buy a copy of your credit score for about $10. Analyze it for errors and omissions. Get started repairing the problems or fixing errors. (If you have serious credit errors or negative issues, it could take you months to fix. That's why I suggest taking a look at your credit at least a year before you think you want to buy a home.)

3. **Gather the information you need ahead of time.** If you know you'll need complete copies of your past two or three tax returns plus a current pay stub (or a current profit and loss if you're self-employed), you should have that information on hand when the lender comes calling. I recommend you buy a file holder to hold all of the relevant documents, so that you'll have what you need when you need it.

4. **Qualify your lender.** Just as you shop for a broker and a new home, it's very important to shop for a lender. Not all lenders are created equal. Loan products, services, style, and personal attention vary greatly. Look for a lender that is best qualified to meet your needs. Look for someone exceptionally well trained and thoroughly knowledgeable in the mortgage type you want to use. Look for someone who is seasoned in the business and can guide you through with a practiced hand. If you're self-employed, you'll want to find someone who frequently works with self-employed borrowers.

For more information on choosing the right lender, see Question 42.

 **FIRST-TIME BUYER TIP:** Most first-time buyers don't know that if they receive money from their parents as a gift toward the down payment, they need to provide a gift letter from their parents (or have their parents sign a gift letter affidavit) stating that the money is a gift and does not need to be repaid. In addition, if your parents or relatives are going to give you money, it's a good idea to have that money in your account six months before you actually go to apply for a loan. Banks will look at your monthly balances for at least the past six months. The higher the balance, the more likely it is that you'll be approved for your loan.

### MARK AND MARLENE'S STORY

Mark and Marlene were first-time buyers in the Seattle area. They had been looking for a home for several months and finally found the house of their dreams. Since they had been prequalified (as opposed to preapproved) for their loan, they knew they could afford the property, and they had the cash for the down payment.

But when they went to apply, they were rejected by the lender. The lender pulled a credit report on the couple and discovered that they had "forgotten" to file their taxes in the two previous years. When he went back to the couple to inform them that they had been rejected for the loan, they were shocked at the news. The lender simply didn't want to have anything to do with them. After all, if they could forget something as significant as their federal taxes, how would they deal with a monthly mortgage payment?

# Question 55: How Do I Get the Best Loan at the Best Rate on the Best Terms?

The most important thing to remember is this: *The best loan for you may not be the cheapest loan you're being offered.*

Your loan should work for your personal financial situation, and that may mean paying a bit more up front for a lower long-term rate, or paying nothing up front for a higher rate. Either way, lenders now offer so many different financial products that it's easy to find the creative solution that's best for you.

After you find it, there are some things you can do to get that loan at the best price possible.

- **Know what you want.** The mortgage market is extremely competitive for conventional loans, which, in 2017, meant loans under $424,100. (The amount adjusts upwards usually every year.) Call a few of the lenders who appear to offer the lowest rates online and have them bid on your business. You can also go online to Bank Rate Monitor's site (BankRate.com) and check out the daily mortgage rate (plus the daily rate on auto loans, credit cards, and a host of other credit products).

- **Stay on top of interest rates.** Interest rates change at least once each day, and sometimes even more frequently. If you decide to float your loan, watch the bond market activity closely. If rates seem to be dropping, react quickly and call in your lock. Then get the confirmation in writing.

- **Watch the points and fees.** The number of points and fees also changes frequently. Martha and Ken watched as the number of points required on their loan rose to four and a half and then fell back to two. They locked in at two and a half points. You might also choose a no-point, no-fee (that's nonrecurring fees, like title cost, not an insurance premium) loan, but be prepared to carry a higher interest rate over the life of the loan.

- **Consider using a mortgage broker.** They usually have access to more than a dozen investors, and their job is to do the shopping around for you. Mortgage brokers can offer a wide variety of choices, but don't be afraid to tell them about other mortgage packages you've discovered elsewhere. Let them offer you a better deal. You'll also want to stay on your guard, since end lenders (also known as investors) pay mortgage brokers a fee for every loan they buy (call it a finder's fee). The only problem is that the lender gets a higher fee for every loan that's above the market rate. So the lender has a real incentive to sell you a loan that's more expensive than you'd otherwise have to pay. This practice is called service fee premiums. Ask your mortgage broker to disclose the service fee premium he or she is being paid by the end lender to do your loan. If it's more than 1 percent of the loan amount, you should look elsewhere.

- **Don't be afraid to negotiate for lower fees.** Ask for detailed explanations of fees and speak up if you don't like something. Once you have a detailed listing of fees and charges from each lender, you can compare apples to apples, then go back to the lender and ask for the elimination of specific fees.

- **Consult with your real estate attorney before you apply for a mortgage.** Some first-time buyers believe a real estate attorney should be called in only if there is a problem. Others call the attorney after the deal has been negotiated. The truth is, your real estate attorney should probably be the first call you make after having your offer to purchase accepted, or maybe even before. Real estate attorneys who do a lot of house closings know the people at the title companies, they know the brokers, and they know the mortgage players. They can give you resources, point you in the right direction, and guide you toward a successful house closing. If you're living in a state where real estate attorneys are not commonly used (like California), you should have to know your stuff even more thoroughly before you meet with the lender.

 20/20 HINDSIGHT: When I first published this book in 1994, loans over $203,000 were considered to be jumbo loans. As we went to press at the end of 2017, the conventional loan limit was $424,100. Jumbo loans range from $424,101 to a million or more. "Superjumbos" are higher than that, and if you need a $3 million loan, well, you probably have a private banker who is going to arrange that sort of thing for you. What's the difference between getting a conventional loan and a jumbo loan? You'll have to pay more fees and a (slightly) higher interest rate. How much? Usually a point (remember, a point is 1 percent of the loan amount), plus the loan will carry an interest rate that is about a half point higher than a conventional loan. You can add another 1 to 1.5 percent to the interest rate for superjumbo loans.

# CHAPTER 7

# Finding a Great Mortgage
# You Can Live With

In this chapter you'll find all the answers to your questions about what types of loans exist, how private mortgage insurance helps home buyers to purchase their homes, and what to do if a lender isn't treating you the right way.

## Question 56: What Are the Different Types of Mortgages Available? How Do I Choose the Right Type for Me?

In the aftermath of the Great Recession, one of the first casualties was creative financing. Pay-option ARMs (where you picked how much you'd pay for the first five to ten years of the loan and then would reamortize with a much higher payment), negative amortization loans (where you paid less than you really owed, with an expensive catch-up later), and other crazy loans that were designed to put someone who earned $50,000 a year into a $500,000 house.

As I write this, some nine years after the Great Recession, it still seems as though there are creative ways to finance residential real estate. In fact, if you start to ask a few questions, you'll soon figure out that your lender is actually offering only six or seven basic mortgage types. And, new "Ability to Repay" rules put in place after the housing crisis require lenders to ascertain that you actually *can* afford your monthly payments. It's just that in today's world of personalized banking, lenders say, everyone wants something that is made to order for his or her specific financial situation.

## Making the Right Choice

Choosing the right mortgage for you will depend on several factors, including your monthly income today and what you expect it will be in the future, the assets you currently hold, and how much debt you're carrying. Other factors can influence your mortgage decision as well. Do you want to pay points up front, or do you prefer to pay them over the life of the loan? Do you want to gamble that interest rates will stay low and get an adjustable-rate mortgage (ARM)? Or would you feel more comfortable paying a fixed amount each month?

Lenders offer a variety of financing options simply because today's home buyers want a cure for every ill. For example, if you plan to live in your house for only three to five years, you might consider a two-step loan, also known as a 5/25 (pronounced "five twenty-five") or a 7/23 ("seven twenty-three") mortgage, or a one-year adjustable- rather than a fixed-interest-rate mortgage.

Here is a quick description of the basic types of mortgages available in the marketplace. The following questions offer an in-depth explanation of these mortgages, along with suggestions as to which type of buyer might actually benefit from which type of mortgage.

- **Fixed-Rate Mortgage**. The original and most popular type of loan. When interest rates are low (as they have been since the early 1990s), a fixed-rate mortgage charges the same percentage rate of interest over the life of the loan. Homeowners repay the loan with a fixed, monthly installment of principal and interest. Fixed-rate loans can be taken out in a variety of lengths, including ten-year, fifteen-year, twenty-year, and the ever popular thirty-year loan. In the mid-1990s, a forty-year version of the fixed-rate loan was introduced. My advice is to take a pass on this. If a lender tells you that you'd do better with a forty-year term, find a new lender and then think about finding a less expensive home to buy. This loan is a complete waste of time and money, since you won't start building up any appreciable equity in your home until somewhere near the twentieth year of the loan.
- **Adjustable-Rate Mortgage (ARM)**. Adjustable-rate mortgages have interest rates that fluctuate and are pegged to one-year Treasury bills or a specific index. The

initial rate of interest is usually quite low, and then the rate bumps up (if the index to which the loan is tied rises) between one and two points per year. There is usually a yearly cap of one or two percentage points, and the loan also has a lifetime ceiling cap, usually around five or six points. The interest rate can also go down. From the late 1980s through the Great Recession (2008–09), ARMs proved to be the best deal around because interest rates sank and then stayed low. Homeowners whose initial interest rate was around 5 percent watched their loans drop to 3 percent, or less.[*]

- **Two-Step Mortgages.** Also known as 5/25s and 7/23s, and they come in two different flavors: convertible (which converts the loan to a fixed loan for the remaining twenty-five or twenty-three years, respectively) and nonconvertible (which converts the loan to an adjustable-rate mortgage, also known as the ARM). They are similar loans with different numbers attached: the 5/25 is a thirty-year loan that has a fixed-interest rate for the first five years and then adjusts into a convertible or nonconvertible loan. The 7/23 is a similar thirty-year loan, except that it adjusts after seven years instead of five. Both of these loans can be amortized over the entire thirty-year period. They are considered riskier than fixed-rate loans, but they are significantly less risky than ARMs during the first five or seven years. As a result, the interest rate is lower than a standard thirty-year fixed-rate loan but slightly higher than a one-year adjustable.

- **FHA Mortgage.** Preset spending limits are the hallmark of an FHA mortgage. The loan amounts are set by the median prices of different cities within a particular area. The difference in loan amounts between rural and densely populated areas can vary by as much as $100,000 or more.[†] The best part about an FHA loan

---

[*] And then the savvy homeowners refinanced to a fixed-rate mortgage. Over the period from the early 1990s to 2016, Sam and I refinanced our primary mortgage down maybe a half dozen times as interest rates dropped. While we paid something to refinance, we saved tens of thousands of dollars by moving to a lower rate. We now have a fifteen-year loan at 3 percent, which we have been prepaying at a fast and furious rate simply by making the same payment we had when interest rates were higher. Friends of ours refinanced to a ten-year rate and locked in at 2.75 percent. Now that's a mortgage you *never* want to pay off.

[†] FHA's loan limit floor—which is 65 percent of the Federal Housing Finance Agency's conforming loan limit—was $271,050 in 2017. The ceiling (the highest amount that FHA will lend in the most expensive cities, like San Francisco) was set in 2017 at $625,500. The administration calculates loan limits annually by using a value worth 115 percent of the median home price in each area. The updated limits kick in on January 1 of each year and are typically announced in November.

is the low down payment required; very little needs to come out of your pocket. In the aftermath of the Great Recession, FHA loans were set with a minimum down payment of 3.5 percent for those with a credit score of 580 or above, or a 10 percent down payment requirement if your credit is below 580.[*] There are still some zero-down loans available (which I'll cover below), and there are some HUD home (FHA foreclosures) programs that allow you to buy a home with as little as $100 down, no matter what the price.[†] However, be prepared: If you use an FHA mortgage, you'll pay a steep mortgage insurance premium (known as MI), and other up-front costs are part of the bargain that must be considered when choosing an FHA loan. FHA loans are still assumable, which means you could simply take over the payments from your seller (provided you qualify), saving a lot of cost and hassle; and are a good choice if your debt-to-income ratios are on the high side.

- **VA Loan.** A VA loan is administered by the Department of Veterans Affairs in Washington, D.C., and is designed to help qualified veterans of the US armed forces buy homes with no down payment. In addition, veterans are not allowed to pay points to the lender, although they are responsible for some loan fees; that sometimes causes a problem because it's usually the seller who ends up getting stuck for the extra bucks. Only veterans who have served a specified number of days qualify for a VA loan. And you must get a certificate of eligibility from the Department of Veterans Affairs.

- **Balloon Mortgage.** These are hardly ever used for residential real estate anymore. The basic idea is that you took out a mortgage for a particular length of time (originally this was five years), made interest-only or interest-and-principal payments and then at the end of the loan term, the entire balance was due in full. Today, balloon mortgages are usually paid in one of two ways: Either the mortgage can be amortized over thirty or fifteen years, and you pay just the first five or ten years of the loan before paying it off or refinancing; or you pay only the interest on the loan (as opposed to interest and principal, which you pay when a loan is amortized) until the end of the loan period. For example, if you borrow

---

[*] The 580 limit is sort of specious, as it's incredibly difficult to find a lender willing to give a mortgage to a borrower with this low a credit score, even with the federal government backing it.

[†] You can search for HUD homes at HUDHomeStore.com, which is the federally sanctioned website (run by a private company) to unload HUD homes.

$100,000 on a five-year interest-only balloon, the $100,000 is due on the last day of the five-year period. Throughout the five years, you'd pay interest only on the money.

- **Graduated-Payment Mortgage (GPM) also known as the Negative Amortization Loan.** The GPM was originally designed for first-time buyers because it offers reduced monthly payments early on in the life of the loan, which become larger as the loan progresses and, hopefully, the finances of the borrower improve. These loans were basically outlawed in the aftermath of the Great Recession (when the most common form was known as a "pay-option ARM"), because after five years you owed more than you originally signed for as the unpaid interest was tacked on to the end of the loan term. FHA eliminated its GPM in 1988, but they could make a sneaky comeback as first-time buyers look for ways to get more house for their cash. If someone offers you an interest-only loan, you should be wondering whether it is actually a form of a negative amortization loan.

- **Shared-Appreciation Mortgage.** A shared-appreciation mortgage is a financial concept borrowed from commercial property transfers. The lender will offer you a below-market rate in exchange for a share in the profits of the home when it is sold. There are significant benefits to this, as you get all the tax benefits, and the lender doesn't make any money unless you do. On the other hand, if the home appreciates greatly, you could end up paying a lot of that profit to the lender. Shared-appreciation mortgages are most commonly coordinated by nonprofit associations seeking to help low-income first-time buyers become first-time homeowners. They use community development block grant (CDBG) money to help make up the difference between what low- to moderate-income families can afford and what the competitively priced commercial products want to see on their borrower's balance sheet. These loans are few and far between now, as I write the fourth edition of this book, but there are so many tech-enabled "new" models of mortgages and real estate developing that I expect to see shared-appreciation mortgages continue to pop up here and there.

- **Biweekly Mortgage.** The name for this mortgage product comes from the number of payments you make per month: two. Each payment represents half of what a regular monthly payment might be, but because you pay every other week, that adds up to twenty-six payments, or a thirteenth month. Making that thirteenth payment, no matter what form it takes, will significantly cut down the amount of interest you'll pay over the life of the loan. The trouble with biweeklies is that while they are easier payments to make (particularly if you get paid biweekly), the obligation to pay twice a month can be onerous, particularly if money is tight or someone in the household loses a job or has his or her income reduced. And, you'll get charged a hefty sum (as much as several hundred dollars) to set up a biweekly loan. That irks me because you can achieve the same effect on your loan by simply making an extra payment a year, or dividing that extra payment into twelve pieces and paying a little extra each month.

## Question 57: How Small a Down Payment Can I Make? Where Can I Find a Zero-Down Loan?

From the 1940s through the early 1980s, if you wanted to buy a house, you had to come up with at least 20 percent in cash for the down payment. (So if you were buying a $100,000 house, you needed $20,000 in cash.) Today, if you're buying the median-priced home in San Francisco, for example, you'd need a little more than $200,000 cash to do so.*

In the twenty-five years I've been writing about real estate, study after study has shown that coming up with the down payment is one of the toughest obstacles for first-time home buyers to overcome. Scraping together that extra cash each month, on top of rent, utilities, child care, student loans, and credit card payments, excluded those whose finances were more marginal from the benefits of homeownership.

Things began to change when the FHA started permitting home buyers to purchase homes with 10 percent down, and then 5 percent down. Studies showed that defaults did increase as home buyers put less and less down on their homes, but the amount was tiny.† Apparently, there was a profitable market to tap. So conventional mortgages followed suit and began offering 95 percent loan-to-value ratio mortgages. Soon, FHA dropped its

---

* In 2017, Zillow reported the median-priced home in San Francisco was $1,195,000, which means a 20 percent down payment would run you $239,000.

† Excluding subprime mortgages, which have been blamed for contributing to the start of the Great Recession.

down payment requirement to just 3 percent. Conventional lenders followed, introducing 97 percent loan-to-value ratio loans. All of this happened before the Great Recession, and helped whip the housing market into a frenzy.

While the down payments were decreasing, lenders (led again by FHA) were increasing their debt-to-income ratios. So instead of allowing a borrower to spend only 28 percent of his or her gross monthly income on the mortgage and up to 36 percent on their total debt, home buyers were permitted to spend up to 42 percent. Industry experts saw that these marginal home buyers (made up of significant numbers of minority and immigrant families) were already spending as much as 50 to 60 percent of their gross monthly income on rent—and were making it work.

Then FHA decided home buyers only needed to put down 2 percent on a house. The rest of the down payment could be a gift from a family member, or a grant. The USDA started offering a zero-down loan for rural areas. In response, conventional lenders went a step farther. The Department of Veterans Affairs had always offered qualified veterans a true zero-down loan, but the loan was expensive. In the late 1990s, conventional lenders began offering true zero-down loans to ordinary home buyers. Some of the programs were either restricted by income or area, and some continue to be available to all home buyers.

**FIRST-TIME BUYER TIP:** Let's be clear about one thing: Anytime you put down less than 20 percent in cash on your home, you'll either pay private mortgage insurance (PMI) or FHA mortgage insurance (if you get an FHA loan), unless you opt for an 80/10/10 or an 80/15/5 loan. I'll talk more about PMI in Question 58. PMI can be expensive, although the cost has fallen throughout this past decade. And while PMI must be canceled automatically by your lender once you've reached a certain level of equity, it could take you ten years or more to get there. You'll pay more in PMI premiums the lower the down payment. It gets particularly expensive when you fall below 5 percent. But if paying PMI is the only way you can buy a home, it's generally worth it. (For a few years during the Obama administration, homeowners could write off their PMI premium paid each year for mortgages taken out January 1, 2007, or later much the same way you're allowed to deduct the interest you pay on your mortgage and your real estate taxes. For the tax year 2016, the deduction was eliminated if your adjusted gross income was above $109,000. The PMI deduction expired after the 2016 tax year, and Congress has yet to renew it.)

## Finding a Low-Down-Payment Loan

Almost any major mortgage banker or broker can do a low-down-payment loan. If you need the extra lending ratios, you may need to go with an FHA loan. But almost all lenders can and will do an FHA loan (although they do require a bit more paperwork). You should simply ask which loan options require that you put 5 percent down, or less.

## Finding a Zero-Down Loan

As we go to press, there are very few true zero-down loan options left. Most of this has to do with the Ability to Repay rule, and the tougher lending standards most mortgage lenders enacted after the Great Recession.

**VA LOANS.** The Department of Veterans Affairs offers a true zero-down loan option for qualified veterans. Contact your local VA office for current requirements, or go to benefits.va.gov/homeloans.

**USDA LOANS.** Offered by the United States Department of Agriculture, a USDA home loan (which is more formally known as the USDA Rural Development Guaranteed Housing Loan Program) is a true zero-down-payment mortgage for eligible rural and suburban homebuyers. For more details, go to eligibility.sc.egov.usda.gov/eligibility/welcome Action.do, and click on the property type.

**NAVY FEDERAL CREDIT UNION.** Navy Federal is the country's largest credit union and it offers a true zero-down loan to members of the military, some civilians who work for the military, some people who work for the Department of Defense, and a few others. Find out more at navyfederal.org/products-services/loans/mortgage.

**PLEDGED ASSETS LOAN.** There was a time when investment companies like Merrill Lynch allowed you to pledge assets to cover the top 20 percent of the loan (your down payment), giving you essentially a zero-down loan. As I was writing this edition, however, I couldn't find any investment companies that advertised these loans online. That's because they're extremely risky,[*] and have to be held in the investment company's portfolio rather

---

[*] If you had a pledged assets loan when the stock market dropped at the start of the Great Recession, the loan would

than getting resold by Fannie Mae and Freddie Mac on the secondary market. Don't count on finding one.

**NONPROFIT ORGANIZATIONS.** Traditionally, nonprofit organizations and housing authorities have used community development block grant funds to help first-time home buyers with either down payment funds or by lowering the interest rate on the loans. When President Trump was running for office, he said that he would change how these grants were made to the states, which could lessen their availability. At press time, that hadn't happened, but stay tuned. To find out more, you can search for "down payment programs" and your city and state (search locations separately). You can also find out about down payment programs at DownPaymentResource.com, which features thousands of programs that are available to first-time buyers (and others) nationwide.

**20/20 HINDSIGHT:** The higher your loan-to-value ratio, the higher your monthly costs will be. Sometimes it's better to not stretch yourself too thin financially. I call this concept underbuying. When you underbuy, you spend less than you can afford because you choose to make your financial life a bit easier. Brokers will often encourage you to overbuy, that is, spend as much or even more than you can comfortably afford today, on the theory that soon you'll be earning more money and will be in a house that is the right size for you and your growing family. Whichever way you go, make sure you think it through first. While you'll be using your leverage if you overbuy, that financial risk won't be worth anything if you can't sleep at night.

---

have been "called," meaning the company would have demanded an immediate repayment or it would have sold your pledged assets to cover the amount of the loan.

# Question 58: What Is Private Mortgage Insurance (PMI)? How Can I Avoid Paying it? How Do I Get Rid of It? Is It Deductible? How Does Private Mortgage Insurance (PMI) Differ from FHA's Mortgage Insurance (MI) and Mortgage/Credit Insurance?

Want to buy a house but don't have the 20 percent to put down in cash? Private mortgage insurance (PMI) is an often necessary expense you'll incur when you buy a house with less than 20 percent down in cash. Although it's expensive, PMI allows you to purchase a home with a small down payment, and helps the lender resell your mortgage on the secondary market to an institutional investor.

By definition, PMI is additional insurance designed to *protect the lender* (not you) from individuals who default on their loans and who have less than 20 percent equity in their property. Mortgage experts say that, compared to home buyers who put down the traditional 20 percent of the purchase price, those who make small down payments are more likely to default on their home loans. Therefore, lenders require those riskier buyers to purchase PMI to insure the lender against the extra risk—and ensuing cost—of foreclosure.

Most states have regulations prohibiting lenders from making a loan in excess of 80 percent of the purchase price without PMI. The difference between putting down 20 percent and, say, 15 percent or even 10 percent, wouldn't seem to make a substantial difference on the surface, but a spokesperson for the Mortgage Bankers Association of America (MBA), a nonprofit trade association serving the needs of lenders nationwide, says that 20 percent provides a necessary cushion for both home buyers and lenders: "If I put down 20 percent and lose my job, and the house has declined in value, I can still sell it and pay off the mortgage and come out even or with a little bit of cash. But if I've only put down 5 percent in the same set of circumstances, then I'll come out of the deal owing money."

Although it's expensive, PMI has its upside for buyers, too. About 30 percent of home buyers, most of them first-timers, can't put together enough cash for a 20 percent down payment. PMI allows many people to purchase property years earlier than they otherwise would have been able to. Buyers who are required to purchase PMI have to pay for that additional security, but they gain from being able to get a mortgage with much less cash up front, which is considered a plus by many real estate experts, who argue that you should buy a home with as little cash as possible.

First-time buyers often wonder whether every lender charges PMI. (Not all lenders advertise it.) "If a customer calls me and says a lender doesn't charge PMI, I ask them to check the interest rate," says Ray, a mortgage banker. "It's always one-quarter or three-eighths of a percent higher than ours. And you'll be paying it for the life of the loan." In other words, pay PMI separately and keep it out of the interest rate.

## The Cost of PMI

Since I wrote the first edition of this book, several things have occurred that will ultimately make it less expensive for home buyers who have PMI. The most important thing is that a new law was passed. The Homeowners Protection Act of 1998 requires all lenders who closed on loans after July 29, 1999, to provide consumers with an explanation of how the homeowner can cancel his or her PMI policy. There are three ways to do it:

1. If you believe your home has reached the 20 percent equity threshold, you may hire an appraiser to appraise the value of your home. The lender may not accept that appraisal, however, and may charge you for an additional appraisal.

2. Each monthly mortgage payment consists of both principal and interest. Each bit of principal you repay goes to build up your equity. Starting with loans that are originated after July 31, 1999, lenders must inform you annually that you may cancel your PMI once you've reached the 20 percent equity threshold. On a thirty-year loan, you might hit the 20 percent threshold somewhere around the tenth year. If you prepay your loan, you'll cross the equity threshold a lot faster. You can run an amortization schedule at ThinkGlink.com to see how fast you can get to the 20 percent market through prepayment.

3. If you do not request a cancellation of your PMI premium once you've hit the 20 percent equity, the lender is now required to automatically cancel your PMI once you hit the 22 percent equity threshold. This will be done whether or not you request it.

But even if your home has appreciated enough in value over two years to hit the 22 percent number, you may not be able to cancel your PMI that quickly. Lenders may require you to keep PMI for a minimum of five years even if your home has doubled in value. If that's the case, you may be able to refinance with a different lender and get rid of PMI altogether.

**FIRST-TIME BUYER TIP:** Canceling PMI as soon as possible can save you hundreds of dollars per year and even thousands of dollars over the life of your loan. If you use the money you save each year (which could amount to $300 to $500 per $100,000 in loan amount), and prepay your loan, you'll save not only a few thousand dollars but perhaps tens of thousands of dollars in interest.

## PMI Premiums

The PMI premium price depends on the purchase price of the home and the type of mortgage you've selected (for example, fixed thirty-year, fixed fifteen-year, ARM, 7/23, or balloon). You can expect to pay anywhere from $45 to $60 per month for every $100,000 of loan amount. Like I said, it isn't cheap, but it's necessary if you don't have 20 percent to put down in cash.

**FIRST-TIME BUYER TIP:** Lenders must tell you at the closing exactly how many years and months it will take for you to pay off enough of your loan to cancel PMI. This doesn't include any rise in your home's equity, which could shorten the time frame considerably. Plus, your mortgage service must provide you with a phone number each year that you can call for information about canceling your PMI.

**20/20 HINDSIGHT:** If your lender balks at canceling your PMI, contact the department or agency that regulates mortgage lenders in your state. If your lender is federally chartered, you can call the Treasury's Office of Thrift Supervision or the Federal Deposit Insurance Corporation (FDIC).

## FHA Loans and Mortgage Insurance (MI)

Frequently, home buyers wonder if they have to pay PMI if they get an FHA loan. The answer is no. But that doesn't mean you're not paying for some form of mortgage insurance.

All government loans require mortgage insurance, which is referred to as MI. But because you're getting a government loan, you get the government version of PMI. Unlike PMI, however, you can never cancel your mortgage insurance on an FHA loan, even if you reach 50 percent in loan-to-value ratio.* The only way to cancel MI on your FHA loan is to refinance into a conventional loan.

## How to Get a Low-Down-Payment Loan Without PMI

There is one way to get a low-down-payment loan without paying for private mortgage insurance. It's called an 80/10/10 ("eighty-ten-ten") or an 80/15/5 ("eighty-fifteen-five") loan.

The concept here is that you're essentially getting two loans simultaneously, a regular 80 percent loan-to-value ratio first mortgage, and a home equity loan. With an 80/10/10, the first mortgage is for 80 percent of the sales price of the home, the home equity loan is for an additional 10 percent of the cost, and the final 10 percent represents your down payment. With an 80/15/5, the home equity loan is for an additional 15 percent of the cost of the home, and you put down 5 percent.

There are pluses and minuses to the 80/10/10 loans. The good thing is that you don't pay PMI. And, because home equity loans to $100,000 are tax deductible, you can deduct the interest you pay. While PMI was deductible for a period of years (through 2016), the deductibility has expired, and there are no indications it will be renewed. Unfortunately, the interest on the home equity loan part of an 80/10/10 tends to be higher than on your regular loan, which means you'll pay more in interest. But since it's tax

---

* For a while, you could cancel MI on an FHA or other government-backed loan. But after the Great Recession, FHA changed the rules (again!) and said that you now have to carry MI for the life of the loan, even if you have 80 percent equity. This was done in part to dissuade buyers from using FHA loans, which became a popular choice when mortgage lenders weren't making many loans.

deductible, the numbers work out almost even between a PMI low-down-payment loan and an 80/10/10.

Who's a good candidate for an 80/10/10? If you work for a company that pays a good bonus once a year, and you know that the size of your next bonus will allow you to entirely pay off the home equity portion of the loan, you may want to go this way. That's because you'll be able to get to a conventional-size mortgage a lot faster, and save yourself the cost of PMI.

Talk to your lender, think about how long you'll have this loan, and work out the numbers before you make this important decision.

## Comparing PMI, MI, and Mortgage/Credit Insurance

As we've just discussed, private mortgage insurance is required whenever you put down less than 20 percent on a house. All lenders will require you to have it, and you won't be able to talk your way out of it. And then there's this: The lower your down payment, the higher your PMI premium.

FHA mortgage insurance (also referred to as MI) is the government version of PMI. It's required on all FHA loans no matter how much you put down in cash. In addition, you can never cancel it. The only way to get rid of MI on an FHA loan is to refinance out of that loan into a conventional loan.

Credit insurance, also referred to as mortgage insurance,[*] is an entirely different animal. This is insurance designed to pay off your bills in case something should happen to you. Depending on the kind of insurance you get, it will either pay off your credit card bills or your entire mortgage.

Sound good? It isn't. Credit insurance and mortgage insurance are extremely expensive. And you're paying a lot of money for something that is a declining liability. What I mean by that is that every month, when you write a check to the credit card company or to your mortgage lender, your check includes principal and interest. So each month, your principal balance due falls a bit (or more than a bit, the further into paying off your loan you get).

---

[*] Just to confuse you, I imagine.

If you take out mortgage insurance to pay off a $100,000 loan when you die, and it's a thirty-year loan, and you don't die for thirty years, you'll have paid off your mortgage before taking advantage of the policy. If you then let the policy lapse, you've paid out for thirty years for nothing. If you die fifteen years into your mortgage, your $100,000 balance may only be $70,000, and yet you're still paying for $100,000 in coverage. After paying off your $100,000 mortgage, you might expect to get the extra $30,000 in cash, right?

Not likely. You've forfeited that $30,000. If you're worried about how your spouse or partner will manage the bills after you've gone, buy a term life insurance policy. It's a heck of a lot less expensive than mortgage or credit insurance, and you'll get everything you're paying for. Also, your spouse or partner will have the option to use the funds in any way he or she wants to, and you can get a policy that will return a portion of the premium to you if you don't wind up using it in the term. Perhaps paying off the mortgage at that time wouldn't be in his or her best interest. Term life insurance provides them with options that aren't available with mortgage or credit insurance.

**20/20 HINDSIGHT:** One of the things we do to show our family and friends how much we love them is to plan ahead in case the unthinkable happens. Planning for how your loved one will live and still be able to stay in the home you're buying (if that's what you feel is best) is something for which you should carefully consider and prepare.

## Question 59: What Is an Assumable Mortgage? Are These Loans Still Available?

Sometimes a broker will show you a property, then lean over and say, "And it's got an assumable mortgage to boot." You nod, knowingly, but inside you're wondering what's up. The broker is obviously trying to tip you off to something, but you're not exactly sure what.

Here's the answer: With an assumable mortgage, the buyer takes over from the seller the legal obligation to make monthly payments of principal and interest to the lender. There is no change to the terms of the loan, which is attractive to buyers in a high-interest-rate environment. The lender, assured of getting repaid on the loan, then releases the seller from his or her liability.

How do you find out if a mortgage is assumable? Most conventional mortgages are not assumable, meaning that they have a due-on-sale clause built into the verbiage of the loan. A due-on-sale clause means that if you sell the home, you immediately owe all of the money to the lender. FHA mortgages are assumable, which is one reason brokers like to show first-time buyers FHA properties.

Another reason you might like an assumable mortgage is that it can be cheaper and easier to assume a loan than take out a new loan. If you, the buyer, decide to assume the mortgage of the seller, you pay fewer closing costs and fees. It's also easier: Provided the buyer qualifies for the loan, there is less paperwork that needs to be completed.

If you purchase property that is subject to the existing mortgage, that means you can take over the loan obligation (as long as you're deemed credit-worthy and you meet the Ability-to-Repay requirements), but the seller remains liable for the mortgage amount. There is no formal transfer of obligation or liability, as with assuming a mortgage. If someone tries to convince you to buy a property subject to a mortgage, make sure the lender can't call in the loan as a result of the transfer of title. If you purchase property subject to an existing mortgage and the lender, upon receiving notice of the transfer of title, calls in the loan, you could be forced to pay the entire loan off immediately.

**20/20 HINDSIGHT:** Since interest rates dropped in the early 1990s, assumable mortgages have fallen out of favor. FHA loans are still assumable, but if interest rates are lower than the rate of the assumable mortgage, you're better off getting a new loan than taking over an older, more expensive mortgage. Also, frequently, you'll pay more for the property (because the home has appreciated in value) than whatever balance remains on the mortgage. Unless you have the cash to make up the difference (between the mortgage balance and the price the seller wants for the house), you'll need a new, larger loan. While some agents and brokers still tout "assumable loans" as being something you need to pay attention to, in reality, you're better off shopping around to different lenders to find the right mortgage program for you.

## Question 60: What Is a Fixed-Rate Mortgage? What Is an Adjustable-Rate Mortgage (ARM)?

The most popular type of mortgage is the fixed-interest-rate mortgage, where the amount of interest and principal repayment is amortized in equal amounts over the life of the loan. Many homeowners like the financial security of knowing that they will pay exactly the same amount of money each month (excluding property tax or insurance payments to an escrow account) until the loan has been paid off in full.

Although the concept of fixed-interest mortgages hasn't changed much, most lenders now offer borrowers a choice in how long a loan they want. While a thirty-year mortgage was, and is, the most popular length, ten-, fifteen-, and twenty-year fixed mortgages are also available, and have become more popular since interest rates have been so low.

One to avoid: the forty-year loan. On $100,000, you might save an additional $50 per month if you went with a forty-year loan instead of a thirty-year. But for that savings, you're facing an additional ten years of interest payments. It's just not worth it. My feeling is that if you have to take a forty-year mortgage because you can't afford to finance your house with any other sort of loan, you're buying a house that's too expensive for your budget. Let it go and start looking for something that costs less.

Because interest rates are low, borrowers are finding that the shorter loan length offers a significant financial advantage over the regular thirty-year mortgage: Homeowners can save thousands of dollars in interest payments if they shorten the length of the loan by up to fifteen years. Of course, the shorter the amortization period, the higher the monthly payment. But the loan is amortized faster, so you pay less interest over the life of the loan.

For example, if you take out a $100,000 thirty-year mortgage at 4 percent interest, your monthly payments toward principal and interest would be around $477.42. If that same mortgage was fifteen years in length, your monthly payment would be around $739.69. The difference is that you're paying off the loan in half the time, so you need to pay more in principal each month.

You'd end up paying $133,144 in principal and interest over the life of the thirty-year loan, but you'd pay only $33,144—$100,000 less—over the life of a fifteen-year loan.

|  | 15-YEAR LOAN | 30-YEAR LOAN |
|---|---|---|
| Monthly Payments | $739.69 | $477.42 |
| Total Payments | $133,144 | $177,868 |
| Total Interest | $33,144 | $71,868 |

**20/20 HINDSIGHT:** When you get a fifteen-year loan, the interest rate is usually lower than if you get a thirty-year loan. So, even if you prepay your thirty-year loan down to the point where it will terminate in fifteen years, you'll save more money by going with a fifteen-year loan because the interest rate on the whole loan is less. Here's what I mean: If thirty-year mortgages are available for 4 percent, you might get a fifteen-year loan for 3.75 percent or even 3.5 percent. That quarter or half-point in the interest rate can produce significant savings over the life of the loan. See below:

|  | 15-YEAR LOAN @ 3.75% | 30-YEAR LOAN @ 4% |
|---|---|---|
| Monthly Payments | $714.88 | $477.42 |
| Total Payments | $128,679 | $177,868 |
| Total Interest Paid | $28,679 | $71,868 |

The difference between paying off a $100,000, fifteen-year mortgage at 4 percent vs. 3.75 percent is $4,465. It's well worth it, if you can afford the payments.

## Who Would Benefit from a Fixed-Rate Mortgage?

Buyers on a limited or fixed income and those who do not like to gamble with interest rates are usually best served by a fixed-rate mortgage. You know you'll pay the same amount (not including real estate property taxes and insurance, which will go up over time) throughout the entire term. But if you can handle the higher payments and want to pay down your mortgage as fast as possible, you should try a ten-, fifteen-, or twenty-year fixed-rate mortgage. The truth is, since the Great Recession, most buyers have been steered toward some form of fixed-rate mortgage. It's stable, predictable, and affordable.

There's no need to worry that your monthly payments will suddenly jump up and double or triple on you.[*]

Still, buyers who choose a thirty-year mortgage for the initial lower payments and want to pay it off faster can make an additional mortgage payment per year—a thirteenth payment—and direct the lender to use that money to repay the principal.[†] This is called prepaying your mortgage. An extra payment a year will significantly lessen the amount of interest you pay over the life of the loan.

There are several ways to successfully prepay your mortgage:

1. Make a lump-sum payment if you happen to come into some cash, perhaps through an inheritance;

2. Divide your regular mortgage payment by twelve and add 1/12 to each monthly mortgage payment you make, directing the lender in writing to apply the difference to the principal balance (you may even have something on your mortgage coupon that you can check off for that purpose);

3. Make one complete extra payment per year, on its own, at any time, although the earlier in the year you make it, the faster you prepay your mortgage and the more interest you save.

If you make a thirteenth payment every year, beginning with the first, on a thirty-year mortgage, you'll effectively cut your mortgage term by years. This works best with a thirty-year loan (more years of payments) than a fifteen-year loan, where much more of your monthly payment repays the principal. It works more effectively with higher interest rates (where you're making larger interest payments) than lower rates. Here's an example of how it works:

---

[*] That's what happened with pay-option ARMs. When the initial fixed payment period of five years expired, mortgage payments doubled or tripled for many homeowners, who found themselves at risk of losing their homes. With their houses still underwater (worth less than the mortgage amount), homeowners couldn't refinance to take advantage of the extraordinarily low interest rates. The Making Home Affordable refinance loans helped some homeowners overcome some of those issues and allowed them to refinance their homes.

[†] For best results, write a separate check, note in the memo section that the check is to be "applied to the principal balance," and include it with your monthly payment.

| Loan Amount | Loan Term | Interest Rate | Monthly Payment | Prepayment | New Loan Term | Total Payments | Prepayment Interest Savings |
|---|---|---|---|---|---|---|---|
| $100,000 | 30 years | 4.50% | $506.69 | $50/month | 25 years | $182,405 | $15,872 |
| $100,000 | 15 years | 4.50% | $764.99 | $50/month | 13 years, 9 months | $137,699 | $3,480 |
| $100,000 | 30 years | 6.00% | $599.55 | $50/month | 24 years, 7 months | $215,838 | $24,569 |
| $100,000 | 15 years | 6.00% | $843.86 | $50/month | 13 years, 9 months | $151,894 | $5,014 |
| $100,000 | 30 years | 8.00% | $733.76 | $50/month | 23 years, 11 months | $264,160 | $39,912 |
| $100,000 | 15 years | 8.00% | $955.65 | $50/month | 13 years, 8 months | $172,018 | $7,433 |

Bottom line: How much can you save by prepaying? A lot.

**FIRST-TIME BUYER TIP:** Use the calculators on ThinkGlink.com (click on the Tools button) to quickly and easily help you calculate your prepayment amortization schedule. Be aware, however, that an extra payment per year does not relieve you of the obligation to meet your monthly payments. Even if you pay twice the amount owed one month, you still must make your regular mortgage payment the next month. Moreover, the thirteenth payment does not lessen future monthly payments. It does alter the end balance on your account.

## Adjustable-Rate Mortgages (ARMs)

An ARM is a mortgage with an interest rate that adjusts at specific times over the life of the loan—usually yearly, every three years, or every five years. But there is even a ten-year ARM, which adjusts once every ten years.

Adjustable-rate mortgages are attractive to a variety of buyers because the initial interest rate is much lower than those on almost any other type of loan. Interest rates on one-year ARMs tend to start out very low—sometimes as low as 3 or 4 percent—and increases in the rate are generally tied to an economic index, such as one-, three-, or five-year Treasury securities. When the time comes for your loan to adjust (either yearly, or every three, five, seven, or ten years), a margin of between one and three percentage points is tacked on to whatever index the loan is tied to. This is how the lender comes up with your next interest rate.

## What Is Your ARM Tied To?

There are a variety of different indexes that your ARM might be tied to, but the most popular are the Constant Maturity Treasury (CMT), the 11th District Cost of Funds Index (COFI), and the London Interbank Offered Rate (LIBOR). Some of these are more sensitive to economic shifts, and might adjust faster than others. LIBOR-tied ARMs[*] tend to move faster than other indexes, so you could expect your ARM to jump up more quickly. Regardless of which index your ARM is tied to, all of them work much the same way. If the CMT is at 2.25 percent and your lender charges a 2.5 percentage point margin, your new adjustable mortgage interest rate based on that index would be 4.75 percent when the loan adjusts.

ARMs are likely to fluctuate with the economy, though you can get an idea of how much your mortgage will adjust by keeping an eye on economic indicators, such as the prime interest rate and the federal funds rate, which is the rate the Federal Reserve charges banks. But even if interest rates soar in the next few years, not that they're expected to, ARM holders are somewhat protected by a lifetime cap on their loan's interest rate. This cap, usually five or six percentage points over the lifetime of the loan, limits how much the interest rate can go up. With a six-point cap, an ARM starting at 5.25 percent could never go higher than 11.25 percent.[†] If you go this route, make sure your ARM has an interest-rate lifetime cap, and that the loan can go up only one or two percentage points per year.

---

[*]  See how quickly you're getting the hang of all this jargon? By the end of the book, you'll be spouting acronyms like a pro!

[†]  But I'd hope that the pro you are means you're thinking about interest rates and if they start to go up significantly, you'd bite the bullet and refinance to a fixed-rate mortgage.

## Going Down

ARMs, the lender likes to point out, can also readjust downward after the first adjustment period. This has happened to Sam's and my loans any number of times and it's like a gift that keeps on giving! We saved tens of thousands of dollars by having our ARMs reduce as interest rates fell. And if that happens to you, you'd reap the benefit of your gamble for years to come. Let's say you need a $100,000 loan. You decide on an ARM, which has a starting interest rate of 6 percent. Let's say it's a three-year ARM with a two-point cap per year (meaning the loan can only go up two points a year) and a margin of two and a half points over the Treasury bill to which it is tied.

For the first three years, your interest payment is $6,000, or $500 per month. At the end of the three years, let's assume the rate rises to 7 percent (just because the interest rate can go up two percentage points doesn't always mean it will). You will then pay $7,000 per year, or $583.33 monthly. (This example isn't exactly precise because I haven't amortized the numbers, but it works for straight interest loans. To create your own comparisons using amortized numbers, try my ThinkGlink.com online mortgage calculator.)

The truth of the matter is this: It's impossible to predict long-term interest rates. No one has a crystal ball. In fact, if you'd bought your home in 1990, your ARM interest rate would have dropped the first year and held steady somewhere around 6 to 7 percent for the rest of the decade, until it dropped a bit further after September 11, 2001, and then much more significantly as the Great Recession began in 2008–09. As I write this, in late 2017, mortgage interest rates have fallen below 4 percent for a thirty-year fixed-rate loan. The much prophesized hyperinflation never materialized post-recession, and it's hard for me to imagine how mortgage interest rates will get back above 6 percent anytime soon.[*]

 **FIRST-TIME BUYER TIP:** Watch the spread between fixed-rate and adjustable-rate mortgages. As the spread diminishes, as it has since the Great Recession, more people get fixed-rate mortgages. If interest rates rise when it

---

[*] There is an entire generation of homeowners who have never experienced a 6 percent interest rate (or higher) and I think there would be a huge revolt from the real estate industry, not to mention another recession. Affordability would plummet, and home prices would likely follow.

> comes time to buy your first home, you can simply choose an adjustable loan. If rates then drop after you've owned your home for a while, you can turn around and refinance into a fixed-rate mortgage.

## Who Could Benefit from an ARM?

Buyers who carry more personal debt (in the form of credit cards, school loans, or a car loan) might benefit from the lower interest rates associated with an ARM, particularly if they can show that they have good job and salary prospects for the future. Conventional lenders will generally allow your housing expense (mortgage principal and interest, private mortgage insurance, and property taxes) to equal no more than 28 percent of your monthly gross income (income before taxes), or up to 36 percent if you have no other debt, unless you get a higher debt-to-income loan.

For example, if your gross monthly income is $4,000, you could afford monthly mortgage and property tax payments of up to $1,120. All debt, including installment and revolving loans (credit cards, car payments), should not exceed 36 percent of gross income, conventional lenders say. And while conventional lenders never calculate a loan on the basis of future earnings, you might find that a mortgage broker or portfolio lender might be willing to stretch the qualifications needed outside normal parameters if, for example, you are a fourth-year medical student with a guaranteed residency in the near future, or a third-year law student with a job offer.

(When lenders stretch the requirements for prospective borrowers, they usually keep the loan within the institution's portfolio of investments, meaning they don't resell the loan on the secondary mortgage market. That way, they needn't worry about Fannie Mae and Freddie Mac's requirements and have additional lending flexibility.)

## Ask Yourself: How Long Do You Plan to Stay?

How long you plan to stay in your new home will have an effect on what you buy, where you buy it, and how you plan to pay for it.

If you know you're going to stay in a home (or keep your mortgage) for only five to seven years, you may want to get an ARM. Lenders acknowledge there is a strong probability that, compared to a fixed-rate mortgage, you will enjoy a lower interest rate over the entire term of an ARM.

---

### ILYCE AND SAM'S STORY

When we bought the 1880s farmhouse in which we've lived for the past decade or so, we decided to use a 5/1 ARM rather than go with a thirty-year fixed-rate mortgage.

It might have seemed a strange choice. We knew we had found the house in which we wanted to spend the next twenty or thirty years. We knew we were going to settle down and raise our family here. Why use a 5/1 ARM?

We guessed, correctly, that within five years of buying the property we would need to refinance our mortgage in order to pay for a "gut-job" renovation of our home. We asked ourselves: "Why get a thirty-year mortgage when we are going to refinance in five years?"

So we went with the 5/1 ARM. The interest rate, as I remember it, was at least one percentage point or more less than the going thirty-year fixed mortgage interest rate.

When we refinanced five years later, it was 1999 (as I was writing the second edition of this book) and interest rates were beginning to go down. From 1999 to 2004, we refinanced our mortgage no less than six times. Each time, we used a 5/1 ARM.

I've never been one to try to "time" the mortgage market (or the stock market, for that matter). But when you refinance so often, you're bound to get lucky once in a while. Just before the Great Recession, our 5/1 ARM was at 4.25 percent. Once interest rates dropped, our ARM kept falling. We finally refinanced into a fifteen-year fixed-rate mortgage at about 3 percent.

Our required monthly payments have dropped precipitously. And, to borrow a cliché, we're making hay while the sun shines. We not only used our "savings" each month (the difference between what we would be paying for our loan and what we are now paying) to prepay our mortgage, but started to add more each month as our income has improved.

The net result? We have very little principal remaining on our mortgage balance. But now that we locked in such a low interest rate, I wish we could have this mortgage forever!

# Question 61: What Is an FHA Loan? What Is a VA Loan?

An FHA loan is often called the "first-time buyer's mortgage." The reason for that is clear: FHA loans require a much smaller down payment than conventional ones. It's common to see an FHA loan with only 3.5 percent down (or less), whereas conventional lenders prefer to see a 20 percent cash down payment, which is often too steep for most first-time buyers. (Conventional lenders will allow you to purchase a home for less than 20 percent down, but you'll have to pay private mortgage insurance. You'll pay the FHA's version of mortgage insurance if you get an FHA loan with less than 20 percent down, although if you can afford a 20 percent down payment, there's no reason to get an FHA loan unless your credit is awful or something else is out of whack with your financials.)

## Almost Everyone Qualifies for FHA Loans

Credit scores are the determining factor with FHA loans. Supposedly, you can have a credit score of 580 and get an FHA loan. Unfortunately, the actual lenders who will do these loans with that low of a credit score are few and far between. And while you don't have to be a first-time buyer, FHA loans aren't the cheapest option, though if you have debt-to-income ratio issues or credit score issues, they may be your only choice.

One big restriction is the amount of money you can borrow. Here is a chart with the current loan limits, as we went to press in 2017. Be advised that these numbers change frequently. You can check out the latest loan limits by going online to the website of the Department of Housing and Urban Development (www.hud.gov) and then clicking through to "Buying a Home."

## FHA Loan Limits

FHA loan limits are not fixed by metropolitan area, though a metro area that covers several counties might encompass various FHA loan limits. Generally, expensive suburbs have higher loan amounts, while more rural areas (where prices are assumed to be lower) are allowed smaller loan amounts.

| Unit Size | 2004 Standard Limits | 2017 Standard Limits | 2004 High Cost Areas | 2017 High Cost Areas |
|---|---|---|---|---|
| Single Family | $160,176 | $275,665 | $290,319 | $636,150 |
| Two-Family* | $205,032 | $352,950 | $371,621 | $814,500 |
| Three-Family* | $247,824 | $426,625 | $449,181 | $984,525 |
| Four-Family* | $307,992 | $530,150 | $558,236 | $1,223,475 |

* Depending on where you live, these might be called a duplex, tri-plex, and four-plex, and they refer to the number of units in a single structure.

NOTE: Loans for properties that contain more than four units are considered to be investment properties. As an investor (even if you plan to live in one of the units), you'll pay a higher interest rate. On the other hand, you might be able to make enough money from renting out the other units to live for free.

WEB RESOURCES: To find out what the specific FHA loan limits are for your county, log on to this website: https://entp.hud.gov/idapp/html/hicostlook.cfm. This page of the HUD website appears to be updated annually, so you will always be able to find out what the FHA loan limit is for anywhere you want to live. You can also just search "FHA loan limits" and the name of the county in which you're looking for a home.

## Who Could Benefit from an FHA Loan?

Cash-strapped first-time buyers with challenging debt-to-income ratios and lower credit scores are the logical choice. FHA loans are a good choice for those who have had credit problems or bankruptcies in their past, because the government does not regard these past financial problems in quite the same light as a private lender would. As long as the loan-to-income ratios are met, and the borrower can pay the mortgage insurance premium (which can be steep), former bankruptees can qualify. As one lender puts it, an FHA loan is a good way to begin to rebuild a credit history. The idea behind the FHA loan is to provide an outlet for people who do not have access to other financial outlets.

**20/20 HINDSIGHT:** If you have severe negative information on your credit history, including a bankruptcy, court judgments, or charge-offs, and you've been slowly rebuilding your credit history, an FHA loan may be the only option available to you. While some lenders will try to entice you with offers of getting a loan within one year of bankruptcy, what you won't be told is that the interest rate you'll pay is about the same as charging your house on a credit card! FHA loans can fill in the gaps until your credit is considered good enough for a conventional lender.

## VA Loans

One of the many benefits that come along with joining a branch of the armed forces is the helping hand Uncle Sam offers when it comes time to buy your house. The Department of Veterans Affairs in Washington, D.C., guarantees loans for veterans, allowing them to purchase homes at favorable lending terms with no down payment.

The VA started the program at the end of World War II, and since it began in 1945, more than 22 million veterans have obtained loans worth nearly $2 trillion (by the time you read this, the amount may well be past that number). Although the program has changed some since its inception, VA loans generally restrict the amount of money the veteran is obliged to pay for his or her loan. However, the veteran is required to pay some closing costs, including a VA appraisal, credit report, survey title, recording fees, 1 percent loan-origination fee, and a VA funding fee.

The VA funding fee is the expensive part. Except for a brief period during the 1960s, when it was used to distinguish "Cold War" veterans from those who had put in wartime service, there used to be no funding fee for obtaining a VA loan. However, in 1981, a .5 percent fee was reinstated, although disabled veterans who receive compensation were—and continue to be—exempt. In 1984, the funding fee was increased to 1 percent, and it was again raised in 1990 to 1.25 percent. As of November 21, 2011, veterans taking out their first no-down-payment loan were required to pay a 2.15 percent funding fee to the Department of Veterans Affairs. Veterans taking out subsequent no-down-payment loans are required to pay a funding fee of 3.3 percent. If the veteran chooses to put down 5 or 10 percent of the sales price, the funding fee is reduced significantly.

In the past, the VA has said that it charges a higher no-down-payment funding fee to discourage veterans from using the program. I think that's nonsense. It's about having the veteran pay the lender a fee for making the loan, and that charge is twice as high (2.15 percent vs. a typical 1 percent fee conventional lenders charge). The whole point of getting a zero-down-payment loan is because you don't have the cash for a down payment. Requiring a 2.15 percent or 3.3 percent funding fee is like asking someone to come up with that amount in cash. If you had the cash, you might as well go to a conventional lender or FHA and put 2 or 3 percent down on a house and get a lower interest rate.[*]

According to the VA, you do not have to pay the fee if you are a veteran receiving VA compensation for a service-connected disability, a veteran who would be entitled to receive compensation for a service-connected disability if you did not receive retirement or active duty pay, or the surviving spouse of a veteran who died in service or from a service-connected disability.

## Reserves and National Guard Veterans Pay Even More

By the way, if you're in the reserves or the National Guard, the cost of getting a VA loan is even more expensive. If you fall into either of these categories, and want a no-down-payment loan, you'll pay a 2.4 percent funding fee for your first loan and 3.3 percent for subsequent loans.

## Who Might Benefit from a VA Loan?

For a long time, a VA loan was the only zero-down option available. Another plus of the program is that the VA worked closely with veterans who had trouble with their finances subsequent to getting a VA loan. In many cases, the VA took over these loans and homes, which is why the VA loan default rate was so high. But, the loan was only available to qualified veterans of the Armed Services, which didn't help the rest of the home-buying population.

---

[*] Which is silly, if you think about it, because the government backs these loans. Since they're for veterans, you'd think the government would at least charge the going interest rate instead of a higher amount. But there you have it.

The recent introduction of super-low-down-payment loans and even the new zeros reduces the need for the VA loan, which has grown to be far more expensive than conventional financing. But there are other benefits: The loans are assumable, meaning a buyer can take it over from the seller for very little money, an added incentive for the veteran-as-seller. And there's the VA policy of "forbearance," which means that "worthy" veterans experiencing a temporary economic setback are somewhat protected against foreclosure. In rare instances, where a lender has decided to foreclose on such a "worthy" veteran, the VA has stepped in and paid off the lender, putting the loan in its portfolio. Today, you can choose from several VA loan programs, including fixed- and adjustable-rate mortgages. And lenders, buyers (the veteran), and sellers may openly negotiate who will pay the loan's discount points. In the past, the veteran was not allowed to pay any points to the lender.

If you're a reservist with six years of duty behind you, you're now eligible for a VA loan—the catch is, you'll pay a funding fee that's three-quarters of a percent higher than your active-duty compatriots. While they're expensive, a VA loan might be just the ticket, especially if you're running short on cash.

To apply for a VA loan, simply take your eligibility certificate to a lender. You're eligible for a VA loan if you served ninety days of wartime service in World War II, the Korean conflict, the Vietnam era, and the Persian Gulf War, and were not dishonorably discharged. You are also eligible if you served between six and twenty-four months of continuous active duty from 1981 through today, and were not dishonorably discharged. Check with your loan VA office for more details on eligibility.

## Question 62: What Is an Interest-Only Loan? Are There Other Loan Programs I Should Know About?

In prior editions of this book, I spent quite a few pages discussing interest-only loans, and how you could benefit from them. But the Great Recession changed all of that. As I was writing this edition, Sam leaned over and said that he hadn't seen an interest-only loan deal in nearly ten years. Why? They basically don't exist. Pay-option ARMs, stated income, negative-amortization, and interest-only loans were blamed for the collapse of the housing market. And while subprime loans did help trigger the Great

Recession, there were so many other reasons that contributed to a world-wide credit freeze. It's too long to go into here, and other wonderful books* have been written on the subject.

## A (Very) Brief History of Interest-Only Loans

Interest-only loans were fairly commonplace during the Roaring Twenties. When the interest-only period expired, homeowners typically refinanced their loans to new interest-only loans. Which worked out fabulously, unless your house lost value or you lost your job and couldn't make the payments. Which is, of course, exactly what happened en masse when the stock market crashed in 1929 and the Great Depression began.

At that time, American banks stopped making interest-only mortgages (and most mortgages in general) and only began making new interest-only loans at the start of the Millennium (2000), some seventy years later. Sound like things were getting better? Just wait . . . by 2008, we had the housing crash.

(Sigh.)

I'll say this about interest-only loans: You only pay the interest that's due each month, and none of the principal. The entire principal is due when the loan either converts into a different sort of loan, or as a balloon payment. They're loans that were primarily used to help buyers qualify for a crazy mortgage amount, one that they had no hope of repaying. Buyers used them to leverage up what they could buy, hoping to resell in two years or less once values had skyrocketed. In short, someone who earned $50,000 would routinely qualify for a $500,000 loan, or ten times his or her income.

Looking back, it all seems sort of insane. And yet, those lessons that ought to have been learned from the Great Depression and then from the Great Recession may in the end dissipate in the face of incredible profits and Wall Street greed. In the name of showing investors just how profitable they could be, publicly traded mortgage lenders and banks pushed the bar on lending until it broke. It didn't take long: just a few years.

---

* Some of the best reads include *Too Big to Fail* by Andrew Ross Sorkin, *On the Brink* by former Treasury Secretary Henry M. Paulson, and *The Big Short* by Michael Lewis (who is one of my favorite storytellers).

If you take away lending regulations (like the Ability-to-Repay rules and others) that were put into place in the aftermath of the Great Recession, I'd fully expect another bubble to form relatively soon, and another financial crisis to unfold, with tens of millions of Americans falling victim.

## Question 63: What Is Seller Financing? What Is a Lease with an Option to Buy (also Known as a Rent-to-Own)?

One of the most flexible sources of real estate financing can be the seller of the property you want to buy. Why are sellers interested in providing financing? For many, the return on their investment (in your mortgage) will be far greater than what they can get for their cash in a bank account (5 percent vs. 1 percent in the bank). For retirees, that acts as a kind of annuity. In addition, sellers who provide financing sometimes sell their property (especially if it's a difficult property to unload) more quickly.

Home buyers should be interested in seller financing because (1) by eliminating any potential red tape that could slow down or mar the closing, it allows you to close more quickly, and (2) you might get financing at a below-market interest rate. Of course, not every seller will help you purchase his or her home. You should look for a seller who is ready to trade down to a smaller property or, perhaps, retire to a rental community, and whose mortgage is paid off. Otherwise, it's likely the seller will need your cash to purchase his or her other home.

### JUDITH AND SCOTT'S STORY

First-time buyers Judith and Scott fell in love with a house. Unfortunately, with their salary (at the time, she sold advertising for a magazine and he was a doctor in his second year of residency), they couldn't qualify for a large enough mortgage to quite make ends meet.

Although Judith and Scott knew it meant scrimping and saving, they were sure they could afford the payments. So they went to their seller and asked her to take back a second mortgage. She agreed and offered them a rate that was a half point cheaper than the rate they got for their first mortgage. They closed on the house. A year and a half later, when interest rates dropped, Judith and Scott refinanced and paid off the seller.

When it works like this, seller financing works beautifully. But consider the experience of one of my regular readers of our syndicated column, Real Estate Matters:

## KAREN'S STORY

Karen was eager to sell her California bungalow. She took the advice of her real estate agent and took back the mortgage for the buyers.

That was the beginning of four years of problems. They missed several loan payments (and finally stopped paying them altogether). They twice failed to pay their property taxes. They went through bankruptcy to avoid foreclosure. They refused to pay the cost of the bankruptcy attorney plus court costs. And they committed homeowners' insurance fraud—twice!

They finally left, and Karen reclaimed possession of the house. It was a disaster inside. She had to spend thousands of dollars fixing up the place.

In the course of the last four years, the housing market in her neighborhood skyrocketed. Karen was able to resell the house at a tidy profit. But even that money, she says, wasn't worth the agony of dealing with a pair of irresponsible buyers.

**20/20 HINDSIGHT:** Seller financing isn't for everyone. And even though it's touted as being a win-win situation for everyone (buyer, seller, and agent), it doesn't always work out that way. Home buyers should recognize that sellers have to protect themselves. If you're seeking seller financing, be ready to allow the seller access to your credit history and to pull a credit report. A savvy seller will also request financial references, such as the name of your superior at work, and may also do a background check.

Here's another letter from a reader of our Real Estate Matters column. For her, like Karen, seller financing didn't work out exactly as she expected.

## NANCY'S STORY

Twenty-two months ago, Nancy purchased a home with owner financing. She paid her mortgage on time each month, and also put $15,000 down on the house. Then, two weeks ago, she found out that the home was going into foreclosure and that the owner had not made any mortgage payments in twelve months on the property. There was a lien on the property for the prior year's property taxes of $1,960, and a lien on the house for $2,100 for nonpayment of federal income taxes from the owner. Property taxes for this were also due ($1,600).

The home appraised for $182,500 and the principal balance was $156,199. Nancy was able to get preapproved for $164,000, so she had no problem buying the house. But this was where everything went downhill.

The mortgage company was not willing to work with her. They wanted $24,952 in late payments and interest for a grand total of $181,151, or $5,000 and another $3,000 a month for twelve months, or she was told to buy the house on the courthouse steps.

With the $6,000 in liens on the property, the cost of the home was near $190,000—way above its appraised value. The existing mortgage company refused her lender's offer for a short sale of $157,000.

Nancy has since moved out of the house and it sold for back taxes on September 3. She had invested about $10,000 in remodeling in the home as well and so lost a total of about $44,000.

What could you have done to prevent this situation? Nancy should have bought this home outright with a mortgage from the seller. This would have required the seller to pay off his loan, and any other liens, and put the title in her name. Barring that, she should have paid the seller's lender directly, with any extra being paid to the seller. That way, at least she'd have known that the mortgage was being paid and that the lender had enough cash to pay the real estate taxes.

Clearly, Nancy could have afforded conventional financing. And, often, conventional or FHA financing is going to be your best and safest choice—if slightly more expensive.

## A Few More Details on Seller-Financing Options

Seller financing comes in many forms. The seller can:

1. Provide all the financing and take a straight first mortgage (eliminating the need for a commercial lender). This is called a purchase money mortgage.

2. Take back a second mortgage that will help provide the down payment (although this must be fully disclosed to the lender).

3. Arrange a purchase by articles of agreement. Also known as an installment purchase, you'll receive an interest in the home, which becomes yours after you pay off the seller in full.

## A Purchase Money Mortgage

A purchase money mortgage is a form of seller-provided financing. With a purchase money mortgage, the seller offers to give a first mortgage to you, the buyer. In taking over the role normally played by a bank or savings and loan, the seller would secure the loan with a down payment, and you would pay the seller monthly installments of principal and interest. Although you get the title to the property, the seller has a lien on the property.

If you default on the mortgage, the seller can reclaim the property. A purchase money mortgage can work well for buyers because you don't pay any points or other costs to obtain the loan, and the seller enjoys an excellent return on his or her funds.

## Articles of Agreement

With the articles of agreement, you enter into an installment agreement to buy the home over a specified period of time. The seller keeps the legal title, but you receive equitable title, which means you receive an interest in the property but do not own it. The benefit to you, the first-time buyer, is that the seller will usually accept a much smaller down payment (perhaps 5 percent of the sales price of the home) and yet will still feel comfortable with the arrangement.

Remember that, with articles of agreement, the seller retains title to the property until you've paid off the loan. If you default on the property, the seller need only evict you to reclaim possession of the home, and you could lose all of the equity you've built up until then.

**HOWARD AND EMILY'S STORY**

Howard and Emily had owned a condo for years, but when they wanted to sell, they couldn't get anyone interested in their neighborhood, which had fallen on hard times. They put an ad in the newspaper offering to sell their property for $3,000 down.

Sally saw the ad, checked her bankbook, and realized she had enough cash to buy the apartment. She moved in and paid Howard and Emily as if they were the bank. Over time, she was able to afford a regular loan and paid off the loan held by Howard and Emily. Until then, Sally got a tax deduction, which helped her save more money.

Although the articles-of-agreement purchase seems similar to a lease with an option to buy, the two methods of buying a home are completely different. With the articles of agreement, Sally does not own the home, but since she is paying the real estate taxes and making payments to the seller with interest, she gains the tax benefits, since the real estate taxes and interest are tax deductible. If Sally leased the home with an option to buy, Howard and Emily would also have retained ownership until Sally had exercised her option. But because they would have paid the taxes, they would have had the tax benefits, not Sally.

 **FIRST-TIME BUYER TIP:** Purchasing a home through articles of agreement can work very well for some home buyers. But it is extremely important that the buyer consult with an attorney who will look after his or her interests. Documents will need to be recorded to protect the buyer's ownership interest in the property that he or she is building up through regular principal and interest payments.

Whatever form the seller financing takes, it's in your best interest to explore this possibility. However, beware the difficult seller who will constantly call you for his or her money. That kind of overbearing behavior is difficult to stomach. If you do opt for seller financing, it would be in your best interest to keep the transaction at arm's length.

## Lease with an Option to Buy

A lease with an option to buy, also known as a lease/option or rent-to-own, allows home buyers to build up a down payment while they're living in the house they think they want to own. Why would you lease a home with an option to buy it instead of buying it outright?

- You're short on cash for the down payment and closing costs.
- Your credit history and credit score aren't good enough for you to qualify for zero-down-payment options.
- You don't have at least one year of work history, or at least two years if you're self-employed.
- You're not sure if you like the area and want to "test" it out.
- Your company may transfer you within two years and you're not sure the property will appreciate enough in value to cover future closing costs. (If you wind up staying, you can buy the house at a later date.)

Lease options can help out if you just need a little extra time to get your financial history in order.

**JENNIFER AND DAVID'S STORY**

When Jennifer and David were twenty-three,[*] they started to prepare for buying their first home. Jennifer wrote to me for advice.

"In a year, we'll have enough for about a 5 percent down payment, and enough income to support a loan of about $170,000," she wrote. "The problem is that I've heard that two or even three years' tax returns are required by lenders to get approved for a loan. I'm only ten months into my first real job and my boyfriend starts his first job this month. We have not filed our taxes in the last two years. As student dependents of our parents with very little income to speak of until recently, we never filed, which now seems like a mistake."

---

[*] That may seem young to buy your first home, let alone get married, but some people manage. If it's easier, just pretend they're thirty-three instead of twenty-three.

In her email, Jennifer acknowledged she sounded immature and financially naïve, but said she and her boyfriend were responsible citizens, if a bit misguided.

"We both have good credit and are now turning our attention to establishing some investment potential. Do we need to worry about our lack of tax returns getting in the way of a successful loan application?" she asked.

My answer to Jennifer was simple. If you want to buy a home, take the following steps: (1) get caught up on your last two years of tax returns, then (2) start talking to lenders about what kind of loan you would qualify for and how long you'd have to wait to get it, then (3) consider leasing a condominium that you like with an option to purchase it in another year.

That way, Jennifer and David would be able to more quickly "accumulate" their down payment, but would know what to do to get their financing in place.

## How Lease/Options Work

The buyer purchases a one-year (or multi-year) option on a home by giving the seller a nonrefundable option fee, which is usually a small percentage of the price of the house. Then, the buyer moves into the home and pays rent each month, a portion of which the seller credits back to the buyer as a future down payment for the home.

For example, if you were to pay $1,000 per month in rent, with 33 percent of the rent credited toward the down payment, you'd accumulate $333 each month, or nearly $4,000 per year, toward the down payment for the home. In addition, your nonrefundable option fee may be credited toward the down payment.

There are no hard and fast rules about how much of the rent can be credited toward the down payment. It's up to you to negotiate. Some sellers will give you credit for 100 percent of your rent payment. Others won't give you anything. Typically, the seller will give you somewhere between 25 to 40 percent.

It isn't just the rent credit that needs to be negotiated in a lease with an option to buy situation. You've also got to negotiate the price and terms of sale of the house, just as if you were buying it outright. Once you and the seller have reached an agreement, the price of the home can never vary, even if it appreciates in value.

Buyers should remember that even though they have an option to purchase the home at a later date, the seller remains the sole owner of the property until the buyer exercises his or her option. This is different from other forms of seller financing, such as a purchase mortgage or articles of agreement, where the buyer has some claim to the property. Since the seller owns the home, the seller retains the tax benefits of homeownership and can deduct mortgage interest and property taxes from the federal income tax form.

One of the nice things about doing a lease/option is that the option is typically renewable—although you may be asked to pay another nonrefundable fee, which you can negotiate to be applied toward your down payment. A home investor at a California home buyers' fair once told me she had been renewing her option on a particular home for twenty-three years. During that time, the house tripled in value. Now she knows what she is buying, and she has nearly paid off the house in rent credits.

Here's the best part about a lease/option: If you decide, at the end of the year, that you don't like the home or the neighborhood, or if you discover the home has a hidden material defect (like a cracked foundation) that will cost thousands of dollars to repair that you don't have, you can pay your last month's rent and walk away.

## Finding a Lease/Option

Some sellers advertise their homes as lease/options in the local MLS or online. You might also find landlords who are looking for long-term renters who might agree to a lease/option agreement.

Look for a seller who doesn't need the cash from the sale to purchase something else. Try sellers who have had their home on the market for a long time, or who have already purchased another home and are paying two mortgages. (Your rent could cover the costs of their former home.) And, ask your agent. He or she may know of someone open to it.

# Question 64: What Loans Exist for Buyers with Mediocre or Poor Credit? Where Do I Get One?

Almost all home buyers who go to get a loan will be graded A or A–. These Grade A borrowers are those who have perfect or very good credit reports, who have been in their jobs for two years, and who always pay their bills on time. Lenders estimate as many as 90 to 95 percent of all borrowers will fall into the Grade A or A− category.

So who is a B or a C borrower?

It could be anyone walking down the street, says Joe, president of a subprime lending company. He likes to share the story of Ed and Vivian as an example of how anyone, including you, your parents, or your next-door neighbor, could fall on hard times quite unexpectedly:

### ED AND VIVIAN'S STORY

Ed and Vivian were just three years away from paying off the mortgage on their home when the Northridge, California, earthquake hit in 1994. Although their home was not badly damaged, Ed's printing business almost collapsed.

Due to severe damage his three largest clients sustained in the earthquake, these companies closed up shop, virtually overnight, and moved out of state. Without the income from these three clients, Ed's once-profitable business started running up the red ink. With the business unable to sustain itself, the couple eventually filed for bankruptcy.

But this story has a relatively happy ending. Ed and Vivian went to see a subprime lender, also known as a B-C lender. This lender helped them refinance their home and use the equity to pay off their debts and get their business going again. Within two years, Ed and Vivian were back on their feet. Their business was once again thriving, and they were able to refinance their higher-interest-rate loan for a conventional mortgage.

Ed and Vivian are the typical B-C loan customer, says Harvey, a subprime lender. "It's someone who, through no fault of their own, got downsized and lost their job. It's someone who went from a decent income to unemployment and couldn't make their credit card payments. Or, they've been thirty days late twice in the past year." Or it could be someone who went into foreclosure or was forced into a short sale.

"Good people who have a bad credit problem" is how Rick, another mortgage banker, describes B-C applicants. "If you've had a bankruptcy anytime within the past seven to ten years, or if you've had medical bill problems, or other situations where your credit score is so low you can't get a mortgage through the regular channel," then you may be right for a B-C loan.

You may also be a B-C borrower if you own too many pieces of investment property, don't wish to disclose all of your income or assets, you've been self-employed for too short a period of time, or you're purchasing a unique piece of property that doesn't fit into the secondary lending market's A-borrower mold.

Subprime lending became hugely popular after the 2001 recession, but has virtually disappeared after the Great Recession. If you have mediocre credit, say 600 and above, you can get a loan with a higher interest rate. But if you have awful credit, it's almost impossible to get what was traditionally known as a subprime loan unless you're working with a hard-money lender or a predatory lender charging credit card interest rates.

# Question 65: Should I Automatically Get a Home Equity Loan or Home Equity Line of Credit (HELOC) When I Close on My Home?

The last time Sam and I refinanced, we were offered a free home equity line of credit at a fantastic rate: One point below the prime rate. Today, the going rates for home equity loans are one point (or more) above the prime rate. In other words, it's a variable-rate loan, but we don't pay anything unless we tap the home equity line of credit.

It doesn't happen very often anymore unless you're putting down an excessive amount of equity, or if you're doing an 80/10/10 (also known as a "piggyback") mortgage.

If you are offered a free home equity line of credit, that won't raise the rate you get on your primary home loan. You should take it, even if you have no plans for the cash—you never know when a medical emergency, job loss, untimely death, or other tragedy will cause a cash crunch in your budget. It can be your rainy-day backup if you've already run through your emergency fund.

# Question 66: What Are Predatory Lenders? How Do I Spot One?

A lender who charges excessive fees. A lender who tells you your loan application won't be approved if you don't buy high-priced credit insurance. A lender who tells you your credit isn't good when it is.

These are some of the characteristics of predatory lenders—bad-apple lenders who prey on unsuspecting or unsophisticated borrowers. And plenty of borrowers have fallen victim over the years. As Biata found out, the dangers include not just losing all of the equity you've built up in your home, but losing the house itself—and it could kill your credit score in the process.

---

**BIATA'S STORY**

A Polish immigrant, Biata came to the United States more than fifteen years ago. She married, got a job, had a daughter, and bought a three-bedroom flat in Chicago. One day, her husband simply walked out. Biata found she couldn't quite make the mortgage payments on her single salary, so she went to the lender, a reputable bank.

The loan agent said, "We can't help you, but I know someone who can," and steered her toward a predatory lender.

Biata refinanced her home loan with the predatory lender. The loan was supposed to be for $200,000. Within four years, she owed—according to the lender—more than $500,000 in interest and principal—even though she had paid the lender more than $300,000 in those four years (and had the receipts from Western Union to back up her claim).

The last time I spoke with Biata, she was on the verge of losing her home. Her credit history had been tarnished, and her credit score was sunk. She was sick with worry over her situation and couldn't find a way to get out.

What was even worse about Biata's situation is that she did everything right. By going to her original, legitimate lender to refinance, she should have been given a good deal. Instead, she was falsely told the bank couldn't help her and was served up as a victim to a particularly awful predatory lender.

---

## Warning Signs

It's difficult to define what a predatory lender is. In some states, a lender is considered "predatory" by the interest rate charged or by the points and fees tacked on to the loan. In other states, a lender is defined as predatory if they continue to remortgage the same house over and over again without benefiting the homeowner.

Several branches of the federal government, including the Department of Housing and Urban Development and the Federal Trade Commission, have been working in tandem with the Mortgage Bankers Association of America, national and local mortgage and real estate companies, and trade organizations to highlight the financial dangers associated with getting a loan from a predatory lender. The Mortgage Bankers Association has published a website (StopMortgageFraud.com) that highlights some important warning signs of predatory lending.

- **False information.** Predatory lenders will often encourage you to include false or misleading information on your mortgage application, in direct violation of federal law.
- **Blank spaces on your application.** Were you asked to leave spaces or signature lines blank on your application? Take a look at your "final" application. Was information changed?
- **Missing information.** Did the lender give you a good-faith estimate, a truth-in-lending disclosure, a settlement statement (at closing), or a special information booklet on lending about borrower's rights?
- **Payments going up.** Has your lender suggested refinancing your home loan several times, ostensibly to take advantage of lower rates, but you find each time you "refinance" that your payment and interest rate rise? Has the total amount you owe on the home risen as well? This is called "serial refinancing."
- **Daily interest rate penalty.** Do your loan documents reveal that your interest rate calculation will change to require you to pay "daily interest" in instances when your payments are late?
- **Loan amount is too high.** Is the loan amount higher than the sales price of the home? Is it more than you asked for? Did you do a "cash-out refinance" but never got the cash?
- **Unexpected costs.** Were you charged additional costs and fees at your closing that were not disclosed previously on your good-faith estimate or your TRID statement? The new TRID rules allow you to back out of the loan if this happens but require the lender to send you the exact closing costs seventy-two hours in advance of the closing so that you have time to review them.
- **Credit insurance tacked on to the loan.** Were you required to buy credit insurance as a condition for getting your loan approved? It is illegal to tell a borrower

that purchasing credit insurance is a condition for approval. While credit insurance itself is not illegal, it is generally a waste of money and can significantly raise the cost of your loan.

- **Hefty prepayment penalties that lock you in for years.** Predatory lenders love prepayment penalties, because they lock in a borrower to a superhigh interest rate for a long, long time. These have virtually disappeared since the Great Recession.

While knowing the warning signs of predatory lending can help, each borrower (including you) must be vigilant to make sure you're not caught in a predatory lender's web. As a spokesperson from the MBA explained, "It's up to each borrower to stand on the front lines and fight predatory lending with knowledge."

In other words, if you know your stuff, you won't get caught. And if you use a conventional lender or a well-known online lender, you should be fine.

## The Last Word in Predatory Lending—for Now

In 2014, the Consumer Financial Protection Bureau's (CFPB) Qualified Mortgage Standards went into effect. They prohibit a creditor or lender from making a higher-priced mortgage without regard to a consumer's ability to repay that mortgage. According to the CFPB's website (in 2017), "The final rule implements sections 1411 and 1412 of the Dodd-Frank Wall Street Reform and Consumer Protection Act (Dodd-Frank Act), which generally require creditors to make a reasonable, good faith determination of a consumer's ability to repay any consumer credit transaction secured by a dwelling (excluding an open-end credit plan, timeshare plan, reverse mortgage, or temporary loan) and establishes certain protections from liability under this requirement for "qualified mortgages." The final rule also implements section 1414 of the Dodd-Frank Act, which limits prepayment penalties. Finally, the final rule requires creditors to retain evidence of compliance with the rule for three years after a covered loan is "consummated."

In short, the final rules require a lender to be able to show that it measured a borrower's Ability to Repay for three years after the loan has been granted.

These rules have put the kibosh on predatory lenders for the moment, and have made it tougher for borrowers to qualify for mortgages. Whether these rules (and even the CFPB) survive the post-Obama years remains to be seen.

# Question 67: What Do I Do If I'm Rejected for My Loan?

After all the hours spent searching for the perfect home, negotiating the purchase price, working with your attorney to perfect the contract, and applying for a mortgage, it's extremely disappointing and frustrating to be rejected for a loan. But before you give up and decide you'll never be able to afford a home, you should know that hundreds of people get rejected for loans every day. Sometimes it's their fault, and sometimes lenders reject them for reasons that seem to defy logic or comprehension. Sometimes the issue is fixable, and sometimes you'll have to let go of the perfect home because you'll need more time to get your finances in approvable shape.

Sam once had a client who was rejected for a loan by several lenders. Her ex-husband had declared bankruptcy, but because her name was on some of the credit card accounts, she was tarnished along with his fall. Another first-time buyer was rejected because she had just bought a new car and the lender decided her debt-to-income ratios were out of whack. A third first-time buyer couple was rejected by a handful of lenders because the husband truthfully stated that his business was being sued for $100,000. As the lawsuit was ongoing, the lenders decided it was too big a risk.

Let's look at the reasons why you might be rejected for a loan:

## 1. Credit Report Problems

When you apply for a mortgage, or any other type of loan, the bank or mortgage broker will pull up your credit report. This report includes all of your financial information, including every credit card with their balances and your payment record, current and past addresses, any bankruptcies or other credit problems, bank and money market accounts, any outstanding loans, and a host of other credit information. The credit report is used to determine whether or not you're a good credit risk.

A recent study showed that as many as 85 percent of all credit histories contain at least one factual error, and 25 percent contain errors bad enough to reject your credit application. Fixing any errors on your credit report can raise your score and help you bypass this hurdle with mortgage lenders.

There are numerous types of credit report problems (which may or may not be your fault) that would cause a lender to reject your application for a loan. First, if you've ever missed a credit card payment, or been late with a credit card payment, or defaulted on a prior mortgage or school or car loan, it will probably show up on your credit report. If you've filed for bankruptcy within the past seven years, that will be on there, too. And if you haven't paid your taxes, or there has been a judgment filed against you (perhaps for nonpayment of spousal or child support), you can bet that will be on there. Failure to pay your landlord, doctor, or hospital may also turn into a black spot on your credit report.

Credit report companies get their information about you from companies that extend credit, like department stores, lenders, banks, and credit card companies. The information is updated on a periodic basis, sometimes daily, sometimes annually. Since people actually enter this information into the company computer, there's a good chance that a mistake has been made somewhere along the line.

If you feel that your credit report is wrong, experts say it's best to take it up with the organization or company that is claiming you owe them money. Try to find documentation that proves the mistake and have it corrected as quickly as possible. If there's a more serious problem, such as a bankruptcy filing, a judgment, or if you've not filed your income taxes or "forgotten" to pay back a school loan, you may have a more difficult time getting the lender to approve your loan application. If you've been late paying your bills, regroup by paying in full and on time for six months to a year to prove to the lender that the late payments were an aberration. Be sure all your taxes are paid in full and on time.

**FIRST-TIME BUYER TIP:** If the credit report contains errors, you should contact the credit bureau immediately. A recent law requires the credit bureau to deal with your written request to correct errors within thirty days.

## 2. Inconsistencies in Information

Sometimes lenders will find inconsistencies between what you've told them on the application and the information that the loan officer discovers. If you say your income is $45,000 annually and the lender calls your employer for verification and finds out that it's only $30,000, that's probably grounds for rejection. The lender figures that if you've lied about something as basic and easily checkable as your income, then you may also have lied about something more important.

Most lenders, upon discovering minor inconsistencies (if you say your income is $45,000 annually and it's really $44,500), will ask you about them and give you a chance to explain. Others won't. The bottom line is this: Be straight with the lender. Answer his or her questions honestly and, if you don't know the answer to a question, say so. Don't make anything up. If you get rejected for providing false or misleading information, consider the lost application fee a lesson that honesty is always the best policy.

## 3. Employed Less than Two Years

Lenders like to see that you're earning a stable income. They like consistency. They like knowing that someone has been employing you and will continue to employ you. That's why most lenders will generally reject you for a loan if you've been employed for less than two years.

As with most rules, however, there are exceptions. If you're a secretary making $50,000 and the company across the hall offers you a job as an executive secretary for $65,000, most lenders will be delighted to see you take the job and earn the extra income, even if it's a couple of weeks before closing. Why? Because lenders like lateral moves (that is, the same job for better pay at a competing company) or a step up the corporate ladder (from vice president to president). Although you're changing jobs, you're changing for the better, and the lender should be understanding.

If, however, you spend a year as a mechanic, then become a short-order chef for six months, then move into used car sales, the lender will probably shake his or her head and reject your application, even if you've moved up in income—too much movement, not enough consistency.

## 4. Being Self-Employed

Self-employment adds an extra twist to the process of getting a mortgage because lenders don't view self-employed workers as being as stable as those who are employed by others. (Although the good news is, you can't be fired!)

Lenders will rarely approve a mortgage unless you have been self-employed for at least two years. When you apply for the mortgage, you'll have to bring profit-and-loss statements, as well as your last two tax returns. The lender won't look at your gross income. Net income (that is, gross income minus expenses) is what's important. This is important to remember when looking for a home, because you may be grossly overestimating the amount of money you'll be able to borrow. For example, if you have gross earnings of $75,000 and $50,000 in expenses, a lender will consider your income to be $25,000, even though you may feel you can spend more. Some mortgage brokers specialize in getting loans for self-employed people, and work with lenders who keep these loans in their portfolio, and therefore have more relaxed lending policies.

If you're self-employed for less than two years, but are taking home a significant and reliable income, you can look for a mortgage broker who specializes in placing loans of this type. Just know that if you're self-employed, getting a mortgage is going to be a long and somewhat arduous task. You may also have trouble if you're employed but all or most of your salary is from commission. Try to avoid paying any fees up front, so that in case you aren't approved, you won't lose any money.

## 5. Losing Your Job

If you lose your job before the closing, it can mean an instant rejection of your loan application. If you're married or are buying with a partner and your spouse earns enough money to support the mortgage payments, then the lender may approve the loan anyway, but in your spouse's or partner's name only. If your application is denied based on job loss, wait until your job prospects change and you've found a new job. Try to find something in the same field, for about the same (or more) money, otherwise you may be subjected to the two-year employment rule.

## 6. Unapproved Condo Building or New Development

Sometimes you'll get rejected for a loan and you won't be the problem. Institutions that buy loans on the secondary market have a specific set of guidelines that lenders must follow. One of these rules is the 50 percent rule for condominiums.* Fannie Mae and Freddie Mac, which buy the vast majority of loans on the secondary market, like their home buyers to purchase condos in buildings in which owners occupy at least 50 percent of the building. Why? It's that stability issue. Lenders believe that homeowners will take better care of property than renters. This makes sense, as owners have more of a stake in a property than renters.

Historically, condo buildings that have a high percentage of renters can lose their value. If you're rejected because of the 50 percent rule, you may want to seek out other lenders who will keep your loan in their own portfolio (instead of reselling it on the secondary market to Fannie Mae or Freddie Mac), and who may be more flexible on this rule. If the building is less than 50 percent owner occupied, you may want to rethink your purchase, unless you're doing seller financing. Or you may want to seek out a lender that has made loans to other homeowners in that building.

Those buyers who purchase new-construction townhouses and condominiums may also have a tough time finding a lender who will approve their loan. Conventional lenders like to see development projects that have been in existence for more than two years. They like to see a new-construction project more than 50 percent owner occupied before they'll grant a loan; otherwise the project could go into default and the properties might drop in value (an anathema to a lender, who wants to protect the investment). If you get rejected for a loan for your new townhouse or condo purchase, check with the developer. They'll usually arrange for some sort of financing package from a lender, who will then keep the loans in-house for one to two years before reselling them on the secondary market.

## 7. Low Appraisal

Another reason people get rejected for loans is that it doesn't "appraise out." When lenders say that a home doesn't appraise out, they mean that the bank's appraiser has determined that the home is worth less than you contracted to pay for it. Let's say you offered

---

* This rule has changed over the years and has been as high as 70 percent in the past.

$150,000 for a home, with 20 percent ($30,000) as a cash down payment, which is all the savings you have in the world. You're counting on the bank lending you the additional $120,000 to purchase the home. But when the bank actually sends in the appraiser, the home is appraised at $120,000, and the bank will only lend you 80 percent (or $96,000). You need to come up with an additional $24,000 in cash to close on the home, but if you can't come up with the extra cash (and first-time buyers are perennially short on cash), the lender will reject your loan application.

## 8. Adding New Debt

Sometimes buyers think they'll be able to get away with making a large purchase after they've been approved for a mortgage. For example, if you get approved for your loan and then two weeks before closing you go out and buy (or even lease) a new car with hefty monthly payments, you'll likely get rejected for your mortgage just before closing. Why? What few people realize is that lenders may do two credit checks: before they approve your loan and before you close on it. Lenders are increasingly watching out for folks who incur large new debts that may interfere with their repayment of the mortgage. So don't buy that new car just before closing. Wait until after.

## 9. Refusal to Provide New Documentation

If the loan officer calls you up and asks for additional documentation, by all means provide it. Not providing information is grounds for loan application rejection. If the loan officer continually asks for additional information, or asks you to send material you've already sent, this may be indicative of an extremely disorganized and pressed office. Or you may have another problem.

## 10. The Gambling Game

As I discussed earlier, this isn't an official scam, but it happens often enough that first-time buyers, repeat buyers, and homeowners looking to refinance their loans should be aware of it. As you have now seen, there are plenty of reasons why a loan application might not be approved. One problem that doesn't get much media attention is this: Some loan officers gamble with your locked-in interest rates, hoping to put more money in their own pockets.

Although that sounds surprising (it is) and perhaps illegal (technically, but the illegality isn't enforced as long as the lender lives up to his lock agreement), a little explanation might help you understand why loan officers might gamble with your rate.

To eliminate the uncertainty of changeable interest rates, borrowers may pay their prospective lender for the privilege of locking in a specific interest rate and a number of points. The lock is good for a predefined time, usually thirty to sixty days. When you lock in your rate, you must close on your mortgage before the lock expires, or you lose the preset interest rate. Experts say that the mortgage loan process can easily go awry, particularly when interest rates are headed up. Lenders, nervous about their investments and eager to charge the highest interest rate possible, are not as excited to close on their loans as when interest rates are dropping.

According to the Office of the Commissioner of Savings and Residential Finance, which regulates and monitors mortgage brokers, mortgage bankers, and financial institutions in Illinois, lenders often "play the float" with your mortgage interest rate. Although you think you've locked in at a certain rate with a certain number of points, lenders will, in essence, gamble with the rate rather than actually lock it in, hoping that interest rates will slip further. The loan officer and the mortgage company will then pocket the difference between the new current interest rate and the rate you locked into.

The problems start when interest rates begin to go up instead of down. If the loan officer has been playing the float with your loan, and the rate goes up, he will have to pay the difference between your locked-in interest rate and the current market rate out of his pocket to close on the loan. And because loan officers are loath to pay out, they will often find something "wrong" with your application at the last minute (such as new documentation that's needed, etc.), forcing you to accept a higher interest rate or more points, says one loan officer.

If you feel as if your loan rejection is without merit, and can prove that you sent all the information required, you may want to complain to your state regulatory body. The squeaky wheel gets the grease. Make sure you are heard loud and clear.

## 11. Illegal Discrimination

Recent investigations and surveys of the mortgage banking industry seem to prove that minorities, specifically African Americans,[*] are twice as likely to be rejected for a loan as Caucasians. And that (rightfully) makes people very angry. If you feel you've been rejected for a loan because of your race or sex or sexual orientation, you should file a complaint with your state attorney general's office, the state office that regulates the mortgage banking industry, and other regulatory agencies, including the Department of Housing and Urban Development (HUD). If the rejection is for an FHA loan, notify your local housing authority office.

---

[*] This happens to other minorities and people of protected classes as well, including Latinos, LGBTQ, and sometimes pregnant women or single mothers.

# CHAPTER 8

# Putting Together the Deal

## Question 68: How Do I Decide What to Offer for the Home? And, How Do I Make an Offer?

If you've been prequalified or preapproved by a mortgage lender, or if you've figured out by yourself how much new debt you can manage, you already know your uppermost financial limit. That's the number you can't go beyond, unless interest rates change or you and whoever is buying this property with you figure out a way to earn more money, win the lottery, or inherit a bundle of cash.

Just remember this: What you can afford to spend has nothing to do with how much a seller is asking for his or her house. The seller wants the most money possible. You want to pay the least amount possible. The rest is subject to negotiation.

But we're getting ahead of ourselves. It's important to determine how much a house is worth before you make an offer. (This would seem obvious, but there are plenty of buyers who get caught up in the heat of the moment—especially in a hot seller's market—and just offer up a number.)

The answer to the question of worth lies with your broker or agent. He or she has access to the sales data that can tell you what homes in the neighborhood are selling for and how long they took to sell. Because of the differences in the fiduciary responsibilities between a buyer's broker and a seller's broker, however, you'll have to proceed on a slightly different course in getting this information and putting it to use.

If you're using a buyer's broker, and assuming he or she is at least competent, if not fabulous, it should be relatively easy to ask the buyer's broker for "comps" (comparable values of like properties that have recently sold in your neighborhood). Once you have the comps, you and your buyer's broker can begin an ongoing discussion about what the comps mean and how they apply to various homes in which you're interested.

If you're working with a seller's broker, he or she is required by law in most states to provide you with everything you need to make an informed decision on how much to offer. However, you may have to specifically request that the seller's broker provide you with recent sale comps, as well as the listing prices for similar homes in the neighborhood. You may also request information on the number of days a particular home has been on the market.

## Tell Me Again Why Comps Are Helpful

Comps are homes that have recently been sold (preferably in the past three to six months) and are similar in size, location, and amenities to the home on which you want to bid. Comps give you an idea of what other sellers have been paid for their homes. Finding out the listing prices is also important, because comparing the list prices with the sale prices tells you exactly what percentage of their sales price sellers are getting. (As an aside, study after study has found that homes sell, on average, for 6 percent below list price. But that assumes that the home is not overpriced, and that the market is well balanced with an even number of buyers and sellers. If a home is well priced it is listed at or just a bit above what comparable homes in the neighborhood have sold for. In the hot seller's market we saw during the latter half of the 1990s, from 2003 to 2006, and in 2016 and 2017, many sellers received list price—or more—for their homes.)

## Figuring Out the Right Offer

Let's say House A was listed at $100,000 and sold for $96,000 (Seller A received 96 percent of his list price). House B was also priced at $100,000, and sold for $95,000 (Seller B received 95 percent of her list price). Home A and Home B are nearly identical homes in more or less the same good physical condition. Seller C, however, put a few extras into his home, such as a wood-burning fireplace and upgraded carpet. His home was priced at $110,000 and he received $104,000 (Seller C received 95 percent of his list price).

Now, you go to a showing at House D, which is in the same condition and is the same size as Houses A and B, but Seller D is asking $110,000 for her house. Based on the sales prices of other homes in the subdivision, how much would you pay for the house? Although Sellers A, B, and C received around 95 percent of their list price, their homes were competitively priced. Seller D's home is not competitively priced. On the other hand, now that several houses have sold at just under $95,000, the owner of House D might be pushing the envelope a bit. And, depending on the market strength, that might not be unreasonable.

But back to you: If you think the true value of House D is around $95,000 or $96,000, and the most you want to offer Seller D for her house is $95,000 (95 percent of $100,000, which is the amount at which the house should be priced), you have to make a decision about how much lower than that you want to offer initially.

Unless you're in a heated situation where several parties may be bidding on the same house you want (see Question 74, What Do I Do in a Multiple-Bid Situation?), or if you're in a tight seller's market (sellers are getting almost exactly what they want for their properties, in a very short amount of time), never offer the list price for a home. Instead, offer between 5 to 10 percent below the maximum price you want to pay for the home. So if you've decided you're not going to pay any more than $95,000 for Seller D's home, then you may want to consider an initial offer of $90,000. That's the start of negotiation.

Of course, the trick is to know what you want to pay for a property before you make your first offer. Instead of emotion, that decision should be based on logic and reasoning. If you can't get a clear idea of how much to offer based on the comps your broker has provided to you, ask him or her for another set of comps. And if your search goes on for more than three months, you'll need another set, as the market continually changes.

If you're working with a buyer's broker, you should feel free to ask what he or she would pay for the house. Buyer's brokers, because they owe their fiduciary loyalty to you as the buyer, should be forthcoming with how much they think a property is worth. If your seller's broker is less forthcoming, ask how much he or she would allow his or her children to pay for the home. Remember that he or she has a fiduciary responsibility to the seller. According to a strict interpretation of the law, the seller's broker can't do anything but suggest you pay list price.

**FIRST-TIME BUYER TIP:** If you have a dual agent (representing both sides), a non-agent, or a transactional agent working with you, it's effectively the same as a seller's broker. Ask for the information you need, and any explanation for data you don't understand. Finally, if you feel lost and can't get what you need from your transactional agent, dual agent, or non-agent, you are entitled to go to the managing broker of the firm and ask to have a buyer's broker assigned to work with you.

## Making an Offer for New Construction

Making an offer for a new home that has yet to be built is in some ways more complex than making an offer for an existing house. At least with the existing home, all of the appliances, tiling, wall coverings, window treatments, and siding are already there. With new construction, you'll often be buying from blueprints, or perhaps after seeing a model home built and decorated for your viewing pleasure.

Part of the offer and negotiation process includes a myriad of choices—everything from what kind of tiles and carpet you want, to whether you want to upgrade to the full basement with the extra-tall ceiling and a concrete floor. Do you want to add on the fourth bedroom upstairs instead of the double-high entryway?* Do you want the three-car garage that is designed so that, in the future, you can turn one of the bays into an office or a mudroom? (This is where your reality check from Question 10 comes in handy again!)

As a standard rule, developers rarely negotiate down on price unless they're stuck with a final unit or two that won't sell for whatever reason. More typically, the lowest prices will be offered when the development first opens for business. As sales activity heats up, the price of homes in subsequent phases (you'll often hear about Phase I, Phase II, and Phase III of a development) will rise.

Being the first to buy into a new subdivision often means you get the best price and perhaps the best upgrade package on the options that are available. The risk you take is that the subdivision will fail to sell out, or the developer will go belly-up and the investors will take over and offer the remaining properties at a price far below what you paid.

When you make your offer, you can try to negotiate the developer down on price. But

---

\* I think maximizing your interior space is always the savvy choice, because adding space is so expensive later on.

you'll probably have better luck asking for more options and upgrades being thrown into the mix. For example, you might pay full price, but receive upgrades on appliances, wiring, carpet, and tile choices. If you're one of the first to buy into a condo development and the parking is being sold separately, you may be able to get the developer to throw in the space for nothing, or to give you two spaces at a discount.

 **NEW CONSTRUCTION TIP:** One of the places developers make a lot of money is in the options and upgrades. It's far too easy to walk into a $300,000, four-bedroom, 2½ bath house and then spend another $100,000 (yes, you read that right) on options and upgrades the salesperson convinces you you just have to have. In fact, new studies show that the average new construction home buyer will spend more than 10 percent of the purchase price on options and upgrades. On a $300,000 house, that's more than $30,000 in upgrades.[*] While it's generally easier and cheaper to add these things at the beginning of the build, you should visit a bunch of competing subdivisions and price out the various packages these other developers give to home buyers, so you can make the most of the leverage you have in the negotiation process. (If this process sounds a lot like buying a new car—only more complex—you're on the right path. The big difference is that new cars depreciate in value and you're hoping that your new home will appreciate.)

**JACKIE'S STORY**

When Jackie was in her early thirties, she became the editor of a real estate section of a major metropolitan newspaper. After working there for a while, it occurred to her she should stop paying rent and instead purchase a home.

She talked to all of the real estate writers to find out which developer had the best reputation and settled on a converted school that was being turned into condominiums. She was one of the first people to buy in the development and, armed with the information from her writers, she negotiated all kinds of extras and upgrades when she purchased the unit.

---

[*] When we bought an investment condo off the plans more than ten years ago, we spent an additional 14 percent of the purchase price on options and upgrades.

But her big coup was getting the developer to throw in her parking space for free. Two weeks later, the developer started charging $15,000 for the spot. Four years later, Jackie got married and sold her unit—for a big profit!

The old cliché is true: Knowledge is power. If you know what other developers are offering in similar developments, and use that knowledge in your negotiations, you're much more likely to get what you want.

## Question 69: What Goes into the Actual Offer to Purchase or Contract to Purchase?

There are three basic pieces to an offer: the address or description of the property, consideration or the price you are prepared to pay, and the date on which the closing will take place.

A valid offer can be written on anything, including a paper napkin, and can read as follows: "I, Ilyce R. Glink, offer to buy 1 Willow Lane for $125,500, to close on July 13, 2018."

Although property has been bought and sold this way for centuries, making an offer today is usually a bit more complex. In some states, it's customary for the broker to use a "contract to purchase" form when making an offer. In other states, the broker has a preprinted "offer for purchase" form. Whichever is used, you'll generally sit with the broker and discuss all sorts of issues, such as:

- Contingencies (see Question 71)
- Earnest money, also known as your Good-Faith Deposit (Question 70)
- Any requests you may have for personal property (such as appliances, lamps, attached bookcases, and so on)

After you fill in the form and sign it, your broker will then present the offer to the seller and his or her broker. If you are buying a FSBO (a home for sale by owner), you will have to make the presentation yourself. If you don't understand the contract and its implications, don't sign it. Consult a real estate attorney first.

**FIRST-TIME BUYER TIP:** As the Internet continues to disrupt the real estate market and facilitate the sale of homes, more sellers may try to sell without a broker's help, and save the 5 to 7 percent commission. If 8 to 12 percent of homes are estimated to sell without a broker's assistance, in ten years perhaps 20 to 30 percent (or more—although agents don't like to hear you say it) of homes could be sold by owner. Savvy home buyers need to know how to make a quality offer that any seller, represented or not, will be happy to accept, and how to sound good while presenting that offer. Essentially, in a presentation, you go over the offer for purchase with the seller, point by point, discussing things like price, closing date, date of possession, and the contingencies along the way. As long as you're calm and professional, and consult with a real estate attorney ahead of time, you'll do just fine if you end up presenting without the assistance of a broker.

Typically, buyers represented by brokers do not attend the offer presentation. But sometimes they wait downstairs. (Though this generally isn't a good idea. You don't want to seem too eager, because it cuts into your negotiating power. And waiting downstairs is "too eager" by half in my book.)

## LEO AND GENNA'S STORY

Leo and Genna looked at fifty homes before they found the one they wanted to buy. It was a nice-looking three-bedroom, 2½ bath house with a big living room, dining room, and sunroom facing a small porch and backyard.

Because there was so much interest in the property, Leo and Genna decided right on the spot (at the first showing) to make an offer. They sat at the kitchen table with their broker and drew up the offer, then waited while the broker went upstairs to present the offer to the sellers.

Although this was their first purchase, Leo and Genna took the time to thoroughly investigate the neighborhood and market before looking at homes. These savvy first-time buyers knew almost immediately how much they were going to offer for the house because they had seen so many similar homes in the neighborhood and knew at what prices they had been sold over the previous six months. That knowledge enabled them to act fast when the time was right.

## The Pressure Cooker

Sometimes, getting what you want hinges on how quickly you're able to act under pressure. Don't allow yourself to be sucked in to a point where you're no longer able to rationally discuss the offer and its implications. If you're finding yourself dragged along by the current, perhaps against your will, take a time-out. *Remember, there is more than one right house for you.*

Homeowners typically move between five and seven times in their life. If you fall prey to the notion that this home is the only one for you, you may offer too much for it, thereby making it an imperfect choice.

 **NEW CONSTRUCTION TIP:** Making an offer for a newly constructed home often means sitting down with the developer's agent and your agent (if you have one) and working out the price plus the upgrades and options that are to be included. If the developer is mobbed with offers, you may have to make a reservation or be wait-listed for a home, and you may not find out until later whether or not you are actually going to be able to purchase it.

## Deconstructing the Offer to Purchase or Contract to Purchase

An offer to purchase is usually a much simpler document than a contract to purchase. Why? Because the contract to purchase must be much more specific about the property description, fixtures, exclusions, all of the necessary legal language for property transfer, rights to sue for specific performance (if the buyer or seller backs out of the contract on a whim), damages, brokers' fees, etc.

Every city and state will have its own real estate or Realtor (member of the National Association of Realtors) association that provides standard form contracts for the purchase and sale of real estate. You should also be able to get the contracts you need from your real estate attorney, if you're buying a house without an agent. In a pinch, there are preprinted forms available online, although you will need to consult with an attorney to find out if these preprinted forms favor the seller or the buyer in the transaction (they're rarely neutral). Though the contracts are similar, real estate laws do vary from state to state.

Just remember that it's likely these contracts were written from the seller's perspective. (Originally, all brokers were seller's brokers, so that bias tends to remain.) As a buyer, you're going to want to look over the forms carefully and, in all likelihood, hire a real estate lawyer to help you sort them out.

**NEW CONSTRUCTION TIP:** If you're purchasing new construction from a developer or builder, you'll probably use the developer's contract, which will likely be written to favor the developer. Some developers will allow attorneys to modify the contract to make it more even-handed. Do not attempt to modify the contract yourself. Engage a real estate attorney to assist you, especially if you are not working with a buyer's agent.

## Offer to Purchase

Let's look at an offer to purchase real estate contract that starts out like a letter. It is addressed:

To: _____

seller(s)

There is a place for the date of the offer. Then:

The property herein referred to is identified as follows:
                    (Here you would fill in the address of the property.)

I hereby offer to buy said property, which has been offered to me by
            (fill in name of seller's broker), as your broker, under the following terms
            and conditions:

The contract now allows you to check off whether you will pay for the property by check or cash. Next comes how much you will pay for the property, and in what stages:

$ _____ is paid herewith as a deposit to bind this offer.

$ _____ is to be paid as an additional deposit upon the execution of the purchase and sale Agreement provided for below.

$ _____ is to be paid at the time of delivery of the Deed in cash, or by certified, cashier's, treasurer's or bank check.

Next comes a statement that tells the seller that the offer is only good until a certain time on a certain date. The seller has until that time to accept the offer, or the offer for purchase becomes invalid. The seller may counteroffer, and then further negotiation would take place. The seller is then notified that the offer is contingent upon the execution of the standard purchase and sale agreement.

Next comes the closing date:

A good and sufficient Deed, conveying a good and clear record and marketable title shall be delivered at 12:00 Noon on [FILL IN DATE], at the appropriate Registry of Deeds, unless some other time and place are mutually agreed upon in writing.

After another paragraph, in which the buyer promises to forfeit his deposit if he or she does not fulfill his or her obligations, and one that says "time is of the essence," there is a space to write in any additional terms and conditions, or to attach any riders.

Finally, the document is signed by the buyers, and the receipt for deposit at the bottom of the page is filled out. The standard purchase and sale agreement forms can be up to two or three times as long as what I've laid out.

Real estate attorneys say that most buyers never read the contract. But you should. The following section walks you through a typical contract, point by point:

- **Parties.** Fill in the name of the seller and buyer.
- **Description.** Give the address, title reference, and description of the property. For example: "the land with the buildings thereon, numbered 391 Waverley Avenue, Newton, Massachusetts, Middlesex County, being shown as Lot B on a 'Plan of Land in Newton belonging to Katherine F. Cameron,' E. S. Smithe, Surveyor,

dated May 1914, recorded with Middlesex South Registry Deeds Book 4741 and more particularly described in deed to Seller dated May 27, 1977, recorded at Middlesex South Registry Deeds in Book 13200, Page 450."

- **Buildings, Structures, Improvements, Fixtures.** This is a general list of the buildings, structures, and improvements that are included with the sale. You should delete, exclude, or add anything appropriate. In particular, list items that the sellers could take with them, but which should be part of the deal, like the dishwasher, washer, dryer, and refrigerator. Some of these items will be decided based on local custom. For example, in downtown Chicago, all appliances stay with the house. In the northern and western suburbs, refrigerators, washers, and dryers generally go with the sellers to their new home. (Hint: Your agent can fill you in on the local custom if you're not aware of it.)
- **Title Deed.** Specifically note any restrictions, easements (rights other people may have to use your property or otherwise restrict your use of the property), rights, or obligations that you are willing to accept on your title and delete those that you are not. Your attorney will help you with this.
- **Plans.** The plans should have already been approved and recorded in advance by the seller, and they should comply with all laws, allowing a clear transfer to the buyer.
- **Registered Title.** There are some states that have a registration system for title.
- **Purchase Price.** Fill in the amount and write out the amount to be paid as a deposit, the amount of the escrow (that is, money held in trust by a third party) "upon execution of this agreement," and the remainder at closing.
- **Time for Performance: Delivery of Deed.** State the time, date, and place for closing.
- **Possession and Conditions of Premises.** Says that the buyer receives full possession free of tenants and occupants at closing, that the property does not violate any building or zoning laws, and that the buyer shall be entitled to inspect the premises before closing.
- **Extension to Perfect Title or Make Premises Conform.** Gives the seller thirty days to correct any problems with the property's title.
- **Failure to Perfect Title or Make Premises Conform.** Should the seller fail to deliver good title, your money will be refunded.
- **Buyer's Election to Accept Title.** If something impairs the property's title, such as

a mechanic's or tax lien, you can elect to take the property as is, subject to the lien, and deduct the lien amount from the purchase price. Should a disaster occur, such as a fire, you can elect to take the home as is and be compensated from the insurance proceeds, or take a reduction in the price of the home to cover the damage.

- **Acceptance of Deed**. Acceptance of the deed at closing means that the seller has fulfilled all duties and obligations under the contract.
- **Use of Money to Clear Title**. The seller may leave behind money at closing to pay off any liens against the property.
- **Insurance**. The seller promises to maintain a certain amount of insurance. The amount is usually negotiated, but should be sufficient to cover the cost of restoring the property after a fire or other disaster.
- **Adjustments**. List of expenses (like water or assessments) and taxes that must be prorated for the portion of the month or year the seller owned the house until closing. You will be credited at closing for these expenses.
- **Adjustment of Unassessed and Abated Taxes**. Taxes that have not yet been assessed for the year are usually prorated based on the prior year's taxes according to a local formula. (Sometimes this is 110 or 120 percent of the prior year's taxes.)
- **Broker's Fee**. Spells out who gets the commission and how much.
- **Broker's Warranty**. Names the brokers and warrants that they are licensed.
- **Deposit**. Spells out the escrow agreement and who will receive the interest on the account.
- **Buyer's Default and Damages**. If the buyer fails to buy the property, the seller gets to keep the escrow money.
- **Release by Husband or Wife**. The spouse agrees to release any claim, even if he or she isn't on the title. Omitted if seller is divorced or widowed.
- **Liability of Trustee, Shareholder, or Beneficiary**. Included if one of the parties is represented by a trustee, otherwise omitted.
- **Warranties and Representations**. Whatever promises the seller makes to the buyer regarding the conditions of the property.
- **Mortgage Contingency Clause**. Standard on some contracts, otherwise added as a rider. (See Question 71.)
- **Construction Agreement**. Legal language that sets up the contract for construction dates and which parties will participate.
- **Lead Paint Law**. Federal rules require sellers who live in properties built before

1978 to disclose that a home may have lead.[*] Some states have gone further. In Massachusetts, if a child under the age of six resides in any residential premises where paint, plaster, or other material contains dangerous levels of lead, the owner must remove or cover the paint to make it safe for children.

- **Smoke Detectors and Other Certifications.** In Massachusetts, the seller agrees to provide a certificate from the local fire department stating the property is equipped with smoke detectors. In Illinois, you must provide a certificate saying that you comply with the local ordinance.
- **Additional Provisions.** This is the place for any additional riders to the agreement.

## Condominium Contracts

There is a difference between purchasing a condo and purchasing a single-family home: when you purchase a condo you are buying real estate plus an interest in the common areas managed by the homeowners' association.

Sometimes real estate sales contracts for condominiums contain special provisions that are not applicable to single-family houses. For example, some condo boards have the right of first refusal when a condo unit is sold. This allows the board to purchase the unit if it decides that's in the best interest of the condo building. In a sales contract, the seller will agree to procure the release or waiver of any option or right of first refusal.

In any case, your condo contract should specify that the seller must give you the condo declaration, condo rules, and association minutes for the past two years, plus the property budget for the past two years, plus the current year within ten days of signing the contract.[†]

---

[*] According to the EPA.gov website, federal law requires that before home buyers are obligated under a contract to buy housing built prior to 1978, they must receive the following from the home seller: (1) an EPA-approved information pamphlet on identifying and controlling lead-based paint hazards titled *Protect Your Family from Lead in Your Home* (PDF); (2) any known information concerning the presence of lead-based paint or lead-based paint hazards in the home or building; (3) for multi-unit buildings, this requirement includes records and reports concerning common areas and other units when such information was obtained as a result of a building-wide evaluation; (4) an attachment to the contract, or language inserted in the contract, that includes a "Lead Warning Statement" and confirms that the seller has complied with all notification requirement; (5) a ten-day period to conduct a paint inspection or risk assessment for lead-based paint or lead-based paint hazards. The buyer and seller may mutually agree, in writing, to lengthen or shorten the time period for inspection and home buyers may waive this inspection opportunity.

[†] But preferably you'll see all of this before your contract is finalized.

## Co-op Contracts

When you purchase a co-op, you're not really purchasing real estate. You purchase personal property in the form of shares in the corporation that owns the building. You become a tenant and pay "rent" (monthly maintenance assessment fee) for the right to live there. Co-op contracts are entirely different from condo or single-family contracts. Still, you'll want to request the co-op version of the condo documents listed above so that you know the building rules and financial situation ahead of time.

# Question 7o: What Is the Earnest Money (also Known as the Good-Faith Deposit)? Who Holds It? When Do I Get It Back?

The earnest money, also known in some places as a good-faith deposit, is an amount of cash that the buyer puts up to show he or she is serious about purchasing the property. The money represents the buyer's commitment to buy and acts as an unofficial option on the property. After receiving an earnest money check, the seller will usually stop showing the property, and wait to see if the buyer can get a mortgage.

Earnest money is important to the transaction because it shows the seller that the buyer is operating in good faith (hence the name). The bigger the deposit, the more reassuring it is to the seller, who thinks, "This buyer is serious." It also ties the buyer to the property and keeps him or her from looking for additional properties.

## How Much Good Faith Do I Have to Show?

Usually, home buyers offer 5 to 10 percent of the sales price of the house in cash as the earnest money. Since the money is typically held by the seller's broker, it's an amount large enough that almost any buyer will think twice about walking away from the house on a whim.

If you don't have 10 percent in cash, then put down 5 percent. Sometimes a buyer will attach a $1,000 check to the offer to purchase to show initial good faith. The rest of the deposit, or earnest money, is due when the contract is signed by both parties, or shortly thereafter.

## Who Holds the Earnest Money?

The money typically goes into an escrow account held by the seller's broker, but this is largely a matter of local custom, or it can be negotiated. The buyer usually receives the interest on his or her money.

## When Do I Get the Earnest Money Back?

If the sale goes through, you don't. The earnest money plus interest is often used as part of the cash down payment and is paid to the seller. If the sale does not go through because of a reason covered by a contingency in the contract (if, for example, the buyer could not get a mortgage), the seller should sign a release of escrow and the earnest money will be refunded to the buyer. The earnest money should also be refunded to the buyer if the sale does not go through because of a problem on the seller's side. If, however, the buyer backs out of the deal for no reason at all, or for a reason that is not covered by a contingency, return of the earnest money may be subject to negotiation.

## What If the Seller Won't Give Back the Earnest Money?

Before you'll get back your earnest money, the seller needs to sign a release of escrow. If the buyer and seller disagree over who is entitled to the earnest money, and the attorneys can't resolve the issue, the broker has two options: to hold on to the money until the disagreement is resolved; or, in some states, to turn over the funds to the state real estate commission or agency for mediation, or local courts for litigation. Ask your buyer's broker to explain your state law and the local customs regarding this matter.

In the real world, brokers hate to be put in this position. Even though they legally can't release the funds until the seller and buyer have resolved their differences, they become the focal point for everyone's frustration at the situation.

**20/20 HINDSIGHT:** If you can't resolve who is entitled to the good-faith deposit, or the seller refuses to release the funds, you may have to sue to get your cash back. If this happens to you, consult with a real estate attorney for details on the legal options available to you.

# Question 71: When We Make an Offer, What Contingencies Should We Include?

When the first edition of this book was published in 1994, my publisher sent me on a book tour. Around the same time, we'd grown tired of our 1920s co-op overlooking Lake Michigan in Chicago and were looking to buy our first house. We had been looking for the past few years for the right house and, as I've said earlier, had probably seen 125 of them. (Who knows? It could have been a lot more. At some point, we just stopped counting.)

While I was traveling on my book tour, Sam continued house-hunting. During one trip, he found a couple of houses he liked very much. Homes were selling very quickly at the time, so we talked on the phone, he described the house in detail, and he made an offer.

He included the usual cadre of contingencies, including an attorney-approval rider, a financing contingency, and an inspection contingency. But he also included an "Ilyce has to love it" contingency. What this special contingency said was essentially this: When Ilyce comes back into town, she has to see the house. If she doesn't like it, we can back out of the deal.

Lucky he put that into the contract, because as it turned out I wasn't wild about the house when I saw it. The sellers had accepted the contingency, and we did back out of the deal.

Although the market in the late 1990s and early 2000s was considerably hotter than in the mid-1990s, this kind of contingency is making a resurgence through the Internet. Couples are now making offers for property online—sight unseen (except for 360-degree photos or a video of the property).

So the "we have to love it when we finally see it" contingency is becoming somewhat more popular. (By the way, I don't recommend making an offer sight unseen on any property. But if you're so inclined, I may have a bridge in Brooklyn you'll be interested in buying.)

## Your Everyday, Garden-Variety Contingencies

Let's start out with a definition: A contingency allows you to back out of the contract for a specific reason. There are typically three contingencies that accompany a contract to purchase: financing or mortgage, inspection, and attorney approval.

## Mortgage or Financing Contingency

A mortgage or financing contingency gives you a way to back out of the contract to purchase if you cannot get a lender to give you a mortgage commitment.

The contingency will generally require you to be specific about the type of mortgage you are seeking and will require you to seek mortgage approval within a specified period of time, generally forty-five to sixty days. You must be reasonable about the mortgage's parameters, and usually you must agree to look for a mortgage at the current prevailing rate of interest.

The contingency is meant to protect you in case you can't find financing. And, to be viable, it must be included in the contract or attached as an addendum.

**FIRST-TIME BUYER TIP:** What do you do if you're in a really tight bidding war, with several other parties all looking for a way to differentiate their bids? If you've been preapproved for your loan, that means that as long as the house appraises out in value, you'll get your financing. The lender has committed to it in writing. In an extreme situation, you could change your financing contingency to read that the purchase of the home is contingent only upon the house appraising out in value by the lender's appraiser. The risk is, of course, that the lender will back out of the deal for some reason, even though you have a written commitment. With a written commitment, the lender has to follow through, unless the company goes belly-up. But this may give you the edge you need to complete a winning bid. Before you do this, however, you'll want to consult with your real estate attorney.

## Inspection Contingency

This contingency gives you the right to have a house inspector come and examine the property before you close on the purchase.

Again, the purpose of the contingency is to protect you from buying a home that may have serious hidden structural problems or material defects. When you add an inspection contingency to the contract, you'll want to make sure it covers both the home and the property on which it sits. You might also want to have a separate contingency for each of the following:

Radon

Asbestos

Lead

Toxic substances

Mold

Water

Pests, including termites, mice, rats, roaches, and so on

 **FIRST-TIME BUYER TIP:** Although federal law requires sellers of homes built before 1978 to disclose if they have lead in their homes, the sellers may not know if it's there, and if they're selling on their own, they may be unaware of the federal disclosure requirements. Just be aware that if the home is old and you're planning to do any renovation work, you may uncover decades-old lead-based paint that could then get sanded into the air, creating a potentially dangerous situation—especially for children. There are inexpensive products available in any hardware store that will help you test for lead (and mold). One of the easiest looks like a cigarette butt. Basically, you swab it over a windowsill, next to a pipe, or anywhere else you suspect lead. If the test swab turns red, there is lead present. There may even be an app for testing lead on the walls and in the water (like there is for everything else). Like asbestos, lead is only dangerous if it is ingested. Babies can and do pick up tiny pieces of paint to stick in their mouths (my first son, Alex, didn't do it, but our second, Michael, couldn't resist). Anyway, it's worth a few bucks to make sure you know what's lurking in the house you're about to purchase.

Generally, the inspection contingency will require you to have your inspection within five to ten days after the seller accepts the offer. Otherwise, you may lose the right to withdraw from the contract. Keep this in mind when scheduling your various tests.

Sometimes buyers hope that the inspection will turn up small, fixable problems with the property so that they can get additional money from the seller at closing. The real purpose of the inspection contingency, however, is to protect you from purchasing property that may have serious, expensive, or unfixable problems. Like the mortgage contingency, the inspection contingency should be either written into the contract or attached to it as a rider or addendum.

## When Don't I Need a Professional Home Inspection?

I'm often asked whether every home buyer should have his or her future home inspected. The short answer is yes.

However, if you've been living in your home for the past five years as a renter, and you've been responsible for the entire upkeep of the property, then perhaps you know what problems exist with the plumbing, heating, and electrical systems. Perhaps you know that the back right burner on the stove doesn't work and the air-conditioning compressor is on its last legs.

But most home buyers haven't lived in the property they're going to purchase. They don't even know where the water shutoff valves are. And if that's the case with you, you should definitely pay for a professional home inspection.*

Some brokers say that if you're moving into a condo or co-op apartment building, you have relatively little risk of something big popping up. That's because with a condo you only own what's inside your unit plus a share of the common elements of the property. With a co-op, you don't even own that. You own shares in the corporation that owns your property and you pay a monthly rental fee (the maintenance or assessment) for the unit that the shares represent.

---

* And if you have suspicions about anything else that doesn't seem to work right, like the HVAC systems, foundation, or whether the property is on a city sewer or has a septic system—yes, I heard from someone who couldn't figure it out—you should get a professional inspector with that specific expertise. It's absolutely worth the money.

In a condo or co-op, the only things for which you're responsible are interior electrical work, appliances, and plumbing fixtures (and sometimes not even those). Your financial liability, should something go wrong, is slight.

So why, you're probably thinking, should any condo or co-op buyer pay for a professional inspection? Because a good inspector will tour the common elements of the property; look at the building's heating, electrical, and plumbing systems; and check out the roof, the foundation, the parking structure, and the windows.

When we moved into our co-op, the inspector found that some members of the building's board of directors had tapped in illegally to the electrical panel, dangerously overloading it. Our inspector was required to report it to the city, which fined the building (and made us, as you can imagine, less than popular). The building eventually corrected the problem, for which it had to assess the residents.

By having the inspection, you learn not only how your own property works, but what problems may exist in a condo or co-op—problems that you'll have to pay for during the time you live there.

## Attorney Approval Contingency (also known as the Attorney Rider)

Full disclosure: I'm married to a real estate attorney. That means I've heard all kinds of horror stories, so I'm a big believer in using a real estate attorney to help close residential deals, even in states where this isn't commonly done.

But before you can hire a real estate attorney, you need to add an attorney approval contingency to your offer. And before you finalize your offer, you should consult with someone who can advise you about the purchase and its legal consequences. In some states, that's the real estate attorney's job. In others, the broker will advise you. Be aware that real estate agents and brokers are not attorneys and are not supposed to give you legal advice. If they give you legal advice about changing the contract, be aware that the advice may not be correct. (And if the advice they give you is incorrect, you may not be able to go back and sue them for giving you bad legal advice. They are not, after all, attorneys.)

The attorney contingency or rider essentially gives your attorney the right to make changes to the contract or to reject a contract that doesn't protect you.

**FIRST-TIME BUYER TIP:** If you are working with a seller's broker and that broker is the person who is supposed to advise you of your legal rights under the contract, there may be a serious conflict of interest. If you have any qualms at all about being counseled by your real estate broker or sales agent, consult an attorney. Spending between $450 to $1,000 (if your first home costs in excess of $750,000, the cost for an attorney may rise as well) for an attorney is a small price to pay when you're making the biggest investment of your life. As all the fees and costs are pinching your wallet, try to imagine how expensive and time-consuming it would be if something *really* went wrong.

 **FIRST-TIME BUYER TIP:** Do not assume that, just because you have an attorney rider, that your attorney can remove you from the deal if you suddenly discover you have made a mistake in the offer (usually offering too high a price for the home). Although some attorneys do try to cover for their clients' mistakes by rejecting the contract, this is unprofessional. If you have any questions about the offer or contract, consult an attorney before making the offer or signing your name.

For more information about why attorneys are important and how to hire a good one, see Questions 77 and 78.

In some states, the offer for purchase is worded in such a way that there is no need for an attorney approval rider. It would say something like "This offer to purchase is subject to a contract that is agreeable to both parties." If you aren't sure whether or not your offer is worded in that way, it is best to attach an attorney rider.

## Other Sorts of Contingencies

There are many other contingencies that might appear in a contract for purchase, including:

- Sale of your prior residence (obviously, this wouldn't apply to first-time buyers);
- Admittance to certain clubs (for example, if you are buying a home near a private golf course, you might make the purchase contingent on your acceptance to the club);

- Approval by the condo or co-op boards;
- Pest inspection, asbestos, radon, lead, water (may be separate contingencies or lumped under inspection);
- Compliance with building codes;
- Liking it in person, if you are bidding on a home sight unseen (except perhaps through the Internet).

You can attach almost any contingency you like to your offer to purchase, but remember, having odd contingencies, in addition to the mortgage, inspection, and attorney approval, could give the seller grounds for refusing your contract. And in a hot seller's market, that's the last thing you want to do.

# CHAPTER 9

# Negotiating the Deal

Whether you're negotiating buying or selling a home, the terms and conditions of a divorce settlement, or what salary, benefits, and bonus you'll accept with your new job, negotiation is all about the give-and-take.

David Falk, Michael Jordan's agent throughout his basketball career, says negotiations are most successful when everyone walks away happy. The person who holds the stronger hand usually gets to give less and take more, but in a successful negotiation, both sides end up compromising.

And that's what you want when it comes to buying your home as well. You don't want the seller to take you for a ride, but you don't want to ride the seller, either, or he'll begin to like you a lot less and can make the move more difficult. Emotions run high in something as personal as selling a home. And when negotiations get tough, emotions become embittered weapons.

In this chapter, I'm going to walk you through the different parts of negotiating the offer and hopefully give you some strategies that will help you and the seller walk away happy.

# Question 72: How Does the Negotiation Process Work?

Unlike a judge's settlement, where both sides may end up profoundly unhappy with the result, a successful house negotiation can leave everyone feeling like winners. And that's the goal: As a buyer, you want the sellers to feel they are getting a fair price for their home. You want them to bask in the glow of having made a good deal so that they'll be nice to you when you want to tromp through with the inspector, your spouse, your friends, your decorator, and your parents.

You want that niceness to extend through to the closing, so the sellers don't make you crazy with all kinds of nonsense at the end. You want the sellers to like you so that they feel good about selling their home to you, someone they hope will love it as much as they have. (As we'll discuss later, the emotional component to homeownership is stronger than for just about any other type of financial investment.)

At the same time, you also want to feel as though you paid a fair price for the home. There's nothing worse than finding out the day after you've signed the contract that you overpaid for the house except for fighting with the sellers over items you thought were included with the price but they intend to take with them. The nastiness can leave a bad taste in your mouth. And, ultimately, in your new home.

## Negotiating Fairly

So how do you negotiate fairly? How do you end up with good feelings on all sides of the table? First, enlist your broker's (or attorney's, if you choose not to work with a broker) help in keeping everyone's emotions at bay. Brokers are good at this. It's probably one of the most important parts of their job. They must present your offer as something worthwhile, not insulting. You must rely on them to make you seem like a serious buyer.

Once you write up the offer with your broker, it's up to him or her to present it. This is the first step of the negotiation. It can take place in an office, but usually your broker will go to see the sellers in their home, where they are most comfortable. And then, perhaps over a cup of coffee, your broker will tell them exactly how much you are willing to pay for their home, the conditions under which you'll purchase the home, and when.

Sometimes it doesn't happen like this. Once in a while, especially if the sellers are out of town, or if they work odd hours, an offer will be communicated over the telephone or by email. But it's usually done in person. After all, as my mother, Susanne the agent, likes to say, this is a very personal business. When your broker leaves, the sellers and their broker will discuss the offer.

Unless it is a full-price offer or they are quite desperate, they will almost never take your first offer. Everyone understands that the first offer is a little bit (or quite a lot) below what you expect to pay for the property. The key to a successful negotiation is to remember that it's a psychological game.

**20/20 HINDSIGHT:** In a bidding war situation, you may get only one opportunity to make an offer. The best-bid offer can be frightening to construct. You want to get the property, but you don't want to overpay for it, either. In that case, you'll have to rely on your broker to steer you through based on his or her years of knowledge and experience in home sales in the neighborhood. See Question 74 for more ideas on how to win in a multiple-bid situation.

## Offer and Counteroffer

Here's how it works: Let's say the home is priced at $100,000. You think that's close, but maybe it's a slightly higher price for the home than you think is fair. You offer $90,000, or 10 percent less than the asking price. The sellers now assume you'll be willing to compromise somewhere in the middle, say $94,000 to $96,000. The sellers then make a calculated guess: Are you willing to go up to $96,000? Or will you only go up to $95,000? Or will you stop at $94,000? If the sellers want to cut to the chase, they may instruct their broker to present a "split the difference" counteroffer. That means that you'd pay $95,000 for the property.

Sometimes negotiations get tough. If the sellers think the $100,000 price is fair and don't want to go much lower, they may come back in much lower increments, say $1,000. Then you have to decide if you also want to match those increments or make a final offer. Making the last offer is like saying "I call" in a card game. The sellers might come down $2,500 and say that $97,500 is a final offer, take it or leave it. Or you might put in your own take-it-or-leave-it offer of $95,000 and put the ball in the sellers' court. If you turn the negotiation into a power struggle, it could quickly turn nasty. Better to keep things on a more even pace, if not downright friendly, to keep the negotiations moving ahead step by step.

But that doesn't mean you shouldn't play up your strengths. If you can't afford to pay more than $95,000, have your broker tell the sellers that you are making your very best offer and, while you can't be more flexible on the price, you really love the house and would be more flexible on the closing date. You're never going to know what the sellers' hot points are. They may be much more concerned about the closing date than the extra $5,000. They may also be more interested in turning their home over to people who really love it. That's where you can use the sellers' emotional attachment to their home to your great advantage.

## The Lowball Bid

If you decide you love a home that's either too expensive or way over your budget, you have a choice: You can walk away and find somewhere else to live, or you can make a lowball offer.

Although there is no one set definition of a lowball offer, it can be described in several ways: First, it's usually more than 10 percent below the asking price of the home; second, sellers usually find them insulting, which means the seller's broker must plead with them to reconsider and make a counteroffer; third, it gives a decidedly negative cast to the negotiation process.

For example, if you decide to offer $80,000 for a home priced at $100,000 and enclose with your offer comps of other like homes in the neighborhood that recently sold for $75,000, the seller may consider your offer. But if you offer $50,000 for a house that's well priced at $100,000, it's the nice seller who would even dignify that offer with a response. As the buyer, you have the right to make whatever offer you want. And your broker must present that offer to the seller. But that doesn't mean you won't tick off the seller.

 **FIRST-TIME BUYER TIP:** Sometimes a lowball offer works and other times it doesn't. A lot depends on the presentation of the broker and the desperation of the seller. It also depends on whether you're in a buyer's market or seller's market. If you're in a hot seller's market, where there are too many buyers for the homes that are available for sale, expect to pay nearly list, list, or in-excess-of-list price for the home. A lowball bid in an evenly paced market might be considered highly insulting in a hot market. In fact, many sellers wouldn't even respond to such a bid, even though you might be perfectly willing to raise your initial offer.

# Bidding Wars

A bidding war occurs when more than one buyer is interested in purchasing the same home at the same time. As I was writing this in 2017, the market in most of the country was so hot that bidding wars erupted over properties that sellers couldn't sell even a few months earlier.

Usually the seller's broker will ask for bids from the interested parties. The broker will then present the bids to the seller, who will decide which offer to respond to. What often happens is that you'll find out there is another interested party and your broker will encourage you to make your very best bid. That is, no negotiation. If you want to offer $95,000, then that's what you put in. If you think the other party is going to offer $95,000, and you really want the house, you need to offer a little more.

 **FIRST-TIME BUYER TIP:** There's nothing I can say about bidding wars and the negotiation process other than I get it. It's extremely pressured. Your broker will tell you to stay close to the telephone so that you won't miss "The Call." You'll be on pins and needles, wondering if your bid is going to be accepted or rejected. Try not to get so worked up about your bid that you can't concentrate on anything else. Take a walk. See a movie. Get your mind off of it. Putting some space between you and your offer, not to mention the whole negotiation process, can only help you keep what little perspective you'll have left once you make an offer for a home. And remember, if you don't get this home, there will always be another.

## MARLA AND DAVID'S STORY

Marla and David were certain that they'd never be able to buy a home. Not that they didn't have the down payment—they had plenty of cash to both make a significant down payment and have extra funds for the closing costs and fees and the cash reserves lenders require. They had excellent credit and had even been approved for a mortgage.

What was killing them was the heat of the market—and their own inability to move fast enough (a common problem for first-time buyers). Every time they went to make an offer on a house, it sold before they could even see it. If they were lucky enough to get their bid considered, it was one of several bids in a hotly contested bidding war.

After losing six houses in bidding wars plus another half-dozen homes they couldn't even bid for, Marla and David sat down for a long talk. They discussed their strategy for finding and bidding on houses with their agent. They asked their agent to be much more aggressive in finding properties for them earlier, almost anticipating the market. And they decided to be much more aggressive in the type of offer they put together.

They got the next house they bid on.

## Negotiation Survival Strategies

Marla and David used some of these ideas when putting together their winning bid. While some sellers and their agents may find some of these strategies to be too aggressive, unethical, and even offensive, they may help you capture the home of your dreams, especially if you're squaring off against a seasoned investor who is paying in cash. Use them sparingly, and only when you're facing a relentless seller's market.

1. **Don't be afraid to initially offer list—or even above list—price.** Yes, you're telling the sellers you'll pay at least that much for their home. And you may even go up from there. But nothing gets the sellers' attention like an offer that contains the number they're hoping to see.

2. **Remove as many contingencies from your offer as possible.** The first contingency to go should be your financing contingency—if you've been approved (and have received the lender's commitment in writing), and if you're sure that the house is going to appraise out and that the lender won't go out of business before you close. In an aggressive situation, some brokers advise their clients that being preapproved

is the same as being an all-cash buyer. The next contingency to go should be inspection contingency. Unless you're worried about a structural element like the foundation or roof, all it takes to fix these things is money. Finally, if you have to, you can let go of the attorney approval rider. Although your attorney (if you're in a state that uses attorneys) can still negotiate your contract language for you, he or she can't yank you out of a deal simply because the contract doesn't protect you.

3. **Make an open-ended offer.** If the seller's agent calls around for a "best bid," make an offer that really counts. Some extra-aggressive folks have won houses in tough bidding wars by offering to pay $1,000, $5,000, or even some sort of percentage more than the highest bid. For example, instead of listing a price, your offer might read: The buyers agree to pay 2 percent more than the highest bid.

4. **Offer to let the seller choose the closing time.** If you line up your ducks ahead of time, you may be able to close within a week or two, rather than in two to three months. By letting the seller choose the closing time that suits him or her best, you're throwing a big bone to the wolves.

5. **Create several offer packages and allow your broker to pick the one that's going to get the job done.** In a multiple-bid presentation, the buyers' brokers will often present one after another, allowing each broker to hear the others' bids. Although it's not quite on the up-and-up ethically, some brokers will have their buyers create multiple offers, which they will keep in envelopes in their briefcases. Then they'll angle to be the last to make their presentation. After hearing the other bids, they'll simply pull the one that'll take the cake out of their briefcase.

**FIRST-TIME BUYER TIP:** Real estate markets can change on a dime. It's rare that a hot buyer's market or seller's market will last for years, although it can happen. The bottom line is that markets do change and real estate is cyclical. It flips from a buyer's market to a seller's market and rarely stays balanced for long. Rather than being overly aggressive and risk purchasing property at the very high end (especially if you're only going to hold it for a short period of time) and then watching your home lose half of its value overnight (as happened in Las Vegas, Phoenix, and other cities during the Great Recession), consider stepping aside for a few months and waiting until the heat subsides. If for some reason it doesn't, you should at least be able to look at the market unemotionally and with a more seasoned eye. Remember, renting for another year isn't the worst thing that can happen.

 **20/20 HINDSIGHT:** When you're in the middle of looking for a home to buy and you've been disappointed time and time again, it's easy to start feeling as though you'll never find the right house, and even if you find it, that you'll never be able to buy it. I know I sound like a broken record, but there are plenty of houses that come on the market every day. If you don't get a particular house, another will come along that will seem even more wonderful and perfect than the house you lost. I know I keep repeating this, but there will always be another house.

## Negotiating into the Future

It's hard to imagine a negotiation for anything, be it an art auction, real estate, or even a lawsuit, that wouldn't take place in person—or at least over the telephone. But that's what appears to be happening.

The late-1990s success of eBay, an Internet-based auction site for just about anything from old stuffed animals and trading cards to furniture, led to an explosion of online negotiation. Everyone's trying to help everyone buy things electronically. There's even a site that allows two sides in a lawsuit to negotiate toward the middle: Each side sends an offer on what they'll pay or accept into the site and the two sides get closer and closer until they're $5,000 or less apart. Then the computer finds the right number in the middle. Both parties pay relatively little and save hundreds, if not thousands (or a percentage of the winnings) in attorneys' fees.

When I first wrote this book, going online and getting an email address from AOL was about the last thing I did (in November 1993) before this book went to press. (Yes, I wish I had thought to buy stock in the company, but alas, I can't lay claim to that one.) At that time, I couldn't have imagined that by the end of the 1990s, millions of people would go online to peruse all of the homes that are listed for sale with Multiple Listing

Services (MLS) nationwide. Or that Zillow and Realtor.com (among many other web-sites) would offer millions of listings for rentals, FSBOs, and Realtor-listed properties. I couldn't have imagined the success of sites like Auction.com (now called Ten-X) or that a company all but unknown in 1999 (Google) would make a $50-million investment in their online auction platform in the last few years. I didn't imagine people would make offers for homes they'd never seen in person. I could barely imagine buyers and owners getting excellent, complete information about the mortgage process, let alone applying online for a home loan.

The Internet revolution, also known as "the Internet of all things," continues. Soon, buyers will tour homes via virtual reality (VR) and may negotiate the contract using artificial intelligence (AI) rather than using real estate agents, brokers, or attorneys.

But at the moment, it's still about people and strategy.

## Question 73: How Do I Make a Counteroffer?

A counteroffer is what happens after the initial contract is presented. You make the offer. The seller responds by countering your offer with another one. Any response from you or the seller, after the initial offer presentation, is *by definition* a counteroffer.

Making a counteroffer is actually simpler than making the first offer, because you're in the driver's seat. A counteroffer means that the seller has responded to your offer. That means that the seller believes you are a serious buyer and that your offer is valid.

Before responding to the seller's counteroffer, make sure you understand the psychological implications behind it. In making your counteroffer, you can either match the seller's decrease in price with an equal increase or jump up more to make the seller feel better about the deal. The choice is yours.

Once you've decided how much to offer in this next round, talk to your broker. It's usually unnecessary to draw up an entirely new contract, although customs vary from state to state and county to county. At this stage, the broker usually modifies the existing offer and calls the seller's broker, who relays the new offer to the seller.

 **FIRST-TIME BUYER TIP:** Once you make your offer, you'll be hard-pressed to do anything until you've heard back from the broker regarding your counteroffer.

> To make sure you hear something soon, consider limiting the time in which your offer is valid. If you put down something that says "this offer expires within twenty-four hours" or "by the end of day Wednesday," you will force the seller to respond to you on your time frame, not his or hers.

# Question 74: What Do I Do in a Multiple-Bid Situation?

Whenever you have a situation where there aren't enough homes on the market for all of the home buyers who wish to purchase them, you have what's known as a seller's market. And when the list price is the starting point for negotiations instead of a home-run finish for the seller, you know you're in a *really* hot market.

In this kind of home-buying climate, many people often bid on the same home at the same time, resulting in a multiple-bid offer. When Sam's cousins, Helene and Ken, were selling a home they owned, the broker held a two-day open house and then accepted bids on the following Tuesday. They had more than three hundred people tour the house, resulting in nineteen offers for purchase. Several of those were "I'll top the best bid by 5 percent" sorts of offers. Now *that's* a hot market.

When you're facing this sort of situation, you have only a few choices:

- **Make an offer at or above list price.** How high you go depends on how badly you want the house. Just don't offer more than you can afford, or you'll never enjoy living in the property.
- **Make your best offer first.** Don't wait for a second round of negotiations. If the seller asks for your "best offer," don't assume there will be a counteroffer phase.
- **Offer a "clean" contract.** A "clean" offer is usually one with few, if any, contingencies. Consider eliminating the home inspection contingency, the financing contingency, and the attorney approval rider.
- **Be as flexible as possible.** Offer the seller his or her choice of closing dates. Consider allowing the seller to take some of the fixtures, like a dishwasher or refrigerator that might have ordinarily stayed with the house.
- **Consider adding an "appraisal" contingency.** If you have to remove the financing contingency, consider substituting an appraisal contingency, which will allow

you to cancel the deal if the house doesn't appraise out in value. That is, if the bank's appraised value of the home is less than the purchase price.

- **Let the seller dictate the closing date and other terms.** If you have flexibility in the closing date, this can be a powerful force in your favor.
- **Write a letter.** Appeal to the seller's emotions. Tell him or her how much you'll love living in the home and how you'll take care of it.
- **Back off.** Often, an agent will counsel a buyer to back off in a multiple-bid situation, reasoning that the likely outcome will be to pay too much for the property. Sometimes, all buyers will back off and the seller's agent will go to the various buyers and ask them to come back and bid, defusing the situation.
- **Don't panic.** You may not get the property at first, but sometimes deals have a way of unwinding. It's possible that the other buyers will drop out of the deal for some reason and the seller will come back to you.

It would be nice if every story had a happy ending. But in a hot market, sometimes things just don't work out.

### MARK AND LISA'S STORY

Mark and Lisa were tired of shopping for their first home. They had spent virtually every moment of their free time looking during the past couple of months. In Southern California, where they were shopping, homes were selling in minutes or hours, rather than days or weeks, and home prices were zooming before their very eyes.

"We felt like we were watching our future profits slip away because we couldn't find a house to buy in our price range," Mark explained.

After losing out on several properties when they didn't offer enough cash, Mark and Lisa made an offer for a townhouse. The townhouse had some good points and some not-so-great-but-livable things. It was in the neighborhood they wanted, but at 1,500 square feet, it was quite a bit smaller than the space they'd hoped to get. It was listed for $300,000, which was about $30,000 more than they wanted to spend, though certainly affordable by a mortgage lender's standards.

This townhouse seemed perfect. Their agent, sensing yet another set of buyers about to throw in the towel, suggested they use a tried-and-true method for getting their offer accepted: Make a full-price offer without any contingencies and write a letter telling the sellers how much they wanted to buy the townhouse and what good neighbors they'd be.

The wife, a television writer, wrote a beautiful letter. So beautiful, in fact, that her agent told her, "This is so great I'm going to have all my sellers use it." ("No, you're not," said the wife, insulted that the agent would use such a personal letter for all her home buyers.)

The agent included the letter with the full-price, no-contingency offer and the promise that the sellers could choose the closing date. The buyers waited. At the end of the day, the sellers countered their offer—$10,000 above list price.

Lisa thought the sellers countered above asking because she and Mark sounded so desperate in their letter, but their broker said that two more offers had come in for the property, each of which was above list price. Lisa and Mark mulled it over and decided to take a pass on the property. In the end, it wasn't worth overpaying for a property that was smaller than they needed.

 **20/20 HINDSIGHT:** Remember your wish list and reality check? If you find that you're getting caught up in the heat of the negotiation, turn back to your wish list and reality check for a dose of objectivity.

## Question 75: What Is a Home Warranty? What Kind Can I Get for New Construction? What About a Previously Owned Home?

The concept of a home warranty sounds pretty good: If something breaks, the foundation cracks, or the roof leaks, all you have to do is call an 800 number and someone will come out and fix it for free. Although existing and new home warranties should work this way in theory, in practice there are often extra headaches and expenses you will incur on the road to fixing your problem.

There are two types of home warranties: one for new construction and one for previously owned (also known as existing) homes. Let's look at new construction warranties first.

# New Home Warranties

New construction basically means you'll be the first person to live in your newly built home. Today, many developers are building semi-custom homes; they allow you to choose your own style of home, décor, cabinetry, floor coverings, appliances, and bathroom fixtures. You may even have a choice of options—a basement, sunroom, attic, two- or three-car garage, extra bedroom—and upgrades like carpeting, floor coverings, cabinetry, fixtures, and so on.

In the past, developers of new construction provided a new home warranty backed by one of two or three organizations, which created a pool of money that covered structural problems with new homes. It worked pretty well until a rash of undercapitalized, sleazy developers built shoddy homes and didn't put in enough money to cover the problems. That left one of the organizations short of funds and unable to pay the claims. In the past few years, other warranty companies stepped in to fill this gap, and have recently begun providing warranties for new construction again. Unfortunately, these pools of cash may not be enough to pay off every claim.

But real estate attorneys say reputable developers of new construction will often back up their own work, and this should be one of the criteria on which you select a new home. Usually, the developer will provide a door-to-door warranty for one year on nearly everything in the home. Part of this warranty is covered by the manufacturers of your new appliances and mechanical systems. The developer might also extend the warranty to five or ten years for specific major components, such as the roof, hardwood floors, or the fireplace.

I can't stress this enough: It's vital to know exactly what kind of service your developer will provide to you once you've bought his or her home, and what structural items and mechanical systems have what kind of warranty. If the developer refuses to warrant anything, watch out. That refusal might mean that the developer is sleazy or has built a shoddy project with something to hide.

## JUANITA'S STORY

Juanita bought a townhouse in a new development on the west side of Chicago. After she moved in, she started having problems with a few minor leaks, which caused her floorboards to buckle.

The paint in one of her bathrooms started peeling, and the deck didn't look like it was connected correctly. She contacted the architect, who happened to buy a unit in the same development (a good sign, I'd say). Before the architect could respond to her complaints and concerns, Juanita hired a professional home inspector to go through her unit, pointing out all the things that weren't built right.

Juanita sent a three-page letter to the architect, the developer, and the developer's attorney. Although the home inspector's final conclusion was that it would cost about $1,000 to fix all of the little problems, his report was so scary to the owner that nothing the developer could say would make it right.

Although the owner had lived in the unit for a year, she decided she wanted out. The developer said fine, he'd buy back the unit and pay for some of her closing costs. He intended to fix the relatively minor problems and resell the unit—this time for an additional $60,000.

What Juanita didn't realize was that the price of her townhouse had skyrocketed in the year she'd lived there, giving the developer a huge return on his investment.

 **20/20 HINDSIGHT:** In Juanita's case, everyone got what they wanted. Juanita got her money back. She bought from a quality developer who backed up his product. The developer was happy because he resold the townhouse and made a huge profit. The architect was happy because she no longer had a neighbor in the development who was unhappy with the work. Bottom line: It's incredibly important to buy from a quality developer, one who will back up his product a year or more after the sale.

 **FIRST-TIME BUYER TIP:** When buying new construction, check out homes built by the developer to see how the homes have stood the test of time. See how happy the homeowners really are. If you're buying in an established—or semi-established—subdivision, knock on doors and ask the owners what they like and dislike about their homes. Ask about everything from how well the mechanical systems work to how quickly the developer fixed items on the punch list (a list of items not finished to your satisfaction by closing). Check out other, older subdivisions the developer has built and see what complaints, if any, turn up. Check for complaints that may have been filed against the developer with your local chamber of commerce, Better Business Bureau, and your local state's attorney's office. Remember: The best defense is a good offense. Find out ahead of time what you're up against.

The time to reaffirm that your new home has a warranty is when you're negotiating for the home. Your attorney can step in and request a new home warranty, then make it a condition of buying the home. Then read the policy so that you know what's covered and what you'll have to do if you have to file a claim. At the very least, not having a home warranty for new construction means you have no recourse (other than expensive litigation) should something go wrong.

## Existing Home Warranties

The majority of first-time buyers will be buying previously owned homes, those that are up for resale. As we've discussed, these older homes are also referred to as "existing" homes in real estate jargon.

More than twenty-five years ago, several companies began providing home warranties for pre-owned homes. Although this type of warranty was slow to catch on at first, it has grown by leaps and bounds in the last few years, fueled by our increasingly litigious society and some recent court rulings that have placed more responsibility on the seller to disclose problems in the home. Millions of people have bought existing home warranties, and it isn't just sellers buying them. Buyers like having a number to call and an insurance policy (because that's what we're really talking about) in case something goes wrong.

Unlike new construction warranties, which cover all types of problems—including expensive structural problems—existing home warranties are typically structured as service contracts. Many people confuse them with insurance, and in many states, they're regulated by the state department of insurance.

But existing home warranties are like insurance in that they cover the costs to repair or replace a broken appliance or plumbing system over and above a deductible, which the home warranty industry refers to as a service fee. However, they are limited in scope. The typical policy covers the furnace, air-conditioning, kitchen appliances, water heater, trash compactor, electrical system (fuses and interior wiring), and interior plumbing, but there are serious exclusions. For example, if a pipe bursts because something gets stuck, it's covered. But if a pipe bursts because it freezes, it's not. Commonly, separate warranties (or extensions) must be purchased for refrigerators, washers, and dryers, not to mention swimming pools and spas.

Homeowner warranties do not, however, cover preexisting problems. If the appliance works on the day of closing, it's covered. Otherwise, it's not. And it's important to note that these warranties don't cover everything in your home, including structural problems like a crack in the foundation walls or basement floor or a leaky roof.

The seller usually purchases a home warranty, which is paid for out of the closing proceeds. The buyer is responsible for the service fees, should there be any need to call the toll-free number. Sometimes, seller's brokers will purchase the warranty for the buyer. And increasingly, buyers who are not given a warranty with the home are purchasing it themselves. The cost runs from less than $300 to more than $600 for a year of coverage.

Neither buyers nor sellers pay much attention to the service fee, but it gets charged every time, and buyers have to foot that bill. On some home warranties, the deductible or service fee can run as much as $150 per call. Most service fees range from $55 to $125 per call.

Are existing home warranties worth it? "If you look at a home in terms of the kinds of things that can go wrong in the first year, it's a pretty good deal [for the buyer]," says a spokesperson for the Home Warranty Association of California. "It's inevitable in a resale house" that some things are going to break down. Water heaters can explode. Furnaces can go out. Air conditioners can break. "Without a home warranty, you'd probably spend $1,000 to repair a furnace or $2,500 to replace it," he adds.

**FIRST-TIME BUYER TIP:** In some states, home warranties are completely unregulated. In other states, the department of insurance regulates them. If the home you are considering comes along with a home warranty, scope out the company to see if there are any reports of nonpayment of claims. Also, check for complaints that have been filed with the Better Business Bureau, your state's attorney's office, and the attorney general's office.

**20/20 HINDSIGHT:** Don't mistake a home warranty for homeowners' insurance coverage. A home warranty typically only lasts for the first year you live in your home. Generally, it cannot be extended. It also doesn't cover the types of damage covered by a homeowners' insurance policy, nor does it have the liability component. The simplest way of putting it is this: Neither new home warranties nor existing home warranties are insurance. They are by-products of the insurance industry. You still need to buy a homeowners' insurance policy.

If you're going to buy a home warranty (or ask the seller to buy one for you), be sure to shop around and find a solid company with a good rating. There are plenty of places where the top twenty home warranty companies are rated. Be sure to read the worst reviews in addition to the best ones—that's where you really learn what issues people are having with customer service.

# Question 76: What Does the Contract Really Say and What Are My Obligations Under It?

The real estate contract, also called a purchase and sale agreement or an offer to purchase, contains certain provisions that deal with the transfer of title to property between two parties. It can also speak directly to what happens to the property if it's destroyed before the deal is closed.

Every contract starts with the price and title (the actual ownership interest in a house). Why? Because you have to know what you're buying and how much you're paying for it:

With a single-family house, you're usually buying a house on land with things in it.

With a condo or townhouse, you are buying the space between the walls, floor, and ceiling of a building with things in it.

With a co-op, you're buying shares in a corporation that owns the property. These shares are equal to the unique value of your unit. (You're actually "renting" your unit.)

The sellers are supposed to deliver good title to the house, condo, townhouse, or co-op to you. If they're including personal property in the sale, like a washing machine or refrigerator, they must also give you good title to these items as well.

How do the sellers guarantee and deliver good title?

Before we get into the meat of it, let's have a definition of good title. Good title means the individual who owns the property owns it free of defects, easements, liens, and mortgages (except your own), and free from any matters that would impair your use of your home as a residential dwelling. There's nothing more complicated about it.

## Basic Elements of a Contract to Purchase

The basic elements of a contract include: the assurance of good title, the deed, conveyance (that is, transfer to your ownership) of personal property like bookshelves or light fixtures, how you're going to pay for the property, the sales price, and where the closing is going to be.

Of all the basic issues, title is the most important. Sarah and Bob's story illustrates one problem that might come up.

### SARAH AND BOB'S STORY

Sarah and Bob went looking to purchase property in the Indiana Dunes, which is on the southern tip of Lake Michigan. It's a beautiful stretch of sand and water, punctuated, at times, with a glimpse of the far-off skyline of Chicago. It's a place where generations of Chicago and Indiana residents have gone to rest, play, and enjoy the shore.

Years ago, as I was writing the first edition of this book, Sarah and Bob decided to purchase a vacation house in the area. They agreed to pay $200,000 and signed the contract. In the contract, the seller sold them the house with a quitclaim deed, which essentially sold Sarah and Bob every interest he owned in the house.

Had Sarah and Bob bothered to do a title search on the property, what they would have found might have made them change their minds. But they were so enamored with the idea of spending weekends and summers in their new vacation home that they neglected to learn what was going on in the community. If they had been reading the local papers, they would have known why the seller was willing to sell them the property at what seemed to be a great deal.

The seller sold them a house he owned on land he leased from the federal government, and the government had decided not to renew the land leases for some of the homes in the Indiana Dunes. This decision, which reversed generations of policy, was made to protect the shore from becoming too populated too close to the beach. Those homeowners, some of whom recently paid big bucks for vacation homes on the beach, had bought limited occupancy; the government leases had just ten years left before they ended.

At a price tag of $200,000 and with only ten years to live there, Sarah and Bob were facing a steep tab of $20,000 per year. They could never resell the property and recoup their investment. They tried to fight the decision, but to no avail.

A purchase and sale agreement usually provides that the seller must give the purchasers a warranty deed. That deed warrants that the seller has good title to the property and that he or she will defend you against others who may claim to have an ownership interest in the home you are buying. If the seller has only a leasehold interest in the property, then he or she can sell only that leasehold interest and not title to the property.

Under the typical purchase contract, you are obliged to purchase the property, for a certain amount of money, at a certain time, provided the seller guarantees good title.

**FIRST-TIME BUYER TIP:** Checking out the title for problems, liens, and encumbrances is the only way to ensure that you'll never have a long-lost relative or friend of the seller laying claim to your home. And to make sure you don't lose out if someone does "pop out of the woodwork," be sure to purchase an owner's title insurance policy that will protect you from anything the title company missed in its search.

## Question 77: Should I Hire a Real Estate Attorney? Should I Sign Anything Before My Attorney Reviews It?

No state requires you to hire a real estate attorney. In fact, real estate professionals in some states—California, Arizona, and Indiana, for example—actively discourage the use of an attorney. Instead, buyers and sellers are encouraged to rely on real estate brokers and the local title or escrow company to close the deal.

Whether or not you need a real estate attorney depends on how familiar you are with the workings of the real estate industry. I've talked to attorneys and brokers all over the country and except in a few states, like California, they overwhelmingly recommend that first-time buyers use attorneys.

There are several good reasons for this. Real estate attorneys:

- Are the only people involved in the transaction who do not have a vested interest in seeing you close on the deal. Real estate brokers and mortgage lenders, for example, don't get paid until the deal closes;
- Act as another layer removing emotion from the deal;

- Can negotiate the finer points of the deal for you;
- Can protect you from getting a bad deal should problems arise or should the negotiation turn nasty;
- Can work with the real estate brokers to organize and finalize details of the closing;
- Can work with the lender to make sure documentation is prepared correctly and is sent to the closing at the right time;
- Can explain the legal consequences of the deal and any terms you may not understand;
- Are a good buy for the money, as you can usually get them to work for a fixed fee;
- May be able to get you a reduced fee from the title company (which works on volume);
- Track all the little details that ensure a smooth closing;
- Provide you with a closing book (or electronic folder) that neatly organizes all the documents involved with your house closing.

## Penny Wise, Pound Foolish

You may think you're making a smart move by cutting out your real estate attorney and saving yourself the fee. But when you consider a $100,000, $200,000, or $500,000 investment (which is the cost of your home), trying to save $400 to $1,000 isn't so smart. Of course, some people could research all of the minutiae involved in selling or buying a home. And they could probably do it themselves and save the expense. But the vast majority of us don't do this on a daily basis, and we won't be prepared to deal with the consequences if something out of the ordinary happens or we've overlooked a detail.

What would you do, for example, if your seller dies the day before closing? What would you do if your buyer lost his job the week before closing and could no longer qualify for his or her mortgage? And what if a long-lost relative of the sellers turns up a few days before closing to lay claim to the home?

On even a $100,000 home, the attorney's fee is minuscule, and on a bad deal, that fee could save you a tremendous amount of heartache, not to mention money, to fix whatever problems crop up.

After all, no one hires an attorney for the good times. It's only to protect yourself in case your dream of homeownership turns into a nightmare. For nearly thirty years, I've watched Sam help literally thousands of individuals purchase and sell their homes. Most of the time, the deals go pretty well. But there's always something that crops up.

There was the case of the sellers who were angry about moving and ripped out all of the wiring in the house just before the closing; the buyer who wanted to sell one property and purchase another doing a 1031 exchange (which is used for investment properties) but didn't want to disclose the owners of the property; the buyer who discovered that the bank didn't wipe out all the liens during a prior foreclosure; and the buyer who discovered that someone other than the seller actually owned the property. Sometimes home buyers and sellers don't know what they're doing, or they fall prey to a bad-apple real estate agent or mortgage lender who uses them to further their own agendas.

There are bad real estate attorneys, too. But a good real estate attorney can help you successfully negotiate the minefield of homeownership, helping you buy or sell—and maybe even enjoy the experience.

In 2004, Sam and I started writing a syndicated column that answers some of the legal questions home buyers, sellers, and owners ask. It's called "Ask the Lawyer." If you'd like to ask Sam a question, email him through my website, ThinkGlink.com, or go to SamTamkin.com.

## Signing on the Dotted Line

You can sign any contract, as long as it contains the absolute right for your attorney to review the document and approve it. If the contract or document does not contain that absolute right, then do not sign it unless you're sure you understand all the provisions contained within.

As I mentioned earlier, most attorney riders give your attorney the limited right to cancel the contract on the basis of your attorney's review of the contract. If you're going to use a real estate attorney, and you're not sure you understand the terms of the contract you're signing—for example, if you're not sure there is an absolute right for your attorney to review and approve the document—then make sure to show it to your attorney before you sign it.

## Question 78: How Do I Find a Real Estate Attorney? How Much Should He or She Charge Me?

Not all real estate attorneys are competent, let alone good. And it's important to find one who will help, rather than hinder, the deal. Finding a good real estate attorney is like finding a good broker. First, ask your broker and your friends for recommendations. You want someone experienced, someone who has handled a minimum of fifty closings within each of the past three years. If you're purchasing new construction, or building a new home on land that you already own, it's important to hire an attorney who is very familiar with new construction contracts and can protect you in case the developer defaults or builds a shoddy product that doesn't conform to code.

After you get several names, call the attorneys up and ask them how much they charge and what they'll do for that fee. Don't be embarrassed to ask about fees. (You may not, however, want to start with the fee. Rather, start by asking the attorney about his or her experience, then move to how they help buyers. You can ask about fees at the end, if the attorney hasn't already offered that information.) It's crucial that you know how much you're getting for your money, and that the attorney understands what is involved with your deal.

### How They Charge

Some attorneys (especially those in medium or large law firms) charge by the hour. And in the largest firms, you can expect to pay $450 to $1,000 (or more!) per hour, depending on who does your closing. (The young associates have the cheap hourly rates and the senior partners charge the most.) You'll also be charged for photocopies, facsimiles, computer research time, and for the time it takes to actually travel to and attend the closing.

Other attorneys, especially solo practitioners, charge a flat fee. You can expect the flat fee to range from $350 to more than $1,000, depending on what you're buying. It's not unusual for attorneys to charge more for new construction, especially if the deal won't close for a year or more. There's a lot of extra work involved in one of those deals. Also, if you're buying a very large or expensive home, typically you'll be charged a higher flat fee because of the work involved in negotiating the contract. I recommend trying to find someone who will charge you a flat fee for his or her time. That way if there's a problem with the closing, you won't be charged for all those extra hours.

## Some Attorneys Work for Free

Really? Sure, you might also find attorneys who say they'll do your closing for free. But before you sign the engagement letter, be sure to ask about title charges and fees. Some attorneys make their money by taking a fee from the closing agent or title company for "reviewing" title or something else. Make sure you understand what the fee is, and what you'll be responsible for, before you say yes.

**FIRST-TIME BUYER TIP:** Sam says that if a buyer calls and tells him, "My closing is a piece of cake," Sam always raises his fee. The reason is that this home buyer has an unrealistic expectation of what is involved in a home closing and may have unknowingly created more problems that Sam will have to untie. Even the easy real estate deals are technical and complicated to close successfully.

**FIRST-TIME BUYER TIP:** Looking solely at how much attorneys charge for their services is not necessarily the best way to choose your attorney. For this, the biggest investment of your life, ask yourself if you feel comfortable telling this person all of the intimate details of your financial life. It's vital that you feel comfortable with, and perhaps even a bit close to, your attorney.

## How Does Your Attorney Respond to These Questions?

When you're interviewing your attorney, think carefully about the attorney's response to these questions:

- **How busy are you right now? How many house deals are you handling?** Some real estate attorneys handle upwards of three hundred transactions per year. That means that they basically don't have time to sneeze—or that you're working with an associate, paralegal, or assistant. You want someone who has enough time to handle you not only for the closing but throughout the entire transaction.

- **How many closings do you do each year?** Make sure your attorney completes at least fifty residential real estate closings each year to know that they have the experience in residential transactions you'll need as you work your way through the deal. Don't hire your cousin the litigator, or your friend Harold who negotiates airplane leases for a living. These folks probably didn't even do their own house deals.

- **How much do you charge?** If it seems as though the attorney isn't charging enough, it could be that he or she is part of a network of attorneys who do their own title work. In that case, they'd also get compensated from a company like Attorney's Title (or another firm that employs real estate attorneys to do title work) if you choose to work with that title company. Is that a bad thing? Maybe not. If something goes wrong with the title, the attorney could be liable. Either way, you won't know what the story is until you ask.

- **Are you doing any deals that would conflict with mine right now?** It's happened more than once. A buyer calls up an attorney only to find out the same attorney is already representing the seller. No attorney worth his or her salt will suggest he or she can handle both sides of the same transaction, even if you agree to sign a document that says you know it and approve it. If there is a conflict, ask your attorney to recommend another real estate attorney to you.

- **Do you have an engagement letter I can sign?** Attorneys should present you with an engagement letter that outlines the things they'll do to help you negotiate and close on your real estate transaction. The letter should also state the fee. The better attorneys do this, although all attorneys should. Ask the attorney you select to prepare one for you to sign.

 **FIRST-TIME BUYER TIP:** If you're buying a foreclosure or short sale, you *must* hire an attorney, no matter where you live. These deals have lots of hidden traps you'll want to avoid. And, if you're buying directly from a seller, you'll need an attorney to help write up the deal, make sure that the seller complies with state and federal disclosure laws, and protect you so that nothing goes wrong. Or if you're buying with a partner to whom you're not married (even if you're in a romantic relationship), you'll want to have the attorney draw up a partnership agreement in addition to the purchase contract.

**NEW CONSTRUCTION TIP:** If you're hiring an attorney to handle your new construction purchase, make sure at least one-third of the attorney's practice is new construction. Not all new construction is the same. For example, a single-family home in a development in the far suburbs is going to be different from new-construction infill development in an urban area. There are practical differences in each type of development. You want to make sure that the attorney knows how to handle your developer no matter where you're buying. As a bonus, if you hire an attorney who has done a lot of work for buyers in the development in which you're purchasing a home, you'll get someone who already knows the legal lay of the land, has already seen and read through the condo declaration, and knows where the developer may be willing to kick in a few extra upgrades or items. It could make the deal go much more smoothly.

## When Complications Arise

If a deal is really complicated, you will almost certainly need an attorney, no matter where you live. Sam once worked on a house closing that seemed pretty ordinary—until he found out there were ten lenders. He had to negotiate a separate deal with each lender until they were all satisfied. This extremely complicated closing took ten hours. Someone in attendance called it the "hour per lender" deal.

Once you hire the attorney, the general idea is to let him or her do the job. If the attorney advises you on certain points, believe him or her. If the attorney tells you to do something, do it. The attorney knows the ins and outs of real estate law much better than you do.

**20/20 HINDSIGHT:** Once again, hiring a real estate lawyer is not the same thing as having your uncle Harry, the tax attorney, do your real estate closing. Real estate law is specialized, and while Uncle Harry may be a whiz at writing wills or finding creative places to put your money, he may help get you nailed to the wall in two minutes if he doesn't truly understand the finer points of real estate law.

## Question 79: Should I Close at the Beginning, Middle, or End of the Month? Does It Matter?

When you choose to schedule your closing will be a point of negotiation between you and the seller. Here are some points to help you clarify why timing is everything:

- **Set the closing date according to when your current lease ends.** If you're living in an apartment, it's foolish to close when you still have six months left on your lease, unless you can easily sublet your apartment or you have an escape clause. If you close at the beginning of a month and your lease expires at the end of the month, and you don't need to do any work in your new home, you'll be paying double rent for one month, which can be costly. Poor timing is one of the biggest mistakes a home buyer can make (see Appendix I for a list of other common mistakes).
- **If you close at the beginning of a month, the lender will require you to prepay the interest on your loan from the day of closing to the end of the month.** Therefore, the cash you would need at closing will be more than what you would need if you chose to close at the end of the month. For example, if you close April 15, you'll have to prepay your mortgage from April 15 to April 30. If you close April 30, you only pay one day's mortgage interest.
- **If you're trying to decide whether to close December 31 or January 2, remember that you get to take deductions for your house in the year that it closes, even if it's on the last day of the year.** If you close December 31, the points you pay at the closing, plus any prepaid interest, are deductible on your income tax statement for that year. But you should make sure, if you choose to close on December 31, that these deductible costs will be greater than the standard deduction allowed to you by the IRS. Talk to your accountant or someone familiar with these real estate tax issues to find out how they might affect your situation.

## Paying in Arrears—Except for Subprime Loans

Mortgage interest and principal payments are paid in arrears—that is, you pay on July 1 for money you've borrowed in June. If you close April 15, you would pay a half month's mortgage interest in cash at closing. You would then pay nothing until June 1, when you would pay the interest for the month of May. On July 1, you pay interest for the month of June. And so on.

The reason for this is that your loan payments are computed at a certain rate, and that rate remains constant, like a fixed-rate loan. The lender must manually (well, actually it's all digital) compute the amount of interest from the day of closing to the end of the month.

The only time this would change is if you're getting a subprime loan. Most home buyers will fall in the excellent or good credit category, and lenders will grade these borrowers "A" or possibly "A−," which means they have a few problems on their credit history, but nothing serious.

If you have serious credit problems, but still have enough credit to get a loan, you might fall into the B, C, or D category of subprime lending. If that's the case, you may get a loan where you have to prepay the interest before you even borrow it. So, if you close on June 15, you'd have to prepay your interest through the end of the month. Then, instead of waiting until August 1 to make your next mortgage payment, you might be required to pay it on July 1. That way, you stay a month ahead.

If a lender is going to require this on your loan, it should be fully explained to you and written into your loan documentation. If you get a subprime loan, ask your lender to fully explain your payment schedule.

**FIRST-TIME BUYER TIP:** The last week of the month is the busiest time for title companies (not to mention moving companies). If you decide to close at the end of the month, be sure that your attorney schedules the closing well in advance. Otherwise, you might find that the title company is booked up and can't accommodate your closing.

**20/20 HINDSIGHT:** If your lease expires the same day as your closing, be sure you have a backup place to live just in case you don't close on the property—

even if it means moving to a hotel or back home with the folks for a few nights. Sometimes properties just don't close. You might have what's known as a "dry" closing, where the paperwork is signed but the money doesn't transfer. In the case of new construction, the house might flunk its final inspection. Or, more likely, it just isn't done yet and doesn't have its Certificate of Occupancy (also called a COO). Either way, make sure you're protected, even if it means paying for an additional month of rent.

# Question 80: What Is Seller Disclosure? How Does It Affect Me?

At the beginning of the 1990s, the term *seller disclosure* was virtually unknown. As the decade ended, it became a buzzword. Today, there are all sorts of written seller disclosures that are required, including some pretty specific requirements for disclosures around lead paint.

So what is seller disclosure? Essentially, it requires the home seller to divulge any known latent material defects in his or her property. That bit of jargon means that the seller must disclose if his or her property has any hidden or unseen defects or problems that could adversely affect the value of the property.

Buyers like seller disclosure because it tells them, up front, about the condition of the property. Some sellers like disclosing the defects, because it protects them from buyers discovering the defects during an inspection and then asking for money to fix the problems. Other sellers don't. They feel uncomfortable with this formal process of baring their home's soul, so to speak.

As a buyer, you want to find out everything you can, in advance, about the condition of the home. If you run into a seller disclosure form (and it is almost certain you will), the form will ask detailed—or perhaps not so detailed, in some cases—questions about the condition of the home. If the seller answers the questions honestly (there usually is an option for "don't know," which is completely useless to a buyer), the form may list such problems as water in the basement. The seller, of course, will say the price of the house takes into account these problems. The buyer will then have to decide if the house is worth the asking price if it also needs a new roof and a new furnace or air-conditioning system.

# A Brief History of Seller Disclosure

Although it seems as though state or federal law should automatically cover seller disclosure, in many cases, it does not—at least, not specifically.

In 1987, California* passed a law that codified the questions the seller must answer. In addition, the agent for the seller, the buyer, and the seller themselves must sign off that they have reasonably inspected the property and disclosed any defect.

By 1992, only California and Maine had some sort of formal regulation requiring sellers to disclose any hidden material latent defects in the property. In Maine, the broker is required to ask specific questions that the state has designated. The broker is required to gather this information at the time the property is listed and provide this information in writing to the buyer prior to, or during, the preparation of an offer.

In 1992, Coldwell Banker, a national real estate company, announced a new policy that required all sellers listing property with the company to fill out and sign disclosure forms. Although some sellers weren't thrilled with the prospect of having to fill out a form that asks specific questions about the house, land, and neighborhood, buyers were generally glad to have it.

State law in Illinois prior to 1993, for example, was silent on the issue. In effect, that meant that if there was a defect hidden in the house and the seller knew about it but didn't say anything, then the buyer was stuck with the problem. *Caveat emptor: buyer beware*. If,

---

* So much of what happens in real estate starts in California, the land of progressive thinking. In addition to material defects in the property, California sellers must disclose dogs that bark; potential hazards from floods, earthquakes, fires, environmental hazards, and other problems in a Natural Hazard Disclosure Statement; and the availability of a database maintained by law enforcement authorities on the location of registered sex offenders. There are many more disclosures required by sellers and their agents, all of which are enumerated in *The State of California Department of Real Estate Disclosures in Real Property Transactions*, 6th edition, 2005 (the most recent edition I could find), which is available online.

however, the seller told his or her broker about the hidden defect, the broker was obligated to inform the buyer.

But by the mid-1990s, things were changing. In Illinois, sellers must now fill out a twenty-three-question seller disclosure form. Since then, nearly every state has enacted laws requiring sellers to make a full, and in most cases written, disclosure about any latent material defects in their property.

According to the NAR's legal counsel, one of the largest areas of controversy in the process of buying and selling homes is the failure to disclose defects in property. The majority of lawsuits after closing, where buyers are unhappy, involve the alleged failure to disclose some condition affecting value or desirability.

The finger is usually pointed in the direction of the broker first, and then to the seller. Because the NAR protects the interests of brokers, it feels sellers, rather than brokers, should shoulder the responsibility for disclosing defects in their house. As the NAR's attorney said: "The agent has the duty to disclose factors that he can observe with a reasonably diligent inspection. The broker doesn't live there. Seller disclosure forces those issues to be addressed."

Ask your broker if your state requires seller disclosure, and whether the seller needs to make that disclosure in writing. You should also ask the seller to answer specific questions about the condition of the property before you make an offer to purchase.

For example, you might ask if there has ever been leaking or moisture or flooding in the basement. If the answer is "yes," then you can ask what caused the problems and if they were fixed. While you can also ask the real estate agent, chances are he or she won't know the real answers: They might just say "not to the best of my knowledge," which doesn't help you at all. To protect yourself, you'll need to ask the seller these questions directly. Don't be shy about asking for copies of the proof of payment if the seller indicates the problem has been fixed. That way, you'll have the name of the contractor or vendor should you have a similar problem in the future.

 **20/20 HINDSIGHT:** Although seller disclosure forms cause consternation for both home buyers and sellers, wouldn't you rather know what's going on before you buy rather than after you move in? And because each state requires a slightly different form of disclosure—but all states require that sellers answer questions truthfully about the physical state of their home—you should ask very specific questions about any problems or defects the home might have or have had.

# Question 81: Do I Need a Home Inspection? How Do I Find a Reputable Professional Home Inspector?

The quick answer is YES! Except in the rare situation—for example, you're buying a home from your parents that you have lived in and know intimately—savvy agents and brokers always advise their buyers to have the home inspected by a professional inspector or someone you know is knowledgeable about construction matters.

But hiring an expert doesn't excuse you from looking at the home carefully before you get to the inspection stage. Remember, the inspector will charge you between $400 and $800 (or more) for each inspection. By keeping a sharp eye out for the following, you may be able to spot some major problems and eliminate a potential property before paying an inspector.

## The Home Buyer's Watch List

When you start visiting homes, watch out for:

- **Wet, clammy, sticky, smelly basements.** A damp feel to a basement can hint at water seepage caused by improperly graded soil, or an improperly laid foundation.
- **Cracks in the basement.** A visible crack line in the interior of the basement or on the exterior foundation could point to more-than-normal settling. Or the house may have been built on new landfill, a hill, or an improperly graded site. It could also point to an area prone to earthquakes or earth movement during heavy rains.
- **Bad smells.** If a house smells bad, it may have a biological problem, like mold growing in the ductwork or behind vinyl wallpaper. While mold can be scrubbed away with bleach and water or other cleaners, you may have to rip out ductwork to get at it.

- **Poorly fitted ductwork.** Heating and cooling systems can be problematic, especially if the original work was done in a slipshod way. Check the duct lines to see that they fit snugly and securely.
- **Discolored spots on walls and ceilings.** Discoloration could be the result of a water problem—a leak from the roof, the walls, or the pipes. Also, beware of a fresh paint job, particularly in the top floor of the house or the basement. It may be covering up a problem.
- **Improperly fitted skylights.** Skylights, which are now extremely popular, are usually one-piece preassembled units that are popped into a hole in the roof. Check for discoloration, peeling paint, or other signs that the skylights were improperly fitted or may be leaking.
- **Damp attic.** Poor attic ventilation can lead to moisture being trapped in the upper recesses, causing dry rot or condensation. The underside of the roof should never be wet.
- **Insulation.** Does the house have adequate insulation? If not, you could be looking at a fortune in heating and cooling expenses. If the home has insulation, ask about the R-factor (the higher the number, the better) and be sure the insulation is facing the correct way.
- **Sloppy masonry work.** Has the homeowner tried to patch up the masonry him- or herself? Or are there holes in the mortar? It could be a sign of a larger problem. If you're looking at new construction, sloppy masonry and detail work can mean that other work was also done in a slipshod way.
- **Do-it-yourself electrical work.** Proper electrical wiring is a must to avoid future problems that could be costly to fix as well as a serious safety concern. If the electrical box is a mess, it could mean trouble for you.
- **Poorly graded landscaping.** Does the landscaping slope away from the house (the high point should be against the house)? If so, great. If the landscaping is sloping toward the point where the house connects with the ground, or if the walk around the side of the home is pitched toward the home, it's a good bet there has been or will be a leaking problem into the basement. Water is a very damaging substance (think about the Grand Canyon), and the constant pressure of water and snow melting toward the house can cause tremendous damage to the foundation.
- **Fuzzy windows.** If the home has double-paned or thermal-paned windows, and the windows appear to be fuzzy or full of condensation, the seal has been broken.

That means that the windows are no longer working properly and will ultimately have to be replaced. And that can be quite a chunk of money.

There are thousands of potential hazards when purchasing a home, and most buyers have no idea where to begin to look for problems. That's why it's so important to have the proper inspections completed before the expiration of the inspection contingency. First, you never know a home unless you've lived in it. Second, most people aren't particularly familiar with the structure and mechanicals of a house, townhouse, or condo. The roof may look fine to your eyes, but a house inspector may see peeling shingles and notice water marks from leaks on the ceiling. Third, a house inspector can be yet another voice helping you to distance your emotions from the purchase of the home.

## New Home Buyers Should Hire Professional Home Inspectors, Too

Just because you're buying a brand-new home doesn't mean you don't need a pro to inspect it. In fact, it's just as important as if you're buying an existing home. Why? Because even though the house may be new it doesn't guarantee that it was built correctly. Inspectors have shared stories with me about new construction projects that have had outlets wired incorrectly, and ground fault interrupters that weren't connected at all. They've seen balconies that are not fully bolted into the side of the building, hot water faucets that only feed cold water, and dishwashers that aren't bolted into the cabinet and begin to rock side to side and leak.

 **NEW CONSTRUCTION TIP:** For new construction buyers, if you're going to hire a home inspector at the end of the project, consider getting a package deal and hiring an inspector at the four critical junctures of the home building process: (1) after the foundation is poured; (2) after the house is framed; (3) after the house has been wired and plumbed (before the walls get finished); and (4) before you close. Coordinate with the builder or developer to make sure you can bring the home inspector through and have someone available from the site to answer any questions that come up. When interviewing an inspector for this task, make sure he or she has done new construction inspections before. And, be sure to let the builder know

> that this is what you're planning to do and write it into the contract so that you don't have problems getting your inspector onto the job site.

## Finding an Excellent Home Inspector

Once you've received the right to have the home inspected (through the inspection clause attached to the contract), you have to hire your home inspector or put together your home inspection team (in the case of multiple inspections, including pest, toxic, and the general home inspection).

If you look online, you'll find dozens, if not hundreds, of people calling themselves "professional home inspectors." Some of them are, some of them aren't. Finding someone who belongs to one of two home inspection trade associations is a good way to begin finding a good inspector.

Some of the most qualified home inspectors are members of the American Society of Home Inspectors (ASHI) or InterNACHI:

**ASHI** is a nationwide, nonprofit professional association founded in 1976. ASHI only admits as members those home inspectors who have performed at least 750 home inspections according to the ASHI Standards of Practice, or 250 inspections in addition to other licenses and experience. Applicants must also pass a written exam, receive approval on at least three sample inspection reports, and perform a satisfactory home inspection before a peer review committee. ASHI's standards have been adopted by many states, and the organization consults with other states thinking of passing laws to license home inspectors.

**INTERNACHI** is an international trade association for professional inspectors, and has a six-step procedure for becoming a Certified Professional Inspector, a process that includes joining the organization, passing an online exam, completing the online code of ethics, submitting four mock or simulated inspections for approval, and signing an affidavit. To maintain the certification, you must pass twelve training courses within the first year of receiving your certification, and complete continuing education requirements.

Where can you find a good inspector? Ask your real estate broker for a list of suggestions. When you call:

- **Compare fees.** Fees should range from $400 to $800 or more, depending on the size of the home. Ask what's included in the fee and how long the inspection should take. Be prepared to allow at least two hours for a thorough inspection of a moderately sized property.
- **Compare telephone manner.** The inspector should be courteous and knowledgeable. Ask for a list of specialized inspectors you might call (for radon, asbestos, electromagnetic power, water quality, pest control, etc.). Ask if the inspector is bonded, licensed, and insured. Ask if the inspector is a member of ASHI or another professional inspection association. Ask for references, and then call them.
- **Make sure you'll receive a written report.** You should receive the report either on-site (many inspectors now do their reports on site using hand-held computers that plug into printers in the car) or by fax or email within twenty-four hours. Get clear answers about when you'll receive the report, what kind of report it is, and how detailed it will be. Will it be a checklist only or will the inspector write his or her overall view? The best inspectors do everything on site and deliver an immediate report digitally, allowing you time to review the report and ask questions while the inspection is still fresh in your mind.

Once you've found your inspector, have him or her come out before the expiration of the right-to-inspection clause in your contract. You will usually have about five to ten days from the time you sign the contract to have your inspection. Don't wait until the last day in case it's raining or the inspection needs to be rescheduled.

**FIRST-TIME BUYER TIP:** For those home buyers living in the northern half of the country, snow can pose huge problems for home inspectors. If there's a big snow the night before your inspection, the inspector will be limited in what he or she can do. The inspector may be able to brush off the snow from the roof to see a small piece of it, but they won't be able to make a thorough assessment, nor will they be able to ascertain the condition of the landscaping. A heavy rain can also make it difficult to properly inspect the home, and you can't properly test out an air-conditioning system in the winter, or a heating system in the summer.

> Finally, try not to have the inspector come in the dark, because you want him or her to inspect the entire property, exterior and interior spaces. Daylight makes the process much easier.

 **20/20 HINDSIGHT:** When interviewing the home inspector, make sure he or she will be inspecting the entire house, top to bottom, inside and out. If the inspector balks at inspecting the basement, crawl space, attic, garage, or anything else, find someone else. If the inspector tells you these places will be inspected and then balks when actually at your home, call his or her supervisor, or consider ending the home inspection at that point. If that happens, the home inspector clearly isn't doing his or her job, nor is he or she giving you what you're paying for.

## The Inspection Report

At the end of the inspection, or perhaps the next day, the inspector will give you a report of what's wrong with the house. The report should be complete and it should be written. It would be even better if the report includes the inspector's written remarks as well.

## Be Sure to Tag Along

One of the smartest things you can do is attend the inspection, walk around the property with the inspector, and ask a lot of questions. The inspector should be happy to explain everything to you. It's an excellent opportunity to learn about the home you're buying and what you'll need to watch out for in the future.

## Watch Out for This Trick

If a qualified, licensed, and bonded house inspector tells you the property may need $20,000 worth of repairs within the first five years, it should change the way you think about it. Is the property still a bargain? Should you look elsewhere? Can you afford to buy a home that will need such a substantial cash outlay within such a short period of time? Is the house a great deal anyway? (If your contract has an inspection contingency, you should be able to terminate the contract and get your earnest money back. Then you can search for another home.)

20/20 HINDSIGHT: If the home inspector offers to complete any work he or she recommends to you, politely decline the offer. While this doesn't happen too often, the inspector could be suggesting there is trouble where there is none, simply to drum up more business.

## The Inside Skinny on Home Inspectors

Over the years, I've received loads of mail from disgruntled home buyers who believe they hired lousy inspectors who did a lousy job. And I've also received loads of mail from disgruntled home inspectors who feel they are being picked on for no good reason.

I believe the truth lies somewhere in the middle. Sometimes home inspectors miss things they should not. Sometimes home buyers have unrealistic expectations about the home they're buying. All home buyers have to understand this truism: Old houses have great charms but expensive problems. The older the house, the more problems it will have.[*]

Brand-new and newer homes have problems, too, but once a house passes its fifteenth birthday, unless it has been flawlessly maintained (and sometimes even if it has), there will be problems you'll need to address and correct as the years go on. That's just part and parcel of homeownership. If you're not ready for that responsibility, either buy a new house or continue to rent for a while.

What you need to do is find a qualified home inspector who won't scare you needlessly. (And believe me, some home inspectors make old grout sound as bad as the roof is caving

---

[*] It may not happen the day after you close, but problems will definitely arise in older and very old homes during your tenure.

in.) But you also need one who will tell you the truth and not kowtow to agents who refer business to them. And if that sounds like a conflict of interest waiting to happen, pat yourself on the back. That's exactly how it works in many places.

I do believe, however, that a home inspector should stand behind the reports he or she has written for clients. Many don't. Many written inspection forms are nothing more than checklists where the options are "Good," "Fair," "Poor," and "Recommend Specialist for Further Inspection." Too many referrals to specialists and you may find yourself wondering what added value the home inspector provides. (The answer is that if the inspector only recommends you to specialists without identifying a real problem, it's a diminishing value that may ultimately not be worth what you paid.) Not only that, but when you sign the agreement for your professional house inspection, you're basically signing away your rights to sue the inspector should he or she have missed something or made an incorrect assessment.

Sam recently had a client who hired a professional home inspector to look at the property she was buying. The inspector did the inspection and took her money, but before he would give her the written report, he made her sign a piece of paper that said, basically, that she wouldn't sue him but if she did, his total liability was the amount he had been paid.

I find that to be outrageous. It's as if the inspector was holding her written report—that she had already paid for—hostage!

Home inspectors should stand behind what they write. And if they can't, they should have insurance to cover their mistakes. Every home buyer should ask the home inspector whether or not he or she carries an E&O policy and for how much. The better home inspectors have them.

Home inspectors are not the only individuals who do professional home inspections. Some contractors and structural engineers may also do home inspections and be able to give you an opinion as to the structural integrity of your home. Both contractors and engineers are typically licensed by your state and carry insurance.

Although I recommend you contact the American Society of Home Inspectors (ASHI .com) for a referral to an ASHI-certified inspector in your neighborhood, you should know that ASHI doesn't appear to police its wayward members, police its ethics code, or step in to mediate trouble between its member inspectors and homeowners who have had problems. Also, there appear to be some home inspection companies that hire anyone off the street to work for the ASHI-trained owner. You may think you're hiring an ASHI-certified inspector when, in fact, you're not getting what you paid for.

There are other national organizations that claim to certify home inspectors. Before you hire such an inspector, check out the requirements for membership and certification. If they don't at least meet ASHI's standards, you have to wonder if the home inspector really knows what he or she is doing.

**20/20 HINDSIGHT:** If you want to see what a great home inspection looks like, I have a twenty-eight-part series on my YouTube channel, ExpertRealEstateTips, with Jamie Dunsing, who has been in the professional home inspection business for more than thirty years. Go to YouTube.com/expertrealestatetips and look for "Home Inspection" under Playlists. (Don't forget to subscribe to my YouTube channel while you're there for more free real estate videos.)

# Question 82: Should I Test for Toxic Substances and Contaminated Water?

Once a rare addition to contracts, toxic substance inspections—including radon, lead, water, and asbestos—have become a regular part of most real estate contracts. Unfortunately, most home inspectors are not qualified to do specialized tests for toxic substances. You must therefore find separate inspectors who specialize, or purchase the appropriate test in your local hardware store.

Here are the major toxic substances for which home buyers are inspecting these days:

**RADON.** A study by the Environmental Protection Agency stated that twenty-two thousand deaths a year are attributed to radon, a gas that seeps through cracks in the house or foundation from the earth. According to an EPA pamphlet, "Radon is the second leading cause of lung cancer in the U.S., after cigarette smoking. As you breathe it in, its decay products become trapped inside your lungs. As these products continue to decay, they release small bursts of energy that can damage lung tissue and lead to lung cancer. It's like exposing your family to hundreds of chest X-rays each year." Of the home buyers and homeowners who actually check for radon, the EPA estimates around 20 percent will find an unacceptable level. Although you can purchase an EPA-listed radon gas test kit in your local hardware store, it may be better to have a professional inspector perform the test, which requires two to four days' exposure in the home. (Or start with a store-bought test and hire a professional should the test indicate higher than acceptable levels.) Radon emissions can be fixed by either sealing the cracks in the basement or crawl space, or installing an air system that sucks the gas out from beneath the home. For more information, call the EPA's hotline at (800) SOS-RADO.

**ASBESTOS.** If you're buying new construction or anything built since the mid-1970s, you probably don't have to worry about asbestos. If you're buying an older home, it's likely there may be some asbestos in the house. Asbestos is a microscopic airborne fiber that is ingested through the nose or mouth; it lodges in the lung and can cause lung cancer. If not disturbed, the threat from asbestos is minimal, if any. You can hire an asbestos specialist to come out and tell you if there is asbestos in the home and how much it will cost to have it wrapped or removed (the two ways to abate the threat). Lori, a first-time buyer in Chicago, said she wasn't deterred from buying her home because of asbestos. She and the seller agreed at closing to give her a cash credit (a payment to the buyer at closing) equal to the price it would cost to remove the asbestos. For more information, contact your local OSHA (Occupational Safety and Health Administration) office of the federal government, or your local office of the federal Consumer Product Safety Commission.

**LEAD PAINT.** High levels of lead in paint and water (see below) have been connected with mental and physical development problems, particularly in young children. Lead is usually only a problem when ingested or inhaled. Lead paint is most often found in older homes (its use has been banned for more than twenty years) and can simply be covered up. In HUD homes, or those financed with an FHA mortgage, lead paint must be removed or covered over. A test by an outside agency can run between $100 and $300, depending on the number of samples tested. The federal government passed a lead paint law, which requires sellers of homes built before 1978 (the year lead paint was removed from the shelves) to disclose that there may be lead paint in the house. There are lead tests you can purchase at your local hardware store that look like a short, white swab. You simply swab the painted surfaces and, if the swab turns red, there is lead present. Again, the problem with lead paint is only serious if you ingest lead paint chips or dust (if, for example, you're renovating your home). For more information, call your local office of the federal Consumer Product Safety Commission or check out the EPA lead website (epa.gov/lead).

**LEAD IN WATER.** High levels of lead in water is another problem, particularly in old homes and apartment buildings. If pipes that were soldered together with lead begin to corrode, lead particles can be released into your water supply. If the water is contaminated at the source (from your local city or municipal water supply), you may want to consider buying a filtering system, or looking for another home in a different area. There are inexpensive water filtering systems you can purchase at your local hardware store that claim to take out at least 93 percent of all lead in water. This is a much more cost-effective solution than either purchasing bottled water or replacing all of the plumbing lines in your house. For more information, call your local office of the Federal Consumer Product Safety Commission or go to epa.gov/lead and search for "lead in water."

**ELECTROMAGNETIC RADIATION.** One of the most recently discovered hazards is electromagnetic radiation from high-voltage power lines. Only a few early studies have been done, and the results are mixed. Some seem to show an increased rate of cancer and other unusual diseases in people who live in homes that are located directly underneath high-voltage power lines. Other studies show no increase of cancer or other diseases. Power companies deny the link, but you may simply want to avoid both the risk that there may be a problem, and that other problems will be discovered later. There's another risk, too: Property prices won't rise as quickly because of the perception that there is a problem—whether or not one actually exists. Since there's no way to shield yourself from the electromagnetic radiation, you must simply find another house to buy. There is a test for electromagnetic radiation, which can cost between $100 to $250, depending on the house.

## And Then There's Mold

When we gutted our home in 1999, the house was basically open to the humid Chicago summer air for about three or four months. In the fall, while we were cleaning up from the renovation, we noticed that mold had begun to grow on an old wood door in our basement. So we hired someone to wash it away with bleach and water.

"That's not a bad way to go as long as you don't have a really large spot of mold, say, an area no bigger than ten feet by ten feet," said Josh, a certified environmental health specialist based in Fort Wayne, Indiana. "But I wouldn't advise doing it yourself if the area is any bigger."

In the past twenty-five years, mold has surpassed all other toxic substances in terms of dollars spent for its removal except for asbestos. But it ranks much higher on a home buyer's and homeowner's list of concerns. The problem has become so severe in the past few years that mold removal (or remediation, as it's known) has become a very big business—so big, not to mention expensive, that many insurance policies have excluded mold removal from the items that are covered if a pipe breaks and your home is flooded.

Let's back up a bit. Every house contains mold spores. You'll find mold on dogs and kids, in the yard, in the bathroom, and in the basement. But most often, you'll find that mold spores cling to wet or damp spaces, like a wet basement wall; the windows of a house that has too much humidity and too little fresh, cool air moving around; or inside the walls, where a roof leak has no chance of drying out. According to the Centers for Disease Control and Prevention (cdc.gov) and the Environmental Protection Agency (epa.gov) websites, mold starts growing within twenty-four to forty-eight hours of being exposed to water or an extremely humid environment.

"If a house has a history of water problems, it could have a mold problem as well. If building materials (at a new construction site) stay damp and conditions are right, mold could start to grow. If the relative humidity of a home is above 60 percent, or if the house is closed up with no air conditioning, mold can begin to grow," Josh explained.

## JULIE AND ADAM'S STORY

Julie and Adam bought a lot across the street from where they lived, and built a new house. When it was done, they moved in and put their house up on the market for sale. A couple made an offer for the house, and the deal closed.

After the house closed, the couple didn't move in right away. It was summer, and the house was closed up and the air-conditioning was turned off. Mold grew like crazy.

When the couple finally moved in, their kids began getting sick. They finally realized mold was the cause and moved out: The house had grown so moldy as to be uninhabitable. The couple sued Julie and Adam for selling them a house that contained mold, but lost the case.

In the meantime, the house basically had to be torn apart, board by board, and rebuilt. As we went to press, it is still uninhabited, some three years after Julie and Adam closed on the sale of the property.

## Harmless Mold, Killer Mold, Black Mold

While there are some forms of mold that are extremely dangerous or even toxic, including *Stachybotrys chartarum* (also known as black mold), most mold spores are relatively harmless. If you have allergies or asthma, you may be more sensitive to mold.

"Mold today is like asbestos was twenty years ago," said Lawrence, a professional home inspector based in Chicago who asked not to be fully named. "In the property inspection business there is always the problem du jour. And consumers are being taken advantage of because of it."

Lawrence says that while some cases of mold are life-threatening, most aren't. But "mold remediation companies are in the business of scaring consumers into doing more (and spending more) than they need to."

"With asbestos, removal caused more problems than good. But asbestos and mold are very emotional [buzzwords] today," Lawrence added. "If you think you have a problem and someone scares you enough, you will sign a contract for remediation services."

When you shop around for your first home, be on the lookout for obvious signs of mold. If the house has a damp, dank, or musty smell, that could be mold. If you see spores clinging to the walls (which might look like a black, gray, or green shadow on the walls) or the ceiling in the basement, that could be a sign of mold. Or, if you see spores (they might look like black, gray, or even colored spots) on the inside of the window, and you still decide to make an offer, then you should tell the professional home inspector to keep a sharp outlook for a possible mold problem.

"In one case I just evaluated, a gentleman was living in the basement and thought there was spray paint on the walls. It turned out to be mold. He had to cover his nose and mouth with his shirt when we went down. I had on a respirator," he recalled.

**MARYA'S STORY**

Marya went looking to buy a house. She came across what she thought was the perfect home. But when she had the home inspected, it turned out to be covered in mold. Apparently, the owners had moved away and locked up the house during the summer without leaving the air-conditioning on. She asked her attorney what she should do. He advised her to back out of the deal.

"No matter how clean you get this house, there could always be a mold problem. There's no reason to stay where there are so many other homes for sale out there," he told her. She wound up buying a different house.

## What You Can Do

Whether you own or rent, if you have a leak, if your home floods, or if you get water in your basement, you can expect mold to grow unless you dry things up quickly. Don't worry about saving money. Control the humidity in your house by using your air conditioner or dehumidifier in the summer or on humid days.

As experts have pointed out, it's far less expensive to keep mold at bay than to do any remediation work. Although Josh's company does not do remediation at all, he estimates that it would cost a homeowner at least $1,000 to start with mold removal. Remediation costs can run as high as several hundred thousand dollars. It just depends on how intrusive the mold has become.

The EPA has an entire microsite on mold. You can access it at EPA.gov/mold.

 **FIRST-TIME BUYER TIP:** Real estate attorneys advise that the language you use in your contract should state that the "sale is contingent upon satisfactory results of the tests." If you don't include this kind of language, you could find yourself having the right to have the tests done, but not the right to back out of the deal if the house fails to pass the tests to your satisfaction. For more details about legal language that would be appropriate in your area, consult a real estate attorney.

## The News on Synthetic Stucco and Mold

Since the late 1990s, one of the biggest sources of mold problems has been with homes made with synthetic stucco, also known as EIFS. There are many different trade names for synthetic stucco, including Dryvit.

The problem seems to be that synthetic stucco is a polymer, which is like plastic. When you coat the exterior of your house in synthetic stucco, it's difficult for air to circulate. If water infiltrates the house between the synthetic stucco and the wood frame or plywood holding the house together, mold can grow because of the lack of air circulation. In other words, the wood gets wet, the moisture is trapped by the polymer, and then the wood can't dry out, causing mold to grow.

Responding to the problems, manufacturers developed a second type of synthetic stucco, with a different drainage system. At press time, it's unclear whether this second type of synthetic stucco was able to prevent moisture intrusion.

If you're buying an existing home or new construction home that contains synthetic stucco, you may want to read up on what kind of synthetic stucco has been applied, who applied it, and where current litigation is with the company that manufactured it. While there are homes made with synthetic stucco that do not have a water infiltration problem, many do. One study suggests that a majority of homes made with synthetic stucco either have, or will have, a problem with water infiltration over time. Search "first generation EIFS defects" for more information.

If you buy a home with synthetic stucco, you should hire a home inspector who specializes in EIFS systems to check your home for moisture infiltration every six months. If there are holes or cracks that develop in the home, you'll need to fix those quickly to avoid causing permanent damage to your home. To find a home inspector who specializes in EIFS, start with the American Society of Home Inspectors (ASHI.com).

 20/20 HINDSIGHT: You'd think that in an extremely dry climate like Arizona or Nevada, you'd be safe buying a home coated in synthetic stucco. But homes in those areas have had issues as well. Until the moisture intrusion problem has been definitively solved, you may just want to steer clear.

### Mold and New Construction: A Growing Issue?

One of the big questions: Why is mold becoming an issue now? One answer appears to be that the new homes being built are much more "airtight" than homes built twenty or thirty years ago.

Windows are double- or triple-paned (making them more energy efficient), caulks that seal joints have improved, house wraps have become more impervious to moisture, roofing materials are stronger, and so on. The speed with which new homes are being built can cause mistakes to be made. Making sure your new home is being built correctly is one reason why you should have a professional home inspector on the premises at least four times during construction. Once the house is built, you may miss the signs of future problems, like a roof vent that was installed incorrectly.

## Question 83: What If the Inspector Finds Something Wrong with the Home I Want to Buy?

It's likely that your home inspector or your toxic substance and pest inspectors will find something wrong with the property you want to buy. Remember, that's their job. Once a problem is found, and it might be a small problem or a big problem, you have to ask yourself two questions:

1. Is the problem fixable or unfixable?

2. At what price is the problem fixable?

Here are some examples of unfixable problems:

The house sits on a fault line.

The house is in a floodplain.

The home's foundation is severely cracked (a major crack is one that is larger than $\frac{1}{8}$ inch).

The house's water supply has been contaminated by the local dump.

The house is located under electromagnetic power lines.

Almost everything else is fixable—even most kinds of earthquake damage.

But is it affordable or smart to try to fix every problem? Is the house worth it? You can fix a leaky roof or replace it entirely, but is the house worth its $100,000 price plus $5,000 for a new roof? What if the house also needs a new furnace and hot water heater? What if it needs upgraded electricity for a clothes dryer? What if the pipes are old and leaking?

If your inspectors find something wrong with the house, you have two options: (1) withdraw from the contract (provided you have the right inspection contingency that allows you to withdraw if the inspection report is unacceptable) or (2) renegotiate the purchase price to reflect the cost of fixing the items marked on the inspection list. If you decide to withdraw from the contract, have your attorney write the letter. If you decide to go ahead, but want to renegotiate the purchase price, talk to your broker and your attorney about what may be customary for your area.

 **FIRST-TIME BUYER TIP:** Often, sellers assume that home buyers want an inspection so as to be able to use the problems to negotiate the price down. If this is your strategy to buy the house at a lower price, don't be surprised if the seller refuses to do anything and you're stuck taking the house in "as-is" condition. Also, in a hot market, many sellers may be unwilling to do more than the bare minimum, if anything at all. That's a symptom of a strong seller's market. In a buyer's market (where there are more homes for sale than qualified buyers), you'll have more leverage. You should find, however, that most sellers are happy to do what's reasonable and fair. If that's all you ask for, you shouldn't have too much of a problem.

## Question 84: What Do I Do If the Seller or Broker Has Misrepresented the Condition of the Home?

If you find out from the inspection that the seller or broker has misrepresented the condition of the home, and you have a properly written inspection contingency, you should have the option of walking away from the deal. You may also report the broker's conduct to the state agency that regulates real estate professionals.

**20/20 HINDSIGHT:** While you may be upset and frustrated, you have to consider yourself lucky not to have bought what could easily have turned out to be a lemon of a house. There's nothing more frustrating than living through one home crisis after another.

If you find out after you close on the home that the seller or broker has clearly misrepresented the condition of the home, or did not disclose everything they knew about the property or should have known about the property, you can take them to court. But be prepared to prove that they did have knowledge of the problem or should have had knowledge.

**ILYCE AND SAM'S STORY**

When we bought our co-op, the seller and the seller's broker told us that everything was working in the unit. But, we forgot to test the dishwasher before closing. (Rule No.1: Always run all the appliances during an inspection.)

The first night we were in the apartment, we decided to turn the dishwasher on. Nothing happened. Sam reached down under the sink and discovered that the sellers had turned off the water—which should have been our first clue. We turned it back on. The next morning we found out why: The dishwasher had leaked all over our new downstairs neighbors' kitchen, ruining their window shade.

We were furious. Obviously, the sellers knew that their dishwasher leaked, which is why they turned off the water. Would we have not bought the unit if we'd known about the dishwasher? Of course not. It cost us only $150 to replace the window shade plus $60 to replace the faulty hose.

But, boy, were we steamed. We wrote a nasty letter to the sellers and felt much better.

**FIRST-TIME BUYER TIP:** Make sure your inspection contingency allows you to withdraw from the deal if the home inspector gives you an unsatisfactory report on the property. But remember, all homes, even new ones, have problems. And old homes often have older and more difficult problems. Keep your expectations in line with what you're buying. If you're buying an older home, don't assume it will be in perfect condition or that the seller will pay to upgrade the house with next-century technology. If that's your assumption, you may be better off renting.

# CHAPTER 10

# Possession and Other Parts of the Offer to Purchase

## Question 85: What Is Possession?

You've heard the cliché: Possession is nine-tenths of the law.

In real estate, possession is when you actually take physical control of the home. Most buyers take possession of the home at the closing. The keys, garage door openers, and other security devices are handed to the buyer from the seller, who has moved all of his or her belongings from the home. At that moment, you have the right to do anything you want with your house.

Sometimes possession is given either before the closing or after. Let's say you need a place to live or want to renovate the home prior to the closing. The seller might let you take possession a few days early so that you can move in or get started on your remodeling. Many real estate attorneys advise sellers not to allow a pre-closing possession by the buyer. It's very risky because the buyer might move in and then decide not to close. At that point, the seller becomes a landlord and may have to pursue an eviction proceeding against the buyer.

Possession issues in a residential real estate transaction usually involve a seller who wants to stay in the house after closing (see Question 86).

Possession and the closing date are closely linked. Sometimes they're used as negotiation points when money isn't the primary issue. In one case in California, a first-time buyer made a full-price offer for a woman's house, but the woman was having trouble accepting the offer. She hadn't found a place to move her family and was worried. The buyer stretched out the date of the closing, in exchange for a few thousand dollars off the sales price, and the deal went through.

 **NEW CONSTRUCTION TIP:** With new construction, you can't close on your new house and move in until the builder has obtained a certificate of occupancy (also known as the COO). This certificate is issued by the local municipality and certifies that the house meets code and that basic necessities (such as the walls, roof, electricity, plumbing, and other mechanicals) are in place and are working. If you're concerned about the condition of the home and the builder says he's received the COO, ask to see it. If you have any questions, call the local building or planning department that issued the COO. While punch list items (small details that haven't yet been installed or need to be fixed) may remain, COOs are only issued once the house is virtually complete.

## Question 86: What If the Seller Wants to Stay in the House After Closing?

When the seller indicates he or she would like to stay on after closing for a few days or weeks, it's called a *post-closing possession*. There are two issues to consider:

1. **Charging a reasonable daily rate.** If you've got a few weeks to go on your lease or if Mom and Dad are gracious about letting you camp out for a few more nights, you might want to grant the post-closing possession. In some states, it's customary to allow the sellers a few days or even a week to move out after the closing. If you do allow a post-closing possession, you'll want to charge the sellers a reasonable rate for the extra time they stay in what will now be your house. This "reasonable" rate (which might be covered by local custom) should cover your daily expenses, including the daily cost of your mortgage, homeowners' insurance, and taxes.

2. **Sellers overstaying their welcome.** The risk with letting the sellers stay after the closing is that they might never leave. And if the sellers don't leave, you'll have to

force them out. At that point, you'll want to make them pay dearly for each extra day they stay, so the sellers realize it will be much cheaper for them to leave.

What happens if you get the nightmare scenario—the sellers never indicate during the contract negotiations a desire to stay post-closing but then announce their intention to stay for a while at closing? Houston, you may have a problem. Real estate attorneys generally advise buyers to refuse to close unless the seller has moved out. Usually, the threat of not closing (plus an extremely stiff financial penalty) is enough to get the sellers motivated to leave.

**20/20 HINDSIGHT:** Schedule your final walk-through after the sellers have moved out, or while they are moving, so you'll know that they're really going to be, or are, gone. The ideal situation is to walk through the empty property so you can see whether there has been any damage caused by the sellers or their movers and then go directly to the closing.

In cases where the sellers ask to stay in the home after closing (either because the sellers' purchase of another home is a couple of days after the sale, or the sellers are arranging a move to another city), you can give them the couple of days (a set number) for a modest fee that will cover all of your expenses of ownership. But when those days are up, you should encourage them to move out fast. An amount of money large enough to convince the sellers it's time to move should be held back at closing, in an escrow account, in addition to the daily fees they will owe you.

If the money is held in escrow, and your sellers turn out to be deadbeats, it's much more likely you'll see that cash.

## Calculating a Daily Fee That Will Motivate Your Sellers

There are several ways to calculate the kind of daily fee that will motivate your sellers:

1. Charge the same prices as an expensive, local hotel.

2. Find out the going rent for the home like yours, then divide by thirty (or the number of days in the month).

In either case, you want the sellers to understand that staying in the home will be a very expensive proposition. Should all else fail, and the sellers continue to stay in your new home, you may have to take legal action. Consult your attorney for more details.

> **FIRST-TIME BUYER TIP:** In some areas of the country, it's customary for the seller to retain possession at no cost for three to five days after closing. Your broker or attorney should be able to advise you on local closing customs during negotiations. Be sure to include any post-closing possession (beyond the customary time frame) costs in the offer to purchase docs.

# Question 87: When Is the Right Time to Terminate the Contract? How Do I Do It?

The question you should really ask yourself is: Why do I want to terminate the contract to purchase?

If you want to terminate the contract because you're feeling buyer's remorse (see Question 88), you can't. That's the tough part about the real estate game. The rules say that when you write,[*] sign, and present the offer, and the seller then accepts it, you have a deal. Unless your inspector finds something wrong with the home, or your attorney rejects the contract, or your lender won't grant you a mortgage, and you have contingencies in the contract for each of these cases, you're pretty much stuck.

Some unscrupulous buyers will tell their attorneys to summarily "reject" a contract if they get cold feet. That's not really fair to the seller, who has allowed you to tie up the

---

[*] All offers to purchase real estate must be put in writing and signed in order to be valid.

property during the negotiation process. In addition, the seller may be able to sue you for something called *specific performance,* which is essentially making you live up to the deal to which you signed your name.

When can you walk away from a deal? You may be able to if you're willing to forfeit your deposit or earnest money. Most first-time buyers have little cash, so the idea of giving up 5, 10, or 20 percent of the purchase price, or even $1,000, seems a little steep. But it's been done many times before. In this case, the earnest money is either split between the seller and the broker, or the seller gets to keep it all.

In all cases, you'll want to walk away from the deal at the earliest possible moment, and you'll need to follow the specific provisions in the contract about notice (usually written) and timing, in order for the withdrawal to be valid.

### Returning the Earnest Money

When you put down a good-faith deposit, also known as the earnest money, it's usually deposited in the escrow account of the seller's broker. The seller's broker may not release that money to you without the seller's permission.

I frequently receive letters from buyers telling me that the seller's broker refuses to release the cash. If you do terminate the contract for valid reasons, the seller should sign off on the release of the earnest money. But sometimes sellers don't—just out of spite.

If this happens to you, your next step will likely be to explore your legal options. Talk to your real estate attorney. You may have to file suit in order to shake your money loose.

## Question 88: What Is Buyer's Remorse and How Do I Cope with It?

"Buyer's remorse" is the sinking feeling in the pit of your stomach that you've made a terrible mistake. It usually occurs within a week after your broker presents your offer to purchase or you sign the purchase and sale agreement—sometimes even that very minute. It keeps you awake at night, tossing and turning in a cold sweat, as you wonder how you're going to make the payments and you agonize over your choice. Did you make the right one?

Pam, a broker in Rock Hill, South Carolina, says that if a first-time buyer has buyer's remorse, the only person to blame is the real estate agent. "If the agent has truly done her job and qualified those people, and found out what they really wanted in their first home, then they should be happy," she says. "But if the agent turns a blind eye to their insecurity about buying a home and doesn't try to help them understand the process, it can be very tough."

---

**SUSANNE'S STORY**

No one is exempt from buyer's remorse—even a top real estate agent like my mother.

My mother, Susanne, has had a more than thirty-year career in real estate and, for many years, she was widely considered to be among the top agents in the Chicago area. In some years, she sold in excess of $20 million in property.

But she has only owned two personal residences in her life: a 1920s co-op that she and my father bought for $35,000 when I was three, and the condo she now lives in that she bought some fifteen years ago in what was then a brand-new complex. She's never had a mortgage.

She has only bought one investment property, even though she has helped thousands of people successfully buy and sell homes throughout her career and has invested in syndicated real estate deals. We had bought a one-bedroom condo in downtown Chicago for Sam to use for his office nearly twenty years ago. Because we bought there, my mother decided to buy a two-bedroom condo. And that's when she came down with a bad case of buyer's remorse.

It was the perfect investment: All of her expenses were covered for the time she owned it. But she couldn't wait to get rid of it. She sold it quickly, and a couple of years later the property doubled again in value.

---

# Fighting Your Emotions

Buying a home is such an emotional process that first-timers often get overwhelmed. Real estate agent Pam says brokers should be understanding and help clients know whether they are making the right decision for the right reason. Brokers should be able to read the personality of that buyer and make sure that the decision is not 100 percent emotion, zero percent common sense.

Pam says that she often helps her distraught first-time buyers with something she calls "the Ben Franklin Close." She advises her buyers to make a list of everything you like about the house and then everything you would change. This, she says, will help you make a rational decision by seeing the pluses and minuses of a home.

## Curing Buyer's Remorse

What's the cure for buyer's remorse? I hate to be the bearer of bad clichés, but "time heals all wounds." Give yourself six months in your new home. If you still hate it, you can always turn around and try to sell it. Chances are, after six months to a year, you'll be settled in and feeling a whole lot better.

 **FIRST-TIME BUYER TIP:** Your best defense against a bad case of buyer's remorse is preparation. If you haven't already created your wish list and reality check, you should do so. Knowing the difference between what you want in a home and what you can't live without will help you understand the important compromises that have to be made when you purchase your first home. And that's exactly what it is—your first home, not your last one. If you hate your house, you can always sell it. Life's too short to do otherwise.

# CHAPTER 11

# Before You Close

G et ready. Life is about to start moving very quickly. Once you've gone through the contingency period and you know you're buying this property (barring something unexpected), there will be a long list of items to get through that will make the closing a smoother experience.

## Question 89: When Should I Schedule My Pre-Closing Inspection? What Do I Do If I Discover Something Is Damaged or Missing? When Should the Seller Move Out?

When it comes to buying or selling a house, the cliché holds true: No good deed goes unpunished.

**PATTY AND FRANK'S STORY**

Patty and Frank agreed to buy a $300,000 condominium from David and Marla. When they negotiated the contract, David and Marla agreed to leave all the fixtures, including light fixtures, refrigerator, sconces, and bookcases that were attached to the wall. Everything was so friendly that Patty and Frank decided to forgo the pre-closing inspection. They felt as though they didn't need to walk through the apartment because David and Marla assured them that everything was in order.

After the closing, everyone shook hands, and David and Marla handed over the keys. Patty and Frank went over to their new condo, opened the door, and discovered that it had been stripped bare: no light fixtures, no refrigerator, no sconces, and huge holes in the wall where the bookcases had been ripped out. They were, understandably, heartbroken.

While David and Marla certainly should have lived up to the contract (they could be sued), Patty and Frank should have taken it upon themselves to have a final walk-through of the apartment before closing.

## Moral of the Story: Never Leave Anything to Chance (or Goodwill)

Most first-time buyers don't realize that they should ask for a pre-closing inspection. Sure, just about everyone understands that they can ask for an initial inspection, and bring a licensed house inspector along to point out what's wrong with the home. But too many first-time buyers aren't told that they should also request the right to a second, *pre*-closing inspection.

To avoid getting burned, schedule the walk-through as close to the actual closing as possible, certainly within the twenty-four to forty-eight hours prior to closing. *If possible, the sellers should have already moved out.* The whole point of the walk-through is to protect yourself and your future property from sellers who aren't as nice as they seem to be, or who are actually as nasty as they appear. By inspecting the premises, you're making sure the seller has lived up to his or her agreements in the sales contract. And if he or she hasn't, you want to know about it in advance of the closing so remedies (both monetary and otherwise) can be agreed upon before money changes hands.

## The Devil's in the Details

What should you look for in a pre-closing inspection? To start with, you want to make sure that the condition of the home hasn't materially changed since you signed the contract several months earlier. Remember, you probably negotiated for the home some sixty to ninety days ago and have spent the past few weeks arranging for your mortgage, packing, and preparing to move. As Patty and Frank discovered, a lot can change in sixty days—or afterward.

Here is a general checklist for your walk-through:

1. Turn on every appliance.

2. Open every door.

3. Make sure nothing's broken.

4. Be certain everything the seller agreed to leave is actually there, and in good shape.

5. Be certain that when the sellers moved out, they did no damage to the home.

It's vital that you turn on every appliance that's being left in the home, including the dishwasher. As you may recall from our very own dishwasher story, Sam and I learned this the hard way. (It's been years, but Sam and I still discuss whether or not our old sellers actually knew that the dishwasher leaked. Regardless, we know we should have tested the dishwasher while we were there and let it run a full cycle even if we were going to eventually redo the kitchen and replace it.)

## Don't Be Shy

It's equally important to open every door. Don't be afraid to poke your head into your seller's messy closets. You're looking for anything unusual or broken. Finally, be certain that everything the seller agreed to leave is actually in place and in the apartment. Check your contract if you're not sure if that window air conditioner was part of the agreement. Are the window shades or curtains supposed to be left? Or did the seller want to take them? If the seller asks you at the pre-closing inspection if he or she can take additional items, simply say, "I have to check with my attorney." That will give you time to think about whether or not you want to give away that chandelier.

**ANOTHER SAM AND ILYCE STORY**

When we went for our pre-closing inspection, our sellers were in the process of moving out. There were boxes everywhere and it was extremely difficult to move through the house.

Our seller looked out onto the backyard and motioned to the swing set. "My son built that," he said.

We looked out and nodded. "It's a fine piece of work," Sam said.

"My grandchildren just love playing on it," our seller said.

"I can imagine they do," I said, looking over the fine construction: two swings, a sandbox, and long blue slide. The top of the slide was built like a small fort, with straight sides. I imagined little children climbing up to the top and hiding out, then escaping down the slide.

"If you're not going to use it, would you mind if we took it with us?" our seller asked.

Sam and I looked at each other and smiled. While it was true that we didn't have children at the time (we now have two, who are in their twenties), we had planned to put that swing set to great use over the next few years.

"I'm sorry," I told our seller. "But we do plan to use it. It stays."

To replace that swing set with one of the same quality would have cost us, at the time, more than $700. I wasn't ready to ante up that kind of cash so that our seller could have a ready-made play area for his grandchildren in his new home. (Though I could have charged him the $700 to take the swing set with him.) And today, twenty-five years later, it still sits in our yard. Our neighbors' young daughters like to come and play on it.

## New Construction Pre-Closing Walk-Through

If you're buying new construction, you'll also want the right to conduct a pre-closing walk-through, but you'll be looking for different things than someone buying an existing home. You want to be sure that everything the developer promised would be done and put in is actually there and working before closing. This includes any sod or plantings, doorknobs, doorbell, window screens, fixtures, appliances, etc.

You also want to be sure that everything works in every room. Take a hair dryer or radio with you and test out the electrical sockets in each room. You can buy a simple device that will tell you if a socket has been wired correctly. Make sure everything has been painted and is in working condition. Turn on the water in the showers and sinks, and flush the toilets. If there is a garage, make sure the electric door opener works.

With new construction, there are always a few last-minute items that need to be finished, and it may not be possible for the contractor or developer to get them finished before closing. That's why you need a *punch list*. A punch list is a list of all items that need to be fixed in the home before you consider it completely finished.

During your pre-closing inspection, write down all of the items that need attention: that loose tile in the master bath, the wall that wasn't painted, the electrical outlet that doesn't work, the tree that should have been planted in the side yard. Have your attorney or broker present the punch list to the developer at closing, or before closing, and have the developer agree to fix these items (in writing) before you actually close. Often, the list of punch list items gets attached to the purchase contract and most developers should be happy to comply with any reasonable request.[*]

## Attendance Is Mandatory

Who should go to your walk-through? My mother, Susanne, makes it a point to go to almost all of her clients' walk-throughs. She says she helps the buyer remember what was where amid the mess and muck of moving. It goes without saying that you, the buyer (or buyers, if you're buying with someone else), should attend the walk-through. You should ask your broker to be there. Beyond that, the seller or the seller's broker may attend. Sometimes, if the buyer is out of town, the buyer's attorney will attend.

If the seller attends and you notice that certain things are missing, try to avoid a confrontation. Have your broker speak to the seller or seller's broker to confirm what was written in the contract.

Some buyers like to have a professional house inspector attend the pre-closing inspection. I think that's overkill in most cases. The pre-closing inspection isn't about finding a leaky oil tank. You should be looking for things like a gash in the wall caused by the

---

[*] Taking care of punch list items can be the most frustrating part of working with a new construction builder. It's also why I suggest you spend time vetting the builder by knocking on doors and talking to people who already live in the community or in homes that were built by the developer.

L-shaped sofa as it was moved out of the home. That gash is something you could ask the sellers to fix before closing, or they could give you a credit at closing for the damage.

## Missing in Action

What should you do if you discover something's missing or damaged during the pre-closing inspection? Make a list of anything that doesn't seem right to you and take photos and call your attorney immediately after you leave the home. You can also call your broker. Your attorney may telephone the seller's attorney before closing, or may present a list of items at closing. Either way, the list will have to be resolved before you'll agree to close on the house.

The list gives you some leverage, because as anxious as you are to move, the sellers are equally anxious and have most likely found another place to live. Perhaps they're scheduled to close on a new home shortly after you buy theirs. At this point, most sellers and the attorneys will find a way to make everyone happy. The seller may offer you $45 instead of fixing the back door. He or she might offer you $600 for the washer and dryer their movers took "by accident." Or the seller might say, "Forget it, I'm not fixing the east window screen."

Just remember that the pre-closing inspection or walk-through gives you your last opportunity to make sure that the property is in the same condition (except for normal wear and tear) as the day you bought it. It's important that you take full advantage of that opportunity.

## When Should the Seller Move Out?

Ideally, the seller is gone before your pre-closing inspection. And unless there are some extraordinary circumstances, you should make sure the seller is completely out of the home before you close on the home. That doesn't mean the end of the business day, as in you close at 10 a.m. and the seller's out by 5 p.m. Your new home isn't a business. Getting the seller out by the closing means that if you're scheduled to close at 10:00 a.m., the seller is packed and gone by 9:59.

After closing (and getting all of his or her money), the seller has little, if any, incentive to move out. If you close and pay money to the seller, and then the seller decides not to leave, well, then, you might have a real problem getting them out. Also, the seller no longer has any interest in the property once the deed changes hands. An unscrupulous seller might be inclined to inflict damage (if the transaction has been a bit hostile), or may be less than careful when moving his or her items out of the home. You want to protect your property, and the best way to do that is to make sure the seller is out before money changes hands.

This said, sometimes buyers and sellers make other arrangements. For example, let's say the seller has had his home on the market for a long time—say, a year—and within the year, the seller went out and bought another home and moved. So the house you're buying is vacant and perhaps empty of furniture, which means the seller probably wants to close as quickly as possible. You don't want to close until your apartment lease is up (so you avoid paying both rent and mortgage), but you do want to get in a little early to do some painting, and would the seller mind? It doesn't hurt to ask. If the seller seems to hesitate, offer to "rent" the house for a few days before closing for a nominal daily fee.

The earliest the seller would probably want to let you into a house would be two to three weeks before closing. When Sam's mom passed away, her best friend Rocky bought the condo. Sam allowed her to have free access to it from the day they agreed to the sale until the closing, and Rocky was able to get the condo repainted and fixed up before she moved in.

There's greater risk for you, the buyer, if the seller wants to stay in the house after closing. Let's look at why a seller might want to do this:

- **No place to go.** The seller may not have found anywhere to live. This is the most dangerous for you because there is no end in sight for when the seller might leave. It could be in a few days, a few months, or never. Also, you're going to be coming from somewhere and will want to—or have to—move into your house.

- **Bad timing.** The seller isn't scheduled to close on his or her new home until a few days after closing. Most sellers are going to turn around and buy something new. In a perfect world, the sellers would attend your closing while they simultaneously closed on their new house. However, this isn't a perfect world, and the sellers will usually want to close first on your home, because then they'll be able to use the funds to purchase *their* new home. So you might be scheduled to close on your house on a Friday, and the seller is scheduled to close on his new place on Monday and may ask to "rent" your house for the weekend. If this is the case, and you have a few extra days you can spend in your current place of abode and the seller will pay you the daily rate you want, then that's fine. (Just so you know, the seller could close on his new place a few days ahead of your closing by using a financial product known as a "bridge loan." A bridge loan is a short-term loan that allows the seller to borrow enough money to close on his new home before he sells his old home. Some sellers get into trouble, however, by buying a new home before trying to sell their original home. If that happens, and they use a bridge loan to fund the new purchase, they could end up paying the equivalent of three mortgages simultaneously: their original home mortgage, the new home mortgage, and their bridge loan.)

- **Change of heart**. Sometimes, after fixing up a house for sale, the seller decides he or she doesn't really want to move after all. Hopefully, this change of heart will come before the seller has accepted an offer. But it has been known to happen a day or so before closing.

## Paying the Piper

How much should you charge for each extra day the seller stays in the home? The first thing to do is to calculate exactly how much the home costs per day.*

Add up your monthly mortgage (principal and interest), taxes, and insurance premiums, then divide by thirty (unless we're talking February). That number is your minimum out-of-pocket cost to own and maintain the home each day. Let's say you have a $100,000 mortgage at 8 percent annually. That's $8,000 ÷ 12 = $666.67 per month. And let's say your real estate tax bill is $3,000 per year, or $250 per month. Your insurance premium is $35 per month.

**$666.67 + $250 + $35 = $951.67 (MONTHLY COST OF THE HOME)**

**$951.67 ÷ 30 = $31.72 (DAILY COST OF THE HOME)**

If this were your home, you can see it would cost $31.72 per day for PITI (principal, interest, taxes, and insurance), which is generally the most expensive part of homeownership. If you think that $31.72 is too cheap for a daily fee to adequately encourage the

---

* In some areas, local tradition dictates that sellers can stay for free up to a week after the closing. But just because local traditions exist doesn't mean you have to follow them.

seller to make his or her after-closing stay a short one, you may increase the daily fee by as much as you think is necessary. Certainly, a few dollars more per day for electricity, heat, gas, water, sewer, and garbage pickup wouldn't be out of line. Also, if there are any assessments (for condos, co-ops, and townhouses), those fees should also be covered. When all's said and done, $50 or $75 per day starts to add up pretty quickly.

 **FIRST-TIME BUYER TIP:** The daily fee and the length of the after-closing stay should be negotiated before the closing. There should also be a stiff daily penalty for each day the seller stays in the house past the agreed-upon deadline. You, or your attorney, should make it completely clear to the seller and his or her attorney that the seller will not receive all the proceeds from the closing until he or she has moved out of the house and you've had a chance to walk through the house to make sure that the house is still in good condition and the appliances and plumbing are still in working order.

## When to Hold Back Money at Closing

How much money should be held back at closing? It's a good idea to retain enough cash to cover the payment due for the after-closing stay, plus at least another ten days' worth. Usually, this amount is equal to 2 to 3 percent of the purchase price of the home, although it may be subject to local custom and, in some cases, state law. If you give the seller all the money at closing, you may have to sue to collect your daily fee from the seller. The money should be given to your real estate broker, the title company, or an unassociated third party, and held in an escrow account.

## Question 90: What Exactly Is the Closing? Where Is It Held?

By now you've probably heard about "the Closing," which is also called "the Settlement," depending on where you live in the country. (For purposes of this book, I'll probably refer to it as the closing, but if you're hearing "settlement" or "escrow closing," rest assured that we're talking about the same thing.)

Real estate industry professionals talk about the closing as if it were (a) a big show on Broadway, and (b) some huge black hole in outer space, sucking buyers, sellers, brokers, lawyers, inspectors, money, and mortgages into a netherworld blender out of which pops a deed that now has your name on it. Those are the two extremes. After it's over, you and your broker will either describe your closing as a dream or a nightmare. Rarely have I heard them described as being somewhere in the middle.

So let's start at the top. Why do we have the closing? Well, one attorney put it this way: If you were the seller, would you take the buyer's personal check, fold it up, and put it in your pocket, and then hand the buyer the deed to your house? Of course not. You would want some security that that check was really going to clear. Conversely, you, the buyer, want some reassurance that the deed you're being given is actually the seller's to give. Your lender, worried that you will take bad title to the home (which could mean trouble down the pike for his loan), also wants that same reassurance. The broker wants some security that he or she will actually get paid the commission. The attorney wants to know that his or her fee will be paid.

Everyone wants to be protected. It is from this point that today's closing or settlement evolved. Closing a transaction has always meant that point in time when the deal is completed. One party has paid another for certain rights, privileges, property, or other goods and services. When the passing of money or other consideration has occurred, and the goods and services have been received, a deal is deemed closed. Kaput. Finished.

Around the country, closings are generally held at the title company, which issues title insurance for the buyer (if you're smart enough to get it for yourself, which I'll talk about in a moment) and the lender. The title company researches the chain of title to the home. Your attorney reviews the information furnished by the title company to make sure you will get "good" title to the home when you close. Once the title issues have been resolved (that is, if they need to be resolved), then the title company will insure title in your name—with any exception shown on the policy—in the amount of the purchase price. But remember, lender's title insurance covers the lender's losses on the property, if some outside claim to the title is eventually upheld. If you want to protect your interests, you will have to purchase a separate owner's title insurance policy that insures your losses.

A title or escrow company facilitates the closing by providing a forum for the free exchange of documents and releasing of funds. Generally, the title company acts as an agent for the lender, meaning that the title company works to protect the lender's best interests. However, the seller generally selects which title company will be used, because he or she is the party that usually pays for title insurance. (Of course, who pays for the title policy is dictated by local custom.) If the title company can act as agent for the lender, and close the transaction, the closing will take place at the offices of the title company. Otherwise, the closing may take place at the office of the lender, or another location acceptable to the lender.

In several states, including California and New York, it's more common to have what's known as an escrow closing. In this case, the title company acts for the benefit of both parties, using a document called an "escrow agreement." The title company will only disburse money after certain steps take place. For example, in an escrow closing, the title company will send someone to the recorder's office (where deeds are recorded). Once the name on the deed has been verified as being that of the sellers, and the transfer of title has been accomplished, the title company will allow the closing to take place. If there are any problems along the way, the title company returns the closing funds to the buyer and seller, and records a deed from the buyer back to the seller.

**20/20 HINDSIGHT:** In states that have escrow closings, typically no one goes to a "closing" the way folks in the northern and eastern parts of the country think about it. In other words, don't expect to go to one place and sign a lot of documents. Instead, you provide the escrow company with your set of instructions, paperwork, and money, as does the other side. Once the instructions from both parties are carried out, monies are collected, checks cut, and monies disbursed, the deal is considered closed. It may happen when you expect it, or it may take some extra time.

## The Closing

From the buyer's perspective, the closing can be generally broken into three pieces:

1. **Review and signing of loan documents**. In the first phase of the closing, you, the buyer, must review and sign all of the loan documents provided by the lender. There may be seven to twenty documents or more, including the actual mortgage, note, affidavits, Truth in Lending statements, estimate of closing costs, and the escrow

statement letter that outlines how much will be paid into the real estate tax and insurance escrows.

2. **The relationship between you and the seller and the title company.** There is an exchange of documents that must be signed by you and the seller, and then other documents that require the additional signature of the title company. Depending on your local customs, the seller will provide certain documents for your inspection to verify that they are correct:
   - The deed
   - Bill of sale
   - Affidavit of title
   - Any documentation that may have been required in the contract, including paid water bills, certificates of compliance with laws pertaining to smoke-detection equipment, lead paint, termite or radon inspection (these items will vary from state to state, and even county to county)
   - Condo assessment full-payment certificate
   - Co-op assessment full-payment certificate
   - Insurance certificate
   - Property survey (except for condos and co-ops).

You may have anywhere from a handful of documents to a dozen or more that will require both your (and your spouse's or partner's) signature and the seller's. After you have finished with these documents, the title company will have more papers for you to sign. These documents generally relate to the title or are papers the title company must send to the Internal Revenue Service regarding the purchase and sale of the home. Your documentation may include these:
   - The RESPA (Real Estate Settlement Procedures Act) "Master Statement" or Buyer's and Seller's statements[*] outline who provides the money and from which sources, and details how the money gets paid out. This document is signed by you, the seller, and the title company.

---

[*] These are new forms since the RESPA/TRID revisions to the closing process. A combined statement may be issued, or the buyer and seller will receive separate statements.

- Disclosure statements about construction contracts or any agreements entered into within the past three to six months for work to be done on the property. This is to ensure that there will be no outstanding mechanics' liens placed on the property.
- Disclosure statement about any tenants who have access to the property other than the buyer or seller.
- Statements about any other matters that could ultimately affect the title to the property, such as lawsuits.
- Internal Revenue Service form 1099, which relates the sales price of the home. Once signed, it will be used to cross-check your IRS form with documentation signed by the title company regarding the purchase and sale of the home. Many of these documents are signed and notarized. (Each state and county has little particular quirks regarding documentation. For example, any document that will be recorded in Hawaii must be typed and signed in black ink only. Otherwise, it will not be accepted. In other parts of the country, the notary stamp must be embossed.) Once the documents are notarized, the closing can proceed to the final step: disbursement.

3. **Disbursement of funds**. Once all the documents have been signed, dated, and notarized, the title company can proceed with the disbursement of funds. It will take the money from you, the buyer, and cut checks to the seller, the seller's lender (if applicable), the brokers, the title company, and the attorneys. Since everyone usually gets paid out of the closing proceeds, it's easy to see why the title company doesn't accept personal checks, even for a few pennies. Title companies accept only cashier's or certified checks or a wire transfer, because that's like accepting cash.*

## And If There's No Lender Involved?

Good question. Almost all first-time buyers will have some sort of financing involved with their purchase, simply because it's expensive to buy a home (even a home that costs

---

* Sorry, but as of this writing, Bitcoin and other digital currencies are not accepted.

$30,000), and most first-time buyers don't have that kind of cash stuffed inside their mattresses. (I'm sure there are one or two, but we're talking majority here.) If there's no lender, or if the seller is acting as lender through seller financing, the buyer and seller can sit down together and exchange and sign documents. Or they can have the title company act as an intermediary between the seller and buyer in an escrow closing. The closing may take less time (most closings that involve financing generally take between thirty minutes and two hours) and will certainly have fewer steps overall.

In the next few questions, I'll dissect some of the more complicated pieces of the closing and explain in a bit more detail why they're important.

## Question 91: What Are My Closing Costs Likely to Be?

It's expensive to close on your house. There are lender's fees, title fees, recording fees, city and state transfer taxes, and so on. Of course, the lion's share of the buyer's closing costs is generated by the mortgage. The lender's points—a point equals 1 percent of the loan amount—which may also be referred to as the service charge, or discount points, or origination fee, are the largest fees paid to the lender and usually run between 1 and 3 percent of the loan amount. Occasionally, the points will run more than 3 percent, and there are some loans available with zero points.

(Remember that for every extra point you pay up front, the lender should decrease the interest rate of the loan. If you have the cash and are planning to stay in the home for a long time, you might want to pay three points to get the lowest interest rate possible. The points are fully deductible on your income tax return in the year you buy your home. On the other hand, if you're strapped for cash today, but know that down the line your prospects are good for a higher income, you may want to go with zero points and a slightly higher interest rate, then refinance down the line.)

If you've been reading this book start to finish, you know that when it comes to calculating closing costs, your lender is supposed to make it easier for you by giving you a written good-faith estimate of all closing costs. This estimate is supposed to accurately reflect the buyer's closing costs. And you're supposed to see the final closing costs seventy-two hours before you close, thanks to the new TRID rules. Still, the sheer number of different closing costs and the dollar amount they add up to often surprise buyers at the closing table.

Here's a list of common closing cost responsibilities. Remember, not every charge will apply to your loan, and your actual fee may be higher or lower depending on your specific situation. Ask your real estate attorney or broker to help you go over this list and identify how much each item might cost.

## Buyer's Closing Costs

This list of home buyer closing costs was accurate as of the day we went to publication. But these costs change frequently, so check in at ThinkGlink.com for updates on Buyer and Seller Closing Costs.[*]

| Fee | Expect to Pay | Your Cost |
|---|---|---|
| Lender's points, loan origination, or loan service fees | Up to 3 percent of the loan, or more. | _____ |
| Loan application fee | $0 to $700 | _____ |
| Lender's credit report | $25 to $65 | _____ |
| Lender's processing fee | $75 to $550 | _____ |
| Lender's document preparation fee | $50 to $250 | _____ |
| Lender's appraisal fee | $225 to $600 | _____ |
| Prepaid interest on the loan | Variable, paid per day from the date of closing until the end of the month. | _____ |
| Lender's insurance escrow | About 15 to 20 percent of the cost of the homeowners' insurance policy for one year. | _____ |
| Lender's tax escrow | About 33 to 50 percent of annual property taxes, depending on the time of year you close. (This is just at closing. After closing, you will begin to make regular real estate tax and insurance escrow payments as part of your monthly mortgage payment.) | _____ |
| Lender's tax escrow service fee, a fee to set up the tax escrow | $40 to $95 | _____ |

---

[*] Yes, sellers also pay a long list of closing costs. To see it, check out ThinkGlink.com and search "seller closing costs updated."

| Fee | Expect to Pay | Your Cost |
|---|---|---|
| Title insurance cost for the lender's policy | Up to $1,500, based on the dollar amount of the home you buy and your location. The cost to the buyer for title insurance may be relatively small because the seller may have paid a basic fee to the title company and the lender's policy is issued simultaneously. In many parts of the country, it is the seller's responsibility to ensure that the home is owned free and clear. So the seller picks up most of the cost of title insurance. When you refinance, you'll find that the cost for title insurance goes up substantially. If you purchase a $100,000 house, your title insurance cost might be a flat $150. If you refinance that house, your title insurance may skyrocket to $415. That reflects the additional $265 that the seller paid to ensure that you received good title to his or her home. | _____ |
| Special endorsements to the title | $100 each or more, but are generally included in the title insurance cost. Depending on the type of property you are buying, your lender may require that special endorsements be added to the title. If the lender requires an environmental lien endorsement, it may cost $100. A location endorsement proves the house is located where the documents say it is. If you choose an adjustable-rate mortgage, that may be another $100 endorsement, depending on the title company. If the property is a condominium, there may be a condo endorsement. For a townhouse, there may be a PUD (planned-unit development) endorsement. As you can see, three or four extra endorsements can really add to your closing cost tab. | _____ |
| Any outstanding house inspection fees | $250 to $400 | _____ |
| Title company closing fee | Up to $2,000, depending on the purchase price | _____ |
| Title company wire transfer fee | Up to $75 | _____ |

| FEE | EXPECT TO PAY | YOUR COST |
|---|---|---|
| Title company receiving lender's package | Up to $75 | _____ |
| Title fee for processing/recording documents | Up to $50 | _____ |
| Title fee for sending the package back to the lender | Up to $75 | _____ |
| Other assorted title charges | Variable | _____ |
| Recording fees, of deed or mortgage | Up $300 | _____ |
| Local municipal taxes: city, town, or village property transfer tax; county transfer tax; state transfer tax | Some transactions will cost nothing while others might have nominal transfer expense of $100, and other localities that rely on transfer taxes, you could pay upwards of 1 percent or more of the sales price. But expect this to vary by county, city and state. | _____ |
| Flood certification fee, a fee you'll pay to determine whether the home you're buying is in a floodplain | $10 to $50 | _____ |
| Attorney's fee | Expect to pay up to $1,000 or more if you're buying an extremely expensive home. Although some attorneys in large firms work solely on an hourly rate, there are many real estate attorneys who do house closings for a flat fee, and then may charge a small amount extra depending on whether your deal turns out to be particularly complicated or difficult. If you live in an escrow closing state, like California, you won't be paying an attorney's fee, because you won't be using an attorney. But you will be paying an escrow closing fee, which would be similar to a title company charging you for the space it takes to close the deal—except that they don't charge for it. | _____ |
| Condo move-in fee | $0 to more than $500 | _____ |
| Association transfer fee (often required for condominium and townhouse buyers) | $0 to more than $500 | _____ |

| Fee | Expect to Pay | Your Cost |
|---|---|---|
| Co-op apartment fees (small fees that may be required by co-op associations for transferring shares of stock since with a co-op you're not buying an apartment, you're buying shares in a corporation that owns the building in which your apartment is located or for doing name searches) | $50 to more than $200, or you might be charged a percentage of the sales price. | _____ |
| Condo and co-op building board credit checks | Variable | _____ |

# Question 92: What Is a Title Search? What Is Title Insurance? Why Do I Need Them?

How do you prove you own something? Generally, you have a bill of sale, or the certificate of title to the item—let's say it's a car—that's registered in your name with the state. If anyone inquires who owns that cherry red Ford Mustang, the state can tell them it's you. Proving that a seller owns a particular home, however, is a little more difficult, and lenders won't allow you to purchase a home without knowing it actually belongs to the person selling it. So how do you prove the seller owns the home you want to buy? You conduct a title search.

During a title search, the examiner looks at the chain of title of a home, working backward from owner to owner until it reaches the point where the land was originally granted or sold from the government to the original owners or developers. If the title has been recorded correctly, you should be able to trace the lineage of a piece of land all the way back to when that area of the country was settled. (As with many of our laws, we derive our methods of recording title from our English cousins, whose records of property ownership stretch back a thousand years or more in some cases.)

How the title search is carried out varies from city to city, and depends on what kinds of records have been kept. Public records that may affect a property's title include records of deaths, divorces, court judgments, liens, taxes, and wills. Public records in a wide variety of county and city offices must be examined, including those in the recorders of deeds, county courts, tax assessors, and surveyors. Since many local governments have not yet computerized their records, the majority of title searches are performed manually, with someone spending hours (in many cases) poring over different documents in various offices. (However, if the municipality in which you are buying has computerized this information, title searches can be done in a matter of minutes.)

## Searching the Title

Title searches are conducted by lawyers, title companies, or title specialists, to discover if there are any problems—called "clouds" in the industry—with the title. The lender wants to know if there have been any liens (a claim made against a property by a person or tax assessor for payment of a debt) or judgments (by a court of law) or easements (known or unknown rights) filed against the property, which might prevent you from receiving good title.

## Top 20 Things Title Insurance Protects You From

There are more than one hundred reasons you should have title insurance. I've included the top twenty things here, courtesy of First American Title Company.

1. Forged deeds, mortgages, satisfactions, or releases.

2. Deed by person who is insane or mentally incompetent.

3. Deed by minor (may be disavowed).

4. Deed from corporation, unauthorized under corporate bylaws or given under falsified corporate resolution.

5. Deed from partnership, unauthorized under partnership agreement.

6. Deed from purported trustee, unauthorized under trust agreement.

7. Deed to or from a "corporation" before incorporation, or after loss of corporate charter.

8. Deed from a legal nonentity (styled, for example, as a church, charity, or club).

9. Deed by person in a foreign country, vulnerable to challenge as incompetent, unauthorized, or defective under foreign laws.

10. Claims resulting from use of "alias" or fictitious name style by a predecessor in title.

11. Deed challenged as being given under fraud, undue influence, or duress.

12. Deed following nonjudicial foreclosure, where required procedure was not followed.

13. Deed affecting land in judicial proceedings (bankruptcy, receivership, probate, conservatorship, dissolution of marriage), unauthorized by court.

14. Deed following judicial proceedings, subject to appeal or further court order.

15. Deed following judicial proceedings, where all necessary parties were not joined.

16. Lack of jurisdiction over persons or property in judicial proceedings.

17. Deed signed by mistake (grantor did not know what was signed).

18. Deed executed under falsified power of attorney.

19. Deed executed under expired power of attorney (death, disability, or insanity of principal).

20. Deed apparently valid, but actually delivered after death of grantor or grantee, or without consent of grantor.

But it doesn't seem possible that this could ever happen to you, right? That's what Roberta and Dave thought.

---

**ROBERTA AND DAVE'S STORY**

Roberta and Dave bought a house in a suburb of Chicago. They had the land surveyed. When they actually moved into the house, they discovered that, years earlier, a neighbor had built a garage that took about ten feet off the back end of their property.

The survey should have noted that the garage encroached on their property. The title Roberta and Dave received to the land wasn't "good" title because the encroachment created a defect on it. In other words, someone was making use of their land without their permission. If Roberta and Dave had bought title insurance, their insurer would have reimbursed them for the portion of land that they paid for but to which they didn't receive good title, had the insurer failed to catch the encroachment.

Title problems don't often come up, but when they do, they can blindside you. One Texas home buyer purchased a single-family house with a swimming pool in the backyard. After a few heavy rainstorms, his neighbor filed a complaint with the local municipality, complaining of flooding. It turns out that there was an easement between the two properties designed to keep the land open, specifically for drainage. When the seller had built the pool, he had filled in the land and altered the water flow. Because the title search didn't turn up the easement, and the survey didn't catch that the property had changed, the title company paid hundreds of thousands of dollars to buy the property, fix the problem (which included removing the pool), and resell it to someone else.

If the insurer notes the encroachment, you, the buyer, are considered to have been notified of the defect and must approach the seller about it before the closing. A title search looks for any clouds on the title to the home. Title insurance protects you and the lender against any mistakes or errors or omissions made by the individual performing the search. If you buy a home from Dan and Shelly, and a long-lost relative turns up with irrefutable evidence (say, a recorded deed from the property's original owner) that she actually owns the home, you'll have to turn over the home to the long-lost relative. Now the title search should have turned up this information, but whoever conducted the search missed this important piece of evidence. What happens in a case like this is the lender finds it has lent you money to purchase a property from someone who didn't really own it. Title insurance protects you, the buyer, from any losses associated with the cost of any errors made. It also protects the lender's interest.

## Paying the Premium

Title insurance is paid as a one-time premium; the cost is based entirely on the sales price of the home. In many communities, the seller pays for the cost of the title search, since he or she wants to guarantee that you, the buyer, will receive good title to the home. The lender will insist that you pay for, or obtain from the seller, title insurance that covers the lender. The lender may not insist that you get an *owner's policy* (which will compensate you if there is an error—title insurance insures the lender against errors), but it's an excellent idea. If you purchase the owner's policy at the same place you buy title insurance for the lender, you may be able to get a discounted rate. In addition, ask your real estate attorney if there is a title company he works with regularly. Your attorney may be able to use his or her economic muscle (he or she probably does a lot of house closings and the title company may be eager to encourage the business) to get you a discounted rate.

Finally, if the seller has owned the home for only a short period of time, say, a few years, you may be able to get a discounted policy by checking with the seller's original title company. They may be able to give you a "reissue" rate, which may have a significantly lower premium.

**20/20 HINDSIGHT:** I'm often asked whether a homeowner can buy title insurance. The answer is no. The only time you can buy an *owner's* title insurance policy is when you close on the home. Many first-time buyers are confused by the purchase of title insurance and mistakenly believe they have already purchased their own owner's policy when in fact they have only purchased a lender's policy. If you have a lender's policy, it's the mortgage lender who will be reimbursed for a loss—not you!

## Question 93: What Is RESPA? What Is TILA/RESPA or TRID? And What Does the Closing Disclosure Form Look Like Now?

The Real Estate Settlement Procedures Act (RESPA) is a consumer protection statute, first passed in 1974. The purpose of RESPA is to help consumers become better shoppers for settlement services and to eliminate kickbacks and referral fees that unnecessarily increase the costs of certain settlement services.

In 1974, Congress decided Americans were suffering from abuses in the title industry. Title companies were giving kickbacks to real estate agents and brokers who referred buyers to settlement agencies, mortgage lenders were paying fees to real estate agents who steered them business, and borrowers were being bartered like pork bellies.

Congress decided that buyers should be free to choose their own title company or settlement agency, and have more power in the entire transaction. So the Real Estate Settlement Procedures Act (RESPA) was passed to address these issues.

Section 8 in the RESPA code is the kickback provision, according to the Mortgage Bankers Association of America (MBA). It makes it a crime to pay or receive any money, or give or receive anything of value, to another person for the referral of any real estate settlement services, which includes making a mortgage loan. (This means that your broker cannot legally receive money for referring you to Jones Mortgage Company down the street.) Sections 4 and 5 of the RESPA code deal with disclosure: Mortgage companies must tell you how many loans they resell on the secondary market before you take their mortgage. Then they are required to tell you when they are actually selling your mortgage. Finally, the company that buys your mortgage must disclose all sorts of information, including a telephone number and a name you can contact if there is trouble with your loan. (These disclosures form the basis of the stack of documents you must sign, sometimes in quadruplicate, before you can close on the property.)

RESPA, which used to be regulated by the department of Housing and Urban Development (HUD), is now administered and regulated by the CFPB. The act requires that borrowers receive disclosures at various times. Some disclosures spell out the costs associated with the settlement, outline lender servicing and escrow account practices, and describe business relationships between settlement service providers. RESPA also prohibits certain practices that increase the cost of settlement services. TILA/RESPA is a newer set of rules that went into effect in 2015 that combines the mortgage disclosures previously established by the Truth in Lending Act (TILA) and RESPA into a single block of rules to make it easier for borrowers to understand.

Under TILA/RESPA, when borrowers apply for a mortgage loan, mortgage brokers and/or lenders must give you three things: a Special Information Booklet, which contains consumer information regarding various real estate settlement services; a Good Faith Estimate (GFE) of settlement costs, which lists the charges the buyer is likely to pay at settlement; and a Mortgage Servicing Disclosure Statement, which discloses to the borrower whether the lender intends to service the loan or transfer it to another lender. It also provides information about complaint resolution.

Thanks to TILA/RESPA, at least three days before your closing, you should get your official Closing Disclosure form, which is a five-page document that gives you more details about your loan, its key terms, and how much you're paying in fees and other costs to get your mortgage and buy your home. Many of those were set when you applied for your loan, and some of the charges shown under the "services you can shop for" line may increase at closing, but generally by no more than 10 percent of the costs listed on your final Loan Estimate form.

According to the CFPB, the Closing Disclosure breaks down your closing costs into two big categories: your loan costs and other costs of closing.[*]

| Your Loan Costs | Other Costs |
| --- | --- |
| The lender's origination costs to make or "originate" the loan, along with application fees and fees to underwrite your loan. Underwriting is the lender's term for making sure your credit and financial information is accurate and that you meet the lender's requirements for a loan. | Property taxes. |
| Discount points—that is, additional money you pay up front to reduce your interest rate. | Homeowners' insurance premiums. You can shop around for homeowners' insurance from your current insurance company, or many others, until you find the combination of premium, coverage, and customer service that fits your situation. Your lender will ask you for proof you have an insurance policy on your new home. |
| Services you shopped for, such as your closing or settlement agent and related title costs. | Any portion of your total mortgage payment you must make before your first full payment is due. |
| Services your lender requires for your loan. These include appraisals and credit reports. | Flood insurance, if required. |

The five-page Closing Disclosure form sums up the terms of your loan and what you pay at closing. You can easily compare the numbers to the Loan Estimate you received earlier. There should not be any significant changes other than those you have already agreed to. If there is, you're entitled to cancel or postpone the closing.

---

[*] I've taken this information directly from the CFPB publication "Your Home Loan Tool Kit," which is available on the CFPB.gov website.

## Question 94: Do I Need Homeowners' Insurance? What Should It Cover?

Insurance is a contract between you and the financial services company that is protecting you against some great unknown. When it comes to homeownership, homeowners' insurance will protect you against the financial realities of a physical catastrophe. If, for example, your house burns down, it might cost more money than you'd earn in ten years (gross, not net) to repair or replace it. Each month or perhaps annually, you pay a premium to keep the insurance in force.

Almost all homeowners buy homeowners' insurance policies. One reason? Mortgage lenders. If you need a loan to buy your home, you will be required to purchase homeowners', or hazard, insurance. The reason is simple: Lenders want to know that you're protecting their investment from harm.

When you take out a mortgage, you're pledging your home as collateral for the loan. The papers you sign say that if you default on the mortgage, the lender may begin foreclosure proceedings and take over the home. So, the lender's primary concern is protecting the value of the home. Issues of concern to the lender are damage by fire, water, tornado, flood, or even a tree crashing in through the roof. Let's say that you have no insurance, you have a $100,000 loan, and there's a fire. In a few hours, the lender's $100,000 has disappeared in a puff of smoke.

There's almost no way (unless you have seller financing and the seller either foolishly or unwittingly fails to insist upon it) that you'll get a mortgage without having to purchase enough home or hazard insurance to cover at least the amount of money the lender has given you. (In fact, you'll have to turn up at the closing with a piece of paper that says you've purchased a policy for at least a year that's effective the day of closing or earlier.)

Even without the mortgage requirement, you should carry homeowners' insurance. That's because, in addition to the mortgage, you likely have a significant personal investment in your home. On a $100,000 property, you may have put down $10,000 to $20,000 in cash, and you may have paid between $3,000 to $5,000 in closing costs. Plus, you may have decorated the interior of the home, or renovated, or built an addition. You have personal possessions. What goes up in flames can be worth double or triple what you actually owe the lender.

**20/20 HINDSIGHT:** The amount you carry should cover the cost of replacing your home today, not when you purchased it five, ten, twenty, or even thirty-five years ago. If you are doing a lease with an option to buy, you should carry renter's insurance that would cover the cost of replacing your personal possessions if they become damaged, stolen, or destroyed in some kind of catastrophe. As part of the option agreement, you should require the owner to carry enough homeowners' insurance to rebuild the house to current building code should it burn to the ground before you pick up your option. Make sure you see a copy of the policy and paid premium before you move into the property.

**FIRST-TIME BUYER TIP:** Condos and co-ops have different types of insurance because the property's common elements (a hallway, an interior staircase, the elevators, the roof, a laundry room, or landscaping in common areas) must be covered separately. Typically, co-op or condo associations will hold a building insurance policy that covers the common elements of the property and will satisfy your lender's desire for a "building policy." But don't be confused. This policy does not cover you. You will still need a separate policy that meets your lender's requirements as well as your own.

## What Kind of Insurance Is Available?

The insurance industry offers this assortment for homeowners:

| Type | Coverage |
|------|----------|
| HO1 | Bare-bones policies, no longer available in most states. |
| HO2 | Basic protection against sixteen known perils, except floods, earthquakes, war, and nuclear accidents. There is a version for mobile homes. |
| HO3 | All known perils (with a few exclusions). This is the most popular type of insurance. |
| HO4 | Renter's insurance. Similar in scope to HO2, but geared toward renters, not homeowners. |
| HO6 | Homeowners' insurance for condos and co-ops. |
| HO8 | Special insurance for older homes, but rarely used. |

Why haven't I included HO5 and HO7 coverage? According to the Insurance Information Institute, they are no longer used. HO3 is the most popular type of coverage for homeowners.

## Choosing the Best Kind of Coverage

In some ways, homeowners' insurance is the easiest type of insurance to purchase. You basically decide (1) what you want to cover and (2) how much you're willing to pay as deductible amount on any claim. These items will dovetail into a policy that's right for you.

What kind of coverage should you get? Most people purchase a general policy that covers the house and its contents. Most policies offer coverage for the structure of your home, your personal belongings, liability protection, and additional living expenses if you are temporarily unable to live in your home because of an insured disaster. Condominium and co-op owners need their own unique policies, but they still cover the unit and its contents.

According to the Insurance Information Institute, a nonprofit information group for the property/casualty insurance industry, your homeowners' policy should cover the sixteen listed perils. A peril is the calamity from which you're trying to protect yourself. The perils most commonly covered include:

1. Fire or lightning

2. Windstorm or hail

3. Explosion

4. Riot or civil commotion

5. Damage by aircraft

6. Damage by car

7. Smoke

8. Vandalism and malicious mischief

9. Theft

10. Volcanic eruption

11. Falling objects

12. Weight of ice, snow, or sleet

13. Accidental discharge or overflow of water or steam from within a plumbing, heating, air-conditioning, or automatic fire-protective sprinkler system, or from a household appliance

14. Sudden and accidental tearing apart, cracking, burning, or bulging of a steam or hot water heating system, an air-conditioning or automatic fire-protective system

15. Freezing of a plumbing, heating, air-conditioning or automatic, fire-protective sprinkler system, or of a household appliance

16. Sudden and accidental damage from artificially generated electrical current (does not include loss to a tube, transistor, or similar electronic component)

*(Courtesy of the Insurance Information Institute, iii.org)*

Floods, earthquakes, and mud slides are never covered on a regular homeowners' policy. A "riot or civil commotion" may or may not be covered. Since the September 11, 2001, terrorist attacks, terrorism insurance has become an issue in some places. If you want coverage, you'll have to purchase separate insurance to cover each of these risks. A "land disturbance" may or may not be covered. What about a chemical or paint spill? Damage from wild animals? Backed-up sewers and drains? Bloodstains? Scorching without fire? What about the additional living expenses you'll have to pay if your home is demolished and must be rebuilt? Be sure to ask.

## Comparing Policies

When comparing policies, you'll want to look at the deductible, what's covered, and what type of coverage you're buying. Replacement insurance guarantees that the insurer will pay for the cost of replacing the home as it stands today, up to the amount of your coverage. Guaranteed cost replacement coverage guarantees to rebuild your home no matter what the cost and has a rider built in to take care of inflation. A cash-value policy will reimburse you based only on your property's current market value—not what it would cost to build it new. Today, guaranteed cost replacement is somewhat limited. Insurers might only pay to rebuild your home up to 120 to 125 percent of your policy amount. It's up to you to stay on top of how much it would cost to rebuild.

 **20/20 HINDSIGHT:** Replacement cost insurance for contents may only reimburse you for the actual, depreciated value of the items. So if you paid $2,000 for a sofa ten years ago, and the insurance company says it's only worth $1,000 today, but it will cost $3,000 to purchase another one just like it, you'll have to cough up the extra cash to buy a new one.

Pay attention to the cost-per-square-foot calculations your insurance company uses. They might estimate that replacing your home will cost only $60 per square foot. In reality, only the cheapest of construction costs that little. Replacing your house the way it is, with all of the tile, hardwood floors, wallpaper, marble, and granite you may have will cost way more than that. A more realistic estimate is $90 to $200 per square foot, depending on where you live. For a high-end home, expect to pay upwards of $255 per square foot.

## Other Sorts of Coverage

Some places call it code-and-contention coverage, and others call it building code coverage, and others call it an ordinance-and-law rider. Either way, what you're after is the cost of meeting new building codes that may have gone into effect after your home was built and to which any new homes built are subject. If you lack code coverage, your insurer will probably only pay what it would cost to rebuild your old home in its original condition. Since you can't do that, you'll pay the rest to bring the house up to code. Some companies include code coverage in their basic policies, but if you don't ask, you won't know.

If there have been changes in zoning, you may be out of luck—unless you have zoning coverage. For example, if you live in a beach house and the zoning law was changed restricting any new development on the beach, you might find yourself unable to rebuild on your site if your house burns down. That's where zoning insurance kicks in. It ensures that you can rebuild where you want to go. The policy should state that you can build your exact house, no matter what the cost, on a different lot. Otherwise, choose another policy.

You should also have a policy that covers the cost of replacing your foundation. (Seems obvious, but some insurance companies don't include it.) A personal articles rider is the official name for extra coverage of your expensive jewelry and fine art. Make sure you have current appraisals to support your claim. And, don't forget home office coverage. If you run a business out of your home, you'll need a rider to cover that, too.

**20/20 HINDSIGHT: If you have a home office, you may also need special liability coverage for your home-based business. Check with your insurance agent about adding an umbrella rider to your homeowners' policy for additional liability coverage.**

**FIRST-TIME BUYER TIP: Pictures speak louder than words, and if your home is destroyed, the last thing you'll want to do is try to prove what you owned and when you bought it. Take a video camera or your phone and record everything in your**

home. Make sure you date it. Back the video up with close-ups of jewelry, furs, rugs, and fine art. Consider storing the video in the cloud with backups on your hard drive.

## They Want to Know What?

When you contact an insurance agent to get a homeowners' insurance policy (or if you do it over the Web), you'll need to provide the insurer with some basic information about your home. Here are some of the questions you'll be asked:

- What is your home made of? (Homes made of aluminum siding or shingles are typically considered to be made of wood.)
- Is your home one story? Two stories? Split level? Other?
- How many rooms are there?
- What is the listing price of your home? What was the purchase price?
- How old is your home? When was it built? What kinds of major improvements does it have (like a new roof, or new mechanicals)?
- What is the square footage of your home? (Multiply the length by the width and then multiply that number by the number of livable stories. Attics and basements typically don't count.)
- How far away is the nearest fire department? How about the nearest fire hydrant?
- Does the home have security devices, including smoke detectors, alarm systems, security lighting, dead-bolt locks, or carbon monoxide detectors?
- Is your home located on a floodplain?
- Are there other structures on the property (like a garage, guesthouse, or cabana)?
- Do you own a dog?
- Do you have any valuable jewelry, fine art, furs, antiques, or silverware? Do you typically keep large amounts of cash in the house? (You may need special insurance riders to protect these items.)
- What kind of deductible do you want to pay? (The higher the deductible, the lower your premium.)
- Do you have a business on the premises? (Typically, homeowners' insurance policies either don't include a home-based business or have extremely low coverage.

If you have a business based at home, you may want to purchase a home business rider or a rider for your computers and other electronic devices.)

- How much liability insurance do you want? (Typically, homeowners' policies include a certain amount of liability coverage. But in these litigious times, you may wish for increased coverage.)

By knowing the answers to these questions ahead of time, you'll speed up the time it takes to find the best deal.

## Discounts and Deductions

Although homeowners' insurance is getting more expensive (a direct result of a spate of disasters in recent years where insurance companies took huge losses), there are ways to cut down on your costs. If you move or refinance, you might be tempted to poke around and see what else is out there. If you've got a good record, you should find plenty of options. You might even cut your premium by up to 35 to 50 percent. Here are some ideas:

1. **Shop around.** Once you have insurance, you'll be tempted to stay the course unless something happens, but you may be able to lower your premiums simply by shopping around. If you can't lower them, at least you'll feel good knowing you got the best deal. Direct insurers sell online (the best place to shop, and there are plenty of websites that aggregate insurance offerings) or over the phone. If you qualify, you'll save—big-time—on the commissions. Even with a great policy, you might be able to drop your premium further with one of the ideas given here.

2. **Raise your deductible.** Some insurance companies will drop you if you make more than one or two claims in a year. Make sure your insurance covers you for the catastrophes and plan on picking up the cost of the everyday expenses. Raising your deductible from $250 to $500 might enable you to shave 10 to 12 percent off your premiums. Raise your deductible to $1,000 and your savings may double.

3. **Tout your improvements.** If you've put on a new roof, and it's made of a flame-repellent material, you might've earned yourself a discount. A new plumbing system, new wiring, or a new heating system might also qualify.

4. **Get connected.** A home security system might qualify you for a small discount of 3 to 5 percent. But connect it to the local police and fire station, and you might lower your premium by up to 15 percent annually. If you put in a sprinkler system or smoke detectors, you might get smaller discounts.

5. **Grow old.** If you're over the age of fifty-five (old for a first-time buyer, but not unheard-of), you can probably get a discount.

6. **Educate thyself.** Your insurance company may offer an education program, or brochures, that will allow you to lower your premium once you've attended or read the material.

7. **Buy your home and auto policy from the same insurer.** Some companies that sell homeowners', auto, and liability coverage will take 5 to 15 percent off your premium if you buy two or more policies from them.*

8. **Insure your home, not the land it sits on.** If a tree falls in your backyard, chances are it won't hurt anything except the grass. So don't include the value of your land when figuring out how much homeowners' insurance you need.

9. **Stop smoking.** The Insurance Information Institute says that smoking accounts for more than 23,000 residential fires a year. Quit. Not only will you save on your homeowners' insurance, but you'll probably save a bundle on health insurance (and health-related costs, not to mention the cost of the tobacco products you won't have to buy over your lifetime).

10. **Is group coverage an option?** Professional, nonprofit, and alumni organizations often offer discounts for association members.

11. **Stick around.** If you've kept your coverage with the same insurer for years, you should ask for special consideration. Some companies will give discounts of up to 6 percent if you've been a policyholder for six years or more.

12. **Look around.** Your home is an appreciating asset; some items in your home are depreciating as the years go by. If you've purchased special riders for certain items,

---

* Some states don't allow discounts on premiums. Why? Most likely it's because the state insurance lobby is strong and deductions lower the insurers' profits. Ah, politics.

you may be able to reduce your coverage if they've lost their value. If you've sold items covered by riders, inform your insurance company so they can remove the rider from your policy.

13. **If all else fails, move.** According to a study by the nonprofit Insurance Research Council, it costs insurers 42 percent more to cover losses in the city than it does to settle claims for those who live five miles outside the city limits. City dwellers may be paying double the amount that nearby suburbanites pay for their insurance. But before you put your home up for sale, consider this: The cost of the 6 percent sales commission you'll likely pay to sell your home would more than make up the difference in city-vs.-suburb insurance premiums, for a long, long time.

## Floods and Earthquakes

Some people, like me, believe in climate change. Others don't. Of those who do believe the planet is warming up, most believe that human beings are causing rising temperatures. Some others think it's just happening on its own. One thing that almost everyone can agree on is that the oceans are rising, and that coastal communities in the United States are suffering from more powerful storms. If you live near a body of water, you've probably noticed frequent hundred-year and five-hundred-year flooding, and the attendant damage caused by that. Floodplain maps throughout the country have been redrawn in the last few years, and continue to be redrawn as weather patterns are changing.

If you live in a floodplain (check with the local municipality for floodplain information) or in a coastal community, your lender will require you to have flood insurance. You can only buy basic flood insurance from the federal government, although most agents sell the policies. When I wrote the third edition of this book, the average cost of flood insurance was about $300 for $100,000 worth of coverage, and the maximum limit as that edition went to press was $250,000 for the structure of your home and $100,000 for the contents. It's higher now—and rising.

But because of the rising expense in dealing with the aftermath of increasingly volatile weather patterns, the true cost of flood insurance should be so expensive that it would be unaffordable to buy flood insurance. Insurance is supposed to guard you against something that may happen that would destroy your home. But flooding happens so regularly now, and is so devastating, that risk-based pricing would put it completely out of reach of the Americans who live in these areas. And if there is no affordable homeowners' insurance, the value of these homes would plummet.

As a result, trade associations have developed a pattern of pushing Congress to artificially keep the cost of flood insurance low for these homeowners. Which would be fine, except that leaves the rest of America picking up the tab.* Of course, if your annual homeowners' insurance bill really cost you the $30,000, or maybe even the $130,000 it should be based on the risk you're taking, you'd probably move. And since few people can afford that kind of outlay, your home would be worthless.

In the meantime, the Federal Emergency Management Agency (FEMA), and by extension all Americans, are picking up the tab. The Biggert-Waters Flood Insurance Reform Act of 2012 was supposed to require a stepped-up procedure to get coastal homeowners paying something that is a lot closer to the actual cost of the risk they're taking. Instead, each year, homeowners and Realtors freaked out and the subsidized flood insurance program was extended once again. In 2014, the Biggert-Waters Act was actually repealed and modified. In 2015, the Homeowner Flood Insurance Affordability Act of 2014 (HFIAA) went into effect to slow some flood insurance rate increases and offer relief to some policy-holders who experienced steep flood insurance premium increases in 2013 and early 2014.† Among other changes, the new legislation limited increases for individual premiums to 18 percent of premiums, limited increases for average rate classes to 15 percent, and imposed an annual surcharge of $25 to $250.

## So What's Covered by Flood Insurance?

Finished basements are not covered by federal flood insurance policies, except for basics like the washer, dryer, furnace, and air-conditioning units. That means that you'll take the loss on any carpeting and wood paneling down there, not to mention items you may have stored there. The cost of your policy depends on the value of your home,

---

*   You wonder why it's okay for all of America's homeowners to defray the insurance tab for homeowners who choose to live in extremely risky communities like the Atlantic Ocean or Gulf Coast, while it's not okay for healthy Americans to defray the cost of health insurance for older or sick Americans.

†   In fact, some refunds were offered to those homeowners who paid what they were supposed to pay.

construction costs, and where your home is located. If it's close to a shoreline, as discussed, you'll pay a lot more money for your policy.

Frankly, flood insurance is about the cheapest kind of insurance you can purchase, and it's well worth what you'll spend, since your *regular homeowners' insurance won't cover anything* if you get flooded because of a rising body of water—and that includes an eighteen-inch rainstorm. (If your basement floods because your sump pump failed, your regular insurance company will probably pay, though you'll want to ask your insurance agent to be sure.) Still, only 20 percent of folks who live in a floodplain have flood insurance.

For details about flood insurance, go to FEMA.gov.

## Earthquakes

Earthquake insurance is offered through private insurers, typically as added coverage (called an endorsement). But the expensive damage caused the last few earthquakes has made this insurance very difficult to buy and relatively expensive. This helps to explain why only about 10 percent of homeowners living in earthquake areas actually have earthquake insurance. You can purchase earthquake insurance through your insurance agent, though it is not available everywhere (by law, insurers in California must offer it). The cost depends on where you live, if you're close to a fault line, what type of home you have, and if the structure incorporates modern anti-earthquake technology. In some areas that are highly seismic (except California), earthquake coverage may not be available at any price.

## Some Final Thoughts on Homeowners' Insurance

When putting together your final homeowners' policy, don't forget these items:

1. **College may not be covered.** Some policies cover your kid's stuff when he or she is away at school. Some don't. Be sure to ask. For a few extra dollars, you can get a rider that will fully cover Junior, plus all the hot-shot computer equipment he's bringing with him, from things that happen in a college environment.

2. **Make sure your stuff is fully insured.** Most policies will give you half the face value to pay for your stuff. So if you have a $300,000 homeowners' policy, most insurers will pay up to $150,000 for you to replace your personal belongings. If that's not enough, investigate additional coverage to fill the gap.

3. **Get under the umbrella.** The general liability portion of a regular homeowners' policy is pretty small. Consider getting additional coverage that will give you an overriding umbrella liability policy—just in case.

4. **Update your policy to reflect the true cost of rebuilding your home.** For a regular house that doesn't include perks like granite countertops in the kitchen and limestone bathroom tile, you should expect to spend $100 to $125 per square foot to rebuild and refurnish your home. That means, if you buy a 2,500-square-foot house today, and it burns to the ground tomorrow, the cost to rebuild your home to current building standards could range from $250,000 to over $300,000—even if you paid less than that to purchase it. If your home does have the granite countertops, four or five bathrooms, or a fancy kitchen, you can expect to pay $150 to $200 per square foot, or $275,000 to $500,000. Will it always be this much? If you live in a small town, or in a condominium or co-op, you may pay less. Live in an expensive city, and you can expect to pay more.

# Question 95: How Should I Hold Title to My New Home?

When Janet and Scott recently bought a house in a suburb north of Chicago, they wondered how they should hold title. Scott, a pediatrician just starting his own practice, is well aware of how litigious patients can be. Industry statistics tell him it's likely he may be targeted in a medical malpractice suit over the course of his career as a doctor. Scott was worried someone could sue him and take away their home.

Other homeowners have the same concerns. Whatever business you're in, there may come a time when your home may be in jeopardy. If you declare bankruptcy, your creditors may be able to attach a lien against your house, possibly even forcing you to sell it. There may be a judgment against you. The time to think about how to protect your home, your largest investment to date, is now, before you buy it.

How you hold title to—that is, the ownership of—your real estate is important. But often, the way in which you hold title is an afterthought. In many cases, you aren't even asked what your preference is.

If you're married, you often get joint tenancy with rights of survivorship. If you're single, you hold property in your own name.

But there are other ways of holding title that might help you in certain situations.

For example, should something go wrong, and one spouse or partner gets sued professionally, how you and your spouse or partner own your home can mean the difference between it being sold to pay off a judgment, and you being allowed to live there until you choose to sell.

Your ownership of your home and other assets can have important estate considerations as well.

 **FIRST-TIME BUYER TIP:** When it comes to holding title, all things aren't equal for married spouses and those partners who are unmarried. In many situations, those partners who are unmarried will need to consult with an estate planner or real estate attorney to make sure their interests are protected under state law.

Here are some ways you may hold title to your home and the effect it may have on your estate:

## Individuals

If you're a single person, your options for holding title to your home are rather limited. You may hold title to your property as an individual or you may hold it in one of a variety of trusts.

If you hold the property in your own name and a creditor comes after you, the creditor may be able to force the sale of your home to pay off your debt. If you die while holding property in your own name, even if you name your heir in your will, your will (and the property you own) will go through probate and be subject to probate fees.

If you're an individual, the best way to avoid probate is to put your property in a trust.

You might also ask your tax or estate attorney if a corporation or limited liability company might be a good choice.

# Joint Tenancy

Joint tenancy with rights of survivorship is the most common way married couples hold property, but two nonrelated individuals may also own a piece of property as joint tenants.

The nice thing about joint tenancy is that it allows you and the co-owner to each own the property as a whole. If you own property as joint tenants with rights of survivorship, your share in the property is immediately transferred to your surviving spouse or partner upon your death. Your share is subject, however, to any debts, claims, and expenses you've left behind.

You should also consider the estate planning issues of how your surviving partner will inherit your half of the property. Depending on state law, your spouse would inherit your half (married couples are usually assumed to own property equally) at the stepped-up basis. That means that your half of the property would be revalued on the day you die, and your spouse would inherit it at its current value.

If you and your surviving partner are not married, the property would be divided based on how much each partner contributed to the purchase of the property. For example, if you each contributed 50 percent of the cost, then your surviving partner would inherit your half of the property and get the stepped-up basis.

If you can't prove how much each of you contributed, state law may attribute total ownership to the partner who died first. That may have grave estate implications. Consult an estate or tax attorney for more details.

The key phrase to look for when considering joint tenancy is "with rights of survivorship."

# Tenancy in Common

Tenancy in common allows each person to own their piece of the same property separately.

For example, you may own 40 percent and your spouse or partner may own 40 percent and your parents may own 20 percent, but you may each use and enjoy the whole property. You can't be restricted to using just the 40 percent of the property that you own. And you may sell your share of the property to anyone you choose, just like you might sell stock in a corporation.

Tenancy in common is available to married couples or to two or more individuals, although it's not usually used for property purchased by married couples. When you die, your share of the property goes through probate before it is distributed according to your will.

## Tenancy by the Entirety

Tenancy by the entirety is similar to joint tenancy in that it has rights of survivorship. However, it is only available to married couples and civil unions.

The key difference between tenancy by the entirety and joint tenancy is this: If you own property as tenants by the entirety, both spouses or partners must agree before the property becomes subject to one spouse's or partner's creditors.

Neither spouse or partner can do anything that would create a claim or lien on the marital property. And as long as the couple is married or in a civil union and owns the property, tenancy by the entirety protects the interest of each spouse or partner in the marital home.

For example, if your spouse or partner gets sued, the creditors could not force the sale of the residence because you and your spouse or partner each own the whole property. The creditors would have to wait until the marriage or civil union is severed, or the other spouse or partner consented to the claim, or the property is sold. Once the property is sold, a claim may be attached to the proceeds.

Finally, tenancy by the entirety is not available in every state. Again, it is only for married couples or those in a civil union.

## Think About a Trust

The only way that you can avoid probate is to put your property into a trust. Here are some alternative ways to hold title that may also affect important estate planning issues.

# Land Trust

A land trust is a legal creation where the sole asset in the trust is the property you are buying, and you are the beneficiary of the trust.

At one time, a land trust might have been used to obscure the identity of the beneficiary. Today, that veil has largely been lifted. Individuals, two or more buyers, married couples, and children may be the beneficiaries of a land trust.

While there are no estate tax advantages to a land trust, and they are only available in a few states, the property will pass directly onto a successor beneficiary (if one exists), avoiding probate.

# Qualified Personal Residence Trust (QPRT)

This is another type of trust that allows you to discount the future value of your home and possibly save on the gift and estate taxes you'd otherwise owe.

Here's how it works: You set the term of the trust and place your home into it. You're allowed to live in the home for the term of the trust. The beneficiaries of the trust (your heirs) will receive the home when the term of the trust expires.

If you put your house in a QPRT for five years, your beneficiaries will own your house at the end of the five years. If you're still living and want to stay in your home, you'll have to rent it.

The benefit of a QPRT is that the IRS allows you to discount the future value of the house according to a preset schedule. You'll pay gift tax on a much lower amount, which will cost you less than the estate tax.

If, however, you die before the QPRT term expires, the property reverts to you. You'll be credited for any gift taxes you've paid but will have lost the fee you paid to an attorney to set up the QPRT.

If you survive the term, a QPRT can be helpful in terms of planning your estate. Typically, you are only allowed to set up two QPRTs, one for your primary residence and a second for a vacation home.

## Living Trust

A revocable living trust is another way to pass assets from one generation to another and avoid probate.

You set up a trust and then transfer assets, such as your home or stocks, into the trust. You may name beneficiaries and leave a list of instructions for the trustee who will administer it.

For many people, trusts take the place of wills. Also, living trusts aren't public documents, so the privacy aspect is appealing.

But because you retain complete control of the assets in a living trust, it does nothing to lower the estate taxes you may eventually owe.

## Family Limited Partnership

By creating a family limited partnership, parents can pass along pieces of their property to their children (or anyone else) by making them small limited partners of a partnership that owns the property.

Limited partners traditionally don't manage the property or have an active role in it. This limited role (hence the name) allows you to discount their share of ownership, resulting in lower estate and gift taxes when the property is transferred.

Another value to a family limited partnership is it allows individuals to give property to their heirs over time, in small amounts, which is less expensive than deeding over small pieces of a particular property.

Unless you own a large ranch, plantation, or other significant residential property, you probably wouldn't use a family limited partnership. Traditionally, they're used to pass down commercial, industrial, or other types of real estate.

## Estate Considerations

If you're unsure about the best way to hold title to your property, consult with a real estate attorney, estate planning attorney, or accountant, who can explain the ins and outs of each type of ownership. There may be some very real reasons to go one way or another, and you should be thoroughly informed before you close on your home. One reason might be the amount of total assets you and your spouse or partner own. Although you may want to share title equally with your spouse, if you have joint assets that exceed $10 million, holding property as joint tenants may not be the economically savvy choice. Tax-wise, or estate-wise, it may be better for you to own the property on your own or to place it into a trust. Emotionally, though, it may be difficult for you and your spouse to accept an unequal ownership of assets. For detailed explanations, your financial planner can help you work through the various options.

## Community Property States

Finally, community property estates include Arizona, California, Idaho, Louisiana, Nevada, New Mexico, Texas, Washington, and Wisconsin. If you live in a community property state, and are married, every asset you purchase during the marriage is assumed to be owned equally between you and your spouse.

For example: Let's say you purchase a house as an investment during the course of your marriage. Only your name is on the deed. When you die, your spouse is assumed to own half of that property. The ownership of the property is divided equally between your spouse and your estate.

There are very special issues involved with community property, especially if you move to a state that doesn't allow it. Check with your estate attorney or estate planner for details.

# CHAPTER 12

# The Closing

## Question 96: Who Should Attend the Closing?
## What Should I Do If I Can't Be There?

The closing contains some of the most important legal contracts you'll sign. You're promising to pay thousands of dollars in exchange for a place to call home. I'm willing to bet that this is the largest single investment of your life.

It's probably a good idea for you to attend.

If you live in an escrow state, like California, you may not have a "closing" the way it is described here. You may give a list of instructions to the escrow company, and then go in and sign all of the documents. The seller will also go in, usually separately, with a list of instructions and sign their documents. When the lists of instructions have been completed, the escrow company will conduct the actual closing, then call you to come and pick up the keys to the house. Usually this happens on a preset day, but it could happen at any time within a two-to-three-week period.

For a buyer, a closing is more like a command performance. All of the buyers—that means you, your spouse if you have one, and any partners who are going into the transaction with you—must attend. There are two compelling reasons for you to attend: First, you have to sign your name a dozen or more times on various documents; second, you have to read those documents to make sure everything is in order.

Who else attends the closing? If you're in a state where attorneys are involved, your attorney and the seller's attorney will generally be there. Also, the seller's broker and the subagent or buyer's broker (who are very interested in making sure everything goes smoothly up until the final papers are signed and the final checks—including theirs—are cut) will often attend. There will also, usually, be a title officer (if you are closing at a title company) or other closing agent, and there may be a representative from the lender. Sometimes the lender will bring along an attorney. Whether or not the sellers attend is up to them. While you need to be present to sign documents, sellers' documents can be signed ahead of time.

Despite marking your calendar two to three months in advance, sometimes there's a last-minute scheduling conflict with the closing. An important business trip comes up, or someone gets sick, or perhaps a family member passes away and you want to attend the funeral in another state. Whatever happens, if you can't attend, call your attorney and see if you can juggle the closing date. It may be possible, especially if the seller already owns another home, or the seller is taking back financing, or is moving to an interim home before going on somewhere else. Moving the closing up or back a few days is the least onerous way to deal with a scheduling conflict.

If you cannot change the date of closing—if, for example, the seller is closing on his or her new property that same day and requires the proceeds from the sale—then consider assigning power of attorney to someone who can step into your shoes and sign your name legally at the closing. A power of attorney is the legal right you give someone (usually your attorney) to act on your behalf. You will usually limit it simply to this transaction. (Power of attorney is sometimes used in the case of an elderly parent or relative, when they are no longer able to manage their affairs.)

In the case of purchasing your home, you're better off giving it to someone who's familiar with the transaction. If the only person who knows it is your attorney, and he or she is willing to accept that designation, then that's who should have it. If a friend or family member is familiar with the transaction, then that person should be designated.

In most cases, it's not smart to give your broker the power of attorney. Many brokers work for and represent the seller, so there's a potential conflict of interest. You wouldn't give power of attorney to the seller, but if you gave it to the seller's broker, in effect you'd be doing just that. If your broker is a buyer's broker, then you may want to discuss power of attorney. But remember, no matter whose broker it is, he or she is not a disinterested third party. In most cases, the broker has a significant amount of money riding on the outcome of the closing. If something comes up at closing (see Question 98), you want the person with power of attorney to look out for your best interests, not his or her own.

 **FIRST-TIME BUYER TIP:** Check with your lender ahead of time to see if he will allow your documents to be signed with a power of attorney. Ask what power-of-attorney form they require. Many lenders will not accept power-of-attorney signatures on their documents. In this case, you'll need to presign your document if, for whatever reason, you can't attend the closing.

# Question 97: What Are Prorations?

Let's say that Ginny makes an offer to purchase Maureen and Mike's home. In the two months until the closing, some bills come due that must be paid. Maureen and Mike pay the water bill (which comes every six months), the second installment of real estate taxes (they're due in March and September), and the gas bill (which comes once every two months). On the day of closing, Maureen and Mike's attorney tells Ginny how much her share of these prorated expenses is.

Almost every closing has some costs prorated, simply because we don't pay for our housing needs on a daily basis. Can you imagine trucking on down to the county clerk's office to pay your real estate taxes every day? What about your electric bills? Water bill? Association dues? Many of these costs are spread out over a long period of time. Depending on where you live in the country, you pay your real estate taxes once or twice a year. It isn't fair for Maureen and Mike to have paid an entire year's worth of property taxes, if they only live in the house for nine months of that year before selling to Ginny. Likewise, if Ginny bought the home just before the second installment of taxes was due, it wouldn't be fair for her to pay for six months of taxes, when she would only have three months in the home.

A little bit of math evens things out for everyone. How do you calculate prorations? Take the number of days covered by the bill and then divide the bill by the number of days. That gives you a daily fee. Then multiply by the number of days up to and including the closing. For example, let's say Maureen and Mike's property taxes are $2,000 for the year, broken into two installments of $1,000 each, half due on March 15 and the other half due on September 15. Each $1,000 represents 183 days per year (it's actually 182.5, but we'll round up): $1,000 ÷ 183 = $5.46 per day.

If the closing is on September 16, Maureen and Mike have already paid the real estate property taxes for the rest of the year. At closing, Ginny would have to reimburse them for the days of that year she's going to live in the house. It's 106 days from September 17 to the end of the year. Multiply 106 by the $5.46 daily fee: 106 days × $5.46 daily fee = $578.76.

Ginny would owe Maureen and Mike $578.76 at closing. It can work in reverse also. Let's say the closing is on September 14. On September 15, Ginny pays the $1,000 real estate tax bill. It's seventy-six days from July 1 to September 14. Multiply 76 by the $5.46 daily fee: 76 days × $5.46 daily fee = $414.96.

If the closing was on September 14, Maureen and Mike would owe Ginny $414.96 for their share of property taxes.

## Asking for a Bit More

In some states, it's common to ask the previous owners to pay a little extra in real estate taxes above the daily fee, because in many areas property taxes rise each year and the exact amount for the next bill may not be known. So instead of asking for the daily fee multiplied by the number of days, the buyer may ask the seller to put up 110 percent of the daily fee to cover any increases. In our example, the daily fee of $5.46 would be increased to $6.01 to cover any increase in taxes.

Your real estate attorney (or your broker, if you're in a state where attorneys are not used for house closings) will calculate prorations for every bill that has some sort of shared time arrangement, including gas bills, water bills, assessments to homeowners' associations, and real estate taxes. This includes any insurance policies (above and beyond hazard insurance required by the lender) or service agreements the buyer will have to pay for. Any bill can be prorated using basic math. (Generally, telephone service is shut off when an owner vacates a home and the new owners must start their own account. The local electric company will generally change the name on the service the day of closing, and begin billing the new owners.)

Sometimes attorneys draw up a reproration agreement. If the sellers reimburse the buyer for more than the actual bill, sometimes the buyer and seller agree to recalculate the bill to reflect the actual amount paid. Here's how it works: If you thought the bill was going to be $100 and the seller's share was 25 percent, the seller would have paid you $25. But if the actual bill ends up being only $80, the seller's share is only $20, so you would owe the seller $5 (which is paid after closing when the recalculation is done).

## Yet Another Escrow Account

Sometimes proration money is kept in escrow (by a disinterested third party), which usually happens only with substantial amounts of money. The escrow then makes payments to the buyer based on the bills that come in and will return any extra money to the seller. The important thing with prorations is that the seller pays all his or her costs before closing. Otherwise, you may have to chase the seller to get your fair share.

 **FIRST-TIME BUYER TIP:** Local custom dictates who pays for, and who receives the benefit for, the day of closing. Your attorney, broker, or closing agent should be able to advise you on local custom.

## Question 98: What Do I Need to Bring with Me to the Closing? What If Something Goes Wrong at the Closing?

The simple answer, "bring yourself," won't quite do here. You also need to bring money, in the form of a cashier's or certified check. You must also bring your homeowners' insurance certificate (to prove you have it) and any documents the lender requires (these should have been spelled out in the commitment for the loan).

On the day before the closing, check with your attorney to see how much money you should have the check made out for. It's not a disaster if you bring too much, as the title company can cut a check to you for the difference. The problem comes if you have too little. In that case, you may find the closing stretched out as you run all over town trying to convert a personal check into a cashier's check. You may also wire-transfer funds, but you'll need to get the proper information to know where, and to what account, to wire the money. And bring a favorite pen. You'll be signing your name quite a few times.

 **FIRST-TIME BUYER TIP:** Usually the check you bring to the closing can be made out to your name and endorsed to the title company at closing.

## What If Something Goes Wrong at the Closing?

Just when you think you've crossed the finish line, it seems to move farther away. That's what closings tend to feel like: You solve one problem and another crops up. And another. And another.

When Janet bought her condo, she discovered that the loan amount on the loan document was incorrect. And then she noticed that some of the documentation didn't have her correct address! Leo and Genna's loan agreement also had an incorrect amount. At the last minute, the developer who built Bart and Michelle's townhouse refused to put $1,500 into escrow to cover the sod and landscaping that was supposed to be part of the deal. One buyer refused to close on a condo for twenty-four hours because the sellers—who didn't live there anymore—couldn't find their mailbox key.

There are at least ten reasons why a closing doesn't happen or is delayed for a few days or is stretched out:

1. **Money.** Money problems are one of the most popular reasons home sales may not close on time. For example, if you're transferring money by wire, it's always a possibility that the money will get tied up, or there will be a delay in the processing of the wire transfer. Sometimes the numbers don't add up and a buyer will find that he or she is short. Since lenders and title companies don't take personal checks, you may have to run across town to get that personal check converted into a certified or cashier's check.

2. **Missing Loan Package.** If the lender's documents aren't there, you're not closing. If the loan package has to come from out of state and it's shipped via overnight

delivery, it's always possible that the package will be lost or delayed. If the loan package is missing documents, they may have to be sent by messenger or faxed over to the closing. In addition to adding more time, the lender may try to charge you for the messenger service or even for use of the fax. (Nowadays, things are usually scanned and emailed, but they might charge you anyway!) You should vigorously deny these charges, particularly if it was the lender who made the mistake.

3. **Disagreement About Documents.** Read all of the documents carefully. It's possible that the loan company may try to slip something in, or has made changes to the documents you didn't agree to.

4. **Incorrect Loan Documents.** Nothing can create problems like incorrect information on loan documents. Check to be sure that you're actually getting the amount of money you agreed to and that your address, phone number, and other personal information is correct. Be certain the interest rate is correct. Bring inconsistencies and wrong information to the attention of the lender. New documents may have to be drawn up, or the lender may try to get by with reprinting certain pages.

5. **Last-Minute Requests.** Sometimes the lender will make a last-minute request for documentation at the closing. At Leo and Genna's closing, the lender requested a copy of the canceled deposit check. To safeguard against time-wrenching delays, it's a good idea to bring everything with you to the closing.

6. **Walk-Through Problems.** If you do the final walk-through (hopefully after the seller has moved out) and find that some items are missing or damaged, it must be brought up at the closing. This is the time to negotiate with the seller (or the seller's attorney or broker, if the seller is not at the closing) for remuneration. You and the seller should agree to a settlement before you close.

7. **Title Problems.** Sometimes, last-minute title problems creep up. A long-lost relative turns up, or the title company discovers the real estate taxes haven't been paid. A contractor may have filed a mechanic's lien. You should insist that these title issues are resolved before you'll close on the home. You don't want to inherit someone else's problems.

8. **Someone Dies.** It doesn't happen too often, but you should know what can happen if either you or the seller dies after the contract is signed and before closing. If the

seller dies after signing the contract, the estate must go through with the sale. However, it may be difficult to close on time, particularly if the seller dies close to the day of closing, or if the estate is in probate court. If you die, the seller may be able to force your estate to continue with the sale, although in the real world, sellers may not force the issue. Check with an attorney for further details about your rights in your state.

9. **Catastrophe Strikes.** In the days (or should I say, nights) before closing, nearly every first-time buyer has a nightmare about his or her new home being destroyed before the paperwork is finalized. Fire, flood, earthquake, lightning—you name it. What happens if a fire actually consumes the home you're supposed to purchase tomorrow? In most cases, depending on what the contract says, you wouldn't have to close if something major happened to the home. Or you can elect to close and take the insurance proceeds (after the seller's lender has been paid off—if the home is underinsured that could mean little or nothing for you). If you have already taken possession of the home when disaster strikes, you may lose the right to terminate the purchase and be forced to close. Again, have your attorney advise you of your rights.

10. **Seller's Deal Falls Through.** Usually, sellers take the money from the sale of their home and use it to pay for another home, so it's likely your seller will do the same. But if the seller's deal (for any number of reasons) falls through, he may have no place to go and might have second thoughts about your closing. In other words, the seller might refuse to vacate the home. If this happens, you have three options: First, don't close until he moves out. Second, close and force him out, which is emotionally, physically, and legally difficult. Third, hold back money from the closing to ensure that the seller gets out by a certain time, and attach a stiff daily penalty for every day he remains in the home. And make that incentive very stiff, so the seller will want to move rather than stay. You actually want the daily penalty to be so stiff it's cheaper for the seller to put all of his or her belongings in storage and go to a hotel.

## Timing the Closing

How long should the closing last? As we discussed early on, most closings take less than an hour. One attorney estimates that 10 percent of his closings take less than a half hour.

An additional 50 percent take less than an hour, and 30 percent take less than an hour and a half. Ten percent take less than two hours. So, all told, 90 percent of all closings happen in less than two hours.

The final 10 percent? Well, it could take ten hours, or ten days, or never happen at all. But most closings happen. And when it's over, and the last fire has been put out, you'll own your very own home.

Congratulations!

# Question 99: What Should I Get from the Seller at Closing?

You've signed your name so often your arm is about to drop off.* You've tallied up the numbers, made fast and furious calls to your office to reassure them you're still living and breathing, and are wired from cup after cup of stale coffee. The last thing to do is to get the keys and last-minute paperwork to your new home from the seller.

Keys are pretty important and they require a bit of good faith. After all, when the seller hands you the keys at closing, you don't know if they work or not. You won't find out until much later, perhaps even next spring, that the seller forgot to give you the keys (or combination) to the tool shed lock. Or the combination on the bicycle room. Or the key to your storage locker.

The seller is supposed to turn over all keys to the home at closing. This includes front- and back-door locks, any dead-bolt locks, window locks, interior door locks, shed or storage room locks, or locks on any part of the property. The seller should also give you any combinations you need to open any locks on the property. Finally, mailbox keys and garage door openers are supposed to be included.

**NEW CONSTRUCTION TIP:** If you're purchasing new construction, you may not get your keys at closing. The developer, or the developer's representative, will give you a letter indicating where keys can be picked up. The broker for the development will usually have the keys.

---

* Though if you used an electronic signature program like Docusign, your arm is likely in much better shape!

## And If They Don't Work?

Just in case your seller doesn't have any good faith left at the end of closing, the brokers (if you used them) can be marshaled in to help the situation. If the brokers have participated, it's likely that they have a set of working keys. They should give you those keys to the home, which you can then use to check against the keys the seller has given you. If the seller refuses to turn over the keys, perhaps your first call should be to the local locksmith.

Sam once had a closing where the sellers had moved out of state several months earlier. The sellers' broker had the condo keys and they left their mailbox key with a neighbor. On the day of closing, the buyer refused to close until the mailbox key had been delivered. The sellers, reached by telephone during the closing, told the buyer to call the neighbor. The buyer did call, but the neighbor wasn't there. After hemming and hawing for the better part of a day and a half, the buyer finally decided to have a locksmith come and make a new key for the mailbox. Fine. But he wanted the sellers to pay for the locksmith. The sellers refused. He closed anyway.

## Warranties and Other Paperwork

If the seller has purchased an existing home warranty, you'll want the paperwork. Ditto for any warranties that may be in force for a relatively new home. Sometimes sellers keep paperwork in a digital lockbox. If that's the case, you'll want that sent to you. Make a list of any warranties that you think should come along with the home and ask your attorney or broker or closing agent to get the seller to put them together for you.

 **FIRST-TIME BUYER TIP:** Have your attorney or broker make sure the seller brings all of his or her keys (including mailbox, garage door, and any safe or locked cabinet that is being left behind) to the closing.

# Question 100: How Does My Deed Get Recorded?

A deed is the physical manifestation of the title to your home. Holding title is an amorphous concept—it's not like holding a handful of dirt and saying, "I own this land." To give you something to show for your money and efforts, our legal system (based on the British system of real estate law) has sanctioned deeds, or pieces of paper that say you own a specific piece of property at a specific address.

Part of the process to formalize your ownership is to record the deed. This gives legal recognition—in other words, puts the world on notice—of your ownership of the property. Anyone can go to the office of the recorder of deeds and find out that you own your home. The deed becomes part of the public record, and your ownership becomes part of the property's chain of title. If a title company looked up your property now, after the closing and after the deed has been recorded, your name would come up as the official owner.

## Recording Your Deed

How does a deed get recorded? If you're closing at a title company, the title company may do it. Or the title company will deliver the deed to you and you'll have to take it to your local recorder of deeds' office. It's as simple as that. But you want to make sure that the deed is recorded properly, and that your correct name, address, and other information are listed. When real estate tax bills are sent out, they are sent to the name and address listed at the recorder's or assessor's office. If there's a problem with your home or with your tax bill, a notice will be sent to the address listed there. If the address, or your name, is incorrectly listed, you may never get your property tax bill or any notices, and you could lose your property.

 **FIRST-TIME BUYER TIP:** Check to make sure your deed is recorded correctly and that the information is listed correctly. Verify that the proper authorities have your correct address for tax bills. Mark down the days you're supposed to receive your tax bill (you should find this out at the closing). If you don't receive it, call the recorder's (or real estate tax bill collector's) office to find out why. Nonpayment of property taxes is an easy (and quick) way to lose your property. Make sure it doesn't happen to you.

 20/20 HINDSIGHT: If you move out of your home but keep it as an investment property, make sure you change the address of your tax bill, and that you keep paying your taxes. Otherwise, you could lose your home.

## Your New Story as a Homeowner

You'll notice in the preface to this book that I invite readers to contact me. I give my email address (Ilyce@thinkglink.com) and my website address (ThinkGlink.com). And really, I'd love to hear from you.

I want to know how it all turned out. Was the book helpful? Do you love living in your home, or have you already decided to sell and go back to renting? Have you bought a second home? Refinanced? Paid off your first home before the term was due? Become a landlord?

I hope you'll let me know. While I do a lot of things in my career beyond writing books, engaging in a conversation with you is my favorite. On ThinkGlink.com, you'll find additional information and updates to the book. Please go there and sign up for my free weekly newsletter to continue to learn and grow as a homeowner.

And don't forget, every once in a while, to look around and remember, "There's no place like home."

# CHAPTER 13

# Happily Ever After

You'd like to think that you'll live happily ever after in your new home, but that's not always the case. Here's some information on what to do if something should prove amiss with your home after you close and move in, and how to lower your property tax bill. Finally, I've added a few thoughts on how to recognize when it might be time to sell your home and buy another.

## How Should I Prepare for the Move to My New Home?

If it feels as if you're the only family you know moving into a new house, maybe you don't know the right people. One out of every five families moves each year (this includes both owners and renters). Forty-five percent of these moves happen during the summer, according to the American Movers Conference (AMC), the interstate moving industry's national trade association, which represents some twelve hundred moving companies worldwide. (It only *seems* as though everyone is moving the same day as you.)

There are dozens of details to think about when you move, even if your new house is across town. It pays to plan and be organized. There are several free, or inexpensive (about fifty cents to $1 each), consumer publications about moving that are available to you.

## Planning Your Move

Here are some things to think about when planning a move:

- **Don't take everything with you.** Sort through, throw out, give away, or sell things you don't need anymore. When you've gotten to the bare minimum, start packing.
- **Save those old newspapers.** As soon as you get your mortgage, start saving your old newspapers for wrapping delicate objects like china and glassware. You may want to double- or triple-wrap each piece, so stack away about three times as much newspaper as you think you'll need. If you don't want to rewash the plates after you move, buy packages of plain newsprint or tissue paper for the initial wrap and then put newsprint over that. Or, you can buy an extra-large plastic wrap and do the initial wrap in that, followed by newsprint.
- **The interim move.** Will your new home be ready on time? Do you need an interim move? Will you be storing your furniture? If you're moving across state lines, it's best to store your belongings near your new home, not your old one. That way, if you need something, you might be able to get it quickly and easily.
- **Schedule repair or renovation work ahead of time.** If you need repair, decorating, or renovation work done on your new house, and have the extra float time, get busy scheduling the work four to six weeks before you move. If you're planning to paint or decorate, you may want to have that work done before you've unpacked most things and settled into your new home.
- **Get your new utility accounts.** Three weeks before the move, you'll want to contact your local utility companies (telephone, electricity, cable, gas, water) and inform them of your move. Arrange to have these services cut off at the end of moving day (if you're moving in the afternoon, it would be nice to be able to drink water and use the bathroom, not to mention the telephone). Don't forget to arrange the hookup of utilities to your new home.
- **Reserve the elevators.** If you're moving to a condominium or a co-op, you'll need to schedule a day to move in with the building's management. Generally, large condos (those with an elevator) require you to "reserve" the freight elevator for your move. Do this way ahead of time or the day on which you'd like to move

may already be booked. There may even be a fee for having the building maintenance men "oversee" your move. Ask your new building personnel about moving-
in rules, and don't be surprised if you're asked to pay for the privilege.

- **Discontinue delivery services.** Two weeks before your move, you'll want to set
the day to discontinue your delivery services, like newspapers, milk, dry cleaning,
or laundry. If you're moving to a new state, your broker may be able to offer a little advice on employing these services in your new town.

- **Change-of-address cards.** Also, around two weeks before your move, you'll
have to fill out and mail your change-of-address cards. Your local post office can
give you some cards to fill out, or you may want to have change-of-address cards
preprinted. If you receive FedEx or UPS packages for your home-based business,
you'll want to inform these companies of your change of address as well.

- **Moving with pets.** If you're moving with pets, you may need to take some special precautions, according to the AMC. Pets cannot be shipped on moving vans.
They should travel with you and wear special identification tags with your name,
address, telephone number, and the name of an alternative relative, in case you
can't be located. If you decide to ship your pet by air, make the arrangements
ahead of time. If you move across state lines, nearly every state has laws on the
entry of animals. Write to the state veterinarian, state department of animal hus-
bandry, or other state agency for information. Most states require up-to-date ra-
bies shots for dogs and cats. If you're moving to Hawaii with your pet, you'll
have to quarantine the animal for 120 days. Some pets must have an entry permit
issued by the destination state's regulatory agency. Finally, your new town (or
condo or co-op) may have restrictions on the number of dogs or cats that can live
at one residence. If this might be a problem for you, check with your new city or
village council.

- **Moving with plants.** You generally won't have a problem if you're moving house-
plants, but some states do require you to have an inspection by an authorized state
department agriculture inspector. Plants are susceptible to shock when moving,
and it may be dangerous to move a plant if the temperature is below 35 degrees or
above 95–100 for more than an hour. The AMC says plants can tolerate darkness
for up to a week, but it's best not to store them. Cuttings of your favorite house-
plants, while convenient, will not last as long or as well as potted plants.

# Finding the Moving Company

Of course, as many as eight weeks before moving day, you'll probably need to find a moving company. Shop around and compare prices. Try to use a licensed, insured, and bonded mover. Be careful of overcharges, and if you're moving across state lines, find out how much the company charges per mile. It's better to get a flat fee, if that's possible.

Movers are required to prepare an order for service for each customer. Keep a copy of this, as it shows the terms of the initial agreement with the mover. Next, the mover must issue a bill of lading, which is the legal contract between the customer and the mover. It is very important, so keep it handy during the move. The Interstate Commerce Commission warns "not to sign the bill of lading until comparing it with the order of service to be sure that all services ordered are correctly shown."

A binding estimate binds the mover to bill only at the price agreed to for the specific services needed. If you make any changes or increase the amount that is being moved, it may void the estimate, which should be in writing and attached to the bill of lading. With a binding estimate, you must pay the mover with cash, certified check, or money order, unless you have prearranged to use a credit card. In a nonbinding estimate, the final price for the move will not be known until everything has been weighed and transportation charges have been calculated. Request a copy of the mover's policy on inconvenience or delay (in case they get lost) in advance of the move.

Make sure you and the mover understand when he or she is supposed to pick up your household furniture and when it is supposed to be delivered. Do not accept a promise like "We'll be there as soon as possible." Get definitive dates and make sure it's in writing. If the mover cannot meet the pickup or delivery dates, he or she is required to notify you by telephone, telegram, or in writing. If you're going across country, be sure to ask the mover to notify you of the charges for the move.

Licensed movers are responsible for loss or damage to your property. You should have a list of all of the items being moved. Number your boxes, and make a list of the contents of each box. Label them clearly with your name and new address and telephone number. You and the mover should agree about the contents being shipped, and make sure the inventory list reflects your mutual understanding. At the time of delivery, note any items that are damaged or missing, and ask the mover for a liability claims form. Finally, you and the mover should agree on the amount of liability the mover will assume for loss or damage to your property.

The mover's liability is limited to sixty cents per pound, so it's wise to add extra insurance if your goods are particularly valuable. The mover can provide you with added coverage, but be sure you understand what's protected and for how much. Likewise, you must declare the value of your goods with the mover before the move. Otherwise, the mover is required to value them at a lump-sum equivalent to $1.25 times the weight of the shipment. So if your goods weigh four thousand pounds, the mover is only required to value them at $5,000. Check with your homeowner's or renter's policy to see what's covered.

 **20/20 HINDSIGHT:** If you have a large or complicated move, it's best to purchase some additional insurance over and above the minimum tagged for your order. Also, invite the mover to inspect the contents of your house. The mover's representative should know how long the move will take, what it will cost, and how big a truck you'll need. You can also negotiate the price of the move with the mover. Ask them, for example, to throw in the wardrobes (large boxes in which you hang your hanging clothes instead of folding and packing them) for free. You'll also want to purchase your own packing tape for fifty cents a roll instead of using the mover's tape at $2 per roll. (You won't believe how many rolls your movers will go through, even if you already have everything all boxed up.) If possible, hand-carry all valuables like cash and jewelry. If you have delicate objects, such as artwork, glasswork, china, or crystal, the movers may not insure it unless they pack it themselves, which is an additional charge. Finally, know where each box should be placed in your new home. While the movers can put everything in the basement, the unpacking will go a heck of a lot more quickly if they put each box in the room in which it is needed.

## Discovering Problems After You Close

The first thing to consider is the problem itself. What happened? Did the boiler blow up? Is a pipe burst? Did the electrical system catch on fire? Is there asbestos in the home? Did you fall through the floor? Did the roof leak? Did the dishwasher break? Did the ceiling paint crack? Is something missing in your new home?

Martha recently bought a home in Washington. She wrote into the contract that the wood-burning stove was supposed to stay in the house. When she moved in, she found that the stove was gone. The seller offered her $100, but when she priced out the stove, she found it would cost her $1,200 to replace it.

If you've bought a brand-new home, I think you have a right to believe everything will work beautifully for a long time. But if something goes wrong, your attorney should have negotiated for a new homeowner's warranty, which covers various items in the home for different periods of time. For example, if your new dishwasher breaks within the first year, the warranty will cover that. If the roof leaks in five years, it may cover that, too.

If you've bought an older or used home, you have to realize some things are going to break. Others may work, but not work well. Each home is different and has its own rhythms. If something goes wrong, you'll have to fix it, unless your seller or the seller's broker purchased a homeowner's warranty plan for your older home (if you live in California, more than 85 percent of the homes are sold with a home warranty plan). If you have a warranty, then you'll be able to have your problems fixed (for the first year) and all you'll be responsible for is the deductible.

The next question you have to ask is, did the seller or seller's broker know about the problem and simply "forget" to tell you about it? Or is it possible they simply didn't know there was a problem? Is it a case of puffery, where the broker may have said, "This house is perfect! You'll love it."

Common sense should tell you that when the broker says, "This house is perfect," he or she doesn't mean everything in the home is in perfect working order. (Or maybe that is what they meant, but even if it is, you'd be foolish to take that claim seriously.) But if the seller and the seller's broker told you that the furnace was new and, a week after moving into the home, you discover it's old, covered with asbestos, and just had a paint job, that could be a problem. If you were told the house was freshly painted, and you find out it wasn't, that could be a problem. If you were told the house's roof did not leak, and a day after the first rain your living room looks like a swimming pool, that could be a problem.

Although disclosure laws vary from state to state, most sellers are required to tell you about "known, material defects" that could affect the value of the home. (I put "known, material defects" in quotes because that's typically the legal standard you need to prove; that is, that the seller knew there were material, or serious, defects in the property that were not disclosed to you.) In some states, homeowners have successfully sued their sellers for not disclosing that someone was murdered in their home, or a former owner died of AIDS. In some states, not disclosing that your house is haunted could be a real problem for the seller. (Nope, I'm not making that up.)

The bottom line is, if you feel you've been wronged, or lied to, in the purchase of your new home, you'll need to consult an attorney to learn about the legal rights and remedies you have in your state.

But if you have outsize expectations—and expect that everything will work perfectly in your home forever—you're setting yourself up for a series of disappointments that may erode your enjoyment of your new home.

## How to Lighten Your Property Tax Load

As a new homeowner, you've probably realized that real estate taxes are about as inevitable as death. You'll eventually get to the end of your mortgage payments, but you'll pay property taxes as long as you own the house.

The good news is, you can do a few things to keep your property taxes as low as possible. According to tax professionals, county and township governments often make loads of mistakes when assessing property. The nonprofit National Taxpayers Union (NTU), a taxpayers advocacy group based in Washington, D.C., indicates that approximately 60 percent of all homeowners are overassessed; in other words, in every group of a hundred angry taxpayers who think their taxes are too high, sixty are overpaying. Of those, says the NTU, only 2 percent appeal their real estate taxes. But, of the 2 percent who do appeal, 50–80 percent (so, one to 1.6 percent of the total; the figures vary based on the source) receive some sort of reduction in their property taxes. Those are good odds.

(More recent studies seem to indicate that more people are filing appeals of their tax assessments. The anecdotal evidence appears to prove this true: In 1999, property tax bills in Cook County were delayed by several weeks because so many homeowners filed appeals. In 2004, property taxes in Illinois were considered so outrageous that the state legislature passed a property tax cap. It remains to be seen which homeowners are actually helped by the tax cap.)

Appealing your property taxes is not a difficult process, but it does require a bit of ingenuity, perseverance, and organization. And the reward—a lower tax bill—is eminently worthwhile.

How worthwhile? That depends on each house, but Jim Siudut, an accountant and real estate tax specialist who has produced a video called *Fight Higher Real Estate Taxes and Win*, says he saved himself $1,500 in one year. The next year he saved himself an even greater amount because the rise in his property taxes was keyed to a lower assessed valuation. (See the glossary at the end of this section for definitions of relevant tax terms.)

The key to successfully fighting your property taxes is solid evidence, presented clearly and concisely. Siudut says all homeowners should make sure they're being correctly assessed, especially if their property taxes are high or if they have received steep increases in the last few years.

The time to appeal is when you get your assessment notice—not your tax bill.

Not acting in time is the biggest mistake homeowners make when appealing their property taxes.

The assessment notice details your home's current and past assessed valuation and its current estimated market value. It should also list your property's physical characteristics. In other words, if you have four bedrooms and two bathrooms and an attached two-car garage, the notice should say that.

The estimated market value is the price the assessor's office attaches to your property based on surveys and studies of neighboring properties. The assessment is a percentage of the estimated market value, and that percentage is usually set by law.

It's important to remember that once you receive your assessment notice, you have a limited time to file an appeal, usually thirty to sixty days, depending on the county. If you are not satisfied with your judgment, you may appeal all the way up to your state's supreme court.

In North Carolina, for example, any taxpayer dissatisfied with the assessment made by the county assessor should arrange immediately for an informal meeting with the assessor to explain why he or she thinks the assessment is excessive. If a satisfactory conclusion cannot be reached, the taxpayer should file an appeal with the County Board of Equalization and Review (Board of County Commissioners), requesting a hearing. A taxpayer dissatisfied with the decision of the county board may file an appeal with the State Property Tax Commission within thirty days of the mailing of the decision by the county board. That decision may be appealed to the Court of Appeals and ultimately the North Carolina Supreme Court.

To effectively appeal your assessment, you'll need your most recent and prior year's tax bill (for new homeowners, this should be available at your local tax assessor's office), your current assessment notice, your current property survey, your purchase contract or closing statements (if you purchased your home within the last five years), a copy of any building plans, and an itemized account of expenses (for any improvements made to the property) and any recent appraisals.

To analyze your assessment, you'll need the following data: your property record card; a list of comparable homes ("comps"), and their property record cards, sale dates, and prices. Experts recommend that you check with a local real estate agent or broker for some of this information. Agents and brokers should be happy to oblige, because it's a good opportunity for them to market their services to potential customers.

The first step is to go to your county assessor's office and take a look at your property record card. You do this by using the parcel number or permanent real estate index number, which you can find on your tax bill. The card lists the physical characteristics of your property, including the number of bedrooms, bathrooms, and fireplaces; garage size; square footage; and lot size.

Many overassessments result from factual errors. That is, the assessor's office may say that your house has four bedrooms when it actually has only three. So check the facts. Factual errors are the easiest to document and the easiest to appeal. If you do find a factual error, you'll need either blueprints or a property survey to "prove" your claim. Your evidence should include recent color photographs of the inside and outside of your house. Or you can also ask the assessor's office to come out and reexamine your house.

In addition to factual errors, Siudut uses four tests to determine whether property has been overassessed: an assessment ratio test, an equity test, a market test, and an environmental factors test. Gary Whalen, a real estate broker and tax consultant who has written a book called *Digging for Gold in Your Own Backyard: The Complete Homeowner's Guide to Lowering Your Real Estate Taxes*, refers to property overassessments due to factors other than factual errors as "judgmental errors."

### Assessment Ratio Test

"In any county, the assessment is based on the home's market value. The assessment ratio is a percentage of market value. What you want to do is determine whether or not your assessment ratio is in line with that of comparable homes in your neighborhood," Siudut says.

Gathering comparable data is the most time-consuming part of appealing your property taxes. Siudut and Whalen recommend that you check for properties that have sold within the last two years and are similar to yours in size and amenities. Armed with the exact addresses of these comps, ask the assessor's office for the property record cards for them. Compare the assessed valuation of the comps with the sale price to see if the assessor comes close in determining the correct market value. Did the homes sell for less money than their market value? Check to see what percentage the assessor used to determine the assessed valuation (before the multiplier was applied). Compare this with the percentage used on your property.

Experts say the biggest misconception is that homeowners think they can go only on market value. The key test to fairness is not market value, it's uniformity.

## Market and Equity Tests

The law of uniformity also helps homeowners construct appeals based on market and equity tests. Homes in the same neighborhood should be assessed at the same rate, proportionate to their size and amenities.

Siudut's market test compares your assessment per square foot with those of comps in your neighborhood. To gain an accurate square footage account, measure from your house's exterior walls. Next, find eight to ten comps so that you will end up with at least four that have lower assessments per square foot. To find out the assessment per square foot, simply divide the assessed value by the number of square feet in the property. Like the market test, the equity test compares the value of other homes similar in age and amenities to yours. And again, the idea is to find comps that have been assessed at a lower rate than yours.

Level out the value of the homes by adding and subtracting the value of amenities one house might be missing but another home has. For example, if your house doesn't have a fireplace, but your comps do, subtract $1,500 from your assessed valuation. A local real estate agent can help you determine the appropriate value for each amenity.

## Environmental Test

Did the state recently build a nuclear power plant in your backyard? Did the railroad just add a new switching station down the street? Are a large number of people in your neighborhood out of work because a plant closed down? Is a new garbage dump being planned within a couple of miles of your home?

These are environmental factors that could lower your property's market value. (Of course, as a new home buyer, you've remembered the broker's maxim "location, location, location," and hopefully not chosen a house next to a garbage dump.) If you put these factors to work for you, Siudut says, you might be able to lower your assessment. Document these changes and how they might work against property values in the neighborhood. Use articles from your local newspapers, editorials, and evidence of any television and radio reports. Clip these together to give added weight to your appeal.

Whalen and Siudut recommend combining any errors—both judgmental and factual—to get the biggest reduction.

"If you're organized and present a clear case, it does not substantially increase the assessor's workload," Siudut says. "The more organized and focused you are, the easier you make their job, and the easier it is to get that reduction."

When researching your case, don't be afraid to ask the person behind the desk for help. Homeowners should also apply for all the exceptions to which they're legally entitled: senior citizens, homestead, homestead improvement, disabled, or disabled veterans. The assessor can reduce your equalized assessed valuation anywhere from $2,000 to $50,000, depending on which benefits you're entitled to.

## Property-Tax-Fighting Tools

The best thing you can do is put it in writing, with photos. Use a camera (here's where that digital camera—or even your iPhone—will prove its use again) to shoot the exteriors of homes that you want to compare with yours. Be sure to get the property address in the photo when you shoot the exterior.

Next, make sure your information is neatly typed under each photo. If you want, use a separate sheet for each house. Bind it neatly together. Your goal is to make the job easy for the person at the assessor's office who is going to help you. The easier it is for him to peruse your information, and understand it, the easier it will be for him to recommend that your property taxes be reduced.

# A Glossary of Tax Terms

Here are a few tax terms to help get you going. You can find more at ThinkGlink.com.

**ASSESSED VALUATION.** The value placed on property for tax purposes and used as a basis for division of the tax burden. It's a percentage of what is deemed the home's fair market value.

**ASSESSMENT RATIO.** The percentage of your home's fair market value that each assessor uses to determine the property's assessed valuation. The ratio can vary from county to county.

**NOTICE OF REVISION.** A notice mailed to the property owner after a property has been reassessed.

**STATE MULTIPLIER.** Also known as the state equalization factor, this is a number the state assigns to each county, depending on the assessment ratio the county uses to calculate assessed valuation. The multiplier either raises or lowers the assessed valuation to the state-mandated level of 33.33 percent of market value. The multiplier ensures that taxpayers in each of the state's counties pay the same amount proportionately in property taxes.

**TAX RATE.** The rate at which property is taxed, usually shown per hundred dollars of the property's value.

**UNIFORMITY.** The legal principle that governs property tax assessments. It states that all property in a given area must be assessed at the same level. That is, you should not be assessed at a higher rate than your next-door neighbor. The principle of uniformity is the basis for many successful assessment appeals.

# Special Help for Seniors

Many communities freeze property taxes for seniors who reach a certain age (usually sixty-two or sixty-five) and have a lower income. Talk to your local county assessor's office or your local village or city hall to find out if your community offers special tax relief for seniors.

## The Next House: Knowing When It's Time to Move On

Although you may think you'll live in your first home forever, odds are you'll be looking for another home within five to seven years.

Why do people move? There are dozens of reasons. You may marry, have children, have an aging parent or relative come live with you, change jobs, care for grandchildren, divorce, get sick, or decide you want to live somewhere else.

How will you know when it's time to move on? You may start to feel cramped, confined, and tight on space. Your house may seem frayed at the edges. Your child may need special services available only in another school district.

Typically, you'll become aware that a subtle dissatisfaction comes over you whenever you walk into your home. If you can't fix the dissatisfaction by remodeling the interior or exterior of your home, adding on, or redoing the landscaping, it might be time to move on.

If that's the case, you need to start creating your wish list and reality check all over again. Your list may be quite different than it was when you moved into your home. But creating a new wish list and reality check is the only way to objectively identify what it is you now feel you need and want in a home.

Once you've identified what you want and need, you can go about fixing up your current home to sell. For more information on how to make the most of your sale, check out my home-selling books: *100 Questions Every Home Seller Should Ask*, or *50 Simple Steps You Can Take to Sell Your Home Faster and for More Money in Any Market*.

Feel free to check out my website, ThinkGlink.com, for news, updates, and further information.

# Top 10 Mistakes First-Time Buyers Make

Borrowing a little from one of my favorite performers, David Letterman, I've created a top-ten list of things first-time buyers tend to do when they're searching for a home. Brokers call them "mistakes." These aren't egregious errors, but if, for example, timing problems aren't worked out or the wrong size home is purchased, they can make the process of buying a home a little more time-consuming and heart-wrenching. At worst, they can cause problems down the line, when it comes time to sell.

I can't tell you how many times I've heard first-time buyers exclaim "Not me!" when faced with the possibility of having made mistakes. Reading about them in this Appendix—presumably after you've read the whole book, but before you've shopped for a house—might help you head 'em off at the pass. While you may not see yourself doing everything on this list, brokers agree that the average first-time buyer makes at least one of the following mistakes:

**MISTAKE #1: INCORRECTLY TIMING YOUR MOVE.** As a first-time buyer, you've probably been renting until now. If so, the best time to close on a house is when your current lease ends. Don't sign another year-long lease if you expect to buy a home before that lease period expires—otherwise you'll end up with a dent in your pocketbook from writing rent and mortgage checks. If you can't time your closing correctly, approach your landlord about a shorter lease—say, three to six months—or, alternatively, a month-to-month lease. Another option is to ask your landlord to include an escape clause in your new lease that will allow you to get out of your lease with thirty or sixty days' notice.

**MISTAKE #2: LOOKING AT HOMES YOU CAN'T AFFORD.** First-time buyers often hear that they can buy a home up to two and a half times their combined income. But that's if interest rates are at 7 to 8 percent. Heck, if interest rates stay in the 4 percent range, you might actually be able to push that number to four times your combined income—or more. Still, as we've already discussed, there are so many other costs you have to factor into the purchase, including the carrying costs on your debt, property taxes (paid once or twice annually or billed to you monthly along with your mortgage payment), insurance premiums (paid separately or billed with your mortgage payment), private mortgage insurance (PMI) if you put down less than 20 percent, and the maintenance and upkeep on the property (if you buy a bigger, more expensive home it'll simply cost more to maintain and keep up). And then there's this: If you look at homes you can't afford, you'll get spoiled by how nice they are. When you finally come to your senses and start looking at homes in your price range, you'll be disappointed by what you can comfortably afford. For example, if you've been looking at four-bedroom homes with attached garages in plush suburbs, a three-bedroom home in a so-so neighborhood with street parking is going to seem, well, not quite nice enough. In order to save yourself the heartache, get prequalified or preapproved for your mortgage by a local lender. That way you'll know exactly how much house you can afford to buy.

**MISTAKE #3: BUYING THE WRONG-SIZE HOME.** Many first-time buyers, especially those who are single and in their late twenties and early thirties, purchase one-bedroom condominiums. Why do they buy a one-bedroom? Usually because it's so much more affordable than a two-bedroom. What Millennials don't realize is how likely it is they will meet someone, fall madly in love, and marry. Unless you marry a next-door neighbor (talk about geographic desirability!) who has a condo that can be combined with yours, that one-bedroom, one-bath apartment will soon seem too small. For nearly the same price, and possibly even the same location, your dollars might buy a two-bedroom, two-bath apartment, which would give you some much-needed, additional flexibility. (At the very least, it will be much easier to host visiting friends.) When you buy property, you should think about how long you intend to live there. Is this a five-year home? A ten-year home? Or, is this the home you intend to die in? The average American family changes residences every five to seven years. If you're in your twenties, anticipate significant changes in your lifestyle within five to seven years. Buy smarter by planning for those changes ahead of time.

**MISTAKE #4: BUYING IN A NEIGHBORHOOD YOU KNOW NOTHING ABOUT.** Sometimes first-time buyers will fall in love with a house in a neighborhood that is inappropriate for them. While shopping for a home, never forget that you'll have to travel through the neighborhood to get to and from your house. Is it a nice neighborhood? Is there graffiti on every wall? Are there gangs? Is there a neighborhood crime watch group? Are the neighbors your age? Are there families around the same age as yours? Is it a transient neighborhood, or do families stay there forever? To avoid making this mistake, spend a lot of time in the neighborhood before you buy. Drive to and from the house. Sit in your car and watch your future neighbors come home from work. Listen to how loudly their children play their favorite music. Or, just play. Walk to the local bar, restaurant, grocery store, and cleaners. Think about whether you'll be as happy in this neighborhood as you might be in the house you're looking to buy.

**MISTAKE #5: OPERATING ON A FIRST-HOUSE-IS-BEST THEORY.** Coming from a cramped, one-bedroom rental, almost any home will look good. And, in a seller's market, you might be tempted to make an offer on the first home you see. But that's rarely a good long-term move. I think you should look at five, ten, or even twenty houses (in person, not online) to see what's on the market within your spending range. Season your eyes by inspecting different types of homes: condos, townhouses, duplexes, and single-family houses. See what type of home generates an internal response—it could be very different from what you're imagining is the right type of home to buy. When you've narrowed down your choices to three or four, visit them again. By this time, some form of objectivity should have returned, and you'll be able to make a sensible choice. Completely spur-of-the-moment decisions often don't work out, and you could wind up paying dearly for your impulsiveness.

**MISTAKE #6: BUYING A PROPERTY THAT'S DIFFICULT TO RESELL.** Although you say you don't mind that the house backs up to the local railroad, you will when it comes time to sell the home. And it's unlikely you'll be able to easily convince another buyer just how quiet and peaceful life is there. When buying a home, try not to buy one that will be difficult to resell. Even though you think you'll be there forever, you probably won't. In fact, I can almost guarantee that you won't spend the rest of your life in that house. Most first-time buyers sell within five to seven years, and there's no reason to think you'll be any different. Before you buy a house, think hard about how you would go about selling it. Walk yourself through and point out all the negatives. Say them out loud. Then ask your agent or broker how long it would take him or her to sell it. Keep in mind that homes that are difficult to resell tend to appreciate at a slower rate than homes without significant issues for buyers to overcome.

**MISTAKE #7: OVEREXTENDING YOUR BUDGET.** Although the lender who prequalifies you for a loan may tell you that you're able to afford a $100,000 home, keep in mind that buying in that price range may stretch your budget beyond your comfort zone. To avoid feeling pinched, or losing ground financially, it's important to understand how you spend all of your money and where those extra few dollars go at the end of the month. You may be comfortable spending 35 percent of your take-home pay on rent, or you may prefer to spend less—say, 25 percent. Write down every amount that you spend (down to that last piece of bubble gum) for two months. Can you live without buying your streaming music service? Would you feel uncomfortable knowing you can go out to dinner only once a month? Or that you must eliminate your annual vacation, or your children's summer camp or piano lessons? As a homeowner, you'll have additional expenses beyond your mortgage payment. There's the maintenance and upkeep of the home, plus property taxes. If you live in a condo, you've got assessments. Buying a less expensive home will give you greater peace of mind, allow for savings, and permit a few extras.

**MISTAKE #8: BEING INDECISIVE.** When you're searching for the right house, you should take all the time you need. Don't let your broker bully you into making a decision before you're ready to do it. Ask to see five, ten, twenty, or fifty homes if you haven't found one you like enough to bid on. Indecisiveness kicks in when you've found a home you would like to live in but you're afraid of making the commitment. First-time buyers often lose two or three homes because they can't bring themselves to actually make the offer.* Or there might be two wonderful properties and they face a tough choice. If you're afraid, admit that fear and conquer it by talking with your broker. You're not the only first-time buyer who's had trouble making up his or her mind.

**MISTAKE #9: CHOOSING THE WRONG MORTGAGE.** Many first-time buyers have heard from their parents that the only mortgage to get is a thirty-year fixed-interest-rate loan. That's because the generation ahead of you didn't have the tailor-made financial options buyers have today. Consider choosing an adjustable-rate mortgage (ARM) to take advantage of superlow interest rates. Or pick a ten- or fifteen-year fixed-interest-rate loan to maximize your mortgage interest deduction and save you hundreds of thousands of dollars in interest. Explore all the options. Have your lender show you on paper how much each option will cost and how they compare with one another.

**MISTAKE #10: UNDERINSURING THE PROPERTY.** First-time buyers know they have to buy home insurance to cover their mortgage. Sometimes they forget to increase the coverage of that insurance as the neighborhood improves and the home appreciates in value. Sometimes they forget to insure the contents of the house. Think about how much it would cost you to replace your furniture, clothing, books, laptops, artwork, and pots and pans. Add up everything and then tack on the cost of actually rebuilding the home (a single family or townhouse) if it were to burn to the ground.† Then add on your mortgage, which would still have to be paid. That's how much insurance you should buy.

---

* The very good news is that this problem often takes care of itself. If you lose two or three homes because you couldn't commit, you'll jump at the next viable property you see.

† A friend of mine works in a furniture store. As I was finishing this book, she told me about a family who came into the store to buy all-new furniture for a 6,000-square-foot house with nine bathrooms—their prior home burned to the ground and they had to start all over again. They'll likely spend more than $150,000 just to buy basic beds, side tables, bathroom fixtures, and furniture for the living room, dining room, family room, and kitchen, not to mention, pots, pans, plates, silverware, table linens, etc. There's a lot of stuff that goes into a home.

# 6 Simple Things You Can Do to Make the Home-Buying Process Easier

It's rare that buying a house is a simple, easy process. Heck, just getting all the paperwork together that you need to qualify for your mortgage is a time-consuming, annoying* process, so buckle up and get ready for a bumpy-ish ride. These six things, however, will help smooth the path.

**1: GET PREAPPROVED FOR YOUR LOAN.** Getting preapproved is the only way to ensure that you're searching in the right price bracket. Too often, people search for homes in a price range they can't afford, either because they don't understand how the numbers work, or because they imagine that they're going to negotiate the seller down to a more affordable number (definitely not happening in a seller's market). Not knowing the true costs involved, or holding out false hope of a negotiation miracle, is a haphazard way to spend several hundred thousand dollars. Instead, spend the time it takes, either online or in person with a mortgage lender, to get preapproved for your loan.

**2: GATHER YOUR PAPERWORK AHEAD OF TIME.** Why wait until the last minute? You're going to need dozens of pieces of paper, so you might as well go ahead and

---

* If I'm being honest, the whole process is more cumbersome and annoying that it needs to be. Perhaps as the digital revolution continues, some enterprising Millennial will figure out a way to truly streamline buying a home. Then again, it's still super-annoying to buy a car, so maybe not.

get them in a folder as soon as possible. You'll need copies of your last tax return, paycheck stubs, bank accounts, investment accounts, etc. If everything is electronic, you'll be one step ahead. Print a PDF file of each document you need, save it to a single electronic folder (in Google Drive or Dropbox or another cloud-based file-sharing system), and then share that with your lender as needed.

**3: WORK WITH A GREAT BUYER'S BROKER.** Would you invest $100,000 in a stock just because you got a hot tip on a cold call? Of course not. But people go out every day and spend hundreds of thousands of dollars on a home without consulting a licensed buyer's broker. This is foolish, particularly since consulting a buyer's broker typically won't cost you anything out of your own pocket. You need someone on your side who can advise you on the neighborhood, demographics, and sales history of other homes similar to yours in your neighborhood of choice.

**4: KNOW THE NEIGHBORHOOD BEFORE YOU MAKE AN OFFER.** You don't just live in the house, you live in the neighborhood. Spend time walking around the area at all times of the day and night before you make your offer. Chat with your prospective neighbors about their experiences in the neighborhood. Pay a visit to the local dry cleaners, supermarket, or coffee shop. Stop in at the local police headquarters and inquire about the local crime rate. Pay a visit to the local schools and observe. No matter how much information is on the Internet, learning firsthand about your future neighborhood is something you have to do in person. And it will pay off in spades.

**5: PROTECT YOURSELF.** Make sure your contract has the right contingencies, and the right language, so that you're protected. If attorneys typically represent buyers and sellers in the state in which you're purchasing a home, then use one. And if attorneys aren't typically used, consider using one anyway so that you have someone advising you who doesn't have a vested interest in seeing the deal close. Buy enough homeowners' insurance, and make sure to increase it as the value of your home—and its contents—increases. Stay on top of your purchase so that there are no unpleasant surprises.

**6: HAVE REASONABLE EXPECTATIONS.** If you buy an older home, understand before you close that it's not going to be in perfect condition. There's no way everything will be perfect, even if the seller has recently gutted and renovated the whole property. But when home buyers pay list (or over list) prices, it's understandable that they might expect something nearing perfection. As a home inspector friend of mine likes to say: "All homes have problems, but older homes have older problems." If you expect perfection in an existing home, you're likely to end up disappointed.

# 5 Mistakes People Make When Buying New Construction

When you build a new house, or buy new construction, it's easy to get caught up in the excitement of creating something out of nothing. Your new house starts its life as a big hole in the ground. Six months to a year later, it's finished and laden with all the amenities you've chosen.

More home buyers are purchasing newly constructed homes than ever before. According to the National Association of Home Builders (NAHB), new home sales exceeded 1 million for the first time in 2003, and were expected to continue trending upwards through the rest of the decade. Unfortunately, the Great Recession killed the new construction industry and the number of new homes sold sunk to about 330,000 per year during the worst years. As I write this, at the beginning of 2018, the number of new homes sold is around 600,000, but more than 738,000 were built. That's a big increase from the depths of the recession, but is still more than a third below where they were in 2003, and more than 30 percent below where they should be in order to keep up with population growth and household formation.*

---

* Developers have been busy building high-rise rental units of all shapes and sizes, including expensive (I think) rentals that look more like fancy college dorms than traditional rental buildings, with a lot of shared services and spaces. Developers tell me that Millennials (and the subsequent cohort) want to live in community buildings that are very much like dorms.

Every year, it gets more expensive to buy a new home. According to the NAHB, you can expect to pay more than $50,000 more to buy the average new home than to purchase the average existing home.

What do you get for all that cash? Let's take a look: For a new house of about 2,200 square feet, a builder would use 3,103 square feet of asphalt shingles and other roofing materials, one fireplace, 8,385 square feet of drywall on the ceiling and walls, 13,837 linear feet of framing lumber, three bathroom sinks, three toilets, two bathtubs, one shower stall, two garage doors, and nineteen windows. The typical kitchen has about fifteen cabinets, five other cabinets, and twenty-three linear feet of countertops. Half of homes have stainless-steel sinks. More than 80 percent have a garbage disposal.

The era of the truly smart home is upon us (finally). If you could open up the walls of the average new home, you'd see that most are built to be Wi-Fi enabled. In the next few years, almost all new homes will have systems like Alexa or Google Home built into the walls, seamlessly allowing homeowners to talk to their homes as if you were talking to a child: "Alexa, add milk to the grocery list." Google's purchase of Nest, which started with Wi-Fi-enabled programmable thermostats, has sped up development of smart home accessories. Demand is high and will continue to grow.

In fact, the average newly constructed house has all sorts of amenities new home buyers in the 1950s couldn't ever have imagined.

For example, in 1950, the average new home had 963 square feet, with two bedrooms and one or one and a half baths. More than half of all new homes built today have more than 2,000 square feet, and 90 percent have three or more bedrooms. Eighty-three percent of homes built have at least a two-car garage, and nearly 90 percent have central air.

In the 1950s, new home buyers were just happy to have a garden. Today, new home buyers are as interested in outdoor living environments as they are in interior space. Outside a newly built home you might find a Jacuzzi, a full kitchen (complete with a grill, cooktop, and refrigerator), a fireplace, and various other outdoor rooms and amenities.

In 2016 (which is the latest data available), new homes look quite different than homes from sixty years ago. Here's a summary from the Census Bureau.

Of the 738,000 single-family homes completed in 2016:
- 686,000 had air-conditioning.
- 71,000 had two bedrooms or less and 336,000 had four bedrooms or more.

- 25,000 had one and one-half bathrooms or less and 273,000 homes had three or more bathrooms.
- 178,000 had stucco as the primary exterior wall material.
- 200,000 had a full or partial basement.
- 61,000 had concrete framing.

The median size of a completed single-family house was 2,422 square feet.

Of the 321,000 multifamily (condos or rentals, typically) units completed in 2016:
- 17,000 were age-restricted.
- 9,000 had a fireplace.
- 167,000 were in buildings with four floors or more.
- 213,000 were heated using electricity.
- 134,000 had one bedroom.

The median size of multifamily units built for rent was 1,085 square feet, while the median of those built for sale was 1,706 square feet.

Of the 13,000 multifamily buildings completed in 2016:
- 2,000 had 4 floors or more.
- 12,000 had laundry facilities located in the individual units.
- 4,000 did not have parking in the building or the complex.
- 1,000 had fifty units or more.

Of the 561,000 single-family homes sold in 2016:
- 500,000 were detached homes and 61,000 were attached homes (townhouses).
- 395,000 were in a community with a homeowners' association.
- 380,000 had a two-car garage.
- 129,000 had brick as the primary exterior wall material.
- 396,000 were paid for using conventional financing and 29,000 were paid for in cash.

The median sales price of new single-family homes sold in 2016 was $316,200, while the average sales price was $372,500. The median size of a new single-family home sold was 2,497 square feet.

## It's So Easy to Forget About Your Budget

Choosing which amenities you want in your new home is easy—you'll want them all. It's a lot harder to make those choices work within your budget. Blowing your new construction budget is one of the most common mistakes new home buyers make. I expand on that one below and have identified four other common mistakes for you, with the hopes that you'll be able to avoid them and make your dream house a reality.

1. **Blowing Your Budget.** Wouldn't it be great to put everything you've seen in the model home on your blueprint? Unfortunately, new construction costs a whole lot more than buying an existing home. Adding all the goodies just increases the total cost. In fact, the average new home buyer spends another 10 percent of the purchase price on options and upgrades. If you're already looking at the top of your price range, adding 10 percent onto the price can quickly blow your budget. Start your search by deciding how much you really want to spend on a home, and then find a way to keep costs under control.

2. **Not Checking Out the Builder.** Sure, Dave the Builder says he can build a great house. He might even have a slick brochure and fancy blueprints. But has he ever built a house? Have you ever talked to anyone who bought from him? Have you asked the homeowner if the home has held up physically and if Dave showed up promptly to fix punch-list items? The only way you'll know if your builder is a good one is to spend time visiting other homeowners who have purchased newly constructed houses from him or her in the past. Knock on doors at other communities the builder finished and ask homeowners to talk to you about their experiences in the house and with the builder. If you're not getting answers like "He's fabulous" or "I'd buy another house from him in a minute," save yourself the heartache and find another builder now. If you get great feedback from homeowners, you should then check out the builder with the state commission that licenses contractors and builders to make sure they are in compliance, carry the right amount of insurance, and have had no complaints filed against them. You should also go online and search the company (and the builder's name individually) and the word "complaint" to see

what turns up. While anyone can get fooled, if you follow these steps at least you'll know you tried to find out everything you could ahead of time.

3. **Choosing Options and Upgrades That Won't Increase the Value of Your Home.** If you can afford it, and you don't care about getting your money out of the property when you sell, add on all the options and upgrades the builder offers. But if you want your options and upgrades to help increase the value of your home, and your budget is limited, you'll need to be smart about what you choose. Pay to add on more space, like a fourth bedroom, home office, extra bath, third garage bay, or turn a crawl space into a basement. While you're at it, pay the extra few thousand dollars to have the basement dug deep enough to enjoy a nine-foot (or higher) ceiling when finished. Upgraded appliances and countertops in the kitchen will always pay off in the long run. Choose upgraded ceramic tile to dress up a bathroom or the kitchen, and play around with how to lay the tiles to make the room even nicer. Building out closets or the pantry is a good move, and try to add in more closet or storage space wherever you can. Finally, landscaping can add dramatically to your home's value, so consider beefing up the landscaping budget. If you can't afford everything now, consider delaying nonessentials like molding and even hardwood floors in the living room. You can always add the finishing touches, like replacing a pedestal sink with a marble-topped vanity, down the line, when you've rebuilt your savings account.

4. **Changing Your Mind.** If you change your mind about what you want in your new home, it's going to cost you. It may cost time or it may cost money—or it may cost both. Each change requires the builder to do something differently, and when you give a change order, the builder will tell you how much longer the house will take to build and how much more it will cost. In general, once you commit to buying new construction, you commit to a production schedule. Certain things have to happen at certain times, or the house won't be delivered to you on time. (The house may not be delivered to you on time even if you don't put in any change orders, but that's another book.) If you decide you want a particular tile and that tile is ordered, but if you don't like it when it comes in and decide to choose something else, you could set back your project by weeks or months. If you suddenly decide you want all the doors in the house to be eight inches higher, rather than the standard 6'8", and the

house is already built, the builder may have to do a whole lot of extra work—and order new doors—in order to get the house the way you want it. The time to make changes is when you're still in the blueprint stage. When a design is on a computer or on paper, it's a whole lot easier (and less expensive) to make changes than when the house is three weeks away from completion. The best thing you can do is to make your decisions and then, if at all possible, stick with them.

5. **Not Putting It in Writing.** A handshake is fine when it comes to friendships or business acquaintances, but it has no place when dealing with contractors or builders. When building or buying a newly constructed home, make sure everything you do is in writing, including the contract and amendments; specifics regarding appliances, tile, carpet, and other upgrades; and any change orders. Once the contract is signed, both you and the builder will have to live up to the terms—so make sure you understand them, and what rights you and the builder each have with respect to the work, delivery date, terms, and payment. Too often, important details are left out of the contract—details that can cost you dearly at closing.

# Glossary of Real Estate Terms Every Home Buyer Should Know

**ABSTRACT (OF TITLE)** A summary of the public records affecting the title to a particular piece of land. An attorney or title insurance company officer creates the abstract of title by examining all recorded instruments (documents) relating to a specific piece of property, such as easements, liens, mortgages, etc.

**ACCELERATION CLAUSE** A provision in a loan agreement that allows the lender to require the balance of the loan to become due immediately if mortgage payments are not made or there is a breach in your obligation under your mortgage or note.

**ADDENDUM** Any addition to, or modification of, a contract. Also called an amendment or rider.

**ADJUSTABLE-RATE MORTGAGE (ARM)** A type of loan whose prevailing interest rate is tied to an economic index (like one-year Treasury bills or LIBOR, the London Interbank Offered Rate), which fluctuates with the market. There are various types of ARMs, including one-year ARMs, which adjust every year; three-year ARMs, in which the interest rate is fixed for three years and then varies each year thereafter; and five-year ARMs, in which the interest rate is fixed for five years and adjusts every year thereafter. When the loan adjusts, the lender tacks a margin onto the index rate to come up with your loan's new rate. ARMs are considered far riskier than fixed-rate mortgages, but their starting interest rates can be quite lower than fixed-rate mortgages, and in the past five to ten years, people have done very well with them.

**AGENCY** A term used to describe the relationship between a seller and a broker, or a buyer and a broker.

**AGENCY CLOSING** The lender's use of a title company or other party to act on the lender's behalf for the purposes of closing on the purchase of a home or refinancing of a loan.

**AGENT** An individual who represents a buyer or a seller in the purchase or sale of a home. Licensed by the state, an agent must work for a broker or a brokerage firm.

**AGREEMENT OF SALE** This document is also known as the contract of purchase, purchase agreement, purchase and sale agreement, or sales agreement. It is the agreement by which the seller agrees to sell you his or her property if you pay a certain price. It contains all the provisions and conditions for the purchase and sale, must be written, and is signed by both parties.

**AMORTIZATION** A payment plan that enables the borrower to reduce his or her debt gradually through monthly payments of principal and interest. Amortization tables allow you to see exactly how much you would pay each month in interest and how much you repay in principal (the amount you owe on the loan), depending on the amount of money borrowed at a specific interest rate.

**APPLICATION** A series of documents you must fill out when you apply for a loan.

**APPLICATION FEE** A one-time fee charged by the mortgage company for processing your application for a loan. Sometimes the application fee is applied toward certain costs, including the appraisal and credit report.

**APPRAISAL** The opinion of an appraiser, who estimates the value of a home at a specific point in time.

**ARTICLES OF AGREEMENT FOR DEED** A type of seller financing that allows the buyer to purchase the home in installments over a specified period of time. The seller keeps legal title to the home until the loan is paid off. The buyer receives an interest in the property—called equitable title—but does not own it. However, because the buyer is paying the real estate taxes and paying interest to the seller, it is the buyer who receives the tax benefits of home ownership.

**ASSUMPTION OF MORTGAGE** If you assume a mortgage when you purchase a home, you undertake to fulfill the obligations of the existing loan agreement the seller made with the lender. The obligations are similar to those that you would incur if you took out a new mortgage. When assuming a mortgage, you become personally liable for the payment of principal and interest. The seller, or original mortgagor, is released from the liability, and should get that release in writing. Otherwise, he or she could be liable if you don't make the monthly payments.

**BALLOON MORTGAGE** A type of mortgage that is generally short in length but is amortized over twenty-five or thirty years so that the borrower pays a combination of interest and principal each month. At the end of the loan term, the entire balance of the loan must be repaid at once.

**BROKER** An individual who acts as the agent of the seller or buyer. A real estate broker must be licensed by the state.

**BUILDING LINE OR SETBACK** The distance from the front, back, or side of a lot beyond which construction or improvements may not extend without permission by the proper governmental authority. The building line may be established by a filed plat of subdivision, by restrictive covenants in deeds, by building codes, or by zoning ordinances.

**BUY DOWN** An incentive offered by a developer or seller that allows the buyer to lower his or her initial interest rate by putting up a certain amount of money. A buy down also refers to the process of paying extra points up front at the closing of your loan in order to have a lower interest rate over the life of the loan.

**BUYER'S BROKER** A buyer's broker is a real estate broker who specializes in representing buyers. Unlike a seller's broker or conventional broker, the buyer's broker has a fiduciary duty to the buyer, because the buyer accepts the legal obligation of paying the broker. The buyer's broker is obligated to find the best property for a client, and then negotiate the best possible purchase price and terms.

**BUYER'S MARKET** Market conditions that favor the buyer. A buyer's market is usually expressed when there are too many homes for sale, and a home can be bought for less money.

**CERTIFICATE OF TITLE** A document or instrument issued by a local government agency to a homeowner, naming the homeowner as the owner of a specific piece of property. At the sale of the property, the certificate of title is transferred to the buyer. The agency then issues a new certificate of title to the buyer.

**CHAIN OF TITLE** The lineage of ownership of a particular property.

**CLOSING** The day when buyers and sellers sign the papers and actually swap money for title to the new home. The closing finalizes the agreements reached in the sales agreement. Also called the settlement.

**CLOSING COSTS** This phrase can refer to a lender's costs for closing on a loan, or it can mean all the costs associated with closing on a piece of property. Considering all closing costs, it's easy to see that closing can be expensive for both buyers and sellers. A home buyer's closing costs might include: lender's points, loan origination or loan service fees; loan application fee; lender's credit report; lender's processing fee; lender's document preparation fee; lender's appraisal fee; prepaid interest on the loan; lender's insurance escrow; lender's real estate tax escrow; lender's tax escrow service fee; cost for the lender's title policy; special endorsements to the lender's title policy; house inspection fees; title company closing fee; deed or mortgage recording fees; local municipal, county, and state taxes; and the attorney's fee. A seller's closing costs might include: survey (which in some parts of the country is paid for by the buyer); title insurance; recorded release of mortgage; broker's commission; state, county, and local municipality transfer taxes; credit to the buyer for unpaid real estate taxes and other bills; attorney's fees; FHA fees and costs.

**CLOUD (ON TITLE)** An outstanding claim or encumbrance that adversely affects the marketability of a property.

**COMMISSION** The amount of money paid to the broker by the seller (or, in some cases, the buyer), as compensation for selling the home. Usually, the commission is a percentage of the sales price of the home, and generally hovers in the 5 to 7 percent range. There is no "set" commission rate. It is always and entirely negotiable.

**CONDEMNATION** The government holds the right to "condemn" land for public use, even against the will of the owner. The government, however, must pay fair market price for the land. Condemnation may also mean that the government has decided a particular piece of land, or a dwelling, is unsafe for human habitation.

**CONDOMINIUM** A dwelling of two or more units in which you individually own the interior space of your unit and jointly own common areas such as the lobby, roof, parking, plumbing, and recreational areas.

**CONTINGENCY** A provision in a contract that sets forth one or more conditions that must be met prior to the closing. If the contingency is not met, usually the party who is benefiting from the contingency can terminate the contract. Some common contingencies include financing, inspection, attorney approval, and toxic substances.

**CONTRACT TO PURCHASE** Another name for agreement of sale.

**CONTRACTOR** In the building industry, the contractor is the individual who contracts to build the property. He or she erects the structure and manages the subcontracting (to the electrician, plumber, etc.) until the project is finished.

**CONVENTIONAL MORTGAGE** A conventional mortgage means that the loan is underwritten by banks, savings and loans, or other types of mortgage companies. There are also certain limitations imposed on conventional mortgages that allow them to be sold to private institutional investors (like pension funds) on the secondary market.

**CO-OP** Cooperative housing refers to a building, or a group of buildings, that is owned by a corporation. The shareholders of the corporation are the people who live in the building. They own shares—which gives them the right to lease a specific unit within the building—in the corporation that owns their building and pay "rent" or monthly maintenance assessments for the expenses associated with living in the building. Co-ops are relatively unknown outside of New York, Chicago, and a few other cities. Since the 1970s, condominiums have become much more popular.

**COUNTEROFFER** When the seller or buyer responds to a bid. If you decide to offer $100,000 for a home listed at $150,000, the seller might counter your offer and propose that you purchase the home for $140,000. That new proposal, and any subsequent offer, is called a counteroffer.

**COVENANT** Assurances or promises set out in the deed or a legally binding contract, or implied in the law. For example, when you obtain title to a property by warranty, there is the Covenant of Quiet Enjoyment, which gives you the right to enjoy your property without disturbances.

**CREDIT REPORT** A lender will decide whether or not to give you a loan based on your credit history. A credit report lists all of your credit accounts (such as charge cards), and any debts or late payments that have been reported to the credit company.

**CUL DE SAC** A street that ends in a U-shape, leading the driver or pedestrian back to the beginning. The cul de sac has become exceptionally popular with modern subdivision developers, who use the design technique to create quiet streets and give the development a nonlinear feel.

**CUSTOM BUILDER** A home builder who builds houses for individual owners to the owners' specification. The home builder may either own a piece of property or build a home on someone else's land.

**DEBT SERVICE** The total amount of debt (credit cards, mortgage, car loan) that an individual is carrying at any one time.

**DECLARATION OF RESTRICTIONS** Developers of condominiums (or any other type of housing unit that functions as a condo) are required to file a condominium declaration, which sets out the rules and restrictions for the property, the division of ownership, and the rights and privileges of the owners. The "condo dec" or "homeowner's dec," as it is commonly called, reflects the developer's original intent, and may only be changed by unit-owner vote. There are other types of declarations, including homeowners' association and townhouse association. Co-op dwellers are governed by a similar type of document. Sometimes referred to as the CCR.

**DEED** The document used to transfer ownership in a property from seller to buyer.

**DEED OF TRUST** A deed of trust or trust deed is an instrument similar to a mortgage that gives the lender the right to foreclose on the property if there is a default under the trust deed or note by the borrower.

**DEPOSIT** Money given by the buyer to the seller with a signed contract to purchase or offer to purchase, as a show of good faith. Also called the earnest money.

**DOWN PAYMENT** The cash put into a purchase by the borrower. Lenders like to see the borrower put at least 20 percent down in cash, because lenders generally believe that if you have a higher cash down payment, it is less likely the home will go into foreclosure.

**DUAL AGENCY** When a real estate broker represents both the buyer and the seller in a single transaction, it creates a situation known as dual agency. In most states, brokers must disclose to the buyer and to the seller whom they are representing. Even with disclosure, dual agency presents a conflict of interest for the broker in the transaction. If the broker is acting as the seller's broker and the subagent for the seller (by bringing the buyer), then anything the buyer tells the broker must by law be brought to the seller's attention. If the broker represents the seller as a seller's broker and the buyer as a buyer's broker in the same transaction, the broker will receive money from both the buyer and the seller, an obvious conflict of interest.

**DUE ON SALE CLAUSE** Nearly every mortgage has this clause, which states that the mortgage must be paid off in full upon the sale of the home.

**EARNEST MONEY** The money the buyer gives the seller up front as a show of good faith. It can be as much as 10 percent of the purchase price. Earnest money is sometimes called a deposit.

**EASEMENT** A right given by a landowner to a third party to make use of the land in a specific way. There may be several easements on your property, including for passage of utility lines or poles, sewer or water mains, and even a driveway. Once the right is given, it continues indefinitely, or until released by the party who received it.

**EMINENT DOMAIN** The right of the government to condemn private land for public use. The government must, however, pay full market value for the property.

**ENCROACHMENT** When your neighbor builds a garage or a fence and it occupies your land, it is said to "encroach on" your property.

**ENCUMBRANCE** A claim or lien or interest in a property by another party. An encumbrance hinders the seller's ability to pass good, marketable, and unencumbered title to you.

**ESCROW CLOSING** A third party, usually a title company, acts as the neutral party for the receipt of documents for the exchange of the deed by the sellers for the buyer's money. The final exchange is completed when the third party determines that certain preset requirements have been satisfied.

**ESCROW (FOR EARNEST MONEY)** The document that creates the arrangement whereby a third party or broker holds the earnest money for the benefit of the buyer and seller.

**ESCROW (FOR REAL ESTATE TAXES AND INSURANCE)** An account in which monthly installments for real estate taxes and property insurance are held—usually in the name of the home buyer's lender.

**FEE SIMPLE** The most basic type of ownership, under which the owner has the right to use and dispose of the property at will.

**FIDUCIARY DUTY** A relationship of trust between a broker and a seller or a buyer's broker and a buyer, or an attorney and a client.

**FIRST MORTGAGE** A mortgage that takes priority over all other voluntary liens.

**FIXTURE** Personal property, such as a built-in bookcase, furnace, hot water heater, and recessed lights, that becomes "affixed" because it has been permanently attached to the home.

**FORECLOSURE** The legal action taken to extinguish a homeowner's right and interest in a property so that the property can be sold in a foreclosure sale to satisfy a debt.

**GIFT LETTER** A letter to the lender indicating that a gift of cash has been made to the buyer and that it is not expected to be repaid. The letter must detail the amount of the gift, and the name of the giver.

**GOOD FAITH ESTIMATE (GFE)** Under RESPA, lenders are required to give potential borrowers a written Good Faith Estimate of closing costs within three days of an application submission.

**GRACE PERIOD** The period of time after a loan payment due date in which a mortgage payment may be made and not be considered delinquent.

**GRADUATED PAYMENT MORTGAGE** A mortgage in which the payments increase over the life of the mortgage, allowing the borrower to make very low payments at the beginning of the loan. Also called an Option ARM.

**HAZARD INSURANCE** Insurance that covers the property from damages that might materially affect its value. Also known as homeowners' insurance.

**HOLDBACK** An amount of money held back at closing by the lender or the escrow agent until a particular condition has been met. If the problem is a repair, the money is kept until the repair is made. If the repair is not made, the lender or escrow agent uses the money to make the repair. Buyers and sellers may also have holdbacks between them, to ensure that specific conditions of the sale are met.

**HOMEOWNERS' ASSOCIATION** A group of homeowners in a particular subdivision or area who band together to take care of common property and common interests.

**HOMEOWNERS' INSURANCE** Coverage that includes hazard insurance, as well as personal liability and theft.

**HOME WARRANTY** A service contract that covers appliances (with exclusions) in working condition in the home for a certain period of time, usually one year. Homeowners are responsible for a per-call service fee. There is a homeowner's warranty for new construction. Some developers will purchase a warranty from a company specializing in new construction for the homes they sell. A homeowner's warranty will warrant the good working order of the appliances and workmanship of a new home for between one and ten years; for example, appliances might be covered for one year while the roof may be covered for several years.

**HOUSING AND URBAN DEVELOPMENT, DEPARTMENT OF** Also known as HUD, this is the federal department responsible for the nation's housing programs. It also regulates RESPA, the Real Estate Settlement Procedures Act, which governs how lenders must deal with their customers.

**INSPECTION** The service an inspector performs when he or she is hired to scrutinize the home for any possible structural defects. May also be done in order to check for the presence of toxic substances, such as leaded paint or water, asbestos, radon, or pests, including termites.

**INSTALLMENT CONTRACT** The purchase of property in installments. Title to the property is given to the purchaser when all installments are made.

**INSTITUTIONAL INVESTORS OR LENDERS** Private or public companies, corporations, or funds (such as pension funds) that purchase loans on the secondary market from commercial lenders such as banks and savings and loans. Or, they are sources of funds for mortgages through mortgage brokers.

**INTEREST** Money charged for the use of borrowed funds. Usually expressed as an interest rate, it is the percentage of the total loan charged annually for the use of the funds.

**INTEREST-ONLY MORTGAGE** A loan in which only the interest is paid on a regular basis (usually monthly), and the principal is owed in full at the end of the loan term.

**INTEREST RATE CAP** The total number of percentage points that an adjustable-rate mortgage (ARM) might rise over the life of the loan.

**JOINT TENANCY** An equal, undivided ownership in a property taken by two or more owners. Under joint tenancy there are rights of survivorship, which means that if one of the owners dies, the surviving owner rather than the heirs of the estate inherits the other's total interest in the property.

**LANDSCAPE** The trees, flowers, planting, lawn, and shrubbery that surround the exterior of a dwelling.

**LATE CHARGE** A penalty applied to a mortgage payment that arrives after the grace period (usually the 10th or 15th of a month).

**LEASE WITH AN OPTION TO BUY** When the renter or lessee of a piece of property has the right to purchase the property for a specific period of time at a specific price. Usually, a lease with an option to buy allows a first-time buyer to accumulate a down payment by applying a portion of the monthly rent toward the down payment.

**LENDER** A person, company, corporation, or entity that lends money for the purchase of real estate.

**LETTER OF INTENT** A formal statement, usually in letter form, from the buyer to the seller stating that the buyer intends to purchase a specific piece of property for a specific price on a specific date.

**LEVERAGE** Using a small amount of cash, say a 10 or 20 percent down payment, to purchase a piece of property.

**LIEN** An encumbrance against the property, which may be voluntary or involuntary. There are many different kinds of liens, including a tax lien (for unpaid federal, state, or real estate taxes), a judgment lien (for monetary judgments by a court of law), a mortgage lien (when you take out a mortgage), and a mechanic's lien (for work done by a contractor on the property that has not been paid for). For a lien to be attached to the property's title, it must be filed or recorded with local county government.

**LISTING** A property that a broker agrees to list for sale in return for a commission.

**LOAN** An amount of money that is lent to a borrower, who agrees to repay it plus interest.

**LOAN COMMITMENT** A written document that states that a mortgage company has agreed to lend a buyer a certain amount of money at a certain rate of interest for a specific period of time, which may contain sets of conditions and a date by which the loan must close.

**LOAN MODIFICATION** A loan modification occurs when a mortgage lender agrees to modify the terms of an existing loan by changing the interest rate, length of the loan, or other payment terms. The loan modification is completed with a written document outlining the change in loan terms. Frequently, homeowners must apply to the lender for the loan modification.

**LOAN ORIGINATION FEE** A one-time fee charged by the mortgage company to arrange the financing for the loan.

**LOAN-TO-VALUE RATIO** The ratio of the amount of money you wish to borrow compared to the value of the property you wish to purchase. Institutional investors (who buy loans on the secondary market from your mortgage company) set up certain ratios that guide lending practices. For example, the mortgage company might only lend you 80 percent of a property's value.

**LOCATION** Where property is geographically situated. "Location, location, location" is a broker's maxim that states that where the property is located is its most important feature, because you can change everything about a house, except its location.

**LOCK-IN** The mechanism by which a borrower locks in the interest rate that will be charged on a particular loan. Usually, the lock lasts for a certain time period, such as 30, 45, or 60 days. On a new construction, the lock may be much longer.

**MAINTENANCE FEE** The monthly or annual fee charged to condo, co-op, or townhouse owners, and paid to the homeowners' association, for the maintenance of common property. Also called an assessment.

**MORTGAGE** A document granting a lien on a home in exchange for financing granted by a lender. The mortgage is the means by which the lender secures the loan and has the ability to foreclose on the home.

**MORTGAGE BANKER** A company or a corporation, like a bank, that lends its own funds to borrowers in addition to bringing together lenders and borrowers. A mortgage banker may also service the loan (i.e., collect the monthly payments).

**MORTGAGE BROKER** A company or individual that brings together lenders and borrowers and processes mortgage applications.

**MORTGAGEE** A legal term for the lender.

**MORTGAGOR** A legal term for the borrower.

**MULTIPLE LISTING SERVICE (MLS)** A computerized listing of all properties offered for sale by member brokers. Buyers may only gain access to the MLS by working with a member broker.

**NEGATIVE AMORTIZATION** A condition created when the monthly mortgage payment is less than the amount necessary to pay off the loan over the period of time set forth in the note. Because you're paying less than the amount necessary, the actual loan amount increases over time. That's how you end up with negative equity. To pay off the loan, a lump-sum payment must be made.

**OPTION** When a buyer pays for the right or option to purchase property for a given length of time, without having the obligation to actually purchase the property.

**ORIGINATION FEE** A fee charged by the lender for allowing you to borrow money to purchase property. The fee—which is also referred to as points—is usually expressed as a percentage of the total loan amount.

**OWNERSHIP** The absolute right to use, enjoy, and dispose of property. You own it!

**PACKAGE MORTGAGE** A mortgage that uses both real and personal property to secure a loan.

**PAPER** Slang usage that refers to the mortgage, trust deed, installment, and land contract.

**PERSONAL PROPERTY** Moveable property, such as appliances, furniture, clothing, and artwork.

**PITI** An acronym for Principal, Interest, Taxes, and Insurance. These are usually the four parts of your monthly mortgage payment.

**PLEDGED ACCOUNT** Borrowers who do not want to have a real estate tax or insurance escrow administered by the mortgage servicer can, in some circumstances, pledge a savings account into which enough money to cover real estate taxes and the insurance premium must be deposited. You must then make the payments for your real estate taxes and insurance premiums from a separate account. If you fail to pay your taxes or premiums, the lender is allowed to use the funds in the pledged account to make those payments.

**POINT** A point is 1 percent of the loan amount.

**POSSESSION** Being in control of a piece of property, and having the right to use it to the exclusion of all others.

**POWER OF ATTORNEY** The legal authorization given to an individual to act on behalf of another individual.

**PREPAID INTEREST** Interest paid at closing for the number of days left in the month after closing. For example, if you close on the 15th, you would prepay the interest for the 16th through the end of the month.

**PREPAYMENT PENALTY** A fine imposed when a loan is paid off before it comes due. Many states now have laws against prepayment penalties, although banks with federal charters are exempt from state laws. If possible, do not use a mortgage that has a prepayment penalty, or you will be charged a hefty fee in some cases if you sell your property before your mortgage has been paid off.

**PREQUALIFYING FOR A LOAN** When a mortgage company tells a buyer in advance of the formal application approximately how much money the buyer can afford to borrow.

**PRINCIPAL** The amount of money you borrow.

**PRIVATE MORTGAGE INSURANCE (PMI)** Special insurance that specifically protects the top 20 percent of a loan, allowing the lender to lend more than 80 percent of the value of the property. PMI is paid in monthly installments by the borrower.

**PROPERTY TAX** A tax levied by a county or local authority on the value of real estate.

**PRORATION** The proportional division of certain costs of homeownership. Usually used at closing to figure out how much the buyer and seller each owe for certain expenditures, including real estate taxes, assessments, and water bills.

**PURCHASE AGREEMENT** An agreement between the buyer and seller for the purchase of property.

**PURCHASE MONEY MORTGAGE** An instrument used in seller financing, a purchase money mortgage is signed by a buyer and given to the seller in exchange for a portion of the purchase price.

**QUIT-CLAIM DEED** A deed that operates to release any interest in a property that a person may have, *without a representation that he or she actually has a right in that property*. For example, Sally may use a quit-claim deed to grant Bill her interest in the White House, in Washington, D.C., although she may not actually own, or have any rights to, that particular house.

**REAL ESTATE** Land and anything permanently attached to it, such as buildings and improvements.

**REAL ESTATE AGENT** An individual licensed by the state, who acts on behalf of the seller or buyer. For his or her services, the agent receives a commission, which is usually expressed as a percentage of the sales price of a home and is split with his or her real estate firm. A real estate agent must either be a real estate broker or work for one.

**REAL ESTATE ATTORNEY** An attorney who specializes in the purchase and sale of real estate.

**REAL ESTATE BROKER** An individual who is licensed by the state to act as an agent on behalf of the seller or buyer. For his or her services, the broker receives a commission, which is usually expressed as a percentage of the sales price of a home.

**REAL ESTATE SETTLEMENT PROCEDURES ACT (RESPA)** This federal statute was originally passed in 1974, and contains provisions that govern the way companies involved with a real estate closing must treat each other and the consumer. For example, one section of RESPA requires lenders to give consumers a written Good Faith Estimate within three days of making an application for a loan. Another section of RESPA prohibits title companies from giving referral fees to brokers for steering business to them.

**REALTIST** A designation given to an agent or broker who is a member of the National Association of Real Estate Brokers.

**REALTOR** A designation given to a real estate agent or broker who is a member of the National Association of Realtors.

**RECORDING** The process of filing documents at a specific government office. Upon such recording, the document becomes part of the public record.

**REDLINING** The slang term used to describe an illegal practice of discrimination against a particular racial group by real estate lenders. Redlining occurs when lenders decide certain areas of a community are too high risk and refuse to lend to buyers who want to purchase property in those areas, regardless of their qualifications or creditworthiness.

**REGULATION Z** Also known as the Truth in Lending Act. Congress determined that lenders must provide a written Good Faith Estimate of closing costs to all borrowers and provide them with other written information about the loan.

**RESERVE** The amount of money set aside by a condo, co-op, or homeowners' association for future capital improvements.

**SALE-LEASEBACK** A transaction in which the seller sells property to a buyer, who then leases the property back to the seller. This is accomplished within the same transaction.

**SALES CONTRACT** The document by which a buyer contracts to purchase property. Also known as the purchase contract or a contract to purchase.

**SECOND MORTGAGE** A mortgage that is obtained after the primary mortgage, and whose rights for repayment are secondary to the first mortgage.

**SELLER'S BROKER** A broker who has a fiduciary responsibility to the seller. Most brokers are seller's brokers, although an increasing number are buyer's brokers, who have a fiduciary responsibility to the buyer.

**SETTLEMENT STATEMENT** A statement that details the monies paid out and received by the buyer and seller at closing.

**SHARED APPRECIATION MORTGAGE** A relatively new mortgage used to help first-time buyers who might not qualify for conventional financing. In a shared appreciation mortgage, the lender offers a below-market interest rate in return for a portion of the profits made by the home owner when the property is sold. Before entering into a shared appreciation mortgage, be sure to have your real estate attorney review the documentation.

**SPECIAL ASSESSMENT** An additional charge levied by a condo or co-op board in order to pay for capital improvements, or other unforeseen expenses.

**SUBAGENT** A broker who brings the buyer to the property. Although subagents would appear to be working for the buyer (a subagent usually ferries around the buyer, showing him or her properties), they are paid by the seller and have a fiduciary responsibility to the seller. Subagency is often confusing to first-time buyers, who think that because the subagent shows them property, the subagent is "their" agent, rather than the seller's.

**SUBDIVISION** The division of a large piece of property into several smaller pieces. Usually a developer or a group of developers will build single-family or duplex homes of a similar design and cost within one subdivision.

**TAX LIEN** A lien that is attached to property if the owner does not pay his or her real estate taxes or federal income taxes. If overdue property taxes are not paid, the owner's property might be sold at auction for the amount owed in back taxes.

**TENANCY BY THE ENTIRETY** A type of ownership whereby both the husband and wife each own the complete property. Each spouse has an ownership interest in the property as their marital residence and, as a result, creditors cannot force the sale of the home to pay back the debts of one spouse without the other spouse's consent. There are rights of survivorship whereby upon the death of one spouse, the other spouse would immediately inherit the entire property.

**TENANTS IN COMMON** A type of ownership in which two or more parties have an undivided interest in the property. The owners may or may not have equal shares of ownership, and there are no rights of survivorship. However, each owner retains the right to sell his or her share in the property as he or she sees fit.

**TITLE** Refers to the ownership of a particular piece of property.

**TITLE COMPANY** The corporation or company that insures the status of title (title insurance) through the closing, and may handle other aspects of the closing.

**TITLE INSURANCE** Insurance that protects the lender and the property owner against losses arising from defects or problems with the title to property.

**TRUST ACCOUNT** An account used by brokers and escrow agents, in which funds for another individual are held separately, and not commingled with other funds.

**UNDERWRITER** One who underwrites a loan for another. Your lender will have an investor underwrite your loan.

**VARIABLE INTEREST RATE** An interest rate that rises and falls according to a particular economic indicator, such as Treasury bills.

**VOID** A contract or document that is not enforceable.

**VOLUNTARY LIEN** A lien, such as a mortgage, that a homeowner elects to grant to a lender.

**WAIVER** The surrender or relinquishment of a particular right, claim, or privilege.

**WARRANTY** A legally binding promise given to the buyer at closing by the seller, generally regarding the condition of the home, property, or other matter.

**ZONING** The right of the local municipal government to decide how different areas of the municipality will be used. Zoning ordinances are the laws that govern the use of the land.

# ACKNOWLEDGMENTS

Twenty-eighteen marks the twenty-fifth year since I wrote the first edition of this book. In the past quarter century, two generations of first-time buyers have moved on (Gen X and Baby Boomers) and Millennials have stepped up as the biggest, newest home-buying cohort. (This much is true: the days are long and the years are short.)

Sure, there are differences (mostly, they're savvy technologists who have time-shifted life milestones by seven to ten years). But there are a lot of similarities, too: hardworking, family-centric, worried about their prospects and the debts they have had to take on. The biggest difference is that the world is shifting faster than it ever has, and that includes the world of real estate. Good thing they can keep up.

For me, keeping up with the changes in the real estate industry takes plenty of help. Over the years, I've interviewed countless agents, brokers, lenders, attorneys, economists, developers, and builders, not to mention the myriad of spokespeople from national trade organizations, lobbying firms, and governmental and quasi-governmental housing agencies. They have been kind, considerate, and helpful over the years, and I am very grateful for their assistance. Many of my longtime friends and colleagues in government are now retiring or turning to the next chapters in their careers. I will miss them all.

I also want to say thank you to the thousands of home buyers, sellers, and homeowners who have sent emails and letters over the years, and agreed to be interviewed over the course of my career as a real estate and personal finance journalist. Whether you were on the record or off, your stories helped shape this book, just as they shaped my columns, blogs, television news segments, and radio programs each week. If you recognize your story, if not your name, in this book, there are a hundred other stories exactly like yours that wound up on the proverbial "cutting room floor." But each of them has informed the advice I give to others, and I thank you for sharing.

Helping to make it all happen—and making sure I don't get lost in the details—are some very talented individuals at Think Glink, Inc., Think Glink Media, and now Best Money Moves. Those who participated in getting this fourth edition completed include Kathlene Boone, Kris Mackenzie, Lauren Kocher, Olivia Orzech, Dustin Pellegrini, Emily Pfund and, of course, the inimitable Angus Carroll, whose usual good humor saved many a long day.

I am also grateful for the friendship, counsel, and support of: Ralph Martire, Ellen Fiedelholtz and Michael Silverman, Thea Flaum, Ellyn Rosen, Leo Shaw, Beth and Mark Kurensky, Sarah and Michael Alter, John and Barbara Byrne, Michael Frenkel, Harry Epstein and Marilyn Perlman, Michael and Shelley Gurin, Crystal Wheeler, Pete Hillan, Perry Yeatman, Richard Kraus, Wendy and Frank Serrino, Josh Lowitz, and Lance Gams. My WGN radio and television family has been wonderful to work with over many years. The Penguin Random House team is, as always, top-notch: My editor, Jon Darga, has been fabulous. And my agent, Alice Martell, is still the best.

My immediate and extended family continues to put up with the best and worst of this eclectic life I've chosen. I especially wish to thank my sisters, Shona Glink Kitei and Phyllis Glink Harris, who are kind, thoughtful, and encouraging, and their husbands, Jon Kitei and Ian Harris, who are such a wonderful part of our family. My mother, Susanne Kraus Glink, who, in her eighties, is still selling property and dispensing great wisdom to buyers and sellers. She introduced me to this crazy business, opened my eyes to some of its deepest and darkest secrets, told me some hilarious (but true!) stories, and repeatedly suggested I write a book (which she now hands out to her first-time buyers). Thanks, Mom!

My two sons, Alex and Michael, Millennials and digital natives, never fail to offer their love, wisdom, tech guidance, big hugs, and exceptional puns. And, finally, I would never have finished this fourth edition without the unstinting help and support of my husband and best friend (of more than thirty years!), Samuel J. Tamkin, the world's best father and real estate attorney, incomparable "Office Dad," and one hell of an editor—he cowrites our weekly, nationally syndicated Real Estate Matters column—who continues to believe all my wildest dreams will come true.

# INDEX

441

Ilyce Glink is an award-winning television and radio personality, a communications and media strategist, an innovator in content marketing, and the founder of four Chicago-based companies. Her websites include ThinkGlink.com, BestMoneyMoves.com, Think GlinkMedia.com, ThinkGlinkStore.com, YouTube.com/ExpertRealEstateTips, and IlyceGlink.com.

She is an award-winning, nationally syndicated columnist, a top blogger for CBS News.com, and a best-selling author. She also hosts podcasts, creates videos, and is a frequent guest on WGN Radio, where she fills in as host for the Wintrust Business Lunch.

Glink is the author of more than a dozen books, with nearly one million copies total in print. She has also published a handful of books for her corporate customers. Her latest ebook/webinar offering is *Intentional Investor: How to Be Wildly Successful in Real Estate*. She was the founder and managing editor of the Equifax Finance Blog until 2016, and is the publisher of several web properties, including ThinkGlink.com, a 7,000+ page site dedicated to helping consumers make the best decisions with their money.

She spent eight years as on-air talent/producer for WGN-TV and nearly eighteen years hosting a top-rated Sunday talk show and filling in for syndicated talk show host Clark Howard for WSB-AM in Atlanta, has hosted two syndicated radio programs, and has appeared on every major network's morning news programs, Oprah, CNBC, CNN, and Fox Business.

More than fifteen years ago, Glink started Think Glink Media, a digital communications, strategy, and content agency that combines technology, creativity, and experience to build online and offline connections through powerful communities, breakthrough native advertising, and first-person social engagement. The result is award-winning work, profitable campaigns, and loyal customers. TGM's clients include Fortune 1000 companies in the financial services, real estate, and health sectors as well as start-ups and non-profits.

Her latest company is the award-winning Best Money Moves, a cloud-based, mobile-first financial wellness solution that companies provide to their employees to help them pay down personal debt and improve their financial lives. The result is lower turnover, absenteeism and financial stress, higher employee engagement and productivity, and better health outcomes. Find out more at BestMoneyMoves.com.

Glink has won numerous awards throughout her career, including Best Consumer Reporter, Best Magazine Report, Best Blog, and Best Television Report from the National Association of Real Estate Editors. She has won several top awards from the Society of Business Editors and Writers (SABEW), including Best in Business Blog and the 2015 President's Award. She also received the first Money $mart Week Award from the Federal Reserve Bank of Chicago and received two Peter Lisagor Awards for Exemplary Journalism from the Chicago Headline Club. In 2006, she was nominated for an Emmy Award. She was cofounder of the Medicare Newsgroup, and part of the team that won the 2012 Web Marketing Association's Award for outstanding achievement in web development for MedicareNewsGroup.com.

Follow her on Twitter @Glink, Facebook, LinkedIn, Instagram, and on Google+, and email her at Ilyce@thinkglink.com or through her website, ThinkGlink.com.